connections 500

2016

PLAYS FOR YOUNG PEOPLE

Blackout

Eclipse

What Are They Like?

Bassett

I'm Spilling My Heart Out Here

Gargantua

Children of Killers

Take Away

It Snows

The Musicians

Citizenship

Bedbug

with an introduction by
RUFUS NORRIS

Bloomsbury Methuen Drama
An imprint of Bloomsbury Publishing Plc

B L O O M S B U R Y

LONDON · OXFORD · NEW YORK · NEW DELHI · SYDNEY

Bloomsbury Methuen Drama
An imprint of Bloomsbury Publishing Plc
Imprint previously known as Methuen Drama

50 Bedford Square	1385 Broadway
London	New York
WC1B 3DP	NY 10018
UK	USA

www.bloomsbury.com

First published 2016

For details of copyright and original publication of individual plays, see page 746.

Introduction copyright © National Theatre 2016
Resource material copyright © National Theatre 2016

The authors have asserted their rights under the Copyright,
Designs and Patents Act 1988 to be identified as the authors of these works.

NATIONAL THEATRE and the CONNECTIONS typographical font style are used
with the permission of the Royal National Theatre. All rights reserved.

British Library Cataloguing-in-Publication Data
A catalogue record for this book is available from the British Library

ISBN: PB: 978-1-4742-8413-4
ePDF: 978-1-4742-8415-8
ePub: 978-1-4742-8414-1

Library of Congress Cataloging-in-Publication Data
A catalog record for this book is available from the Library of Congress.

Typeset by Country Setting, Kingsdown, Kent CT14 8ES

Contents

Introduction

Twenty-one years ago the National Theatre launched Connections in response to a demand for good, new, relevant plays for young people to perform. Two decades later, it's still at the heart of the National Theatre's work for young people and one of the most exciting and important projects we do.

The Connections formula is simple. The National Theatre asks playwrights, both established and emerging, all of them writers whose work we love, to write short plays for young people. And each year we invite youth theatres and school theatre groups to perform them, offering support and training to their directors and the chance to present their production at a Connections festival in a major UK theatre.

Over the past two decades we've built an entirely new repertoire of more than 150 plays for young performers.

Being involved in my local youth theatre was the single most formative experience of my teenage life. So when I became Director of the National in 2015, I was determined that we should celebrate the twenty-first anniversary of Connections.

We decided to take a year out from commissioning new plays and delve into the back-catalogue to select twelve fantastic plays to revive for the 2016 festival. We spent months reading and arguing the case for the most popular plays and our own favourites. This collection is the result: twelve plays, commissioned between 1995 and 2013, which represent the diversity and excitement of all the plays we've commissioned over the past two decades and which will appeal to a new generation of young performers.

This year we've also doubled the scale of the Connections festival, with almost 500 youth theatres and 45 partner theatres across the UK joining us to celebrate the twenty-first anniversary year.

As I write, the collection of new plays for Connections 2017 is being worked on and we're starting work on 2018. We think it's vital that young people, wherever they are in the country and whatever their future path, have the chance to get involved in theatre. Connections is one of the ways the National helps to make that happen.

I hope you'll enjoy reading these plays – and more importantly, that you choose one or more to produce. And if you'd like to join a future Connections festival, get in touch:

nationaltheatre.org.uk/connections

Acknowledgements

Connections has been made possible over the past two decades by the dedication of many people and organisations. This anniversary is a chance to thank them all: the teams at the National Theatre including the Connections teams since 1995, first part of Education and now the Learning Department; the theatres across the UK who support the young companies and programme Connections festivals; the many generous companies, charities and individuals who have supported the programme since its inception and the very many brilliant playwrights who have written for Connections. And finally, on behalf of the National, our thanks to all the young companies – youth theatres, school theatre groups, and their directors and staff – whose creativity, talent and sheer hard work make Connections possible. To all of you, our thanks.

RUFUS NORRIS
Director of the National Theatre

Blackout
by Davey Anderson

Inspired by the true story of a young offender from Glasgow who had committed a violent crime, a hard-hitting play about getting bullied, fighting back, trying to make a name for yourself, turning vicious, doing something stupid, losing everything, then finding your way again.

Age suitability: any age

Cast size
ensemble piece

Davey Anderson is a writer, director and musician. His plays include *Snuff*, *Wired*, *Liar*, *Blackout*, *Clutter Keeps Company*, *Playback*, *Scavengers* and *The Static*. His work with the National Theatre of Scotland includes *Enquirer*, *Peter Pan*, *Be Near Me*, *Mixter Maxter*, *Architecting*, *Rupture*, *Black Watch* and *Home*. Adaptations include *Dead Man Dying* by Estebán Navajas Cortés, *Thieves and Boy* by Hao Jingfang and *The War Hasn't Started Yet* by Mikhail Durnenkov. He was co-writer of *The Jean Jacques Rousseau Show*, *Demons* and *The Deficit Show* for A Play, A Pint and a Pint at Òran Mór, Glasgow. His short plays for Theatre Uncut include *True or False* and *Police State*, a co-production with Theatre Dot, Istanbul. He recently co-created and performed *How to Choose* at The Arches, Glasgow, and is currently collaborating with American company The TEAM on *The Scottish Enlightenment Project*.

A Note on the Text

This play does not come with a blueprint or a set of instructions for staging. As you will see, there are no distinct stage directions and no markings in the margin to indicate who says what. Neither does it present a verbatim transcript of my interviews with the young person whose story it tells, although most of the words are his rather than mine. The text printed here is rather intended to be a piece of verbal storytelling, left bare to invite different visual and theatrical interpretations. The words can be spoken by any number of actors, from one to one hundred. The lines may be altered, where appropriate, to suit the dialect of the performers. And the staging can be as simple or elaborate as you like. My only request is that some things are left to the audience's imagination.

One

Imagine
You wake up
You open your eyes
And you're like that
Where am I?
A small room
Bright lights
White walls
A metal door
Oh my God!
Imagine you wake up and you're in a jail cell.
You go up to the door.
You bang your fists.
Screaming
Shouting
What am I doing in here?
And imagine the polis guy comes up to the door.
And he's like that
Keep it doon.
And you're like
Whit did I dae?
Aw, do you not know?
You shake your head.
Whit?
And the polis guy just looks at you like you're a pure thug or
    something.
Imagine he just looks at you and he goes
You're getting charged with attempted murder, wee man.
You'd be like that
Aw naw
What did I do?
And you'd start remembering
Everything
Right from the beginning
You would try to remember
How did I get here?

Two

So you'd start remembering your dad.

He was a woman-beater.

He beat up your mum every day

From the day they got married right up to the day they got
  divorced.

He used to beat her to a pulp.

So she stopped working.

She wouldn't go out the house.

Cos she was embarrassed.

She didn't want to walk down the street with her face all
  black and blue.

And you'd remember that your ma didnae want you to grow
  up to be like him.

She wanted you to be a famous lawyer

Or a famous doctor

Or a famous whatever.

And you'd remember that you were poor.

But you weren't poor poor.

Cos your mum still made sure there was a dinner on the table
  every night.

She'd give you her last penny

She didn't care about herself.

But you'd remember that you never really spoke to her.

Cos you'd come home from school and go straight up the
  stairs.

James?

Aye.

Your dinner's out.

You'd come down.

Grab the plate.

Thanks, Ma.

Back up the stairs.

So you never really spoke to her.

Three

But you'd remember your granddad.
He was the closest thing you had to a proper father.
He put you under his wing.
He did everything a dad would do.
He'd hold your hand
He'd walk you down to the shops
He'd play daft wee games with you
But best of all, he'd take you to the Rangers game every
    Saturday.
He'd take you to see the Orange Walks.
You'd remember how he taught you to play the flute.
But you'd not to play 'The Sash'
Or hang the Ulster flag out the window.
He taught you to keep that kind of thing to yourself.
But then he got his cancer.
You'd remember that.
So every night you'd go and sit with him.
Play a game of cards
Help him do a jigsaw
Have a cup of tea and look out the back window.
You'd remember that that was where the boys fae your scheme
    used to fight with the boys fae the scheme doon the road.
They'd run at each other with bottles and bricks.
Then it would be poles and baseball bats.
And then it would be knives.
You'd be looking out the window going
Is that a wee boy with a sword?
Am I really seeing this?
And you and your granddad
You would just sit there and go
What are they fighting for?
Cos your grandda never went out and started hitting people.
He got his point across with his mouth, not with his hands.
He would just have to talk to you and people would listen
    to him.

And you'd remember you always wanted to grow up to be
    just like him.

Four

But when you were growing up, you didnae have that many
    pals.
Cos you were too quiet.
You were shy.
You were the wee, shy, nerdy boy.
You didnae fit in with anybody.
And the pals you did have, they just used you, if you know
    what I mean.
Cos, know if it was a pure brilliant sunny day, they would all
    go away and leave you in the house.
But know if it was raining outside, they would come roon tae
    your bit and go
Hi James
I've no seen you in ages.
How have you been?
Can we come in and sit for a while?
They didnae care about you
They just wanted somewhere tae sit.

Five

And say it was at school
You would get beaten up for being a goth
Just cos you had long hair and wore black combats.
They used to call you
The gimp!
Haw, look at him.
Ya dirty goth!
Dae you shag deid people?
Whit?

You go up the graveyards and hing aboot there, din't ye?
Naw.
Aye ye dae. I've seen ye.
Pure digging up the coffins and raping the corpses.
Ya dirty beast!
And you'd remember the beatings.
One of the bullies would take off his belt
He'd wrap it round his knuckles
And whack you with it.
Ahh!
Then they'd throw you down the stairs
Don't!
Kick you in the ribs
Stop it!
Death to the gimp!
And they would swagger off
And leave you there, lying on the ground
Curled up into a wee ball.
You'd remember that.
You'd remember every punch.

Six

And you'd remember you had nobody to turn to.
Cos your grandda was in the hospital.
So you'd just sit in your room and watch horror films
Night after night.
Or read books about serial killers.
Or just look at all the pictures.
You had a bloodlust for it.
It gave you a thrill
Reading about killers.
Cos they're normal people.
But they're mysterious.
What makes them tick?
What makes them go insane?

What can make somebody dae it tae somebody?
It fascinated you.

Seven

Imagine
You're in a jail cell
And you start remembering all this.
But you can't remember what you've done.
And then they take you to a Secure Care Unit.
And they take away your belt.
And they take away your laces.
And they take away anything you could use to try and kill
     yourself.
Then this key worker guy comes in to speak to you.
And you ask him
What did I do?
Son, I can't tell you.
How can you no tell me?
You need to ask for a file.
So you ask for the file.
And he goes away to get it.
Imagine waiting for him to come back.
Your mind would be racing.
Remembering . . .

Eight

Wan night
You got beaten up, just for having long hair.
These boys chased you home with meat cleavers and
     machetes
Shouting
Death to the gimp!
Trying to chop you up

All the way to your front door.
Hi James.
How was school?
Straight up the stairs.
Into your bedroom.
Slam!
You look in the mirror.
I'm not a gimp.
You get a pair of scissors.
You cut your hair pure short.
Shave it right to the skin.
James?
Then you look at yourself.
Your dinner's out.
I'm coming.
I'll show them no tae mess about wae me.
Grab the plate.
Thanks, Ma.
Wait a wee minute.
What?
What happened to your hair?
You shrug.
I got rid of it.
She looks at you funny.
You look like a skinhead.

Nine

That's when you started watching films like *Romper Stomper*
And *American History X*
And you thought to yourself
That's whit I'll dae.
So you started wearing the big Doc Martens boots
The bomber jacket
The braces
Everything.

Ten

And then you went into school.
And people would just look at you like
Ooff
He's a pure psycho.
But it felt good.
Cos you were getting tae them.
And then you'd dae the Nazi salute.
And the teachers were like
Stand outside this room.
What have you got this on for?
Cos I like it.
Go home and change into your uniform.
You're not allowed back into the school until you change
    your clothes.
So you went
Fine. It's my life. I'll wear what I want. I'll say what I want.
    I'll dae what I want.
And you sparked up a fag
And started walking about the school
Smoking
Acting like a hard man.
Haw, look
Check the state of him.
And when the bullies saw you, instead of running away, you
    went
Right, who's first?
Whit you gonnae dae, ya daftie?
Two seconds.
Whit?
And you went
Fsssssssssssss.
You put the fag out on your bare skin.
Who's first then?
Are you aw right?

C'mon, who's gieing me the first punch?
James . . .
Go. I'll put my hands behind my back.
You need tae get your heid sorted oot, mate. You're no right.
Then you pick up a chair
And throw it at the fucker.
So he starts punching you
Fists flying
They all start battering you.
James!
What are you doing?
That's not like you.
But you're standing there
With your face red raw.
Aw, it feels great, but din't it?

Eleven

And you'd remember that that's when you started loving the
    pain.
The punches didnae hurt any more.
You just got used to having that energy flow
That feeling of blood pumping through your veins.
And you'd sit there in your room
With the big Nazi posters up on the wall
And you'd listen to music
With that guitar
And that beat that gets you intae it
And you'd wonder what it was like to burst somebody's lip
Or to slice them open
To butcher them.
It made you feel high and mighty just thinking about it.

Twelve

And you'd remember the night that it finally happened . . .
It was raining.
James?
That's your mum.
Shouting up the stairs.
You turn off the music.
I'm just away up the hospital to see your granddad.
You don't respond.
D'you want to come with me?
No the night, Ma.
Are ye sure?
Nah, I want to stay in and watch this film.
Well, d'you want to go up and see him the morra night?
Aye, Ma. Fine.
Right.
I'll tell him you were asking after him.
See you later.
She goes out into the rain.
You put on a slasher film.
Slash
Chop
Rip
Stab
Blood and guts.
You look at it blankly.
It's not enough for you any more.
Then there's a knock at the door
You press pause.
Open the door.
Awright, James.
Awright.
Whit ye daeing?
Nothing. Just sitting in my room.
Is yer maw in?
Naw.

Are you on your own?

Aye.

Yas, man, big Jim's got an empty!

Yas!

They all crowd in.

C'mon.

D'ye want a joint?

Emmm, no the noo.

Whit ye watching?

Nothing.

What's this?

That's a swastika.

Whit ye daeing with a swastika on your wall?

Are you a Nazi or something?

Snigger.

Aye.

They all look at you.

Whit ye intae all that for?

Cos I'm an Aryan. I need tae protect my white blood.

Oh aye. And how are ye gonnae dae that?

Wait till you see this.

You slip your hand under the bed

And you pull out a sword.

Fuck's sake.

What is that?

A Black Mamba.

Where d'ye get it?

I found it.

Did ye fuck?

How much did that set ye back?

You shrug.

I'll buy it aff ye for a fiver.

Nut.

A tenner then.

Fuck off.

Twenty quid.

Check the damage ye could dae wae that.

Have ye chopped somebody yet?
You smile.
So proud.
Look at him
The psycho.
Then . . .
Keys in the door.
Quick
Hide the blade.
Footsteps on the stairs.What's going on here?
Nothing, Mum.
Suspicious.
You only call her 'Mum' when you've done something
    wrong.
We're just watching a film.
I think it's time your friends went home.
See ye after.
Bye, James.
Catch ye.
They disappear.
And your mum just looks at you.
James, sit down, I've got something to tell you.
Don't, Ma.
I'm sorry, James.
Ma, don't!
James, calm down.
Don't.
I'm sorry. It happened.

Thirteen

That's what you'd remember.
You'd remember the night that your grandda died.
That's when you died inside.
You'd remember how you wanted to hold somebody down to
    the ground

And stab their eyes out.
Or get a baseball bat
And skelp it aff somebody's heid.
Just to get the anger out of you.
Cos it was building up
All this anger.
And you didnae have a way to let it out.

Fourteen

Imagine that all this is going through your head as you're
     waiting in a wee room with no belt and no laces.
And then the key worker guy comes back with your file.
He hands it to you and you start to read.
But you can't concentrate on the words
So you ask him to read it for you.
What does it say?
Gonnae just tell me!
Do you really not remember?
You shake your head.
Assault.
Arson.
Attempted murder.
Do you remember now?
Some of it.
Why don't you tell me what happened?
I'll try.
So you start to tell the story . . .

Fifteen

Where were you?
You were in the town.
Who were you with?
You were with your pals.

Your pals' pals.
People they knew.
But you didn't know them?
Naw.
Where were your friends?
They all went away and left you with these folk you didnae
    know.
Why?
You don't know.
But it starts coming back to you.
One of them hands you a bottle of vodka.
Here, d'you want a stank?
And you're like
Aye.
Drink it straight.
How?
Just drink it straight.
So you went
You took a wee bit of it.
It tasted weird.
Naw, here
Something's wrang wae this.
And they went
Just down it.
And you went
Fine.
Cos you didnae want tae look like the wee nerdy boy.
And you took a big stank of it.
And there was ecstasy
And there was Valium
And you didnae know what was in it.
And by the time your pals came back, you were in some state.
James?
You were like Dr Jekyll and Mr Hyde.
Awright, mate?
Cos wan minute you'd be fine.
Where have ye been? I've been pure missing ye.

And then the next minute
Aye, where have ye been, aye, where have ye been, aye,
    where have ye been?
Like that.
Leaving me here, aye? D'ye want me to come over there and
    smash ye aboot?
Calm doon.
And you were looking at people.
But you were nae just looking at them.
You were looking at them like you were picking a victim.
James, come on
We need to get you hame.
And you remember them taking you hame.
But then . . .

Sixteen

All you can remember is
Screaming
You could hear screaming.
It was like being in a dream
But still being awake at the same time.
And all you can hear is
James?
Are you alright?
And you can feel your blood boiling over.
What's happened to you?
What have you took?
James?
And you start punching
James, don't!
And kicking
James, stop it!
And you feel your hands around somebody's throat.
What are you doing?
Squeezing.

Don't!
Stop it!
Please!
James!
Don't!
And then screaming
And then
Everything went black.

Seventeen

Imagine you did that to somebody.
And you don't know why you did it.
You just
You wanted payback.
You were hurting so much
You wanted to hurt somebody else.
But the payback you done, you didnae mean.
You just needed a friend.
You just needed someone to talk to.
But instead you nearly killed somebody that night.
Aye
You remember
You remember it all.

Eighteen

Now imagine this
They take you to a courtroom
And they put you in front of a judge
And the judge says
Son, I see thousands of boys like you
Every year
Getting charged with these exact same crimes.
And most of them end up in jail for anything up to ten years.

And you're standing there
Shaking like a leaf
Thinking
God.
Ten years.
Please don't.
That's me finished.
Then she says
But some of them
I look at some of them standing there
And I know they don't belong in jail.
I know they just made a stupid mistake
And what they really need is somebody to give them a
    chance.
And she looks you right in the eye.
You're one of the lucky ones.
I'm going to give you a probation sentence.
Three years.
And you're like
Thank you.
But if you mess up during that time, you'll do ten years in jail.
Do you understand?
Yes.
You may leave my courtroom.
That's you free to go.

Nineteen

You step outside
Into the sunshine
You take a deep breath
And there's your mum
Waiting.
She looks at you.
You look at her.
How is she ever gonnae trust you again?

But she walks towards you.
Mum, I'm sorry.
And she bursts out greeting.
Then she goes
What are you going to do with yourself?

Twenty

Imagine.
Imagine if all that happened to you.
What would you do?
You know what I would do?
I would start to talk.
I would tell people my story.
Cos when I got angry
I nearly lost everything.
And all I really wanted was somebody to sit up and take
    notice.
And then you would go home.
You would take down all your Nazi posters.
You'd get rid of all your knives.
You would look in the mirror and try to imagine
What comes next?
And then you'd get into bed.
You'd pull up the covers.
And you'd turn off the light.

Blackout.

Blackout

BY DAVEY ANDERSON

*Notes on rehearsal and staging drawn from a workshop
with the writer held at the National Theatre, October 2015*

*Workshops led by Esther Baker and Bijan Sheibani,
with notes by Tom Hughes and Cheryl Gallacher*

How Davey came to write the play

'I wrote the play seven years ago. I was commissioned to
write something in response to the issue of violent crime in
Glasgow. As part of the writing process, I was set up with
the charity Barnardo's to work with a teenager who was
serving a probation sentence. I spent a lot of time with him.
I asked lots of questions, recorded his answers and made a
twenty-minute piece out of it, which is how short the play
can be if you just read it straight through. I then worked on
the text with a group of young people at the Citizens
Theatre and we presented the play at the National Theatre
as a springboard for debate about the issues it raises.

'The character of James felt very familiar to me. He grew up
in a housing scheme on the outskirts of a city. It's a place
where large numbers of people are unemployed and trying
to fit in and create an identity for themselves. It also has a
whole history of sectarianism between Protestants and
Catholics, which is very similar to where I grew up. James
was someone in a difficult situation and I thought, "That
could be me, actually, that could easily be me".'

Approaching the Play

FACTS

Because *Blackout* offers so much potential for interpretation,
directors are advised to stay rooted in the text and to base
their creative decisions upon a close and rigorous analysis
of it. In the workshop, it was suggested that directors begin

their work by listing the 'FACTS' of the play. You should keep these factual and specific. For example, the first facts of the play might include:

- There is a small room.
- There are bright lights.
- There are white walls.
- There is a metal door.
- He is in a jail cell.
- There is screaming and shouting.
- There is a male police officer.

For the beginning of your process, you are working from the bare bones of the play. Because this is a storytelling or memory play, it might seem more challenging to list the facts than with a more naturalistic play. It was suggested that you use your best judgement, even if you have to cheat the exercise by including details that might not strictly be facts, to give yourself bare bones to work with. However, descriptions that are clearly emotional or fabricated should be avoided at this stage in the process.

You could do this exercise as part of your preparation, or with your company early on in rehearsals as a way of inviting actors to enter the world of the play.

IMAGES

Esther recommended that directors should read through the text and pay attention to its images. These can be written down – either images that are directly referenced in the text, or any images that arise in the director's imagination – and will be helpful in conversations about design. You should do this for the entire script, as it will help you to build a picture of the whole play rather than make decisions that will only work for some parts.

The group had the following suggestions for images:

- a cage
- whiteness/brightness
- dark/light
- cancer and images of cancer (for example, frailty or family members)
- the Orange Walk
- colours (these change between different scenes – it could be helpful to decide the colour of each scene, as this could help you make decisions about its tone or rhythm)
- loneliness and waiting
- meat cleavers and machetes
- visceral blood and guts
- smells (for example, smoke or hospital)

You do not need literally to express every image in your production. The image can be expressed verbally or audibly, for example. It is, however, excellent to be aware of a play's entire image structure.

It is helpful to be very specific. Rather than identifying 'violence' as an image, you should be specific about the exact image of violence – for example, *where* on your body do you burn yourself?

You could, for example, choose one image or object (in the workshop, we suggested Doc Martens as a single image) that is featured and has a journey throughout the whole production. You should be aware of the importance of everything that you put on stage – especially in a storytelling play such as this – and how it will help to resonate particular themes or ideas within the text.

Locations

As part of your preparation, you could make a list of the play's different locations. These should be specific, and, as in the images exercise, will allow you to see the play as a whole. The workshop group identified the following locations:

- cell
- street
- house (kitchen and stairs)
- grandad's house
- school
- bedroom
- secure unit
- corridor of school
- town
- streets on way home
- court
- outside court

Some of these locations feature more than once. Directors should be very specific about the location for each individual scene, and find a way to communicate this to the audience (again, like the images, this does not need to be literally communicated).

Timeline

It could be useful to create an accurate timeline of events narrated in the play. Work out the specifics – how many days and weeks between scenes of the play – with the cast, so their performances are grounded in detail and reality.

As an exercise, you could write each event of the play on a different sheet of paper, then order these pages on a physical timeline from present day back to year zero. You can do this alone in preparation and as an early rehearsal exercise with your cast. The important thing is to keep the decisions specific and rooted in the text.

The workshop discussed how the play has two time frames: 1) the time frame of the events that are narrated; and 2) the time frame of the narration. Companies are advised to be very specific about both time frames and, with the second, to be specific about from where and when the story is being told. In answering this question, you are choosing a dramatic frame for your production.

Units / sections

Esther suggested that units would be helpful in approaching work on this play. She acknowledged that everyone has their own system for working on this, but that she suggests separating units on rhythm shifts or thought changes. Separating out discrete units will allow the audience to experience and understand the storytelling shifts clearly. Esther suggested titling each unit, perhaps with a quotation from the text.

Storytelling

Blackout is very much a storytelling play. Storytelling was at the heart of the play's genesis and development, and this should be reflected in the style and technique of the production. When breaking the play into sections, it could be helpful to discuss and be specific about what response the storyteller wants to provoke in an audience, and to identify the areas in which that may change.

Exercises for use in rehearsals

STORYTELLING EXERCISE

You could start work on the play by asking actors to tell a story from their own lives. This will help you to observe how your actors naturally tell a story and will allow your company to feel comfortable in telling stories to an audience, and to experience the different ways in which you might tell a story.

Divide your group into smaller groups. Ask them to tell a mundane story – for example, how they got to school that morning, or a time at which they made a good or bad decision. Each group was given a different instruction that would affect how they told their story. For example:

- Everyone tells the same story, and the audience have to guess who the story actually happened to.
- The group tells the story twice, but to two very different imagined audiences.
- The group tells the story together.
- One narrator tells the story, and the rest of the group physicalise the story somehow.
- A group tell different versions of the same story.

In all the stories, we discovered that a story feels believable when it has more detail in it. The storyteller has to be able to see the detail that they are describing, without necessarily physicalising it all. A version in which every gesture and action of the story is physicalised could overload the text. The simpler the performance of the text, the more evocative it becomes. Doing less, Bijan said, means that when a performer does do something, it means so much more.

Companies should be aware that pulling out very specific details – like with the images discussed earlier – can be most helpful.

Improvising

Early on in the process Bijan would encourage actors to act out everything that is described in the text first, so that when they come to tell the story, it feels real; as if they have experienced that event. For example, in the play, there's the line in which *she stopped working*. Bijan would encourage the actors to act out that event of when Mum stopped working. This will mean that when they are saying the line, it will feel more real, because they can draw upon what that felt like in the improvisation.

After you have broken the play into sections (separating each event in the text) you could focus on a particular scene and ask your actors to improvise each section within that scene. Ask them to act out each event as it happens, in order, and add in anything that would be useful to the improvisation if it isn't already in the text. By doing this you can discover with your company what are important images and feelings in the text, and what isn't necessary to perform. This is also helpful in discovering the importance of the order of events and in helping the actors visualise the story. This then helps the audience see the story too.

The performance of *Blackout* must involve the audience directly and actors should find ways to bring the audience into the story as fully as possible. It is useful to consider the simplest form of storytelling – a person can involve you in the moment by telling it to you directly. How can you bring this simple directness to *Blackout* and incorporate ideas about staging that do not get in the way of the audience really feeling each moment?

FREEZE-FRAME

Split the company into smaller groups. Ask the group to choose five (or however many people are in the group) key moments from the character's life. Each member of the group should choose a freeze-frame that expresses that key moment, and the five freeze-frames should be ordered according to when they happened in the character's life (*not* the order in which they happen in the play).

This exercise will help a company to focus in on the crucial moments of storytelling. It allows you to find the moments that you will really want to highlight in your production.

CREATE A CHARACTER'S BEDROOM

You could ask an actor to (using material from the rehearsal space) create the character's bedroom. You should then challenge them to think of and embody three different things that the character may do in their bedroom. This exercise is designed to help the actors to embody the characters when they are at their most boring, so simple ideas will be much more effective than complex ones.

EMOTIONAL LEVELS

You can create an imaginary 'emotion-o-meter' that runs across the length of the space – it runs from –10 to +10. Then ask the company to walk through the whole play emotionally – discovering when a character is at a +10 (experiencing very high emotions) or, conversely, when they are at a –10. This is designed to help you and your company discover the rhythm and texture of each scene and situation, and to pitch each scene carefully in production.

Themes

- loneliness / detachment
- different sorts of pain
- gender – femininity and masculinity
- violence
- oppressor/oppressed
- crime
- guilt

Davey Anderson suggested that the theme of identity is at the heart of *Blackout*. It is a story about a person trying to find out who they are.

On whether there is a message at the end of the play, Davey said:

> I don't think there's a message to the play; I think it ends with a question. I want the audience to care about the subject matter. I want them to think about: who is to blame for crime? Is crime the result of a personal choice or society? I want people to explore those questions. I don't want people to come away with a simple message.

Davey talked further about the key themes of crime and guilt in the play:

It made sense to focus the play on the experience of the perpetrator of the crime, rather than the victim. I had to keep the victim a mystery. But I also think that the most interesting characters are the ones you disagree with, and with this play I wanted to create room to disagree with James. There's a whole question around who is to blame – is it his fault or society's? It's interesting, because I think a lot of people aren't one way all the time. Their behaviour swings and changes; sometimes you're not a nice person to be around, and sometimes you are. So I wanted the audience to think for themselves, to be able to judge him the way they wanted to.

Structure

Davey Anderson spoke about his love for detective stories, which informed how the play unfolded. 'There's something interesting about a single person (James) being a victim, a perpetrator and a detective all at once.'

In terms of the structure of the play in performance, Davey said: 'The things I'm going to insist on are where the full stops are. It's also important to me that there are twenty different sections. Line breaks tend to show that there's a new image or a new thought.'

Characters

It is important that the company undergo extensive character work when producing *Blackout*, in order to make all the characters, even those who are on stage for a tiny amount of time, feel real and well-rounded. It is important that a production humanises all of the play's characters, rather than judges them.

CHARACTER PREPARATION EXERCISE

1   With an unmarked script, highlight everything that James says about himself.

2   In a different colour, highlight everything that others say
     about James.

3   In a third colour, highlight everything that James says
     about others.

It may help to read these three different lists out loud. Be
careful not to paraphrase or summarise the lines, but to read
them out in full. You should repeat this for each character
in the play.

It is interesting to observe that James talks about himself in
a very removed and detached way. He switches between
talking about 'I' and 'you', and Esther suggested that you
really interrogate and pull out the differences in how he
talks about himself, because they are significant. Davey said:
'I was interested in how the "you" serves to cast the
audience as the main character.' Other characters speak
about James in a very negative way. (Does anyone say
anything entirely positive about him?) James says loads
about other people, and perhaps it is interesting to discuss
why. He also demonstrates no emotion about very strong,
dark things, such as extreme violence.

CHARACTER BACK-STORY EXERCISE

Esther outlined some key questions that directors could ask
actors to consider about their character's back-story. Even
though the answers are not all given in the text, directors
and actors should use reasonable deduction, building on the
impression of the character that you've got from the text.
Remember that a simple answer is usually much more
helpful for an actor than a complicated answer, which will
be difficult to play.

1   How old is the character?

2   Who does the character trust?

3   Who doesn't the character trust?

4   Who is the closest person to the character?

5   Who is the character afraid of?

6   What is the character's secret?

7   What does the character want from life?

8   Where does the character live?

9   Who else lives with the character?

10 Does the character have any siblings?

11 What's the area in which the character lives like?

PHYSICALITY

In the workshop, Esther outlined some questions about physicality that will help your actors to embody their characters. When you are thinking about physicality, you should consider where a character holds their tension. Do they have a physical characteristic? Be aware that body language could change as a character develops or if we discover them in a different situation.

JAMES

James is based on a real person whom Davey met when he was researching the play. Davey discussed how, over the course of their meetings together, sometimes 'James' would be very cogent and clear, and would demonstrate surprising articulacy and vocabulary. On other occasions, however, he would be closed off and wouldn't want to talk. It was always very difficult to pinpoint what had caused this extreme change in his manner and personality. Davey and Esther, based upon their experiences with young people in comparable situations to the protagonist, described how young people often hold an internal conflict that pulls them in different directions.

Davey spoke in detail about the importance of James's transition from goth to skinhead. If these sub-cultures aren't relevant, it is worth considering what the equivalences are

now. 'Seven years ago when the play was first written, the
term goth had connotations of softness, of wearing your
sensitivity on your sleeve,' Davey said. 'That decision to
shave his hair after growing it long as a goth represents a
different approach to the world, becoming more hard,
someone to be feared. Being a skinhead is so tied into a
certain philosophy on the world, so try and hang on to that
however you can in production.'

GRANDAD

Davey discussed how it is important that the Grandad
character emerged from a trade-union context. He worked
in heavy industry all his life, in the type of job that would no
longer exist for a boy like James.

THE DAD

The influence of father figures is great. 'Once he's gone, he's
not really gone; he's inside James somewhere,' Davey said.
Is there a way of exploring this theatrically?

NARRATORS

If you decided to cast and create narration roles, Davey
stressed the importance of giving narrators as much thought
in terms of characterisation as the characters with dialogue.

There is a temptation to treat narration as journalism,
with narrators being quite detached, talking from a place
of absolute knowledge. But I think it's more interesting to
make the narrators as real as the characters. Just as you
work with characters you can work with narration, too.
One option is to investigate what a narrator is trying to
say to the audience – are they trying to seek something
from the audience?

To unlock the live-ness of narration, Davey spoke about
how the actors playing narrators might not play all the
knowledge in advance: 'Perhaps they find out the story as

they go, just as James discovers things along the way. They can have the same journey. It has a more dramatic effect.' For example, in the opening section, the narrators could be commenting on things they see, not fully realising the importance of certain details until information is revealed later. It could be that important information cascades, so that one person finds something out, and perhaps another finds out more, and so on.

An ensemble is most effective when it is being used to highlight key moments. The narrators should support James rather than draw attention to themselves, and there are different qualities of narration lines (some are factual, and some are emotional, for example) which might inform the way lines are divided between performers.

Casting

Davey said that the play is flexible; he aimed to write a play that could be performed by one or forty performers: 'The play is about one central character, but it's open enough for it to be played in different ways.'

In the spirit of the play's openness, companies should feel free to cast a female or male actor in the role of 'James'. You should feel free to do this without necessarily changing the gender of the character – the openness and theatricality of the text will withstand a bold casting choice. Indeed, it may be that a company want to have the whole ensemble playing James at a different point in the production. If a company did want to change the character's name to reflect the gender of the actor, then it is acceptable for the character to be called 'Jay'.

Production/staging/design

Blackout can be performed by any number of actors. It has the potential to be performed as a monologue or as a huge ensemble piece.

Davey spoke about how when he was writing the play he was in the habit of making work without sets, lighting and sound. '*Blackout* focuses on storytelling, bodies in space, and painting pictures with words,' he said. 'The play is so fluid as a piece it requires minimal objects.' Being economical in terms of production, staging and design would be especially effective due to the number of location changes, and of the play's demand for pace.

Davey suggested that the design needs to have openness to allow for the audience's imagination.

PERIOD

Davey said he was happy for the play to be brought into the present day by making changes to the text – changing the name of the film to a more recent horror film, changing mention of DVDs to YouTube, and so on.

CONTEXT/ACCENTS

Davey is happy for actors to perform the play in their own accent – they don't need to attempt Glaswegian. 'It's not necessary or appropriate,' Davey said. 'I'd rather see young performers exploring their own identity and their own location over trying a Glaswegian accent.'

The sectarian context – for example, the references to Ulster and to the Orange Walks – is crucial for *Blackout*. It is possible to edit the references to the Orange Walk to best suit your group, but it is worth bearing in mind that if you are clear in your storytelling, the audience will understand and connect them to their own context. Either way, you need to fully interrogate what the Orange Walk is and explore its meaning with your company before making any changes.

Style and technique

Davey stressed the importance of creating a show that has a high energy. He also stressed paying attention to the 'here and now' of the actors performing onstage.

A crucial production choice for the director and cast to make is 'who' is telling the story and 'who' is being told the story. The play is not written in the first person – it is a constant challenge to the audience to imagine the story and to imagine that you are this person within the story. The 'you' that is repeated throughout the play is a slippery 'you': sometimes it speaks of a specific 'you', at other times it is a 'one'. The director and cast should be rigorous in their interrogation of the language.

The production should be very specific therefore in who is telling the story, to whom and why. In the workshop, the following suggestions were made:

- A monologue
- One person telling the story back to James
- A group of people telling the story to each other
- James telling the story to himself
- James telling the story to his mother
- A writer reading the story back to James
- James's mother could be telling the story
- A judge could be telling the story
- A room full of people – perhaps a group therapy session – could tell the story to each other
- A therapist could be telling the story

The choice of who is telling the story and who is being addressed will help resonate different themes within the production. It was strongly recommended that companies play with different options in rehearsal. Esther suggested that the audience don't necessarily need to know the choice you've made, but that the director and actors should make very specific decisions to ensure that everyone is performing in the same play!

Language

'The rhythm of the language is deliberate, so it's important to retain that,' Davey said. 'James revealed information in tiny nuggets rather with eloquent descriptions. Try and catch the natural inflections of how James spoke. There's the shortness of some of the sentences.'

Davey said that he's happy for the word order to be changed if it needs to be translated into British Sign Language, as long as the order of events is the same. He said that in translation the text might not be true to each word, but it's important to stay true to the order at which moments are revealed.

MOVEMENT AND CHOREOGRAPHY

Blackout works best as a high-energy and physical performance. Davey said that the play suggests and wants movement to be a part of it. However, *Blackout* is explicitly designed to be twenty discrete scenes – that number is important and should not be increased. Therefore, any movement should be integrated into the existing scenes rather than devised and added as a new scene.

MUSIC

Live music and soundscapes could integrate extremely well into *Blackout* to help create the high energy required for the production. Directors are advised to listen and feel for the play's rhythm very carefully when integrating these elements: the text has its own very specific rhythm, which can be amplified, but will work less well if it is altered.

Interpretation

Every word written in the play is intended to be spoken – there are no stage directions or instructions for actors. Davey stated that this includes the final 'Blackout' in the text.

The lines have deliberately not been assigned to different characters in order to allow for interpretation and debate in rehearsal. The process of deciding who will say what, and to whom, should be a part of the creative process and companies should feel liberated in interpreting this as they wish. Openness and democracy are at the heart of this play, and should be celebrated in the process and production.

AMBIGUITY

Blackout purposely creates a significant amount of ambiguity, and Davey wants the company and the audience to ask questions about truthfulness. There is a lot of information telling in the play, and so there can definitely be a tension between what a character says and what the audience see happen. For example, there is no stage direction saying that he takes down the poster, and this can definitely be open for interpretation. Davey suggested that he made a deliberate choice in the writing for the audience to not know what James has done, or to whom he's done it.

How much can the narrator be trusted? This is something to be questioned, analysed and debated with your company. Part of the joy of storytelling is that every storyteller has their own idea and opinion about the story that they are telling: you should encourage your company to find their own attitude towards the story and allow them to express this in the production.

LIGHTNESS AND HUMOUR

Davey suggested that companies search for the lightness in their performance. One way into the lightness may be to find the moments of connection in the play: *Blackout* is about a character who feels very disconnected and lonely. You could, therefore, emphasise the brief moments when they do feel connected (and this has the added effect of increasing the sense of loneliness, because we know it is possible for them to feel connected).

Eclipse
by Simon Armitage

Six friends are interviewed by the police after the disappearance of Lucy Lime, a strange unnerving girl – 'I am a walking Universe, I am' – whom they met beneath the cliffs on a Cornish beach, just before the total eclipse of the sun.

Age suitability: any age

Cast size
seven named characters:
four girls, three boys

Simon Armitage was born in 1963 and lives in West Yorkshire. He is Professor of Poetry at the University of Sheffield and in 2015 was appointed Professor of Poetry at the University of Oxford. He is the author of over a dozen collections of poetry, most recently *Paper Aeroplane: Selected Poems 1989–2014*, drawing on twenty-five years of published work. His translations of medieval verse include *The Death of King Arthur* and his acclaimed *Sir Gawain and the Green Knight*. His translation of *Pearl* will be published in 2016. He is the author of two novels and three best-selling non-fiction titles: *All Points North* and *Walking Home*, in which he walked the Pennine Way as a modern-day troubadour giving poetry readings along the route, and a companion volume *Walking Away*. He writes extensively for radio and television. *The Last Days of Troy*, his dramatisation of Homer's *Iliad*, was performed at Manchester Royal Exchange and Shakespeare's Globe in London in 2014 and a new dramatic version of Homer's *Odyssey*, commissioned by English Touring Theatre, toured in autumn 2015. His awards include the Sunday Times Young Writer of the Year, a Lannan Award, one of the first Forward Poetry prizes, a Cholmondeley Award, the Keats Shelley Prize, the Hay Medal for Poetry, and for his lyrics for the BAFTA-winning film *Feltham Sings* he received an Ivor Novello Award. He is a Fellow of the Royal Society of Literature and in 2010 was made CBE for services to poetry.

Characters

Six friends

Klondike, *the oldest*
Tulip, *a tomboy*
Polly *and* **Jane**, *twins*
Midnight, *male, blind*
Glue Boy, *a glue-sniffer*

A stranger

Lucy Lime

Scene One

A police waiting room. Seven chairs in a row. **Glue Boy**, **Polly** *and* **Jane**, **Midnight** *and* **Tulip** *are sitting in five of them.* **Klondike** *enters the room and sits on one of the empty chairs.*

Klondike   Tulip.

Tulip   Klondike.

Klondike   Midnight.

Midnight   Alright.

Klondike   Missed the bus, then couldn't find it. Sorry I'm late.

Midnight   Are we in trouble?

Klondike   Anyone been in yet?

Tulip   No, just told us to sit here and wait.

Klondike   Oh, like that, is it? Glue Boy.

Glue Boy   Klondike.

Klondike   Extra Strong Mint?

Glue Boy   Bad for your teeth.

Midnight   Klondike, tell me the truth.

Klondike   And how are the split peas?

Polly *and* **Jane**   We're the bees' knees.

Polly   Yourself?

Klondike   Could be worse, could be better.

Midnight   Klondike, we're in bother, aren't we?

Klondike   Three times. Who am I? St Peter?

Off, a voice calls 'Martin Blackwood'.

Midnight   Me first? I thought we'd have time to get it straight.

Polly   Say as you speak . . .

Jane   . . . speak as you find.

Klondike   Say what you think, speak your mind. Clear?

Midnight   Not sure.

Klondike   Glue Boy, show him the door.

Tulip   Klondike, why don't you tell him what's what? He's pissing his pants.

Klondike   Let's all settle down. Midnight, stick to the facts.
The oldies were up on the flat with the van,
we were down in the crags.
They were waiting to gawp at the total eclipse of the sun,
we were kids, having fun.
It was August eleventh, nineteen ninety-nine,
they were pinning their hopes
on the path of the moon,
they were setting their scopes and their sights
on a point in the afternoon sky
where the sun put its monocle into its eye.
The first and last that we saw of her. Right?

Tulip   Right.

Polly *and* **Jane**   Amen.

Midnight   Just tell me again.

Off, a voice calls 'Martin Blackwood'.

Tulip   Stick to the facts. You were down on the sand . . .

Midnight   I was down on the sand.
The mothers and fathers were up on the land.
Was it dark?

Exit **Midnight** *into the interview room.*

Tulip   What a fart.

Klondike   Oh, leave him. Blind as a bat. Sympathy vote.
He'll be alright. Anyway, who's said what? Tulip?

Tulip   No fear, kept mum like those two did.

Klondike   Polly, Jane?

Polly   Thought we'd keep schtum till you came.

Klondike   Good move.

Glue Boy   What about you?

Klondike   What about me? What about you?

Glue Boy   No, nothing.

Klondike   Well, that's alright then.

Jane   What can you hear through the crack?

Polly   He was egging himself, I know that.

Tulip   Shh. No, not a word.

Klondike   Can you see through the glass?

Tulip   Give us a leg-up . . . No, it's frosted.

Polly   Moon came up. Sun was behind.

Jane   Nothing to say. Nothing to hide.

Klondike   Correct. Let's get a grip. No need for anyone
losing their head.

Tulip   The copper who came to the house said we're in this
up to our necks . . .

Klondike   FOR CRYING OUT LOUD . . .
They were on the tops,
we were down in the rocks.
Stick to the facts.
Pax?

Tulip   Pax.

Polly *and* **Jane**   Pax.

Glue Boy   Pax.

Klondike   Stick to what we know and we'll be fine.
Now a moment's silence for Lucy Lime.

All   For Lucy Lime.

Scene Two

A police interview room.

Midnight   Martin Blackwood, they call me Midnight – it's
a sick joke but I don't mind. Coffee please, two sugars, white
– don't ask me to say what I saw, I'm profoundly blind, but
I'll tell you as much as I can, alright?

Cornwall, August, as you know. There's a beach down there,
seaside and all that, cliffs with caves at the back, but up on
the hill there's a view looking south, perfect for watching a
total eclipse of the sun. The mums and dads were up on the
top, we were down in the drop – we'd just gone along for the
trip, killing a few hours. You see, it's like watching birds or
trains but with planets and stars, and about as much fun as
cricket in my condition, or 3D. There was Glue Boy, Polly
and Jane, Tulip and Klondike and me. Thing is, we were
messing around in the caverns when Lucy appeared. Her
mother and father were up with the rest of the spotters; she
wasn't from round here. Thing is, I was different then, did a
lot of praying, wore a cross, went to church, thought I was
walking towards the light of the Lord – when it's as dark as it
is in here, you follow any road with any torch. Lucy put me
on the straight and narrow. There's no such thing as the soul,
there's bone and there's marrow. It's just biology. You make
your own light, follow your own nose. She came and she
went. And that's as much as I know.

We were just coming up from one of the smuggler's coves . . .

Scene Three

A beach in Cornwall, 11 August. At the back of the beach a broken electric fence dangles down from the headland above. There are cave entrances in the cliff face. **Polly** *and* **Jane** *are sitting on a rock, combing each other's hair, etc. They are heavily made up and wearing a lot of jewellery.*

Polly   Your turn.

Jane   Okay. The three materials that make up Tutankhamun's mask.

Polly   Easy. Solid gold, lapis lazuli and blue glass.

Jane   Yes.

Polly   Hairbrush. Thanks.

Jane   Now you.

Polly   Proof of man's existence at the time of extinct mammals.

Jane   Er . . . artwork carved on the tusks of mammals.

Polly   Correct.

Jane   Nail-file. Thanks.

Polly   These are a doddle. Ask me something harder.

Jane   Who swam through sharks with a seagull's egg in a bandanna?

Polly   A bandanna?

Jane   Alright, a headband.

Polly   The birdmen of Easter Island. Easy-peasy.

Jane   Lemon-squeezy.

Polly   Cheddar-cheesy.

Jane   Japanesey.

Polly   Pass me the compact.

Jane   Your go, clever clogs.

Polly   On the same subject. The statues were studded
with . . . which mineral?

Jane   Er . . . malachite. No, marble.

Polly   No, white coral.

Jane   Sugar. When's the test?

Polly   Monday next, I think he said.

Jane   Oh, I should be alright by then. (*Pause.*) What time do
you make it?

Polly   Twenty past. Another couple of hours yet, at least.

Jane   Mine must be fast.

Polly   Let's synchronise, just in case.

Jane   It might be yours. Yours might be slow.

Polly   I don't think so. Anyway, it's solar-powered – it's
been charging up all summer.

Jane   Look out, here come the others.

Klondike, **Tulip** *and* **Glue Boy** *come running out of one of the
caves.* **Glue Boy** *is sniffing glue from a plastic bag, and continues to
do so throughout.* **Klondike** *wears a leather bag on his back and is
carrying the skeletal head of a bull.* **Tulip** *is wearing Dr Marten boots
and a red headscarf like a pirate's.*

Klondike   Bloody hell, it's a cow's skull.

Tulip   How do you know it's not from a sheep?

Klondike   You're joking. Look at the size of it. look at the
teeth. Some caveman's had this for his tea. Hey, girls, fancy a
spare rib?

Polly   Take it away, it stinks.

Jane   And I bet it's crawling with fleas.

Klondike   It's a skull, you pair of dumb belles, not a fleece.

Tulip   He found it right at the back of the cave.

Klondike   I reckon it fell through the gap in the fence – it's been lying there, waiting for me.

Polly   It gives me the creeps.

Glue Boy   It's a dinosaur. Ginormous Rex.

Klondike   I'm going to frame it or something. Put it in a case.

Tulip *takes off her red headscarf, unfurls it and uses it as a matador's cape.*

Tulip   Come on Klondike. *Olé. Olé.*

Polly   Where's Midnight?

Tulip   Still coming out of the hole. Let's hide.

Jane   Don't be rotten. That'd be really tight.

Polly   Why don't we just stay here like statues? He can't see us.

Klondike   He'd hear us, though. He's got ears like satellite dishes.

Glue Boy   Like radar stations.

Tulip   Everyone scarper and hide.

Glue Boy   Everyone turns into pumpkins when Midnight chimes.

Exit **Glue Boy**, **Polly** *and* **Jane**.

Tulip   Wait, my scarf.

Klondike   Leave it.

Exit **Klondike** *and* **Tulip**, *leaving the scarf behind. Enter*
Midnight *from the cave, wearing dark glasses and a crucifix around*
his neck, which he holds out in front of him in his hand.

Midnight   Klondike? Tulip? That skull, what is it?

Enter **Lucy Lime**.

Midnight   Klondike? Glue Boy. Come on, don't be
pathetic. Tulip? Tulip?

Lucy   Selling flowers, are we?

Midnight   Polly? Jane?

Lucy   Penny Lane? Singing now, is it?

Midnight   I'm Midnight. Who are you?

Lucy   I'm twenty-to-three. Look. (*She makes the position of a*
clock's hands with her arms.)

Midnight   I can't look. I can't see.

Lucy   Oh, you should have said. I'm Lucy. Lucy Lime.

Midnight   I thought you were one of the others. They said
they'd wait for me somewhere around here.

Lucy   No, I'm not one of the others. And you can put that
thing down. I'm not Dracula's daughter either.

Midnight   What, this? Sorry, I'm a believer. It's Jesus,
watching over.

Lucy   Well, don't point it at me. It's loaded.

An animal noise comes out of one of the caves.

What was that? A bat?

Midnight   More like Klondike messing about.

Lucy   Klondike?

Midnight   Him and Tulip and Glue Boy and the twins. We all came here in a van to do this star-gazing thing, or at least everybody's parents did, but it's boring.

Lucy   So you've been exploring?

Midnight   Yes. Pot-holing.

Lucy   How did you . . .?

Midnight   Go blind?

Lucy   Lose your sight, I was going to say.

Midnight   Looked at the sun through binoculars when I was ten.

Lucy   By mistake?

Midnight   For a bet. Burnt out. Never see again.

Lucy   Sorry.

Midnight   Not to worry. I've got Jesus, and the truth.

Lucy   Truth? What's that?

Midnight   When you can't see, it's better to follow one straight path.

Lucy   Oh, right. (*Pause.*) Do you want them to come back?

Midnight   I told you, they're written off.

Lucy   No, the others, I mean.

Midnight   Oh, they won't. They think it's a good crack, leaving me playing blind man's buff.

Lucy   Ever caught moths?

Midnight   What have moths got to do with it?

Lucy   Oh, nothing.

She sets fire to the silk scarf and tosses it up in the air. It flares brightly and vanishes.

Enter **Klondike**, **Tulip**, **Polly** *and* **Jane**.

Klondike   Midnight, what's going on?

Tulip   We thought we saw something burning . . .

Polly   Or a meteorite falling . . .

Jane   A maroon or whatever they're called, like a rocket . . .

Klondike   Or sheet lightning.

Glue Boy   Air-raid warning. Keep away from the trees. The strike of midnight.

Midnight   Er . . .

Lucy   It was a will-o'-the-wisp.

Tulip   Who the hell's this?

Midnight   Er . . .

Lucy   Lucy Lime. Mother and father are up on the top with your lot. I've been keeping your friend company – thought you'd be looking for him.

Klondike   Er . . . that's right. We got separated.

Lucy   Lucky I was around, then. Wouldn't have wanted the electric fence to have found him.

Polly (*aside*)   Strange-looking creature.

Jane   Not pretty. No features. Hairy armpits, I bet.

Polly   Yeah, and two hairy legs.

Midnight *sits on a stone away from everyone else and puts on his Walkman.*

Lucy   Mind if I join you?

Klondike   Sorry?

Lucy   Mind if I stay?

Tulip   Feel free. Free country.

Jane   I'm bored. Let's play a game.

Klondike   Let's trap a rabbit and skin it.

Polly   You're kidding. Let's play mirror, mirror on the wall . . .

Jane   Spin the bottle. Postman's knock.

Glue Boy   Pin the donkey on the tail.

Lucy   What about hide and seek?

Tulip   British bulldogs. No, numblety peg.

Lucy   What's that?

Tulip   That's where I throw this knife into the ground between your legs.

Klondike   I know. We'll play bets. I bet I can skim this stone head-on into the waves.

Polly   We know you can. I bet if we had a vote, I'd have the prettiest face.

Jane   I bet you'd come joint first.

Tulip   I bet I dare touch the electric fence.

Klondike   Easy, you've got rubber soles. What do you bet, Evo-Stik?

Glue Boy   Tomorrow never comes.

Klondike   Sure, you keep taking the pills.

Lucy   I can get Midnight to tell a lie. That's what I bet.

Tulip   You're off your head. He's as straight as a die.

Glue Boy   Straight as a plumb-line.

Klondike   You've got no chance. He's a born-again Mr Tambourine Man. A proper Christian.

Polly   Says his prayers before he goes to bed . . .

Jane   Goes to church when it's not even Christmas.

Lucy   I don't care if he's Mary and Joseph and Jesus rolled into one. He'll lie like anyone.

Tulip   What do you bet?

Lucy   I bet this. Two coins together – it's a lucky charm – a gold sovereign melted to a silver dime.

Klondike   It's Lucy Locket now, is it, not Lucy Lime?

Lucy   It's worth a bomb.

Tulip   We can sell and split it. Okay, you're on. I bet this knife that you're wrong.

Lucy   I've no need of a knife. I'll bet you your boots instead.

Polly   I'll bet you this bracelet. It's nine-carat gold.

Jane   I'll bet you this make-up case. It's mother-of-pearl.

Glue Boy   I'll bet Antarctica.

Lucy   You can do better than that, can't you?

Glue Boy   Okay, the world.

Tulip   What do you bet, Klondike?

Klondike   My skull.

Lucy   Not enough.

Klondike   And these Boji stones, from Kansas, under an ancient lake.

Lucy   Not enough.

Klondike   Alright, if you win – which you won't – you can kiss this handsome face.

Lucy   Everybody shake on it.

Klondike   All for one, and once and for all.

Glue Boy   And one for the road. And toad in the hole.

Lucy   Glue Boy, is that your name?

Glue Boy   One and the same.

Lucy   Come with me, you're the witness.

Polly   Why him? He doesn't know Tuesday from a piece of string.

Lucy   Sounds perfect. Everyone else, keep quiet.

Lucy *and* **Glue Boy** *approach* **Midnight***.* **Lucy** *taps him on the shoulder.*

Lucy   Listen.

Midnight   What?

Lucy   Can you hear a boat?

Midnight   Nope.

Lucy   Listen, I can hear its engine. I'm certain.

Midnight   I think you're mistaken.

Lucy   There, just as I thought – coming round the point.

Midnight   There can't be. Which direction?

Tulip (*to the others*)   What's she saying? There's no boat.

Lucy   Straight out in front. Plain as the nose on your face. See it, Glue Boy?

Glue Boy   Er . . .? Oh, sure.

Lucy   It's a trawler. Is it greeny-blue, would you say?

Glue Boy   Well, sort of sea-green, sort of sky-blue, sort of blue moon sort of colour.

Lucy   I'm amazed you can't hear it, it's making a real racket.

Midnight   Well, I . . .

Lucy   Too much time with ear-plugs, listening to static.

Midnight   My hearing's perfect.

Lucy Fine. Okay. Forget it.

Midnight I'm sorry. I didn't mean to be rude.

Lucy You weren't. I shouldn't have mentioned it. It's my fault – I should have thought. You can't hear the boat for the sound of the seagulls.

Midnight Seagulls?

Polly (*to the others*) There isn't a bird for miles.

Jane This is a waste of time. It's her who's telling the lies.

Lucy All that high-pitched skriking and screaming. Must play havoc with sensitive hearing like yours.

Midnight How close?

Lucy The birds? Three hundred yards, five hundred at most. Black-headed gulls, Glue Boy, don't you think?

Glue Boy Well, kind of rare breed, kind of less common, kind of lesser-spotted type things.

Lucy Don't say you're going deaf?

Midnight Who, me?

Lucy Glue Boy can hear them, and he's out of his head. Come on, Midnight, stop clowning around. I bet you can hear it all. I bet you can hear a cat licking its lips in the next town, can't you?

Midnight I don't know . . . I think sometimes I filter it out.

Lucy Yes, when you're half-asleep. But listen, what can you hear now?

Midnight Er . . . something . . .

Lucy That aeroplane for a start, I bet.

Midnight Yes. The aeroplane.

Lucy I can't see it myself. Where would you say it was?

Midnight   Er . . . off to the left, that's my guess.

Lucy   What else? That dog on the cliff, half a mile back. Can you hear that?

Midnight   Yes. The dog. Sniffing the air, is it? Scratching the ground?

Lucy   Amazing. Wrap-around sound. What else? The boy with the kite?

Midnight   Yes, the kite.
The wind playing the twine like a harp.
It's a wonderful sound.

Lucy   And Klondike and Tulip, coming back up the beach. What are they talking about?

Midnight   They're saying . . . this and that, about that eclipse, and how dark and how strange it'll be.

Lucy   And down by the rock pools, the twins?

Midnight   Chatting away. Girls' things. Boyfriends, that kind of stuff. It's not really fair to listen in on it.

Lucy   You're not kidding. You're absolutely ultrasonic. Glue Boy, how about that for a pair of ears?

Glue Boy   Yeah, he's Jodrell Bank, he is.

Lucy   And one last noise. A siren or something?

Midnight   Car alarm.

Lucy   No. Music.

Midnight   Brass band. 'Floral Dance.'

Lucy   No. It's there on the tip of my tongue, but I just can't place it. You know, sells lollies and things.

Midnight   Ice-cream van. Ice-cream van. I can hear it.

Lucy   You can?

Midnight   Can't you?

Lucy   No. Not any more. What was the tune?

Midnight   Er . . . 'Greensleeves.'

Lucy   'Greensleeves', eh? Thanks, Midnight, that should do it.

Midnight   Sorry?

Tulip   Nice one, stupid.

Midnight   What? I thought you were . . .

Tulip   Yeah, well, you know what thought did.

Polly   Pathetic, Midnight.

Jane   You should see a doctor, you're hearing voices.

Midnight   But, all those noises . . .

Klondike   She made them up, you soft bastard. I tell you what, you should take more care of those ears.

Midnight   Why's that?

Klondike   Cos if they fall off, you won't be able to wear glasses.

Midnight   I didn't invent them.

Polly   You lying rat.

Jane   You just lost us the bet, Dumbo. Do us a favour – stick to your Walkman.

Lucy   Midnight, I'm sorry.

Midnight   Get lost. Keep off me.

Polly   Where are you going?

Midnight   Anywhere away from here.

Klondike   Well, get me a ninety-nine will you, when you're there.

Tulip   And a screwball as well.

Midnight   Go to hell.

He takes off his crucifix and throws it in the direction of **Lucy**. *She picks it up and puts it in her bag.*

Lucy   Well, I think that clinches it, don't you? The bracelet, the case, the boots, and the skull and the stone, if you please.

Everyone hands her the items. **Lucy** *puts on the shoes and puts everything else in her bag.*

Klondike   Forgetting something?

Lucy   I don't think so.

Klondike   A kiss from me, because you did it.

Lucy   No thanks, Romeo. I was only kidding.

Polly   What a cheek. Not to worry, in the glove compartment I've got more jewellery, too good for that gold-digger.

Jane   But you've got to hand it to her. I'll come to the car park to check out the courtesy light and the vanity mirror.

Exit **Polly** *and* **Jane**.

Glue Boy   What did I bet?

Lucy   The Earth.

Glue Boy   I've left it at home in my other jacket. Double or quits?

Lucy   No, I'll take it on credit.

Glue Boy   A whole planet. In a top pocket.

Tulip   Hey, where do you think you're going?

Lucy   To see Midnight, make sure he's okay.

Tulip   You've got a nerve.

Lucy   Why? It was only a game.

Glue Boy   Klondike, the sun . . .

Klondike   Don't you think you've lost enough for one day?

Glue Boy   No, the shadow. Here it comes.

Lucy   It can't be. It's too early to start.

Tulip   He's right, it's going dark. Klondike?

Klondike   ECLIPSE, ECLIPSE. EVERYONE INTO POSITION. EVERYONE INTO POSITION.

Tulip   We're short.

Klondike   Who's missing?

Tulip   Midnight. Gone walkabout. And the twins, where are the twins?

Klondike   Get them back. Polly. Jane. POLLY. JANE.

Scene Four

The police interview room. **Polly** *and* **Jane** *make their statement, sometimes talking in unison, sometimes separately, one sister occasionally finishing the other sister's sentence.*

Polly *and* Jane
They were up on the tops, we were down on the deck,
kicking around in pebbles and shells and bladderwrack.
They were watching the sky, we were keeping an eye
on the tide, hanging around, writing names in the sand,
turning over stones, pulling legs from hermit crabs.

We're two of a kind, two yolks from the same egg,
same thoughts in identical heads, everything half
and half, but it's easy enough to tell us apart:
I'm the spitting image; she's the copycat.

They were up on the top looking south, we were down
on the strand looking out for something to do. She came
and she went in the same afternoon, saw the eclipse, like us,

but musn't have been impressed, so she left. Straight up.
And a truth half-told is a lie. We should know, we're a Gemini.

Oh, yes, and we liked her style and the way she dressed.
We were something else before daylight vanished.
Whatever we touched was touched with varnish.
Whatever we smelt was laced with powder or scent.
Whatever we heard had an earring lending its weight.
Whatever we saw was shadowed and shaded out of sight.
Whatever we tasted tasted of mint.
Whatever we spoke had lipstick kissing its lips.
We were something else back then, alright, muddled up,
not thinking straight, as it were. But now we're clear.

Same here.

Scene Five

The beach. **Klondike**, **Tulip**, **Glue Boy** *and* **Lucy** *are standing looking at the sky.*

Tulip   False alarm. Just a cloud.

Klondike   Thought so. Too early.

Tulip   What now?

Glue Boy   I-spy.

Tulip   Boring. Hide-and-seek. Come on, Klondike, hide and seek.

Klondike   Okay. Spuds up.

Lucy   What, like this?

Klondike   Yes, that's it.

They all hold out their fists, with thumbs pointing skyward.

One potati, two potati, three potati, four,
Five potati, six potati, seven potati, more . . .

Tulip   There's a party on the hill, will you come?
Bring your own cup of tea and a bun . . .

Glue Boy   Ip dip dip, my blue ship,
Sails on the water, like a cup and saucer . . .

Klondike   It's here, it's there, it's everywhere,
It's salmon and it's trout,
It shaves its tongue and eats its hair,
You're in, you're in, you're in . . . you're out.

The dipping-out lands on **Lucy**.

Tulip   You're it.

Lucy   Okay, how many start?

Klondike   Fifty elephants and no cheating.

Glue Boy   Fifteen cheetahs, and no peeping.

Lucy   Off you go then.

She turns her back and begins counting. Exit **Tulip** *and* **Klondike**.

Lucy   One elephant, two elephant, three elephant . . .

Glue Boy   Filthy underpants and no weeping.

Klondike *returns and drags* **Glue Boy** *off. Enter* **Polly** *and*
Jane.

Polly   Hey, there's what's-her-face.

Jane   What's she playing at?

Polly   Practising her times-tables, by the sound of it. Let's
tell her to get lost.

Jane   No. I've got a better idea. Let's give her a shock.

Lucy   . . . fifty elephants. Coming ready or not.

Polly *and* **Jane**   BOO!

Lucy   Don't do that. You'll give someone a heart attack.

Polly   We're the two-headed . . .

Jane   . . . four-armed . . .

Polly   . . . four-legged . . .

Jane   . . . twenty-fingered monster from the black lagoon.

Lucy   And one brain between the pair of you.

Polly   Now, now. No need to be nasty.

Jane   Yeah, no one's called you pale and pasty, have they?

Lucy   I just meant it's hard to tell you apart.

Polly   We like it that way.

Jane   It's scary.

Lucy   Anyway, this is the natural look.

Polly   What, plain and hairy?

Lucy   No, pure and simple. Basically beautiful.

Jane   Says who?

Lucy   Says people. Boys. Men.

Jane   You got a boyfriend then?

Lucy   Yes. Someone. What about you two?

Jane   No one to speak of . . .

Polly   We're not bothered. All those round our way are
filthy or ugly and stupid.

Lucy   Maybe you should do what I did, then.

Polly   What was that?

Lucy
Well, three men fishing on the towpath wouldn't let me past;
called me a tramp, threw me in and I nearly drowned.
I was down in the weeds with dead dogs and bicycle frames.
Couldn't move for bracelets and beads and rings and chains.
Don't know why, but I ditched the lot in a minute flat,
took off my clothes as well: cuffs and frills and scarves,

heels and bottoms and lace and buckles and shoulder-pads,
climbed out strip-jack naked on the other bank, white-faced
and my hair down flat. The three men whistled and clapped
but I stood there, dressed in nothing but rain. They stopped
and threw me a shirt and a big coat, which I wouldn't take.
One of them covered his eyes, said it was somebody's fault;
a fight broke out and I watched. All three of them cried,
said they were sorry, said they were shamed. I asked them
to leave, and they shuffled away to their cars, I suppose,
and their wives. I put on the coat and shirt, and walked home,
but never went back to dredge for the gold or the clothes.
This is me now. Be yourself, I reckon, not somebody else.

Jane What a story.

Polly Jackanory.

Lucy Well, that's what happened. You should try it. You
might be surprised.

Jane You're kidding. Us?

Polly Not on your life.

Lucy Why not?

Jane How do we know we'd look any good?

Polly We wouldn't.

Lucy You would. Well, you might.
Anyhow, better to look the way you were meant to be
than done up like a tailor's dummy and a Christmas tree.

Polly Better to look like us than something the cat wouldn't
touch.

Lucy No cat curls its nose up at good meat.

Polly No, but I know what they'd go for first if it's a choice
between semi-skimmed or full cream.

Lucy Suit yourselves.

Polly We will.

Lucy   Don't blame me when you're twenty-three or thirty-four or forty-five, and left on the shelf.

Polly   We won't.

Klondike (*off*)   You haven't found us yet.

Lucy   Am I warm or cold?

Klondike (*off*)   Cold as a penguin's chuff.

Tulip (*off*)   Cold as an Eskimo's toe.

Glue Boy (*off*)   Yeah, cold as a polar bear's fridge. In a power cut.

Klondike *and* **Tulip** (*off*)   Shut up.

Jane (*to* **Polly**)   Why don't we give it a go?

Polly   No.

Jane   Why not?

Polly   Because.

Jane   It won't harm. Just for a laugh.

Polly   I haven't put all this on just to take it all off.

Jane   Come on, sis, do it for me.

Polly   What if we're . . . different?

Jane   What do you mean?

Polly   What if we don't look the same? Underneath?

Jane   Don't know. Hadn't thought. Put it all on again?

Polly   Straight away?

Jane   Before you can say Jack Robinson. Before you can say . . .

Polly   Okay.

Jane   Lucy. We're going to give it a whirl.

Polly   Just for a laugh, though. That's all.

Lucy   Excellent. Down to the sea, girls. Down to the shore.

She sings.

> Oh ladies of Greece
> with the thickest of trees,
> covered with blossom and bumble,
> snip off the bees
> and there underneath
> two apples to bake in a crumble.

> Oh ladies of France
> with warts on your hands,
> come down, come down to the waters.
> And where you were gnarled
> at the end of your arms
> two perfect symmetrical daughters.

> Oh ladies of Spain
> at night on the lane
> in nightshirts and mittens and bedsocks,
> strip off those duds
> and ride through the woods
> on horses carved onto the bedrock.

While singing, she strips them of their jewellery and some of their clothes, and washes their hair in the sea. She puts the jewellery and a few choice items into a bag.

How does it feel?

Jane   Unreal. I feel like someone else.

Lucy   Polly?

Polly   Not sure. Up in the air.

Jane   I feel lighter and thinner.

Lucy   Polly?

Polly   See-through. Like a tree in winter.

Lucy   You look great. You look like different people.

Polly   Sorry?

Lucy   I mean . . . you still look the same, alike. Just different types.

Jane   Here come the others. See if they notice.

Polly   Oh no. Let's hide.

Lucy   Say nothing. Just smile. They'll only be jealous.

Enter **Klondike**, **Tulip** *and* **Glue Boy**.

Klondike   Couldn't you find us?

Lucy   No. You win.

Tulip   We were down in the caves with the dead pirates.

Klondike   How hard did you look?

Lucy   Oh, about this hard. Feels like I've been looking for hours.

Tulip   We were camouflaged.

Glue Boy   Yeah, we were cauliflowers.

Tulip   Oh my God.

Klondike   What's up?

Tulip   It's those two. Look.

Klondike   Wow. I don't believe it.

Jane   What's the matter with you? Never seen a woman before?

Tulip   Never seen this one or that one. What happened? Get flushed down the toilet?

Lucy   They've changed their minds.

Tulip   You mean you changed it for them. That's all we need, three Lucy Limes.

Glue Boy   Three lucky strikes. Three blind mice.

Polly   Shut it, Glue Boy.

Klondike   I think they look . . . nice.

Tulip   Nice? They look like bones after the dog's had them.

Lucy   They had a change of heart.

Glue Boy   Heart transplant.

Klondike   I think they look . . . smart. Sort of.

Tulip   Yeah, and sort of not. They don't even look like twins any more. Don't look like anyone.

Polly   I told you we shouldn't have.

Jane   Don't blame me. You don't look that bad.

Polly   Me? You should see yourself. You look like something out of a plastic bag.

Jane   So what? You look like an old hag. You look like a boiled pig.

Tulip   Glue Boy, what do they look like? Mirror, mirror on the wall . . .

Glue Boy
Mirror, mirror on the wall,
Who's the worstest of them all? . . .

Jane   Glue Boy . . .

Glue Boy   This one looks like a wet haddock . . .

Jane   I'll kill you.

Glue Boy   But this one looks like a skinned rabbit.

Polly   Right, you've had it.

Polly and **Jane** *pull* **Glue Boy**'s *glue bag over his head and start to kick him. He wanders off and they follow, still kicking him.*

Klondike   They'll slaughter him.

Tulip   He wouldn't notice.

Lucy   What a mess.

Tulip   Yes, and you started it.

Lucy   Me? It was all fine till you came back and started stirring it. Now it's a hornets' nest.

Klondike   Leave it alone. It'll all come out in the wash.

Lucy (*holding up some of the clothes left on the floor*)
What about these? Needles from Christmas trees.

Klondike   Tulip, go and put leaves back on the evergreens.

Tulip   Why me? What about her – Tinkerbell?

Klondike   I don't think that'd go down too well. Please?

Tulip   Okay, give them here.

Lucy   Take this, a brush for back-combing their hair.

Tulip   Beach-combing more like. How kind.

Lucy   That's me. Sweetness and light. Lime by name, but sugar by nature. Isn't that right?

Klondike   Eh? How should I know? Got everything?

Tulip   S'pose so.

Klondike   Won't take a minute.

Tulip (*to* **Klondike**, *privately*)   You'll wait here, won't you?

Klondike   Course.

Tulip   Don't let her . . .

Klondike   What?

Tulip   Doesn't matter.

Klondike   Go on, what?

Tulip   Talk to you, you know.

Klondike   No, I won't do.

Tulip   Don't let her . . . Lucy Lime you.

Klondike   Don't be daft. Go on, I'll time you.

Exit **Tulip**.

Klondike   Enjoying yourself?

Lucy   I've had better.

Klondike   Where are you from?

Lucy   All over.

Pause.

I'm a walking universe, I am.
Wherever the best view comes from,
wherever Mars and the Moon are in conjunction,
wherever the stars and the sun are looking good from,
wherever the angles and the right ascensions and declinations
and transits and vectors and focal lengths and partial perigons
are done from, that's where I come from.
Traipsing round with mother and father. What about you lot?

Klondike   Yorkshire. Came in a van.

Lucy   Bet that was fun.

Klondike   I meant it, you know.

Lucy   Meant what?

Klondike   About that kiss. If you want to.

Lucy   What about her? Don't you think she'd mind?

Klondike   Tulip? No, she's alright. She's just . . .

Lucy   One of the lads?

Klondike   Something like that. Well, what about it?

Lucy   Ever played rising sun?

Klondike   Don't think so. How do you play it?

Lucy   Well,
A light shines bright through a sheet or blanket,
Somebody follows the sun as it rises,
It dawns at daybreak above the horizon,
The one looking east gets something surprising . . .

Klondike   Really?

Lucy   Something exciting. Something to break the ice with.

Klondike   Let's try it.

Lucy   Sorry, no can do. We need a torch for the sun.

Klondike (*producing a torch*)   Like this one?

Lucy   And we need a sheet.

Klondike (*taking off his shirt*)   You can use this shirt.

Lucy   And it needs to be dark. Sorry, can't be done.

Klondike   I'll put this blindfold on.

Without taking it off, he lifts the bottom front of his T-shirt over his head.

Lucy   Okay, here it comes.

Klondike *kneels on the floor and holds his T-shirt up in front of his face.* **Lucy**, *on the other side, presses the torch against the shirt and raises it very slowly.* **Klondike** *follows the light with his nose.*

Lucy   Rain in the north from the tears of Jesus,
Wind in the west with its knickers in a twist;
Flies in the south sucking blood like leeches,
Sun coming up in the east like a kiss –
(*Whispers.*) – from Judas.

Repeat.

Scene Six

The police interview room.

Tulip   When she left us for good I was nine or ten.
Ran off with the milkman, so Dad said. Ran off
with the man in the moon, as far as I care.
Grew up with uncles, cousins, played rugby football,
swapped a pram for a ten-speed drop-handlebar,
played with matches instead, flags and cars, threw
the dolls on a skip and the skates on a dustcart,
flogged the frills and pink stuff at a car-boot sale,
burnt the Girl Guide outfit in the back garden,
got kitted out at Famous Army Stores and Top Man.
And Oxfam. I'll tell you something that sums it up:
found a doll's house going mouldy in the attic –
boarded it up, kept a brown rat in it.
Put it all behind now, growing out of it, Dad says, says
I'm blossoming, and I suppose he must be right. Klondike?
No, not a boyfriend, more like a kid brother, really,
known him since as far back as I can remember.
Kissed him? Who wants to know? I mean, no, sir,
except on his head, just once, on his birthday.
Him and Lucy? Well, she took a shine to him,
he told her some things and I think she liked him.
She just showed up and wanted to tag along,
make some friends, I suppose, mess about, have fun;
she had a few tricks up her sleeve, wanted . . . alright,
if you put it like that . . . to be one of the group.
It's not much cop being on your own. Which was fine
by us. It's not that we gave it a second thought,
to tell you the truth. She just turned up that afternoon
like a lost dog. She was one of the gang. Then she was
gone.

Scene Seven

The beach. **Lucy** *and* **Klondike** *playing rising sun.*

Lucy   Rain in the north from the tears of Jesus,
Wind in the west with its knickers in a twist;
Flies in the south sucking blood like leeches,
Sun coming up in the east like . . . piss.

She throws water in his face.

Klondike   You bitch.

Lucy   Something to break the ice, you see. It's a riddle.

Enter **Tulip**, *unnoticed.*

Klondike   It was a swindle.

Lucy   Oh, come on. You can take it. Here, dry off on this.

She hands him his shirt and kisses him on the forehead.

Klondike   You shouldn't joke.

Lucy   What about?

Klondike   Rhymes and religion. Old things. Things in the
past.

Lucy   I don't believe in all that claptrap.

Klondike   It's just the way you've been brought up.

Lucy   Yes, in the twentieth century, not in the dark.
Anyway, what about your lot? They're up there believing in
science and maths.

Klondike   No, with them it's the zodiac.

Lucy   Oh, I see. It's like that.

Klondike   They've come to take part, not take
photographs.

Pause.

Lucy   What's in the bag?

Klondike   Bits and pieces.

Lucy   Show me. Or is it a secret?

Klondike   Just things I've collected.

Lucy   Suit yourself. Only, I was interested.

Klondike   Well, it's just that . . .

Lucy   Oh, forget it then, if it's so precious. Makes no difference.

Klondike   Alright then, since you've asked.

He opens his bag, and reveals the contents, slowly.

This is the skin of a poisonous snake,
this is a horse stick, cut from a silver birch,
this is bear's tooth, this is a blue shell,
this is a wren's wing, this is a brass bell,
this is a glass bead, this is a fax tail,
this is a boat, carved from a whale bone,
this is a whistle, this is a goat's horn
this is driftwood, this is a cat's claw,
this is a ribbon, a mirror, a clay pipe,
this is a toy drum, this is a meteorite,
this is fool's gold, this is buffalo leather –

Lucy   All done?

Klondike   And this is the moon and the sun:
a hare's foot and an eagle's feather.

Lucy   How do you mean?

Klondike   That's what they stand for.

Lucy   Well, quite a bagful. When's the car-boot sale?

Klondike   You couldn't afford them.

Lucy   Wouldn't want them. Anyway, what are they for?

Klondike They're just things, that's all.

Lucy Things from a mumbo-jumbo stall?

Klondike Things for dreaming things up.

Lucy What?

Klondike I said, things for dreaming things up.

Lucy Tommy-rot. You're just an overgrown Boy Scout. Next thing you'll be showing me a reef knot.

Klondike Get lost, Lucy.

Lucy Dib-dib-dib, dob-dob-dob.

Tulip Klondike, show her.

Klondike No.

Tulip Why not?

Lucy Because he can't.

Tulip Show her.

Klondike Why should I?

Lucy Because he's a big kid, playing with toy cars.

Tulip You don't have to take that from her.

Lucy But most of all, because he's full of shite. Eagle's feathers? Chicken more like.

Klondike Alright.

Lucy This is the eye of a bat, this is a leprechaun's hat, this is the spine of a bird, this is a rocking-horse turd –

Klondike I said alright.

Lucy This is a snowman's heart, this is a plate of tripe –

Klondike ALL RIGHT. Pick something out.

Lucy Well, well, well. All this for little old me. I don't know where to start.

Eenie, meanie, meinie, mo,
put the baby on the po . . . no, not my colour.

Scab and matter custard, toenail pie,
all mixed up with a dead dog's eye,
green and yellow snot cakes
fried in spit,
all washed down with a cup of cold sick.
Here's what I pick.

Klondike   The eagle feather.

Lucy   None other.

Klondike   Put it in the bag, then on the rock, then –

Lucy   Let me guess. Light the blue touch paper and stand
well back?

Klondike *performs a ceremony around the bag. There is a deafening
roar and a brief shadow as a low-flying jet passes overhead.*

Lucy   Is that it?

Tulip   What?

Lucy   Is that it? A jet.

Tulip   Oh, only a jet. What do you want, jam on it?
Klondike, you were brilliant. That was the best yet.

Lucy   Hang on, let's get this straight. It's the feather that
counts, right? You made that plane come out of the clouds by
doing a voodoo dance around a bit of feather duster in an old
sack?

Klondike   Not quite. Something like that.

Lucy   Well then, how do you explain . . . this. (*She produces a
rubber duck from the bag.*) Quack, quack.

Klondike   What . . .

Tulip   Where did you get it?

Lucy   Down on the beach, washed up. Klondike, say hello to Mr Duck.

Tulip   You're a bitch.

Lucy   Sails on the water, like a cup and saucer. So much for the jet, lucky you didn't conjure up the *Titanic*, we might have got wet.

Tulip   I'm going to break her neck.

Klondike   No, Tulip.

Lucy   Rubber Duck to Ground Control, Rubber Duck to Ground Control, the signal's weak, you're breaking up, you're breaking up.

Tulip   You think you're really fucking good, don't you?

Lucy   I'm only having some fun. What else is there to do?

Tulip   Oh, it's fun, is it? Well, I've had enough. I hope you're either good with a knife, or I hope you can run.

Klondike   Tulip, leave her.

Lucy   Sorry, neither. You'll just have to do me in in cold blood. Mind you, I'm strong.

Tulip   Where, apart from your tongue?

Lucy   Here, from the shoulder down to the wrist. This right arm doesn't know its own strength.

Tulip   Looks to me like a long streak of piss.

Lucy   Ah, well, looks deceive. For instance, you don't have to look like a man to be as strong as one.

Tulip   And what's that supposed to mean?

Lucy   What will you do when your balls drop, Tulip? Grow a beard?

Tulip   Right, you're dead.

Klondike   Just stop. Knock it off, I said. If you want to show off, why don't you arm-wrestle or something, there on the rock?

Lucy   No thanks, I don't play competitive sports.

Klondike   Not half you don't.

Tulip   Now who's chicken?

Lucy   I've told you, I'm just not interested in winning.

Tulip   Not interested in losing, more like. Come on, arm-wrestle, or maybe I just smash your face in anyway, for a bit of fun, for a laugh.

Lucy   Alright, but don't say you didn't ask for it.

Klondike   Both of you down on one knee, elbows straight and a clean grip. Ready?

Tulip   Yep.

Klondike   Lucy?

Lucy   As I'll ever be.

Klondike   When I say three. One, two –

Enter **Midnight***, carrying a melting ice cream in both hands.*

Midnight   Ice cream. I got the ice cream.

Klondike   Not now, Midnight.

Midnight   'Greensleeves', up the road. A screwball and a ninety-nine. Or was it a cone?

Klondike   Midnight, we're busy. Just wait there for a minute. And count to three.

Midnight   Why?

Klondike   Just do it.

Okay then. One. Two. Three.

With her free hand, **Lucy** *takes hold of the electric cable.* **Tulip** *is thrown over backwards with the shock.*

Midnight   What was that? Lightning?

Lucy   No, something like it. Is she okay?

Klondike   Just frightened, I think.

Lucy   Ten volts, that's all. Hardly enough to light a torch, but it's the shock I suppose.

Klondike   How come?

Lucy   Meaning what?

Klondike   How come her, and not you?

Lucy   Easy. Insulation. Good shoes.

Klondike   She was the earth?

Lucy   Yes. Here, she can have them back – not my style, rubber boots. (*She takes off the boots and tosses them on the floor.*)

Klondike   She was the earth.

Lucy   Certainly was.

Klondike   Just for a laugh.

Lucy   No, self-defence.

Klondike   I see. (*He picks up* **Tulip**'*s knife.*) Well, that's enough.

Lucy   What do you mean?

Klondike   I mean enough's enough.

Lucy   Klondike, that's real. That's a knife.

Klondike   That's right. That's right.

Midnight (*facing the opposite way*)   Klondike. No heat.

Klondike   No heat. Ice cream. That's right.

Midnight   No, no heat, on my face. No . . . no light.

Klondike   No light?

Midnight   No light. No sun.

Lucy   Eclipse.

Klondike   Eclipse? ECLIPSE. Everyone into position. Who's missing?

Tulip   The twins.

Klondike   Polly. Jane. POLLY. JANE. How long left?

Tulip   A minute. No, fifty seconds. Less.

Klondike   Who else? Midnight?

Midnight   Here, right next to you.

Enter **Polly** *and* **Jane**.

Klondike   Six of us. Six of us.

Tulip   Glue Boy. Where's Glue Boy?

Klondike   Where's Glue Boy?

Polly   We saw him up by the tents.

Jane   Out of his head.

Klondike   Idiot. How long left?

Tulip   Twenty. Less.

Klondike   Okay, okay. (*To* **Lucy**.) You. It'll have to be you.

Lucy   I'm going back to the −

Klondike   Stay there and don't move.

Tulip   Where shall we stand?

Klondike   Don't you remember, the plan? (*He begins to move them into position.*) You there, you there, you there . . .

Midnight   What about me?

Klondike   You stand here.

Lucy   Look, I'm not really sure . . .

Klondike   Just stay put. You've had it your own way all afternoon, now let's see what you're made of.

Tulip   Ten seconds.

Lucy   Huh, me at the back, then?

Klondike   Pole position. Right where it happens.

Facing towards where the sun grows darker, they stand in a triangular formation, with **Tulip**, **Klondike** *and* **Midnight** *at the front,* **Polly** *and* **Jane** *behind them, and* **Lucy** *at the back.*

Polly   Look out, here it comes.

Jane (*elated*)   Oh yes.

Polly   Time for the shades. Time for the shades?

Klondike   Yes, the shades. Put them on.

Klondike, **Tulip**, **Polly** *and* **Jane** *put on their protective glasses.*

Midnight   What?

Polly   The specs.

Midnight   Oh yes. (*He takes his off.*)

Tulip   Five seconds, less. Three. Two. One.

Except for **Lucy**, *they begin to chant.*

All   Fallen fruit of burning sun
Break the teeth and burn the tongue.

Open mouth of the frozen moon
Spit the cherry from the stone.

Scene Eight

The police interview room.

Klondike   Dusk and dawn, like that, in one afternoon.
For all the world, this is as much as I know.
We were standing there watching the most spectacular show
on earth, a beam of light from the bulb
of the sun, made night through the lens of the moon;
ninety-three million miles – point-blank range. Strange,
the moon four hundred times smaller in size,
the sun four hundred times further away;
in line, as they were for us for once for a change,
they're the same size. We were set. We were primed.
Like the riddle says, 'What can be seen as clear
as day, but never be looked in the face?' This
was a chance to stand in a star's shade,
to catch the sun napping or looking the wrong way –
the light of all lights, turning a blind eye.
I'm getting ahead of myself – it's hard to describe.
When the shadow arrived from the east like a stingray,
two thousand miles an hour, skimming the sea spray,
two hundred miles across from fin to fin,
we felt like a miracle, under its wingspan.
We said nursery rhymes, like frightened children.
Midnight bats came out of the sea caves, calling,
birds in the crags buried down in their breasts
till morning, crabs came out of holes in the sand
with eyes on stalks to watch for the tide turning.
When it was done . . . we looked about, and she'd gone.
Never thought for a second she might be lost,
just reckoned she wasn't impressed with planets
and stars and shadows . . . figured she wasn't fussed.
Thought that she'd taken her lime-green self up top,
sidled away, shuffled off. Came as a big black shock
when they called and said she never showed up.
She wasn't us although we liked her well enough.
She told us things, showed us stuff. It's almost

as if she did us a good turn by putting us all
on the right track. Sad. And that's the whole story.
I wish I could tell you more but I can't. I'm sorry.

Scene Nine

The police waiting room. **Tulip**, **Polly** *and* **Jane**, **Midnight** *and*
Glue Boy, *sitting, waiting. Enter* **Klondike** *from interview room.*

Tulip   Well?

Klondike   Well what?

Tulip   Any problems, or not?

Klondike   No, none.

Polly   What did you tell them?

Klondike   Same as everyone else, I presume.

Jane   What do they think?

Klondike   How should I know? I'm not a mind-reader.

Tulip   Well, I don't care. I don't see what else we're
supposed to say.

Polly   Nor me.

Jane   Me neither.

Midnight   So we can go home?

Klondike   No.

Midnight   Why not? We're all done, aren't we?

Glue Boy   Except for one.

Midnight   Oh yes. Sorry. Forgot.

Off, a voice calls 'Paul Bond'.

Glue Boy   That'll be me, then.

Tulip   Why are they asking him?

Klondike   It's his turn. Everyone has to go in.

Polly   Fat load of good that'll be. He can't remember his own name at the best of times.

Jane   He was out of his brain that day, weren't you, Glue Boy?

Glue Boy   High as a kite. Cloud Nine.

Off, a voice calls 'Paul Bond'.

Oh, well. Cheerio.

Klondike   Glue Boy?

Glue Boy   What?

Klondike   Whatever you know, get it straight.

Glue Boy   Like you, right?

Klondike   Right.

Exit **Glue Boy** *into interview room.*

Tulip   See the news?

Polly   No. In the paper again?

Tulip   Yes, and on the telly as well this time.

Midnight   *News at Ten*?

Tulip   Don't know. I was in bed by then, but I saw it at six on the BBC.

Jane   What did it say?

Tulip   Said that they'd called off the search. Said they'd had aeroplanes over the sea, locals walking the beach, boats in the bay, dogs in the caves and all that for over a week, but they'd called it a day. Said that she might be thousands of miles away by now.

Polly   Anything else. Anything . . . new?

Tulip   No. Oh yes, they showed her mum and dad.

Klondike   I saw that. Him in the suit, her in the hat, going on and on and on.

Jane   How old?

Klondike   Don't know, but you could see where she got it from.

Pause.

Tulip   They're talking about a reconstruction.

Jane   What's one of those when it's at home.

Tulip   We all go back to the place and do it again, see if somebody remembers anything or seeing anyone.

Polly   And they do it on film, don't they?

Jane   Oh yes, and someone will have to dress up as her, won't they?

Polly   With her stuff, and her hair.

Tulip   That won't be much fun.

Pause.

Klondike   Not a problem, can't be done.

Midnight   You sure.

Klondike   Certainly am. Not without the moon, and not without the sun.

Pause.

Tulip   Anyway, when's the next one?

Polly   Next what?

Tulip   Eclipse. Klondike?

Klondike   Don't know, I'll have to look at the list. Why, are you up for it?

Tulip   Can a duck swim?

Klondike   Polly? Jane?

Polly   In.

Jane   In.

Tulip   What about him in there – Mr Pritt Stick?

Klondike   Mr Dipstick more like. Don't worry about him, he'll be alright.

Tulip   What about you, Midnight?

Midnight   Sorry, I wasn't listening.

Tulip   Don't play the innocent with me, sunshine. The next eclipse – yes or no, sir?

Midnight   Lunar or solar?

Klondike   Solar. Total.

Midnight
Two days in a van with my mum's barley sugars and the
   old man.
Two minutes at most of afternoon night when I'm already
   blind.
Hanging around with you lot calling me names, playing tricks
of the light and stupid games, then egging myself for a week,
can't eat, can't sleep, then twenty questions by the police,
and all the rest, enough to put a normal person in the funny
   farm . . .

Go on then, you've twisted my arm.

Scene Ten

The police interview room.

Glue Boy
I suppose you've heard it needle and thread five times.
Saying it over and over again – not much point, right?
Any road, I was all of a dither back then,
disconnected, fuse blown in the head, loose ends,

nobody home, fumes on the brain – know what I mean?
Hard to think of it all in one long line, it's all
squiggles and shapes. Fits and starts. Kills the cells,
you see, after so long, so that you can't tell. Well,
nothing to speak of coming to mind just yet. Except . . .
no, nothing, nothing. All gone funny. Not unless
you mean the bit between the last bit and the rest?
You should have said. Let's think. Let's think.
No point saying it over and over to death, no sense
wasting breath. Bits and bobs. Chapter and verse.
Unless . . .
No, nothing. What the others said. Just that. Oh yes, then
   this . . .

Scene Eleven

The beach. **Klondike**, **Lucy**, **Tulip** *and* **Midnight**, *as before.*

Lucy   Klondike, that's real. That's a knife.

Klondike   That's right. That's right.

Midnight *(facing the opposite way)*   Klondike. No heat.

Klondike   No heat. Ice cream. That's right.

Midnight   No, no heat, on my face. No . . . no light.

Klondike   No light?

Midnight   No light. No sun.

Lucy   Eclipse.

Klondike   Eclipse? ECLIPSE. Everyone into position.
Who's missing?

Tulip   The twins.

Klondike   Polly. Jane. POLLY. JANE. How long left?

Tulip   A minute. No, fifty seconds. Less.

Klondike   Who else? Midnight?

Midnight   Here, right next to you.

Enter **Polly** *and* **Jane**.

Klondike   Six of us. Six of us.

Tulip   Glue Boy. Where's Glue Boy?

Klondike   Where's Glue Boy?

Polly   We saw him up by the tents.

Jane   Out of his head.

Klondike   Idiot. How long left?

Tulip   Twenty. Less.

Klondike   Okay, okay. (*To* **Lucy**.) You. It'll have to be you.

Lucy   I'm going back to the –

Klondike   Stay there and don't move.

Tulip   Where shall we stand?

Klondike   Don't you remember the plan? (*He begins to move them into position.*) You there, you there, you there . . .

Midnight   What about me?

Klondike   You stand here.

Lucy   Look, I'm not really sure . . .

Klondike   Just stay put. You've had it your own way all afternoon, now let's see what you're made of.

Tulip   Ten seconds.

Lucy   Huh, me at the back then?

Klondike   Pole position. Right where it happens.

Facing towards where the sun grows darker, they stand in a triangular formation, with **Tulip**, **Klondike** *and* **Midnight** *at the front.* **Polly** *and* **Jane** *behind them, and* **Lucy** *at the back.*

Polly   Look out, here it comes.

Jane (*elated*)   Oh yes.

Polly   Time for the shades. Time for the shades?

Klondike   Yes, the shades. Put them on.

Klondike, **Tulip**, **Polly** *and* **Jane** *put on their protective glasses.*

Midnight   What?

Polly   The specs.

Midnight   Oh yes. (*He takes his off.*)

Tulip   Five seconds, less. Three. Two. One.

Except for **Lucy**, *they begin the chant.*

All   Fallen fruit of burning sun
Break the teeth and burn the tongue;

Open mouth of the frozen moon
Spit the cherry from the stone.

Enter **Glue Boy** *from opposite direction, still with glue bag on his head. He collides with* **Lucy**, *who takes him to one side and takes the bag from his head. She holds his hands as he hallucinates.*

Glue Boy   Seeing things. Dreaming things.

He blurts out his dream as **Midnight** *leaves the group, retrieves his crucifix from* **Lucy**'s *bag and puts it on.*

Glue Boy
head through a noose dreams
    lasso roping a horse
needle threading itself
    bat flying into cave
mole coming up through a grave
    cuckoo's head through the shell of an egg
dog on a leash dreams

Midnight *rejoins the group, who are still facing the eclipse, chanting.*
Tulip *leaves the group and begins putting on her boots. She produces*
another red headscarf from her pocket, and ties it around her head.

Glue Boy

sea-horse   trying on its shoes
      tom cat   tortoiseshell   stood up
mermaid scaling the beach
      finding its feet   ditching its tail
square of the sky   shepherd's delight
      pulled down   worn as a crown
poppy blazing in a field of corn
      dead volcano   blowing its top
matchstick wearing heat to its head like a hat
      dream things   hings like that

Tulip *rejoins the group. The twins go to the bag to retrieve clothes,*
jewellery and make-up.

Glue Boy

   double-vision dream   two trees
      Dutch elms coming back into leaf
two snow-leopards   trying on furs
      leggings coats of sheep that were shorn
two African rhino   stripped to the bone
      locking horns
nude Aunt Sally   birthday suit on a tailor's dummy
      rose-petal lips   ivory teeth
dreams   dolled up like Russians
      dressed to the nines   clothes of their mothers
those dreams   others

The twins rejoin the group. **Klondike** *goes to the bag to retrieve the*
skull and the Boji stones.

Glue Boy

nutcracker man coming out of his shell
      great auk treading thin air
phoenix roasting   driftwood fire
      unicorn meeting its match   point of a spear

head of a griffin   worn as a hat
    beak of a dodo worn on a boot
as a spur
    tusk of a mammoth   torn from its root
a tooth   a tree
    white hart hung by its hooves
Franklin's men   out of the deep-freeze
    dream things those   these

Lucy *and* **Glue Boy** *have become stuck together with the glue. They spin round violently trying to free themselves from each other.*

Lucy   Let go.

Glue Boy   It's the glue. It's the glue.

Lucy   LET ME GO.

The rest of the group are still chanting. The total darkness of the eclipse descends, then sunshine returns and **Glue Boy** *is found to be standing in the position where* **Lucy** *stood.*

Klondike   That's it.

Tulip   Blown away.

Polly   That was strange. Really strange.

Jane   Funny, I've gone all cold.

Midnight   I feel sick.

Klondike   Happens to some people. I've read about that.

Tulip   Come on, everyone up to the top.

Klondike   Glue Boy?

Glue Boy   Hello.

Klondike   Where did she go?

Glue Boy   Where did who go?

Tulip   Princess Muck. Lady Di. Who do you think? Lucy Lime.

Glue Boy   Er, don't know. Lost her in the light.

Polly (*picking up* **Lucy**'s *bag*)   She left her bag.

Jane   Here, Glue Boy, better give it her back.

Glue Boy *walks off with her bag.*

Klondike   Come on. We're wasting time.

Jane   It seemed to go on for hours. How long did it last?

Tulip   Two minutes thirty-five.

Polly   Not according to mine. Yours must be fast.

Tulip   So what did you make it then?

Polly   Well . . . less.

Klondike   Come on. Last one to the top gets a Chinese burn.

Midnight   I feel sick.

Klondike   Somebody give him a hand. Polly and Jane.

Tulip   Hang on.

Klondike   Now what?

Tulip (*looking around*)   Nothing. Just checking.

As everyone pauses, **Klondike** *runs in front of them.*

Klondike   Last one up's a chicken!

They all exit, **Polly** *and* **Jane** *dragging* **Midnight** *with them.*

Scene Twelve

The interview room. **Glue Boy** *holding* **Lucy**'s *bag, examining it.*

Glue Boy
Sorry, I just wanted to be sure. Yes, this is the one,
the one that she had on the beach. It's been a bad week.

We're all cracking up with thinking what to think.
We've made up a rhyme to say at the service tonight,
something that fits, we reckon, kind of a wish or a prayer
to cover whatever's gone on, wherever she's gone.
I could run through it now, if you like? You'll say
if you think we've got it all wrong? Okay then, I will.

*As he begins, he is joined in the chanting at various intervals by the others
in the waiting room.*

under the milk token of the moon
under the gold medal of the sky
under the silver foil of the moon
under the Catherine wheel of the sun
born below the sky's ceiling
at home with the moon's meaning
nursed on the dew's damp
twilight for a reading lamp
tribe of blue yonder
Cub Scouts of Ursa Minor
the east wind for a hair-dryer
Mercury for a shaving mirror
a-bed afoot Jacob's ladder
head down on Jacob's pillow
Heaven's sitting tenants
meteorites for birthday presents
Masai of the stone deserts
stage-lit by daffodil heads
Orion's belt for a coat peg
Uranus for an Easter egg
tumbleweed of the world's park
hearers of the world's heart
ears flat to the earth's floor
thawed by the earth's core
needled by Jack Frost
high priest of the long lost
passed over by Mars
pinned down by the North Star
some type of our own kind

branded with real life
Lobby Ludds of the outback
seventh cousins gone walkabout
Navaho of the tarmac plains
snowdrifts for Christmas cakes
groupies of the new age
Venus for a lampshade
Jupiter for a budgie cage
Saturn for a cuckoo clock
guardians of the joke dogs
Jack Russells in tank tops
Sirius for a pitbull
Pluto for a doorbell
Neptune for night-nurse
civilians of the universe
Eskimos of the steel glaciers
St Christopher's poor relations
citizens of the reservations
under the bullet-hole of the moon
under the entry wound of the sun
under the glass eye of the moon
under the bloody nose of the sun
under the cue ball of the moon
under the blood orange of the sun
under the sheriff's shield of the moon
under the blowtorch of the sun
under the stalactite of the moon
under the nuclear blast of the sun
under the hammered nail of the moon
under the cockerel's head of the sun
under the iceberg tip of the moon
under the open heart of the sun
under the cyanide pill of the moon
under the screaming mouth of the sun
under the chocolate coin of the moon
under the chocolate coin of the sun

End.

Eclipse

BY SIMON ARMITAGE

*Notes on rehearsal and staging drawn from a workshop
with the writer held at the National Theatre, October 2015*

*From workshops led by Michael Longhurst and Michael Buffong,
with notes by Audrey Sheffield and Guy Jones*

How Simon came to write the play

Eclipse, written in 1996, was the first play that Simon had ever
written, and was published in the middle of a book of poems.
He was curious about the life of poetry and how it could find
its way on to the stage, so he wanted to try a piece of verse
drama.

At the time of writing the play, Simon was transitioning from
being a probation officer in Greater Manchester to working
as a poet, and was also very interested in stargazing, mysticism
and archaeology – and you can see the influences of all of
these rolled into this play.

The play was actually inspired by the real-life disappearance
of a girl called Lindsay Rimer, in Hebden Bridge, West
Yorkshire: she went missing through the winter of 1994, and
her body was found in the canal six months later. Despite
repeated appeals for information from the police, the murder
remains unsolved. Simon mentioned that knowledge of this
shouldn't necessarily influence your approach or production
in any way.

When the play was written, the eclipse hadn't happened yet,
it was in the future (1999), but there was a palpable level of
hysteria surrounding the event, with people planning to make
something of a pilgrimage to Cornwall, which became like a
sort of Bethlehem for them. Simon was very interested in the
eclipse, and in people's reactions to and fascination with it, at
a time of pre-scientific enlightenment, where they believed
the idea that the 'sky had gone out'. The eclipse was a symbolic
and potent indication of something mystical, frightening and

inexplicable. With this event, for millions of people, everything stopped and they all thought about this one thing. It was a moment where everyone came together to reflect. It was something like a quasi or substitute religious event, and there was a lot of mental energy around it.

Crudely speaking, the through-line for Simon was that these children were obsessed with ritual, magic and superstition, and he was interested in playing with this, and in their similarity to the community of people in Hebden Bridge.

Simon wasn't interested in tying things up neatly, and recognises that this is not a play with a clear linear narrative. He is aware of its ambiguities, confusion and vagueness – and said that he wanted to write a whodunit where even the playwright didn't know whodunit! He is keen not to be prescriptive about the meaning of the play, and wholly understands that every company's process of exploration is a large part of the enjoyment of it all. He strongly encourages directors to be as creative and inventive as they want to be – 'the job of each director is to find the play within the play'.

*

Below are a number of exercises that focus on work that can be done with your cast early on in the rehearsal process. These are all designed to help your company get close to the material, to open up and create a vivid world of the play, and to help make the storytelling clear and the characters rich and specific.

Approaching the play

The play is set in August 1999, before the eclipse had happened, so an important decision is whether or not to treat the play as a 'period piece' – are there possibilities opened up by researching other eclipses in the past or future?

Michael Buffong and the group explored the implications of treating the piece as a play specifically about 1999. This obviously has a bearing on costume and design choices. But what about its impact on the way young people will read the play? The play was written before all young people had phones, and is a depiction of a *community* before the internet changed our sense of what that word meant.

There is an interesting ambiguity about the amount of time that has elapsed in the play between the eclipse and the interviews in the police cell. Is it in the immediate aftermath of Lucy's disappearance ('It's been a bad week')? Or could the investigations have started after the search for Lucy was over and it had been decided that she was likely to be dead? The memorial service referred to in the closing moments of the play might not actually take place until some time after the event. Playing with this ambiguity might be an interesting starting point for a production of this play today – particularly in the light of when you decide the play is set.

Themes

LIGHT AND DARK
To Simon, the eclipse of 1999 was a time when people 'wanted to look at nothing, they wanted to experience that weirdness of night during the day'. The young people of the play are experimenting with dark shamanistic forces, and Lucy comes along representing enlightenment. She sheds light on their darker side – but in the eclipse there is something larger and inexplicable at work: the mystery of the universe persists.

CRUELTY AND PLAYGROUND GAMES
Simon sees the cruelty of the young people depicted in the play as very true to the way young people behave with one another: 'Nursery rhymes can be cruel. Kids can be cruel. I saw the whole play as a game – a playground game being acted out.'

GROWING UP AND ADOLESCENCE
The characters are in the process of moving from childhood to adulthood. To Simon, Lucy represents the adulthood they are moving towards. There is something seductive about that,

but also something scary. The friends are a group of misfits –
they are linked by their outsider status, and they are off their
parents' leash, inventing themselves outside of their parents'
jurisdiction.

RITUAL
Ritual is an important part of these characters' lives –
Simon's suggestion is that they are inspired by shamanistic
practices, and the mystery of the eclipse brings out these
impulses. Klondike is the self-elected shamanic leader, but
there is a sense that he has bitten off more that he can chew.

Structure

The play depicts a group of young people experimenting with
dark and mysterious forces. Lucy Lime comes along to
challenge their old-fashioned views. At the moment of the
eclipse, the group rearm by taking back the talismans that
Lucy had taken from them. The eclipse represents a force
bigger than the play's characters – and is so powerful that
Lucy disappears. In this structure there is a sense that
although Lucy challenges the young people's mysticism, her
rationality is in turn challenged by something more powerful.

There is a structural question posed by the play about how
the characters have changed over the course of the eclipse,
and what the impact of Lucy's visit has been. They have
rejected her to the extent that she disappears, and in doing
so have moved away from the zone of young people playing
games. They feel a sense of guilt or responsibility, and in the
play's final moments are offering up what Simon calls a
'secular prayer'.

Exercises for rehearsals

Michael Longhurst highlighted the many thoughts and
objects of attention that directors can have when reading
through a script; being concerned with what he described as
thinking 'from the top down' – that is, picking up on certain

themes, impressions and a sense of the world of the play –
while at the same time also thinking 'from the bottom up' –
that is, identifying more practical concerns as we go along,
such as potential staging difficulties, questions about design
and props.

THEMATIC OBSERVATIONS AND STAGING CHALLENGES

He suggested it would be beneficial to read through the play,
stopping after each scene to make a note of several things.
First, if there is a particular line that stands out or is striking
to you, make a note of it. You can also highlight anything
that might pose as a staging challenge to you, and you could
mark it in the margin next to that point in the text with 'SC'.
This could refer to any practicality within the script, a specific
locational change, a costume item, an aspect of a character
and so on.

EVENTS AND THEIR UNITS

Michael Longhurst also explained that he finds it helpful to
work out the 'events' within the play. Katie Mitchell refers to
an event as 'something that changes everyone's intention'.
Michael encouraged the group that when looking for the
event(s), find out what it is that involves everyone. So that
even if a character is in a scene but doesn't speak in that part
of the play, this event can be seen as something that clearly
affects them as well as any of the other speaking characters in
the play at that time.

The point from which one event starts until the next event
comes in can be marked and referred to as a 'unit'. Breaking
the text up in this way can be helpful as you are both dividing
the text into manageable chunks, and locating and labelling
the events. Once you have noted an event within the play,
you can draw a line on to the script to indicate where this
happens, and you can title the event – for example, 'Klondike's
entrance' – and if helpful, look ahead to the action of the next
section. As director, you can then decide to 'turn up' or
similarly, 'turn down' that event and what happens at that

point in the play. Of course, the events you identify and locate will always be a result of your interpretation – there is no right and wrong.

Facts and questions

Michael Longhurst also explained how you can collect facts as you read through the text, and how these facts in themselves can inspire a set of related questions. For example, a fact could be that Klondike missed his bus, which could then lead to questions such as: What bus was it? Why did he miss it? How long ago did he miss that bus? Did he get the next bus? Was he annoyed about missing the bus?

Michael emphasised the need to make sure that you are extracting the dramatic juice out of the facts found within the text. By asking and then filling in the answers to these questions, you can begin to get a fuller and richer picture and sense of these characters and the world of the play.

He also encouraged you to ask yourself when you are rehearsing a scene: 'Is this reading how I want it to?' For example, if looking at Scene One and the section where Martin Blackwood is called for a second time, you can check the time and place – that is, ask yourself: Do I believe the time? Do I believe the place? In other word: Do I believe the passage of time between the first and second calls for Martin Blackwood to go through to the interview room? Has a sense of urgency and perhaps panic arisen since that officer's first call? Is there sufficient pressure between the first and second call? Do I get a clear sense of these friends being in a waiting room? And could I stage anything differently to make this clearer, if necessary?

With any questions you have that have been inspired by facts within the text, it is up to you to decide whether these ambiguities or contradictions are something that the playwright might have missed, or whether you can make a logic for this that is useful to you and your production.

Also, with facts, you always have a question as to whether the characters are telling the truth. So if a fact isn't clear, you can land it as a question if that's more helpful. For example, are Polly and Jane identical twins?

Every time you read the script, you will pass and collect different things from the text, so Michael Longhurst suggested reading through the play, scene by scene, noting any themes, staging challenges, facts and questions as they come up, and marking any events and their units as you go along.

Below is an example of this process applied to the first three scenes. Please note that it is in no way a definitive list, but representative of what was discussed during the workshop.

SCENE ONE

Thematic observations. What do we need to know here? Why has the writer chosen to give Klondike a monologue near the start of this scene? The use of verse and structure as an expressive means conveys a sense of ritual, mysticism. The seventh empty chair highlights the significance of someone being missing.

Staging challenges. Where is the interview room – is it offstage? What can we see of it? How to design and stage this separate room in relation to the police waiting room? What is the position of chairs in the room? How will the voice from offstage be done? Live, with an actor offstage? Played as a pre-recorded call?

Events. Event 1: Klondike's entrance (at the very top of the play). Event 2: The summoning of Martin Blackwood. The interrogation is starting (page 47, *'Off, a voice calls "Martin Blackwood"'*). NB: The second call of Martin Blackwood could be seen as another, small event or as Event 3: Midnight exiting into the interview room (page 48).

Facts. We are in a police waiting room. There are seven chairs in a row. There are six friends waiting there. Klondike missed his bus. Klondike has Extra Strong Mints. Polly and Jane are

twin sisters. Midnight's real name is Martin Blackwood. The
incident they are being questioned about, and the eclipse,
happened on 11 August 1999. They were down on the beach,
with their parents up on the flat. Midnight is blind. There is a
separate interview room, off. The interview room has a window
of frosted glass. They knew someone called Lucy Lime.

Questions. Why are there seven chairs when there are only six
friends waiting there? Why did Klondike miss his bus? What
bus was it? How long ago was that? Was he annoyed about
missing his bus? Did he catch the next bus? Where does
Klondike live? Do they all live near each other? How often
do these friends see each other? How close are they? Where
did Klondike get his mints from? Are Polly and Jane identical
twins (or do they or others just refer to themselves as 'identical'
for other reasons)? How did Midnight go blind? Was he blind
from birth? How does he feel about this? What can Tulip
hear through the crack, and see through the frosted glass
window to the interview room? What happened on 11 August
1999? What is each person's relationship to the incident?
Who is Lucy Lime and why are they all here at the police
station? How long ago did the incident happen? What is the
hierarchy within the group? Is Klondike the self-elected
leader? What are the group agreeing to conceal? How much
do they know?

SCENE TWO

Staging challenges. Location change to police interview room.
What is the convention you set up for every time the location
shifts? Will you overlay the scene within the previous setting?
Will you clear the stage each time? Will you use different
parts of the stage to represent the different locations within
the play? And do you need to use the same language each
time? Is it necessary to keep this same established convention
for each change? Or will it be clear to the audience, so
that you'll need to show less and less to the audience every
time? Midnight's blindness: how do the other characters
deal with this? How will this affect the research you do,

exercises you introduce into rehearsals? Is the police
interrogator seen, or will you stage this with only Midnight
visible in the room?

SCENE THREE

Thematic observations. Some of the staging challenges and
decisions can help to be determined by whom you decide
Lucy is, and what her motives are. That is, is she manipulative
or just being playful? How menacing is the bullying of
Midnight? How dark or light is the play and what style and
expressive means will you use? What is the group dynamic
between the friends? Is it light banter or cruelty? Ideas of the
friends being representative of old-fashioned ways, ritual,
mysticism, faith, sociology, anthropology, versus Lucy's
psychology, science. When Lucy takes a characteristic item
from everyone, is she affecting, taking away their identity in
some way? Is Lucy controlling the group in some way? Is she
'catching moths' – setting fire to Tulip's scarf to attract and
draw the others back?

Staging challenges. The scene change to the beach is a massive
locational shift. How to represent the electric fence and the
entrance to the caves? Will different levels be necessary in the
design? How to stage the twins? Are they literally identical, or
do they just think of themselves as such because of how they
behave, and like the idea of being identical? How to represent
Glue Boy's glue sniffing? Being aware of your responsibility as
a director, how can this be shown? Do you need to show this?
How can you get an actor to that place, to that altered state
of consciousness? How regularly does he sniff glue through
the scene? Where are his peaks?

How to represent each character in the play? As in the first
scene, there's no description of how they look, though in the
flashbacks, from Scene Three onwards, every character
(except for Lucy Lime) is described in detail and has specific
items that might tell us a little about their personalities. Will

you use particular character props to help give your actors related character traits that they can play? How to establish each character's identity and beliefs, in order for Lucy to be able to come in and challenge or change them? How do you want your actor to embody Midnight holding his crucifix? What was the animal sound that came out of one of the caves? Is it a natural sound, or Lucy making the noise? How will this be made, and how will it be linked with the enigmatic element within the text? How to stage the setting fire to the scarf moment safely?

How does Lucy trick Glue Boy (if she does) and Midnight into hearing the sounds they hear? What is Lucy doing here? And how will this be staged so she can set this all up without Midnight hearing? Can Glue Boy actually hear these sounds, so goes along with it completely innocently? Or is Glue Boy deliberately tricking Midnight? Or can Lucy conjure up these sounds? All these are directorial decisions that will need to be made regarding the mystery of the play and how and to what extent you choose to manifest/represent this. Will you hear all the sounds that Lucy says she can hear, and if so, will they be actual or abstract sounds?

Events. Event 1: Klondike, Tulip and Glue Boy enter from the caves (page 52). Event 2: Midnight comes out of the cave, alone (page 54). Event 3: Lucy's entrance (page 54). Event 4: Lucy is allowed to stay (page 56). Event 5: Everyone's agreement to honour the bet (page 58). Also, there will be an event every time that Lucy describes a sound she can hear, while all the other characters can't hear anything. Event: The bet is lost (occurs after Tulip's 'Nice one, stupid', page 62).

Facts. The setting is a beach, in Cornwall on 11 August 1999. There is a broken electric fence dangling down from the headland above. There are entrances to the caves in the cliff face. The twins are sitting on a rock. Jane and Polly are combing each other's hair. They are wearing jewellery and have lots of make-up on. The twins have a hairbrush, a nail file and a compact between them. They have knowledge of

the ancient world. They have a test next Monday. The time is
twenty past something. Both Jane and Polly are wearing a
watch. Glue Boy is a glue-sniffer. Klondike and Tulip enter
from one of the caves. Klondike has a leather bag, and is
carrying the skull of a dead cow. Tulip is wearing Doc
Marten boots and a red scarf on her head like a pirate. The
skull stinks. Midnight is still in the caves after the others have
come out. Midnight has very good hearing. Midnight is
wearing a crucifix around his neck and has dark glasses on.
The group all came here in a van together. Midnight lost his
sight by looking directly at the sun through binoculars when
he was ten years old. Tulip wants to play 'numblety peg' – an
old-fashioned game involving throwing knives in the ground.
Tulip has a knife, and she's wearing rubber boots. Midnight is
a Christian and goes to church. Midnight has a Walkman and
headphones. Lucy has a lucky coin, made of a gold sovereign
melted into a silver dime. Klondike has some Boji stones from
Kansas. Midnight's hearing is perfect. There are no birds
around. Midnight is very straight, honest.

Questions. What is the significance of this date? Are they on
their summer holidays from school? Whereabouts exactly are
they and where are their parents? How heavily made up are
Polly and Jane? What have the twins been studying? Why are
they studying in August? And why do they have a test on this
next Monday if there's no school? Are they studying for
summer school? Why is Midnight holding a crucifix? How
good is Midnight's hearing? Did someone bet Midnight to look
directly at the sun through his binoculars? If so, who was it, and
was it someone from this group? Why did he follow it? What
were the group repercussions of Midnight losing his sight?

What is the group's relationship to betting? Do they bet
often? What are the group dynamics? How well do they know
each other? Do they know each other through school, or
through their community? Did they choose to be friends, or
just come together through their parents' gatherings as a
group? How long have they known each other? How old are
they all? How interested are they in stargazing? Are they

urban children, or do they know their environment and the elements very well? Are their games youthful and playful and is it something they do all the time? Or, do the group play games because they are bored, or as part of an initiation and ritual? Are Lucy's parents up on the top? How well do we believe her? How do the group receive the stranger? What does Lucy look like? Why do the other girls feel the need to attack her? Is it because of how she looks, because she's an outsider, because she looks weird or beautiful?

Why do the characters have the names they do? How knife-handy is Tulip? Has she played this game ('numblety peg') before? When do the twins enjoy being the same, and when do they want to be different from each other? What's their relationship? Is one more dominant than the other overall? Has Midnight always been a Christian? If not, when did he convert? What is the relationship between his faith and his blindness? How often does he go to church? How did Klondike get hold of his Boji stones? Are they really from Kansas? Why is Lucy trying to propose this bet? What does she want to achieve? What is Lucy wearing on her feet? What are Klondike's feelings for Lucy? How much does he like her? What does he want? How offended is he? Why are the others all angry with Lucy and her treatment of Midnight, especially after their having been mean to him? What is the group's 'eclipse position' that they seem to have agreed on or discussed beforehand? What actually happens the first time they think the eclipse is happening and it gets darker? Has the sun just gone behind a cloud?

You can then continue to read through the play, noting any of these elements that come up as you go. Sometimes you will naturally focus more on particular aspects than others.

Characters and characterisation

Simon said that his 'characters are almost nursery rhyme characters'. Although the characters are inspired by young people from Yorkshire, there is flexibility here. There is also room to decide what kind of socio-economic background they might be from. The important thing is that they are not from the area they have found themselves in for the eclipse.

THE GANG

Though this play was written in the mid-1990s, Simon was thinking about his childhood in the 1970s when he created this gang of slight misfits. He described the gang to be a bit like the Back Street Kids, representative of what childhood was like pre-internet and the digital age. They embody the idea of 'playing out'; they are inventing the world. He imagined their parents as all 'hippy dippy', getting together often in these places at similar times of ritual gathering. The children are an impromptu gang, brought together because of their parents' common interests, and perhaps playing out the same dynamic as the adults.

The gang believe that if they chant their chant while the eclipse is happening then something will happen. If they believe in the occult, mysticism, zodiac, then the eclipse sees the coming together of all of that, all at once. And they want to harness its power. A total eclipse is probably a once-in-a-generation occurrence, so this is the gang's first experience of it.

In the police waiting room and interrogation room scenes, where the characters are talking to the police, Simon wanted to give the impression that each individual felt guilty about the event – they feel that whatever they did contributed to the fact that Lucy Lime has gone missing. They are worried about going through things with the police, in case anything might incriminate them. The group believe that if they hadn't been involved in that final ritual, Lucy's disappearance might not have happened. Simon also wanted to inject a little more irony into the play – Lucy's intervention with each of the others has moved them on as people, but at the same time they're all still wondering whether their ritual had 'disappeared her' or not. Each individual in the group feels that their interaction with Lucy was significant, though of course it doesn't mean that her disappearance was their fault.

None of the characters are aware that they are speaking verse when they do.

Simon thinks there is something mischievous about the children towards the end of the play.

LUCY LIME

Lucy is like an enlightenment. She challenges the group's notions of religion and superstition, and dispossesses them of the things they were wrapped up in. To Simon's mind, Lucy is representative of contemporary normality. She is a very confident girl/young woman. Her strength is in her language, she knows how to manipulate people, and very quickly becomes ringmaster. She reads social situations very well, and has Psychology over the groups' Sociology and Anthropology. However, her hesitation when told to take her place in the prearranged eclipse formation shows her to be less confident when it comes to manipulating the planets and such. The point at which Lucy puts her hand on the electric fence tells us a lot about her. Her making Tulip do the same, knowing she'll get an electric shock, is a very cruel thing to do.

Simon also mentioned that he was pushing on with the conceptual idea that she knows how currents work. She is Science. Simon said that he imagined Lucy's parents to be members of the 'chattering classes'. The event that Lucy describes to the twins (with the three men, and her jumping into the river) really did happen to her in the past. Through that experience, she learned something incredible about human nature; she stands up to the men and confronts them with what they have done, in her vulnerability. Although Simon is clear about what Lucy might represent, the question of who she is – whether she is real or imagined – is for the production to decide.

KLONDIKE

Simon mentioned that he used Klondike's name as referring to something that comes out of a cave – Klondike is a bit of an amateur archaeologist.

MIDNIGHT

The use of his name was intended to be ironic (as the character has lost his sight).

GLUE BOY

Glue Boy is something of a shaman here, because he is already experiencing a different kind of consciousness.

TULIP

Her name was used ironically, as the character is very much a tomboy. Her last look around at the end of Scene Eleven is just that – she's checking that she hasn't left anything behind.

*

Playing cards are really useful as a rehearsal technique and as a way of expressing 'scales' of different variables. Character status exercises can be helpful in showing how to keep the scene alive, especially when you are working with a lot of actors on stage.

CHARACTER EXERCISE I: LOW/HIGH STATUS

Hold some cards, all the same suit and numbered from two up to ten. Select five actors and ask each to choose one card, and not reveal to anyone else what value they have. Whatever number they get indicates their status – the higher the number, the higher their status. Give a context – for example, it is fifteen minutes before this workshop is due to start, and they are waiting in this room. (NB: Let the actors know that they don't have to try to be funny.) The actors step into the space, and begin to embody their status. The improvisation plays out, and at the end, each actor reveals their card to the rest of the group.

CHARACTER EXERCISE 2: USE OF SPACE TO MANIFEST STATUS

How can you use space to express a character's status at a particular time? You can apply this game to setting up the space of the police waiting room in the play.

- Start with five chairs set up in a line, from the lowest on one end, to the highest on the other. Bring the characters into the space, and let the scene play out.

- Repeat this exercise with one character sitting next to another, first playing the scene as low status as possible, then again as high status as possible.

CHARACTER EXERCISE 3: GUESS YOUR STATUS

Take five cards, give one to each actor, and tell them to lick the back and stick it to their forehead, not looking at the number themselves. The space is still set up with five chairs in a line. All actors can see each other's cards, but not their own. The scene plays out, and at the end, ask the actors to place themselves in the line where they guessed their status number was on the scale of high to low. This version of the exercise forces your actors to learn from each other, and focus on the group dynamic.

CHARACTER EXERCISE 4: SCALE OF NERVOUSNESS

The next stage of this exercise was to replace status and have the scale representing how nervous an individual character was. The actors look at their cards this time, and the higher their number, the more nervous they are. The context is that they are waiting in the police waiting room to be called for their individual interrogation. The scene plays out. At the end, they are asked to order themselves in levels of nervousness – from most to least, without looking at each other's cards. This exercise encourages actors to be very active from the start.

CHARACTER EXERCISE 5: INTEREST IN A NEW CHARACTER

Next, the scale was changed to represent how interested each character was in the new character who enters the room. That is, if you choose a high-numbered card, your character is very interested, and vice versa. Or you could change it to play that if you receive a red card, you like the new character, and if you get a black card, you dislike them – still using the scale to express how much you either like or dislike this new person entering the space.

These exercises can also be really helpful in establishing a common language between you and your cast during rehearsals, and can be used to illuminate elements of the play. For example: 'You're playing that at a two, could you try it as a four?' You might choose to apply this to an actor's manifestation of Glue Boy's 'high-ness' in a particular scene.

CHARACTER EXERCISE 6: STATUS LADDER OF CHAIRS

Use your line of chairs as a ladder down the middle of the space, highest status represented at one end, down to lowest at the other. The actors play out a section from a scene in the play, and move up and down the ladder accordingly as they go. For example, using Scene Three, from the point where Midnight and Lucy Lime both enter the space, on page 54, ask your actors to choose a chair to stand by as they first enter. You can repeat and refine this exercise by asking your actors to be very specific about where they move to and when. Characters' status can be further clarified by repeating the exercise once more, and this time artificially slowing down their lines, to encourage them to take their time and not rush, and to help make their decisions clearer.

All these exercises can be really beneficial in rehearsals. They help to clearly express a character's attitude to other characters at each moment, which can be a way for you to introduce changing certain elements of each character (whether it is the intensity, affinity or an actual characteristic that you are focusing on), by suggesting and encouraging actors to try different things. These games are especially useful when using ten chairs, as this gives even more of a scale for your actors to move between.

Casting

The play is written with seven speaking roles, but there is room to incorporate more people into the chorus sections – which Simon says are references to the chorus in Greek drama. People could also be used to generate some of the frenzied atmosphere of the eclipse in Cornwall that was the inspiration for the piece.

There was also a discussion about how to deal with a cast where the genders do not match those of the characters. The group discussed which characters might be the easiest to re-gender, and in general Glue Boy and one of the twins were popular choices. There are issues created by all re-gendering which may be interesting or challenging for individual productions to explore.

The twins don't have to be identical – they might not even be twins, but just called twins by their circle of friends. To Simon 'it is the language that twins them – their conversation is intertwined'.

Language

Simon identified three elements to the text in this play: 1) dialogue, 2) monologues and blank verse, and 3) the chants, songs and nursery rhymes. It is very important to differentiate between these, to make them distinct from one another. Otherwise, it will all be on one level, and you will lose the sense of it.

With regards to the dialogue interchanges between people, Simon encouraged that 'it's best to keep the P (for Poetry) out of the room', reassuring everyone that the rhymes will happen anyway. He advised to keep any verse sections of dialogue as naturalistic as possible; if you don't, the meaning of the text will be lost. He also suggested that directors need to be aware of any actors being self-consciously performative with the verse sections within the text, and to help them avoid this.

The chants, songs and nursery rhymes are all up for grabs in terms of who says what – a little like Greek chorus pieces. He proposed there could be a slight change of perspective with these sections – perhaps they are spoken to the audience, and you could use the idea of getting others involved in these more choral parts of the text too. (It could also help to convey how many other people were involved in these mystical group events at the time too.) Simon suggested trying everyone in the chorus being in unison on the verb – releasing the active sense of the line. He advised that the interesting words are the verbs and noun objects that occur, and for him, these are the moments of emphasis in the line.

It is important to privilege the language. Clarity is key and it would be a mistake to do the play so quickly that the lines are lost. While the production should be well paced, this shouldn't be at the expense of hearing the language. As a general note, where there isn't punctuation at the end of a line, just continue reading on to the end of the sentence.

Simon encouraged companies to explore changing volume of speech, speed of delivery, the number of people speaking and so on, to avoid becoming monotonous in any way.

With the group's chant at the end, Simon wanted to give the impression that they had written some sort of a secular prayer for Lucy Lime, so that all the imagery used was to expose people outside of their group to their world. This chant is made from the last few sweepings of their beliefs, and they have cobbled something together that they can say at a service. It feels like a concerted effort at a created prayer, and Simon mentioned that this can be said as much to the audience as to anyone else, like a large performance piece, even imagining the group might be coming forwards at this point, like a Greek chorus.

Simon guided that the pronunciation of 'Uranus' should sound like 'Urin-us'.

Michael Longhurst. advised the group against colouring the language for the sake of it, and encouraged them to try and help the audience to imagine the object, atmosphere or emotion they were describing at each point. Tell the story. You, as director, need to decide what you want to achieve, and what you want your actors to do, and to bring the sense through it.

LANGUAGE EXERCISE 1: SPONTANEOUS SPEECH

This exercise can be very beneficial when looking at dividing up the text between two or more characters. Ask your actors to read the section without having decided beforehand who will read which part of the text at any point. For example, you can try this with the twins, Polly and Jane, in the interrogation room in Scene Four. This exercise really allows you to express their individual personalities and rhythms, which is the 'stronger' or 'weaker' twin. It can be very funny, and dark.

As director, you might decide consciously to divide up the text in any of these sections, or you may prefer to create accidents – with some or all of the actors being able to chip in as and when. In this way, the text can take on a different quality and tone, and you may find that certain, different words jump out each time. It's a fun exercise, and allows the cast to be spontaneous, as well as pushing against the form of the text.

LANGUAGE EXERCISE 2: PUNCTUATION DIRECTION CHANGE

To help show the real conflict Glue Boy has about whether to tell the police interrogator something or not, using Scene Ten and Glue Boy's police interview scene as an example, ask your actor to read the monologue standing up, and to change direction with every punctuation change, slowly. Glue Boy's text here is disjointed, and purposefully not connected or logical, to give us a glimpse of his state of mind at the time.

LANGUAGE EXERCISE 3: CONFLICTING CHAIRS

Place two chairs, side by side, and label one: 'I've got nothing to tell you', and the other: 'I've got something I want to say'. Your actor can then re-read Glue Boy's monologue, this time sitting and moving chair, every time his thinking changes from one sentiment to the other.

With both of the above exercises, give yourself enough time –
be very strict to make sure that you've fully moved before
starting the thought.

LANGUAGE EXERCISE 4: VISUALISING THE TEXT IN PICTURES

Actors get into pairs, A and B. They use the text from the
final, chanted section in the play. B closes their eyes, and A
has to whisper each word of the text to B, line by line. B can
only give the thumbs up to continue reading, once they have
fully heard and are able to picture the image(s). In this
exercise, you need to give yourself the space and time to
conjure up and see each beautiful image. This exercise really
helps to highlight the power of the images within the text.

Production, staging and design

There are many practical and creative challenges and
opportunities created by *Eclipse*. Here are some issues and
questions that productions may want to explore. Both
Michael Buffong and Simon were very clear that this was a
very open text, open to interpretation, and these were only
intended as starting points for discussion.

DESIGN

This does not have to be literal or representational. The play
could be performed on a bare stage, so any elements of set
should really help to tell the story. In such a production,
sound and light might become an even more important
element of the storytelling language. What kind of visual
language could move us from the interview room to the beach?
Is the interview room always in the same place on the stage,
or does it move? How do you represent the electric fence?

SOUND

How would sound support the creation of the dual locations?
How might sound be used during the eclipse? There were
reports that birds stopped singing. Might Midnight be more

sensitive to the aural? Could sound be used to tap into characters' psychological state, and used in a more abstract way? Is there a danger of being over-reliant on sound in a play that requires its audience to tune into the poetics of the language? Is the ritual an opportunity to use live music or rhythm for some companies? Silence is as important a tool in thinking about this play's sound world.

LIGHT

This is worth thinking about, in a play in which light is a central metaphor. Can light be used to differentiate locations? Is there a lighting solution to some of the play's technical challenges – for example the fire? How do you represent the eclipse dramatically, without just using a blackout? Is there a way of approaching the transitions between the scenes without using blackouts?

Simon suggested that Lucy's burning of Tulip's headscarf didn't involve naked flame, but was more a conjuring trick of sorts.

THE ELECTRIC FENCE

This could be represented in a number of ways. A hazard warning sign could be put up, with the electric fence running all around this small area, sectioning off part of the beach. You could bypass the actual fence altogether, giving the actor who played Lucy Lime a joke-shop electric buzzer, which still gave out a shock, and could be equally as effective.

In Scene Eleven, where the action returns to the same scene on the beach as earlier in Scene Seven, and certain dialogue between the friends is replicated in the run-up to the actual moment of eclipse, Simon is happy for any groups to choose where they decide to pick up that repeat of the scene on the beach again. That is, he leaves it to the discretion of each director and company to cut into that text at whatever point they feel appropriate.

If any part(s) of the play feel contradictory, Simon is happy for you to leave them out, if helpful for your production.

THE ECLIPSE

It might be useful to explore practically the way an eclipse works. Draw circles on the floor to represent the orbit of the earth and the moon. Using tennis balls to represent the earth and the moon, and a football as the sun, move the balls around in their orbits until the moon comes between the sun and the earth. Use the exercise to discuss the improbability and infrequency of such an event, and as a starting point to explore some of the mysticism surrounding eclipses in general.

STAGING AND DESIGN EXERCISE: LOCATIONS AND TRANSITIONS

Divide your cast into smaller groups, and focus on the three different locations referred to within the play: 1) the police waiting room; 2) the police interview room; 3) the beach.

Ask all groups to come up with three variations of how to stage and transition between each of these three locations. After exploring different options, the groups come together again and share their options.

It is interesting to see how literal, naturalistic or stylised these different staging versions can be. For example, whether people choose to use chairs, blocks, rocks, stools or no set at all, how they think about lighting and sound, and how these choices all go to affect the overall atmosphere, style and storytelling.

Style

Simon highlighted that there were moments for comic relief within this play.

He also mentioned that he was very conscious of this taking inspiration from J.B. Priestley's *An Inspector Calls* and Shakespeare's *A Midsummer Night's Dream*.

With these influences in mind, the play is like a dream environment and the heightened, non-naturalistic language should be celebrated along with the lightness and humour.

Suggested references, reading and viewing list

www.jimmulligan.co.uk/interview/simon-armitage-eclipse

A Midsummer Night's Dream by William Shakespeare

An Inspector Calls by J.B. Priestley

The Doors of Perception by Aldous Huxley

Lord of the Flies by William Golding

Let the Right One In (film, dir. Tomas Alfredson, 2008)

In Lucy's story about emerging from the canal in Scene Five, Simon says that he was trying to suggest that Lucy had experienced 'the power of the naked truth'. The story was inspired by this experience he had on a late train from Manchester:

> Two lads got on and they were very drunk and very aggressive, and everyone in the carriage was a bit on edge, and a bit nervous, and it just looked like something awful was going to happen. There was a woman on the train with a baby. It was a very vulnerable situation, and she looked scared. They were getting louder and more violent and she stood up and said 'Would you like to hold my baby?' and she gave one of the lads the baby. He didn't know what to do, but he couldn't not take it. She defused him by giving him the thing she was most worried about losing. I thought of that moment when Lucy talks about what happened in the canal: of confronting somebody in that way.

What Are They Like?

by Lucinda Coxon

Adolescence is a rough ride. You've got existential angst, mood swings, fashion fiascos, terrifying physical changes, never enough money . . . And that's just the parents. How well do you know yours?

Age suitability: any age

Cast size
twelve named characters:
seven girls, five boys

Lucinda Coxon's plays include *Herding Cats* for Theatre Royal Bath and Hampstead (Theatre Award UK nomination 2011); *The Eternal Not* and *Happy Now?* (Writers' Guild of Great Britain Best Play Award 2008, Drama Desk and Lortel Award nomination, NY 2010) at the National; *Nostalgia* and *Vesuvius* for South Coast Repertory; *Improbabilities* at Soho Poly; *Wishbones* and *Waiting at the Water's Edge* at the Bush; and *Three Graces* at Lakeside Theatre/Colchester Mercury). Her adaptations include *The Shoemaker's Incredible Wife* from Federico García Lorca and *The Ice Palace* from the novel by Tarjei Vesaas, both for National Theatre Connections. Screenplays include *Wild Target*, *The Heart of Me* and *The Danish Girl*, now in production, being directed by Tom Hooper and starring Eddie Redmayne. Her four-part version of Michel Faber's *The Crimson Petal and the White* was screened on BBC2. She is currently adapting Sarah Waters' *The Little Stranger* and Ian McEwan's *Sweet Tooth* for film and developing a series for BBC Television.

Author's notes

The stage directions given in this play are sometimes very specific, sometimes very loose. They should, by and large, be viewed as suggestions. They are a way of scoring the play. The most useful approach in rehearsal may be to discover the intention behind the direction rather than adhere to it. This is not the way I work ordinarily, but much of the pleasure of this play will lie in exploring its physical life.

What Are They Like? features twelve performers who play twelve characters. The transition from performer to character occurs on stage. There might be a value in staging a short warm-up in view of the audience before 'the play' commences. A sense of bonding in the performer company might usefully inform the various forms of isolation and community found in the characters' experiences.

The toy box can be approached at any time by any character within the time bracket specified in the text. Characters might approach more than once, changing their minds about taking their toy. They do each have a special toy, but what that toy might be (cuddly toy, ball, skipping rope, musical instrument, remote control helicopter, doll, puppet, etc.) is something to be discovered in rehearsal. Attachment to or absorption in a toy might halt or interrupt the action of the play. Toys might be deliberately or inadvertently shared. The toy might or might not be referred to when the character is speaking.

Characters

Alison
Frances
Gary
Grace
Indira
Johnny
Meera
Nick
Patrick
Robert
Sarah
Steph

One

Lights up. A circle of shoes on the floor, widely spaced, neatly arranged in pairs, pointing towards the centre – five pairs of men's, seven pairs of women's. They might be formal or utility wear, but they are the shoes of people aged over thirty.

In the centre of the shoe circle is a large cardboard box. We cannot see inside it.

Twelve performers enter, stalk in an insistent rhythm around the shoes, eventually stopping, each in front of a pair. When the moment is right, they step into the shoes. The shoes (and thus, characters) and the performers do not need to share a gender. Nor do the shoes have to fit.

Once all shoes are on, the circle becomes ominously energised. Something is about to begin:

Robert   Tick.

Frances   Tock.

Steph   Tick.

Grace   Tock.

Nick   Tick.

Gary   Tock.

Johnny   Tick.

Indira   Tock.

Alison   Tick.

Patrick   Tock.

Sarah   Tick.

Meera   Tock.

Robert   Get up! Come on, you're going to miss it!

Frances   For the last time, can you just go to bed!

Steph   Go out, go on, and get some fresh air /

Grace   I want you back in the house by /

Nick   You're not still doing that . . . ?

Gary   Haven't you even started yet . . . ?

Johnny   You need to eat something /

Indira   Who's eaten all this?

Alison   You need to work harder /

Patrick   You'll wear yourself out.

Sarah   You've got to take it seriously /

Meera   Hey, it's not the end of the world . . .

Nick *confesses.*

Nick   Y' lie t'them – of course – don't you? Right from the start! You've got to – you don't mean to, but really . . . Come on! As soon as they're born, y' start lying.

It's like when they're little, you say . . . 'There's nothing to be frightened of.' But there is. Of course. There's plenty.

Meera *looks out at the audience.*

Meera   There's plenty.

Nick   I remember when Alex was – what was he? – three, maybe? He got obsessed – I don't know where that came from – obsessed – with the idea of death. The idea I was going to die. He'd wake up screaming . . . some terrible dream: 'Hey – hey!' I'd tell him: 'I'm not going to die! I'm not going t'die! I promise.'

He looks at **Meera**.

Nick   Not *ever*.

He moves away.

Indira   She borrows things. I don't mind. Well, I do. A bit. Not really, you know, but . . .

As she speaks, **Nick** *looks into the cardboard box. At intervals during the play, each of the characters will approach the box and remove a child's toy. The rate and rhythm of this process is something to be discovered.*

Indira   She's always wanted to wear my clothes. But then her brother was the same!

The high heels – 'clip-clop shoes', they called them.

I think that's just normal. Kids like dressing up, don't they?

But now it's different. At least . . . it seems different. I mean, there's an element still, of dressing up, but . . .

She'll try things on of mine, and she'll look in the mirror . . . and . . .

The way she looks . . .

She shies away from something.

It's cold.

So . . . critical.

And part of me thinks: good for you – not kidding yourself. Not making *that* mistake.

And part of me thinks:

Please . . . Don't be so hard on yourself.

Don't be so hard on me.

She leaves. **Gary** *begins – shy, almost apologetic:*

Gary   There's a sense, I suppose, of . . . of a clock ticking fast once they're born. You're . . . you're so conscious all the time of these things that you won't get to do again. All these *first* things. First steps, first words . . . you know! They feel so . . . precious.

Robert *chimes in . . .*

Robert   And you've got to hurry to keep up with them.

Gary   I think that's why you take all those pictures – it all feels so sort of . . . fleeting.

Then, I don't know, it flattens out a bit in the middle . . .

Robert   It's true . . . you relax a bit. Life settles down.

Gary   And then all of a sudden . . .

Robert   Tell me about it!

Gary struggles a moment, then:

Gary   He talks now, sometimes, about the years until he leaves. And I feel . . .

I feel at sea, if I'm honest.

I feel . . .

But he's interrupted as **Sarah** *rushes in, furious.*

Sarah   This is the worst it's ever been. Actually, the other day, I just went in and said: Okay, I've done everything I could do. From now on, it's on you. That's it. It's on you. When the results come out on August 23rd and you've not got enough to stay on in the sixth form, it's

All

On

You.

She seems exhausted now. **Robert** *goes to speak but before he can:*

Sarah   It's impossible. Of course his dad basically left school with nothing but a cycling proficiency badge so he says 'he'll be alright' – and it makes me so angry! Because you don't know that.

You don't *know* that!

And then I think, why do I have to be the bloody bad guy all the time. Why is it always me?

She storms off.

Robert *takes his chance.*

Robert The most important thing is to let them know you get things wrong. Admit to your mistakes, don't try to keep your end up. Cos they see it anyway.

Our parents didn't do that. They belonged to a generation that thought you had to be . . . totally infallible. Or look that way at any rate. No way my kids think that about me. They've seen me mess things up too often.

He ambles off. **Johnny** *remembers with enormous pleasure.*

Johnny I used t'go on trains all the time. I'd say to my parents:

'I don't know what time I'll be back, I'm going on the train!'

People think they're unreliable now – they were a lot worse then. I'd go all over – as far as I could afford. My parents didn't even know what county I was in!

If mobile phones had existed, I suppose they'd've been calling and asking. That would've ruined it – completely!

Patrick Okay: I find the height thing difficult. If you'd told me before, that one day I'd . . .

Well I'd've laughed in your face.

But it matters. It just does.

I've always been tall. I'm not used to looking up at anyone.

Never mind my own son.

Johnny Kira tends to be quite slow returning texts. Within an hour, I consider acceptable.

I tend not to bug her so I get more of a response, whereas her mother . . . well . . .

Frantic's not the right word, but . . .

For me, if she picks up, that's fine. I don't need to know where she is and who she's with. I just need to know she's alright.

He shrugs, sneaks off.

Robert   Get up! Come on, you're going to miss it!

Frances   For the last time, can you just go to bed!

Steph   Go out, go on, and get some fresh air /

Grace   I want you back in the house by /

Nick   You're not still doing that . . . ?

Gary   Haven't you even started yet . . . ?

Johnny   You need to eat something /

Indira   Who's eaten all this?

Alison   You need to work harder /

Patrick   You'll wear yourself out.

Sarah   You've got to take it seriously /

Meera   Hey, it's not the end of the world . . .

Frances   Blah blah blah blah.

Grace *is on the phone. It might be a toy phone. Or a random toy being used as a phone. Or there might not be any kind of prop-phone.*

Grace   Hi, Arun, it's me. Can you give me a call?

Frances   I just feel like a broken record sometimes.

Grace   Hi, Arun, it's me again. Can you call home please?

Frances   I laugh in the middle of saying things sometimes, cos I've said them so often!

Grace *is testy now:*

Grace   Yep, me again. Phone. Please, Arun.

Frances   Or cos I sound like my own mum.

Grace *gives up.*

Steph   I *hate* that.

Grace *tries again. No joy – gives up.*

Frances   Except no way would she have put up with what I get!

Steph   I hear myself, you know? And I just think: shut up! That wasn't true when she said it to you, and it isn't any truer now!

Frances   I say to my girls: you see that word that just came out of your mouth, I wouldn't have even let it come into my head with my mother!

It's because they've never been battered – they've never feared that immediate reprisal. I've had to really *look* for ways to punish them!

Honestly, because we don't hit them – I know some people do, and that's their business – but because we don't, the question is, *what can you do*?

I said to Jasmine (it's always Jasmine) after this last incident:

Okay – here's the deal . . . you know I'm on flexitime, so that means I can choose my work hours . . . ? Let me promise you this: if you continue with this behaviour, even though you are fifteen years old, I will walk you to school every morning, and collect you every afternoon. I really mean it.

That worked.

Grace   He's got a girlfriend. He goes to her house all the time. Every day, straight from school.

She seems very nice, and in some ways we're thrilled – I mean that he's managed to make a relationship – but . . .

Well, we never know what time he's coming back!

I tell him: we only need a bit of communication. Just return our texts. But he doesn't even have his phone turned on when he's round there.

Steph   You can remember things about yourself at that age, that's what makes it hard, I think.

Grace   In the end, I rang her dad and said: 'Look, we really appreciate you having Arun so often. But would you please ask him to keep his phone on, and it would be great if we knew that when it got to half past nine you'd send him home.'

Steph   You don't remember your own first tooth, or learning to read – of course not. But your teenage years – you can remember that – O-levels . . . parties . . . *kissing*!

The recollection excites her . . .

Grace   When Arun found out, he went mad: 'I'm so embarrassed, you've embarrassed me so badly! I can't believe you did this!' On and on.

Completely out of control.

Steph   I remember the taste of boys who smoked! And I never want my kids to smoke – of course I don't – or their friends, but . . .

To be fifteen and kiss a boy who tastes of smoke . . .

It knocks your socks off!

Grace   'You've made me look like a complete idiot! It's so embarrassing!'

I said –

No!

What's embarrassing is

this

you

right now.

You're embarrassing yourself!

He said, it's different – there's no one here to see. I said *I'm* here, aren't I?

He looked astonished. As though that hadn't occurred to him.

He said, well if I can't embarrass myself in front of my own mother, what's the use of anything?

She falters.

'My own mother'. He said that.

Her tone changes.

And I was so relieved. Because . . . Because I'm always waiting for that whole thing to kick in.

'You're not my real mother.'

I'm always waiting for that.

Alison   For my eighteenth birthday, my parents bought me a set of suitcases.

They said it was traditional.

And when I left home, they did this thing where – I mean straight away – they redecorated. Completely. Everywhere.

And they started going on all these really . . . *different* holidays.

I was so . . . wounded. Honestly. I just . . . I just couldn't believe it.

Gary   He got mugged.

Meera   Zack did – they all do. The boys, that is.

Gary   It's as if there's a little window of opportunity where the bigger boys can pounce. Like when crabs shed their shells and all the birds are just waiting.

Meera   'A man stood in front of me, told me to give him my bike.' So he did. Just like that.

Gary   Some bigger boys just walked up to him and his friends, broad daylight, y'know . . . ?

Meera   'This boy asked me the time, so I took out my phone . . . '

She gestures the inevitable consequence.

Gary   Took what was in their pockets. They just let them, rather than lose face, make a fuss . . .

Meera   I said, good boy. Some things aren't worth fighting over.

Indira   She's not fat – I'll say that straight off. But she's not thin, either. Not like some of the skinny-skinny ones. I tell her it doesn't matter. At their age, your body's changing all the time! And what a person looks like is a very small part of who they are!

I can see she doesn't believe me. I don't believe myself sometimes. But it's what you're meant to say.

My husband used t' tell me I was beautiful, and I'd think – what are you –

A liar, or just stupid?

In the end, it made me hate him.

Meera   We're a tight little unit. We've not had much choice with their dad out of the picture.

So when I was diagnosed, I just told them: I'd had a test that said I needed an operation, and the operation would be in ten days' time.

I told them I wasn't going to die.

I felt pretty confident about that – we'd caught it very early, and my doctor seemed really positive. So I told them that. It seemed important to just say it.

I asked them to think if they had any questions they wanted me to ask the doctor – because I had lots of questions too – and if we pooled our questions, we might understand the illness better.

Zack didn't ask anything.

Nadia asked two things: 'What colour is the tumour?' and 'After they take it out, can I have it?'

Sarah   He hates me at the moment – really hates me.

I look on his computer.

There was a problem for a while, with what he was watching. I had to talk to him about it. I had to tell him:

This is nothing like the real world. This isn't what real women look like. Those women aren't enjoying it. They're just doing it to pay for a drug habit or feed their children.

I check his search history.

I tell him, if you've cleared it, I'll just assume that's what you were doing, and we'll be having this conversation again.

Frances   So last summer one day she came home in a rare old state – this is Jasmine again, I hardly need say. She could really hardly breathe to get her words out –

'They've been caught shoplifting – Darcy and Jenny-Rose! I knew they were going to do it, so I went next door to Boots.'

It was a proper saga . . . the parents were down at the police station and the girls were banned from H&M.

She shrugs.

That was all that happened in the end.

A shift.

But I had to have the talk with Jasmine.

I had to say:

Alright let me tell you, if *you* had been caught, it wouldn't have been the same.

It would have been a completely different outcome, and this is why:

Because you're black. And you need to learn this lesson:

You would have been treated completely differently.

You always will be.

Sarah   I know I'm hard on him, but . . . At least that's what he thinks. But you've got to draw the line. I'm just not always sure the line's in the right place.

Frances   I called a meeting in Costa with the other mums. I said I'm sorry, I really like your girls. But when my daughter's with them, when they're all together, there's something goes wrong. So my daughter won't be coming to your house again, and your children are no longer welcome in my home.

I've never regretted that.

You want them to learn the lessons, that actions have consequences. But they can be very hard lessons.

Robert   Our lives, before we had the boys . . . if they knew, it would kill them.

Drugs, for example. We've taken just about everything, both of us. I've never told them that. I don't want to endorse that behaviour – I mean, we don't take drugs now, and I don't think it did us any harm, but that's not the case for everyone.

So they need to understand it's not behaviour I approve of.

I think it's dangerous behaviour.

Johnny   I deliberately don't ask, to be honest. I'd rather not know. Who's this, who's that? How long have you known them?

The truth is there's a distance between us, and I quite like that. We respect each other's boundaries.

Once, in the kitchen, I found a lighter. I wondered about it.

But I just left it alone and it disappeared.

I think that's my policy really. Do nothing if you can. And things just tend to resolve themselves.

He looks down for a moment, then:

I still don't know whose lighter it was.

Patrick   If I'm honest, I've noticed myself competing with him more.

We'd always done running races in the park, but . . .

I started to make the distances shorter so I could still beat him.

Gary   I like to think he still needs me. I don't know if it's true. He'll ring for a lift sometimes, and actually, he's just being lazy – he doesn't want to walk, but I go.

And I'm glad to go. Cos how many more chances will there be? 'Thanks, Dad,' he says. But I'm doing it for me, not him.

I think more about my dad now. You think more about your parents when you're older. When they're not around any more.

Robert   Get up! Come on, you're going to miss it!

Frances   For the last time, can you just go to bed!

Steph   Go out, go on, and get some fresh air /

Grace   I want you back in the house by /

Nick   You're not still doing that . . . ?

Gary   Haven't you even started yet . . . ?

Johnny   You need to eat something /

Indira   Who's eaten all this?

Alison   You need to work harder /

Patrick   You'll wear yourself out.

Sarah   You've got to take it seriously /

Meera   Hey, it's not the end of the world . . .

Alison   For years, I was so jealous of people whose parents had kept their room the same for them. Their old posters on the walls even, some of them. Because honestly, mine . . . well, they couldn't disguise how excited they were . . . to be losing a daughter but gaining an en-suite.

So now, I just feel totally guilty. Because, if I'm honest . . .

I really badly want them out.

All of them.

I can't wait.

Grace   He doesn't ever want to talk about his birth family. He can remember it, that life – of course. He'll never forget it . . . But he keeps it to himself.

It's left him bad with change. Uncertainty. He worries.

He still hasn't called.

Sometimes, I think, if I did to him what he does to us . . . kept him hanging, in the dark, his world would just collapse.

Nick   Once or twice, I've admitted to something, from when I got it wrong, round about their age.

They're shocked – they can't handle it. They think they know everything about you. You're the one thing in the world they know everything about, that doesn't change.

It's 'cannot compute' when you introduce stuff that doesn't go with that picture.

I think they want you to lie. They lie too, of course. It's how we all protect each other.

Robert   I once, when I was young . . . seventeen, it was . . . I made a big mistake with something I took, something I got given at a club.

I had the classic bad trip – I was terrified, utterly. Completely out of my depth – it could have ended really badly . . but no way was I going to call my parents.

He shakes his head at the thought.

So what I say to mine is this:

If you're ever anywhere with people you feel unsure about, or where you start to feel uncomfortable, or if you just don't like what's going on – I don't care what it is – girls, drugs, police – doesn't matter.

You call me. I won't judge you.

Any time, day or night. You call me, and I sort it out.

Patrick   I asked him to show me how to get the iPod to play through the speakers.

He laughed at me. Then he did it really fast, so I couldn't see how.

Now I've got to ask him again.

Meera   When I was growing up, all I wanted was to get away.

It wasn't that I didn't love my parents . . . but . . . I hated that whole extended family thing you get in immigrant communities. I needed to get out – get on . . .

I know they've got to separate from you, but . . .

I can't bear the idea of a slow drifting away.

Johnny   She's not getting on with her mum. Occasionally, there's like a glimmer of some kind of bonding, but mostly they're at each other's throats. I'm the mediator.

I try not to lose my temper. I didn't know I had a temper until we had Kira!

She's quite a forceful character. When she was two, I'd use hostage negotiation techniques on her . . . But she still made mincemeat of me.

She can still turn the tables. Her mum can't do anything right . . .

But if she was here now, with you, she'd be absolutely charming.

Meera   When I told them I was having chemo, Zack asked if my hair would fall out. I said, yes. And it'll look weird at first, but you mustn't be frightened. It won't be for ever. He said:

I never ever want to be seen with you in public with no hair.

I said: I don't blame you. I'll always wear a hat or scarf.

And I did.

Nick   Apart from personal history, then, money and food would be the other main things.

I mean, like, they'll say, 'What's for pudding?' and we say a piece of fruit. Then, once they're gone, it's out with the Dairy Milk. Yeah, we lie about that.

And about how much Margaret earns. We tell them it's less. They can't understand what money's worth anyway. And I don't want them feeling too cosy.

We're not rich. It just sounds like a lot to a kid.

They're going to need to try in life. You look at the world now . . . they're going t' have to *really* try.

Gary   I remember the feel of his hand, small, in mine. The smell of the top of his head. Being able to pick him up!

When he was a tiny baby, I went to Mothercare in the High Road. They had these sleepsuits with the sun, moon and the stars on. I just thought they were fantastic.

I bought them in all the sizes: 0–3 months, 3–6 . . . all the way up to 36 months.

I went a bit mad, I suppose.

Alison   My greatest fear for the future is that if I don't watch it, by the time the last one moves out, first one'll be wanting t' move back in. The idea of that . . . well, it keeps me awake at night.

Gary   He wore them for years. You can imagine. I can see him in them, still . . .

Indira   I don't know how to help her. To make her understand that she is beautiful. Because she really is.

That's the hardest thing, I suppose.

I look at her and realise I was beautiful at her age. But I couldn't believe it then. And it's too late to start now.

Gary   It's like sand running through an hourglass . . . Near the end, it looks like it's going much faster. It isn't – I know that – but still . . .

Steph   It makes you feel totally out of control.

Gary   I'm making it all sound sad. It's not. I don't know why it sounds like it is.

Steph   I think that's all you can say about sex and so on: warn them that the body . . . the senses, if you like . . . have a mind of their own.

And they don't always want what's best for your long-term future.

You will not always feel in control of yourself. And nor will other people.

I said: 'I'm going to buy some condoms. Leave them in the bathroom, with the Tampax and the rest.' They were up in arms about it!

David went bonkers at me. He thinks of them as little girls still. I said, I'm not trying to encourage them to do it! But I don't want them too embarrassed to go and buy Durex and then . . .

You know.

They say –

We don't want to 'discuss' sex and drugs and stuff! We just want a rule. Why can't you be more like Grandma . . . ? Just tell us:

'No – You can't do *anything*! At all! Ever!'

I say: well you two are evidence of how well that approach worked.

Sarah   This year, when his birthday was coming up, I was hating him so much. I couldn't even stand the idea of making him a cake. Not that he'd ever admit to wanting one. Honestly. Really hating.

I thought, I've got to get out of this – for my sake as much as his. I've got to find a way to remember what it was like – before. What *we* were like.

So I thought I'd make him a photo album. Of his life, to date.

Then I worried – I thought, am I being mean, you know? Am I going: Oh, look you hate me, but see how much I love you with all my cutting and sticking, and . . . ?

And then I thought, Oh, just get on with it. He won't think that. He won't even be interested. So I did it.

I made him open his presents sitting on our bed, with Kelly there as well. I saved the album till last.

Beat.

Well, he couldn't stop looking at it. That was what he did, for about an hour. Just look through the pictures.

I said: there are plenty of pages in the back . . . for the future. We'll do it again when you're eighteen.

And twenty-one.

Patrick   I bought some clothes like his. I can't believe I did it.

Frances *starts to laugh, just thinking of what she's about to say.*

Frances   If Rick and me have a row –

Patrick   God knows what I look like in them.

Frances   – like one of the really vicious ones –

Patrick   He's been very nice about it.

Frances   – she says, 'I know I'm only sixteen, but I don't understand why you don't divorce him. Do it before you're too old to get someone else. Honestly, what do you see in him?'

That's when they're in a phase of hating their dad! Of course, sometimes, it's the other way, and I'm the villain.

Robert   The thing is, they've got to experiment with life. I know that. And they've got to feel as though they're doing something you disapprove of – because half the time that's the whole fun of it. So you've got to sort of take positions. On things you're not that bothered about.

They've got to think you're a bit of an old fart. That's sort of the job.

He shrugs, walks off.

Grace   He announced he was going on holiday with his girlfriend. Her grandma's in Croatia, near the sea. I said – hang on, we need to talk about this first! And there's the cost . . .

In the end, we agreed – if he paid half.

We set up jobs for him – cat-feeding, lawn-mowing, car-washing – all that.

Well, he didn't seem that interested. I felt riled. I really did. That he wouldn't make more of an effort. Time was getting on. I started nagging him. Then it dawned on me . . .

I talked to him about it, in the car. It's the best place. I said:

If you don't really want to go, it's alright. I'll say I've changed my mind, you're not allowed. I'll be the bad guy.

She notices that the others are now listening to her . . .

Silence. For miles. So I said:

Okay. I'll tell them. You're not going. It's alright, it's over.

The slightest nod he gave me.

What do you want for tea?

By this stage in the play, all of the characters have collected their toys.

Steph   I bought a new dress the other day. The youngest said: You can't wear that! Not at your age! I said: Don't think of me as thirty-six. Think of me as the same age as you but with twenty-two years' more experience!

Johnny   She changes so fast. She's really like a different person . . . You get used to one Kira, and six weeks later there's a new Kira. She's really like a different person . . . New . . . friends, new music, all changed. And you worry, but . . .

Well, you'll worry for the rest of their life, won't you?

Alison   I suppose the only thing worse is if they all move out and I'm too knackered by then to enjoy it.

Bloody hell.

Frances   The main thing is, they make me laugh. They really, really make me laugh. I can't tell you.

If I'm honest, I just think they're brilliant. That's the thing, in the end.

I just think they're great.

I really do.

Johnny   She looks older than she is. We went to the pub the other day. She asked for a pint of lager and I bought it for her.

It's the first drink we've ever had together.

He fails to stifle a smile.

She didn't finish it.

He looks at the others. A sense of something inescapable . . . a mood growing within the group, fear and excitement in the face of the unknown, as:

Robert   Tick.

Frances   Tock.

Steph   Tick.

Grace   Tock.

Nick   Tick.

Gary   Tock.

Johnny   Tick.

Indira   Tock.

Alison   Tick.

Patrick   Tock.

Sarah   Tick.

Meera   Tock.

The characters brace, clutching their toys as a SONIC BOOM *flowers in the air . . . announcing, simultaneously, an end and a beginning.*

Shoes should be removed and hurled away for any curtain call.

What Are They Like?

BY LUCINDA COXON

*Notes on rehearsal and staging drawn from a workshop
with the writer held at the National Theatre, October 2015*

*From workshops led by Ned Bennett and Orla O'Loughlin,
with notes by Kirsty Patrick Ward and Andy McNamee*

How Lucinda came to write the play

'This was my third play for Connections, and previously I was
conscious of not wanting to write a play that was preachy . . .
I avoided this by first doing an adaptation, and then doing a
translation. By the time I was writing this play I had quite a
lot of experience of going to see Connections plays, all over
the country and abroad . . . It also coincided with my own
daughter turning thirteen. I realised that I'd reached a stage
where people who had kids the same age were starting to talk
about the issue of lying, and lies creeping into your relationship
with your child. You had this (possibly an) illusion that you
knew everything about one another, and all of a sudden you've
got to start lying, you start deciding what you will reveal about
your personal history to one another . . . so there's this whole
question about disclosure and personal history at a time when
your children most need your advice and guidance – how much
are you really going to tell them about your sexual history or
history with drugs? How much do they need to know? How
much is useful? That seemed to be quite a big question.

'I talked to kids in schools who said they occasionally lied to
their parents – one of them said, "I only lie about one thing:
where I am, what I'm doing and who I'm with." I asked the
children, "Do you think your parents lie to you?" and they
were emphatic that they did not (unless they were trying to
protect them from trouble in the family). So there was this
extraordinary sense that they didn't want to think or believe
that their parents could lie to them, and found it very hard to
see that their parents might be withholding information from
them. This seemed particularly interesting, because when

I went to see all these Connections plays, the people in the audience were of course the parents! So I wanted to write a piece about the anxiety of children becoming teenagers, but also a piece that included the parents. In a sense it's a kind of community play, and is very active in fostering conversations between parents and kids.'

Physical warm-up game

- Get into pairs.

- Facing your partner, first slap your thighs with both hands.

- Next, using both hands choose to move your hands once to the left, to the right, or above your head (one move, not one of each).

- After each move, slap your thighs again.

- The object of the game is not to mirror each other, but if you and your partner do mirror one another, then you must do a double high-five before your next move.

- By doing these moves (a slap on the legs, followed by a slap to the left or right or up, etc.), you will almost be creating a dance with your partner.

- Once you've hit your stride, try increasing the speed.

- Then start again with a new partner.

- Once you've mastered this with a new partner, try repeating the exercise from a long distance across the room – not in straight lines, but all over the space.

- Finally finish with another close round.

This warm-up is excellent for focusing a group, as well as breaking the ice.

Challenges of the play

The following challenges were shared most within the group:

- How to approach the stage directions, when and why are they are specific or interpretable?

- Is the script locked down?
- How to approach ensemble chorus work?
- How to tackle casting if the gender ratio is different?
- Design ideas/how to use the props?
- How to create a safe space in the rehearsal room, and tackle the issues within the play safely (given some young performers' potential backgrounds and familial experiences)?

The exercises below are designed to address these various challenges and offer starting points for the development of your production.

CHARACTER AND CHARACTERISATION

'If you ask kids to play a dragon they find that very easy, but if you ask them to play a forty-five-year-old branch manager of a bank in Leek, they feel very differently: the poetry of the ordinary is hard to pull off, and is a massive challenge.'

Therefore, allowing time for detailed character work is vital.

CHARACTER EXERCISE 1: CHARACTER LISTS

Orla split the participants into pairs and assigned them a character. They were asked to go through the text to find everything that each character said about themselves and everything that was said about them. Participants were encouraged to find literal descriptions or direct lines from the text before more abstract, indirect conclusions. For example:

Jonny

> I used to go on trains all the time.
>
> I'd go all over, as far as I could afford.
>
> I'm the mediator.
>
> I deliberately don't ask.
>
> There a distance between us, I like that.
>
> I found a lighter once.

I still don't know whose lighter it was.

I try not to lose my temper.

I didn't know I had a temper before we had Kira.

That's my policy, do nothing if you can.

I tend not bug her so I get more of a response.

I don't need to know all who she's with, I just need to
know she's alright.

One member of each pair was then asked to stand and say
aloud everything their character said about themselves,
before the other member of the pair said aloud everything
that was said about them. Because the whole play is spoken
from a first-person perspective, there was very little said about
each character, which meant that we were forced to really
investigate vague mentions or indirect references to themselves
from other perspectives.

This exercise can highlight both the indisputable facts about
the characters and the subjects on which a cast and director
will have to make decisions on.

For most characters the exercise revealed: 1) the practicalities
of the characters' key relationship – generally with their
children, but sometimes with their spouse; 2) a collection of
facts – are the children biological/adopted, general age of
the children involved, how many children the character has;
3) some clear, basic character traits (worrier, laid back,
competitive, etc.) With this knowledge, you can begin to paint
a detailed picture of each character and start to build them
on a more complex level.

Using the example of Jonny, the group in the workshop
described him as:

> Laid back. A conflict avoider. Self-deprecating. Was he
> someone who, having had a child, mourned the loss of his
> own freedom and control over his own life? What is his
> relationship with his partner like (who he mentions a lot in
> reference to his child)? Is he happy in his relationship?

Questions like these are all drawn from the text. You can begin to answer them either via clues in the script or through invention based on what you know from the script. For example, to use another character, Grace, we learnt that nearly everything she says is in relation to her adopted son Arun and she makes a point of mentioning (with some pride) when he refers to her as his mum. This is a discovery that includes facts (he is adopted) but also leaves room for actors and directors to make decisions about who she is based on contextual knowledge.

Every character in *What Are They Like?* goes on a journey. They are rooted in reality but are most definitely fictional. They are unique and worthy of their own exploration as individuals. The play offers a lot of opinions but not a huge number of facts, which means that you and your company, through discussion and detailed analysis of the text, can be free to make choices about who these people are.

CHARACTER EXERCISE 2: TABLEAUX

In small groups, create a tableau that wholly sums up a character's relationship with whoever they talk about within the play. Then as a whole group, look at each one in turn and see if the group can identify who is who in the image and why. There is a huge amount to consider in these tableau, both for the people creating them and for the group analysing them – physicality, tension, use of height, display of effort, eye contact, use of any props, and so on.

Creating tableaux can be useful in condensing often very complex emotions and relationships into a single image and can form the early building blocks for an actor when making decisions about character.

CHARACTER WORK: RESEARCH

It is important to ground the characters in reality; Orla suggested having your cast find pictures of real people to represent the other characters; for example have the person playing Frances find a real-life version of Jasmine. In the same way, as a company, it might be worth finding one or two visual representations of the world the production exists in. If, for example, you decide it is school that connects these characters, you could find a picture of a school to share as a reference point. You could find opportunities for further 'shared experiences' – for example by challenging your cast to create family trees for their characters. Allowing a company to discover their characters' pasts through imagination and beyond what is directly referenced in the script could help to create a more rounded and truthful performance.

CONTEXT AND RELATIONSHIPS

This is a useful exercise in which to explore the open playing style. Ned asked the participants in small groups to choose a section of text and explore its context: 'Where literally are they, and whom is the speaker targeting? Is the speaker confiding in a journal? Are they speaking to their own child, or their partner?'

Next the groups acted and directed these sections, and explored how this specificity (of how and whom the speaker was targeting, affected the dynamic of the scene.

The scenes included conversations in supermarket queues, coffee with friends, confessions over a drinking game and while watching a football match. The exercise opened up the play's limitless possibilities, how a large cast could easily be incorporated, and how a preoccupation within a conversation (e.g. driving a car, or taking a yoga class) could add different dynamics within sections. Some groups played scenes naturalistically (overhearing a conversation on a crowded tube), others shared more abstractly and repeated lines, thus creating a chorus which spoke directly to the audience.

By changing the perspective of whom each character is talking to the point of focus will be moving throughout, and the individual atmosphere of exchanges can be found and honed during rehearsal.

RELATIONSHIP BETWEEN CHARACTERS AND AUDIENCE

This exercise is about specificity of intention (adapted from Declan Donnellan's *The Actor and the Target*, 2002). In pairs, Ned asked the group to choose one person to be person A, and the other to be person B. He explained there would be four lines used in this exercise, and to think of them as four different thoughts. They were:

- 'No'
- 'There's you'
- 'There's me'
- 'And there's the space'

First, person A would say all these lines to person B. Next, person B would reply by saying the same four lines back to person A.

'Use these lines as if the other person doesn't understand the difference between yourself, them and the space . . . It's like they are an alien that has landed, and doesn't understand that you are one thing, they are another thing and that the space is a third thing.'

Once the groups had mastered this, Ned asked the pairs to repeat this exercise and say the same lines, but this time with one person playing a parent and another a child.

Then they repeated the exercise but chose a scenario from the text (or a specific relationship between a parent and a child) as a stimulus. They were asked to think about the different ways the speaker was trying to affect the person they were speaking to, the tactics they employed and how specific the performer needed to be in order to execute the task. This exercise is a way of 'looking at the relationships without using improvisation (or the text)', that keenly exposes the need for real specificity when relating to each other physically and emotionally, in order to encapsulate these relationships.

CONTRADICTIONS IN CHARACTERS' PERCEIVING EACH OTHER

In pairs, the group explored a piece of extended text. Ned charged the group to find contradictory ways to endow to their partner and how this can change even within a single speech. For example: 'How a father might speak to his son – in one moment he might speak to him as if he thinks he's being a brat, in another he might speak to him as if he's his best friend.' This exercise was a great way to quickly activate the text, find motivations for characters and to tease out the themes within the play. It was also a good way to explore different statuses in characters, and expose that even parents have moments of self-doubt and fear.

How to approach choral work

Ned asked participants to create groups of four and to choose a piece of text to focus on. One person was charged to read the text and the other three to 'create some action that has a literal response to what is happening'. Ned encouraged the groups to explore pulling the spoken text in and out of focus. One group chose an excerpt from Robert's speech on page 142 where he recalls a bad trip, and created a tableau of a house party where others were using drugs. They played with the focus of the text in both staging (having the speaker in the middle of the group), but also with the tableau moving in front of and around the speaker, thereby altering and exploring the volume of the text. Some lines were even repeated by the chorus, or spoken in unison: this instantly created a clear and unified chorus, which supported the text, and could easily utilise many more performers.

Using the same section of text, Ned then challenged the group to 'create with your chorus an abstraction of what is going on [in the text], by using some kind of movement that is looping . . . So it's not about showing what is happening in the scene this time, but rather representing the inner life of the character.' There was still one speaker and three chorus members, but this time it was about capturing and representing the atmosphere in the scene through movement. Ned encouraged the groups to explore and heighten or soften the tempo within the scenes, and to connect with how the character is feeling internally – maybe this is incongruous to the language they are actually using?

One group explored Grace's speech on page 147–8 where she talks to her son in the car (as he is having second thoughts about going on holiday with his girlfriend). The speaker stood to the side of the chorus, and the chorus pushed one performer (representing Grace's son) from one performer to another. This effectively captured both characters' fears and pressures within this difficult and tender moment, without pulling focus from the text. Another group explored Sarah's growing sense of separation from her son, as a result of their quarrelling on page 147. They used the bodies of the chorus to create a physical barrier separating the characters. Each of the groups utilised pacing (some representations played out in slow motion, or with a heightened energy), staging levels, strong gestures and repetition of key words.

Approaching the use of toys within the play

Deciding what the toys are and how they are used is very important. They will work best when anchored to the rest of the production and when working in tandem with other decisions a team has made. Lucinda suggested that 'deciding whether the toy represents a happy memory or a sad memory for that character' can be really useful.

> For me, the meaning of the toys shifts through the play. In a sense it's a meditation on mortality. The question of whose toy it is, is important. Is it the child's toy? Is it the adult's old toy? Or is it the adult's toy from when they were a child? At the beginning the performers are teenagers, then (via the shoes) they become the adults so the toys locate the past, present and future in an object.

To explore how transformative the toys could become, in pairs Ned asked the group to choose a piece of text and, using an actor/director partnership, choose a toy, and explore how these objects could become many different things throughout the speaking of the text – 'Don't just think in terms of illustrations, but also how these objects can bring out the inner life of the characters.'

This resulted in a skipping rope becoming a telephone, a snake, a noose, a tug of war and a tightrope throughout the course of a speech. What this brought to the text was fascinating, and the representations were a mixture of the literal and the abstract. One pair chose Indira's speech 'She's not fat' on page 138, and explored a character comparing themselves to a doll, eventually pulling the doll apart while the text was spoken. The groups explored personification with the toys, but also what they meant as objects to the characters using them – it gave the scenes an intriguing new point of focus, but did not overwhelm the text.

This exercise really helped to explore the characters in detail, and also demystify the idea that there is a set of 'rules' on how best to use the toys – it was all up for grabs, as long as it is supporting the text and the characters.

EXERCISE: ENDOWING OBJECTS WITH MEANING

The group was presented with twelve randomly selected objects. In pairs, they selected an item without putting too much thought into it, and had a few minutes to apply the item to their character, searching for meaning within them. They then discussed their results with the rest of the group. How relevant did they find the item they selected; did it surprise them? Did they find meaning they didn't expect to find? Did they find anything particularly exciting? Did the object frustrate them (in reference to their character)?

This exercise is a good starting point to encourage each person to go out and find an object that feels exactly right for their character. This can be helpful in allowing actors a sense of creative ownership over their characters.

One of the participants randomly selected a deflated rubber ring for the character of Meera. In just a few minutes it was endowed with the idea that Meera connects to the idea of a buoyancy aide that helps to keep people (her children) afloat in the world. However, when considering this item as it is, deflated, it also serves to represent her cancer diagnosis and how she is struggling to keep everyone up. This is a really useful exercise in highlighting the power an object can have.

The shoes

Lucinda really wanted a sense that the young people/actors arrive in the space as teenagers and then 'become' the characters by literally 'stepping into someone else's shoes'. The shoes are a wonderful device through which you can explore and experiment with the style of the piece – the performance of stepping into a pair of shoes and 'becoming' someone else and the moment when they kick off the shoes and break out of their performance. How does this relate to the roles we play as parents and children?

You should also remember the practicalities of the shoes – performing in shoes that don't fit/are uncomfortable could be distracting for an actor and may affect their performance.

Finding the right shoes

The group was presented with twelve different pairs of shoes. As in the previous object exercise, the random nature of what was provided was key to the participants getting the maximum from this exercise. Each pair selected a pair of shoes for their character. Some found there was a perfect pair for them; others found the exact opposite. They then discussed the reasons for their choice and why or why not the shoes worked or didn't work for their characters. One again, the cast could then be given the task to go away and find a pair of shoes that feels right for their character.

Style and technique

The play is non-traditional in its structure and is very much an ensemble piece. Each production can be as different as the next. Lucinda spoke of each character's *need* to talk; these are not casual conversations, and whom they are talking to is something for each company to discuss and agree upon. For example, if the characters are all in the same place (and the design reflects this), then are they talking to each other? If it all takes place in a blank, abstract space, then do they talk to the audience? If they are talking to the toys – what toys might you pick? The style of the piece can be anything it wants to be; it is wide open to interpretation.

The onstage warm-up, the walking in other people's shoes and the sonic boom are all significant theatrical devices that help to establish a 'play within a play'. This idea is a powerful force and one that productions can choose to play up or down as they wish. How much of a performance can be made of the teenagers being onstage to start with? Are they themselves when they are warming up? Or are they a version of themselves? Or are they someone else? Does the warm-up need to be something specific to say something specific? All these questions are worth considering in the context of the style of the whole piece.

The humour in the play is very important and directors are really encouraged to find the fun and lightness to balance against the heavier themes.

Production, staging and design

There is no 'right way' to stage the play but remember that there is real power in simplicity. Lucinda noted: 'You have twelve characters on stage, telling twelve individual stories, which are braided together within the play, and actually that is a lot of material for the audience to keep in their heads.'

The production should allow the audience to see the characters as clearly as possible. In the spirit of simplicity and clarity, there could be real power and significance in exploring what is possible with just the shoes, the toys and actors in space. Having a more complex set could be distracting and directors are advised to avoid video/projections as these can often provide a split focus for an audience. Make sure that whatever you are adding to the play (be it a concept, a chorus or movement) is really supporting the storytelling, and not detracting or clouding the stories. It is a play where you have to do a lot of listening. It is fine to set it wherever you want,

but don't lose sight of the clarity required to share all these
stories fully..

Stage directions

The stage directions within the play are open to interpretation
and should be considered suggestions just as much as
directions; they are a guide for you to use and interpret in
whatever way is meaningful for your company.

The final stage direction of a 'sonic boom' being heard is
an exception. It crucially signifies the moment where the
pretending has to stop. Along with the hurling off of the shoes
it allows productions to really put an end to the play and for
the performers to leave their characters behind.

Music

Music could be a powerful and evocative tool in a production
but, as with the design, participants were advised against
overloading the play with music. Any choice of music should
support the storytelling and the characters.

Casting

'It's nice to have written something that acknowledges the
parents, and where the performative elements are exposed;
we all know that they're teenagers playing adults, and that's
part of the trick of the play. For once you can cast the best
actor and not just "who's the tallest", we know they are
acting, and that's the universe that the play exists in.'

The play was written to be performed by young people of any
age and allows for a diverse and exciting mix of ethnicities,
gender, body type, age and so on. Orla commented on the
possibility of casting against the script and experimenting with
what that might do to the meaning of some lines. For
example, females could play male roles and vice versa, or the
shortest actor could play Patrick (who is so concerned with his
height!) Such choices might allow for a really interesting
interpretation of the character. The form of the play

acknowledges and actively embraces the fact that these are teenagers playing parents and not the parents themselves.

The play can work with more than twelve actors onstage and there are a variety of interesting ways of making a larger cast work that preserves the integrity of the play. For example, extra (silent) cast members could act as the people the written characters are talking to, or two characters could play the same part (i.e. one as the character themselves and the other providing the voices of everyone who speaks back to that character). If you have less than twelve in a company, your actors could play more than one role by swapping shoes throughout. Whatever your circumstance, the clarity of your storytelling needs to be favoured. Inventing a new character so you can split up the lines or merging two characters together is not encouraged.

Language and text

The play is deliberately not set in any particular region, or with any accent, so you are free to embrace the accents you have within your company. But the text should be performed in the order that it is written and should not be moved around.

Bassett
by James Graham

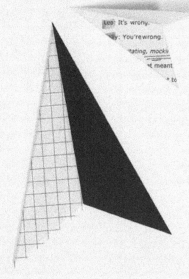

Leo: It's wrong.

...ly: You're wrong.

...tating, mocki...

...t meant

...t to

At Wootton Bassett School the supply teacher has done a runner and locked the pupils in their classroom. Dean needs the toilet, Aimee needs a coffee, Amid needs to pray, and Leo . . . well, Leo really, really wants to escape. Outside, only yards from their confinement, a repatriation of fallen British soldiers is happening along the high street, as it has over a hundred times before through this quiet Wiltshire town. But this one is more personal than most. As factions form and secrets are revealed, maybe Leo is not the only one who'll want to get away. An exhilarating and startling snapshot of a generation who have inherited a world at war.

Age suitability: 15+

Cast size
fourteen named characters:
seven girls, seven boys

James Graham is a playwright and screen-writer whose play *This House* had its premiere at the Cottesloe Theatre (National Theatre) in September 2012, directed by Jeremy Herrin, and transferred to the Olivier in 2013 where it was nominated for the Best Play at both the Evening Standard and Olivier Awards. *Tory Boyz* for the National Youth Theatre was performed at Soho Theatre; and *The Whisky Taster* had its premiere at the Bush Theatre in early 2010. He has written the book for the Broadway musical *Finding Neverland* produced by Harvey Weinstein with music and lyrics by Gary Barlow and Eliot Kennedy. It opened in Boston in summer 2014 and transferred to New York in spring 2015. His play *The Vote* was aired in real time on TV in the final ninety minutes of polling during the 2015 general election. His first film for TV, *Caught in a Trap*, was broadcast on ITV1 on Boxing Day 2008, and he was picked as one of *Broadcast* Magazine's 'Hotshots' in the same year. He is developing original series and adaptations with Tiger Aspect, Leftbank, Kudos and the BBC. His film *X and Y* produced by Origin Pictures and BBC Films, it opened in cinemas in spring 2015 starring Rafe Spall, Sally Hawkins and Eddie Marsan. He is currently working on an adaptation of *Mrs Queen Takes the Train* for Harvey Weinstein, and *1984* for Scott Rudin and director Paul Greengrass.

Characters

Leo, *boy*
Kelly, *girl*
Spencer, *boy*
Rachel, *girl*
Amid, *boy*
Joanne, *girl*
Russell, *boy*
Shanti, *girl*
Jonathan, *boy*
Aimee, *girl*
Dean, *boy*
Lucy, *girl*
Graeme, *boy*
Zoe, *girl*

Notes on the text

A slash mark (/) indicates that the character who speaks next should begin their line, overlapping with the preceding one.

An ellipsis (. . .) indicates hesitation.

A dash (−) indicates a change in thought or broken speech.

(Text in brackets) indicates a line spoken almost privately, to oneself, but still aloud (just).

A classroom in Wootton Bassett School.

A map of the world on the wall, a whiteboard, a window, some tables, some chairs.

We open in darkness.

A school bell rings for lunch.

Lights up just as the classroom door is slamming shut.

A class of Year 11 pupils is dotted around the room, all standing, staring at the closed door – except for one boy, **Spencer**, *who is against a wall, facing it.*

The sound of keys rattling as the door is locked from outside.

Leo *is standing closest to the door, staring at it. A short pause . . .*

Leo   She hasn't.

Rachel   She has.

Leo   She hasn't, she wouldn't dare.

Russell   She has though, you know.

Leo   She's still on the other side of the door, she's just joking – Miss, we know you're still there!

Kelly/Rachel/Dean/Shanti   Leo!

Spencer   Don't!

Rachel   She'll keep us after school if you carry on.

Zoe   She can't do that.

Kelly   She will.

Zoe   She wouldn't!

Kelly/Spencer/Graeme/Dean/Amid/Jonathan
SHE WILL!

Joanne   Shush! Listen.

They all stop and listen. The sound of a plane flying over.

Jonathan   It's coming in to Lyneham.

Leo   We're gonna miss it!

He goes to the door and tries the handle. It's locked. He tugs at it hard, banging and kicking the door.

AAARRRGGHHH! You bitch!

Russell   Leo! Leo, calm down mate, yeah.

Zoe   This must be against the law or something.

Joanne   It's against thingy, isn't it? Human Rights – what's that thing?

Aimee   What thing?

Joanne   Convention thing.

Jonathan   Geneva Convention?

Joanne   Is that the one I mean?

Jonathan   I don't know, what do you mean?

Leo (*paces around*)   God's sake.

Zoe   Yeah, Joanne's right, it's against the Geneva Convention, locking us in at lunchtime. We could get her put on trial and banged or something.

Jonathan   I don't think / she's –

Kelly   Well, she clearly can do it because she has, so.

Jonathan   I don't think she's breaking the Geneva Convention, but I think it probably is against health and safety, though.

Kelly   What?

Zoe   See.

Jonathan   Fire safety.

Leo *sits. Head in his hands.*

Shanti   I can't believe that just happened. She just completely flipped.

Rachel   She completely lost it – went mental.

Russell (*going to* **Leo**)   Mate, you all right?

Kelly   I'm not surprised she went nuts, all you lot teasing her.

Zoe   Who?

Kelly   Everyone.

Jonathan   I wasn't –

Graeme   I wasn't –

Zoe   Oh what, because *you* handed *your* project in, did you, Kelly?

Kelly   There's a difference / between not handing a –

Zoe   Did you? Did you hand your project in? No.

Kelly   Zoe, there's a difference between not handing something in and taking the piss out of the teacher for an hour / so that she goes all –

Zoe   Who took the piss, Kelly?

Kelly   Like you all coughing when she was talking all the time.

Russell   That was funny.

Aimee   I actually do have a cough, though.

Kelly   Well, that's interesting because you're not coughing now.

Aimee   It comes and goes.

Zoe   Why you so bothered, anyway? It isn't even a proper class and she isn't even a proper teacher.

Aimee *coughs*.

Kelly   I'm bothered because thanks to you lot I'm missing the repat. Everyone else, all those people and tourists and journalists and whoever all out there lining the street and I'm locked in here? I think that's a bit not right, I do. Is all I'm saying.

Amid (*looking out the window*)   Look. At the bottom of the drive.

A few of the other pupils scramble and join **Amid** *at the window.*

Spencer   What? What is it?

Amid   They've already started stopping the traffic.

Spencer   Who?

Shanti   Police.

Joanne   Already? That's early.

Jonathan   It's because it's busier today. Because of Charlie.

Leo *holds his head, and groans.*

Russell   Oy, fella, what is it?

Rachel   What's up with Leo?

Zoe   Leo?

Russell   Nothing, just leave him for a bit, all right?

Leo   I just wanted to be there.

For when he came home.

That's all.

Kelly   What, and you think I didn't? We're all missing it.

Zoe   Kelly. Just –

Leo   Uh, sorry, Kelly, but at what point did this become about you, eh?

Kelly   This isn't about me, you're making it / about you.

Leo (*standing*)   Pretending like you even knew him when you didn't.

Rachel/Aimee   Leo.

Leo   It's wrong.

Kelly   You're wrong.

Leo (*imitating, mockingly*)   'Urgh, you're wrong.'

Kelly   Pff. Is that meant / to be me?

Leo   'Pff, is that meant to be me?'

Russell   Oy, oy, oy, can we just chill out and calm down, yeah?

Leo   And you can shut up, Rachel, Aimee; why does everyone listen to her, why does everyone believe her lies, you didn't know him, / I knew him.

Dean   No one really knew him, he was like five years above us.

Kelly   I knew him pretty intimately actually, mate, / if you know what I mean.

Leo   Oh what, and it's nothing to do with there being more people out there today, then?

Kelly   What do you mean, what kind of people?

Leo   You know what kind of people.

Kelly   What kind of people?

Leo   Cameras. Photographs, kind of people.

Rachel   Leo.

Kelly   No, I don't get what he's saying. What are you saying, / I don't get it.

Leo   I'm saying, I'm just saying, I think it's interesting the way you look today, that's all.

Rachel   Leo.

Kelly   And what's the way I look today?

Leo   I dunno, just a little different. In the face.

Rachel   Leo!

Leo   Stop saying 'Leo', Rachel. 'Leo, / Leo, Leo' . . .

Kelly   In the face? What? This is just my face, what are you talking about?

Leo   It isn't just me, Spencer said he thought you had more make-up on today, didn't you, Spence?

Kelly   What?

Spencer (*still facing the wall*)   What?

Leo   You did.

Kelly   Spencer?!

Spencer   No, I said you looked . . . you know. No. I meant . . . nice. Today.

Leo   Erm, well, no, you didn't, but . . .

Rachel   I think you look nice, Kelly.

Kelly   And Spencer, what the hell would you know about what I look like, you've been facing the wall all bloody morning, nearly.

Russell   Spencer, you muppet, why are you still doing that?

Spencer   Miss Kirmani told me to.

Rachel   She's not here, idiot, she stormed out –

Spencer (*shouting and stamping*)   SHE TOLD ME TO FACE THE WALL AND THAT'S WHAT I'M DOING! (*Brief pause. Calmer.*) I'm sick of being in trouble all the time. I'm sick of other people getting me in trouble all the time. I'm sick of getting detention every other lunchtime and after school 'cause of mucking about or other people mucking about and making me laugh or making me join in or making me do things that get me in trouble, I'm just sick of it. OK? She told me to face the wall until she said otherwise and she hasn't said otherwise yet, so I'm facing the wall! OK?

Russell   Man, that is fucked up, Spence.

Spencer   I DON'T CARE IF IT'S FUCKED UP! I don't care. This is what I'm doing. I don't want to fail any more.

A slight sense of calm descends. Momentarily.

Dean   Erm. I don't want to worry everyone, but I really need a piss.

Russell, **Kelly** *and* **Rachel** *laugh.*

Kelly   Dean's gonna wet himself.

Dean   It's not funny!

Russell   Mate, you'll be fine, hold it.

Dean   That's what my hand was up for, to go to the toilet, and then it all kicked off, thanks to you lot.

Kelly   Leo, I want to know what you meant about looking different today.

Jonathan   Oh God, can't we just drop it?

Kelly   I look exactly the same as I always do and that's that.

Zoe   Aren't you a bit colder today, though?

Kelly   What? Why?

Zoe   In that skirt.

Kelly   No. What do you mean?

Zoe   Not exactly boiling today, is it?

Kelly   You're wearing one, Zoe – you're wearing a skirt.

Zoe   Yeah, but you're only *just* about wearing one.

Russell   Ha ha! (*Snaps his fingers.*) Yes, Zoe. One–nil.

Kelly   Zoe, I think I'd rather you just came out with what you think that . . . (*Stumbling over her words.*) And say what the thing what – is that / you're thinking –

Leo   What? What? What's that, Kelly? Got your false teeth in today, as well?

Kelly   Piss off! It's you lot, all looking at me and judging me, making me all . . .

Leo   Making you what? Guilty?

Joanne   Leo.

Kelly   Back off, Leo, I mean it.

Leo   Oh why, what, you gonna come round mine with your big brother? Because I'll tell you something, he isn't as tough as everyone thinks he is.

Kelly   I don't go down Eveleigh Road, Leo, because I don't want to get stabbed.

Zoe (*at the window*)   God, there is literally no one about, we're like the only ones here.

Leo   Oy, Zo, does that window open?

Zoe (*tries it*)   No.

Jonathan   It needs a key.

Zoe   Where's the key?

Jonathan   Dunno. I suppose Miss Kirmani will have it.

Leo   Right.

He empties his rucksack on to a table – some books, crisps, a rounders bat, paint spray cans and other crap falls out. He takes hold of the bat.

Leo   I'm smashing the window in.

Dean   Leo, no!

Leo   Then I can drop down from here.

Russell   Yeah, go on, Leo. (*Laughs.*)

Rachel   You idiot, it's too high.

Leo   No, it's the second floor, not too high.

Kelly   Oh, just let him, Rachel, do us all a favour.

Russell (*looking out*)   Actually, mate, that does look quite high.

Shanti   Why have you got a baseball bat in your bag?

Russell   It's rounders, we're gonna have a game, Noremarsh Park, after school.

Dean   Are you?

Russell   Yeah, come, Dean, if you haven't pissed yourself by then.

Dean   Awh, don't, I'd almost forgotten.

Russell   Well you can't be that desperate, then, can you?!

Leo   I'm doing it.

Spencer   Don't, Leo, we'll get in trouble.

Leo   Spencer, it's all right, if anyone asks, you don't even have to lie, just tell them you didn't see anything.

Jonathan   Leo, you'll get suspended.

Aimee   If not expelled.

Spencer   The rest of us will get in trouble, we'll all be expelled.

Leo   I'll say if was for health and safety, right. Jonathan?

He raises his bat . . .

Graeme/Dean/Kelly/Amid/Shanti   Don't!

Leo *holds the bat in the air. He thinks. He lowers the bat, and drops it on to the desk, smiling at the others, wandering around.*

Zoe   Still can't believe Miss Kirmani's done this.

Leo   She's not allowed. She can't stop us from going to a repat, when she's not even from here!

Shanti   She lives here, Leo.

Leo   I meant from Bassett, Shanti, she's not from Wootton Bassett.

Rachel   I'm not from Wootton Bassett, I'm from Swindon, so / what? Does that mean –

Leo   It's the same thing, you know what I mean, you go to this school, don't you, this is our town, it's our thing that we do, this is for us –

Jonathan   Well, it's for the families.

Leo   You know what I mean! What's this, pick on Leo day?

Russell   Mate –

Joanne   It's been completely ruined now, anyway. I don't think we should do any more. I don't like it.

Zoe   Oh God, you're not one of them, are you, Joanne?

Aimee   I know what she means, though.

Leo   Shut up, both of you. 'Completely ruined'.

Joanne   Don't tell me to shut up, Leo. / I mean it.

Aimee   It's just turned into a media circus. Loads of people just turn up to see what's happening and they shouldn't.

Leo   You don't know what you're talking about, Aimee, you're just chatting shit.

Aimee   Oy, it's my opinion, it's not chatting shit, it's / just my opinion.

Leo   It's about being respectful, it's about paying your respects.

Aimee   I pay my respects, whenever I've seen one, I just don't want to go to them all the time, I don't think it's for me.

Zoe   It's not about 'wanting to', it's about 'should do'. I always go to them. If we're off.

Dean   So do I.

Aimee   Fine. Good for you. I just don't like to see all the men crying. The dads. It makes me upset. And I'm pretty sure they don't all want me standing there gawping at them either.

Graeme (*quietly, speaking for the first time*)   This mor— This morning. On the way here. There, erm . . . there was this . . . a, a photographer man.

Kelly   Pap. Paparazzi. That's what they are.

Graeme   He –

Rachel   Paps are for celebs, Kelly.

Kelly   Yeah, it is a celeb.

Leo   Not celebs. Soldiers. Better than celebs. Celebs are scum, celebs are dogshit.

Kelly   I meant like our town, like our town is a celebrity now. That's all I meant.

Leo   I need to get out of here. You – none of you know what you're . . .

Graeme   I was walking to school and the vans with the satellite dishes had started turning up and I was walking down the High Street and he came up to me and asked me to give him a leg up on to the branch of the tree so that he could scramble up on to the roof of the whatsit – the thing. The shelter thing. So he could get a better view. But I didn't.

Rachel (*sarcastically*)   Wow, good story, Graeme.

Russell   Oy, leave him alone. Well done, Graeme.

Amid   Well done, Graeme.

Russell   Don't help the bastards, let them break their necks. Ha ha.

Leo   Why are they all here today, he was just a normal soldier, wouldn't have wanted all this attention, just to be treated like everyone else, all he would have wanted.

Joanne   He *wasn't* like everyone else, he was amazing.

Shanti   Oh my God, do you remember him as Danny Zuko?

Joanne/Rachel/Aimee/Shanti (*swooning*)   Awwwwwh.

Joanne   My God.

Rachel   So fit.

Aimee   We were only Year 7, what was he? 11?

Leo   Ten.

Aimee   What?

Leo   Ten. Deafo. He was Year 10 when we were Year 7.

Rachel   I always thought he was older, looked older.

Leo   He was Year 10 when we were Year 7! Listen, I played football with him, we were mates.

Kelly   'We were mates', yeah right, now who's chatting shit.

Leo   We. Were. Mates. Fuck. You. Kelly. You. Silly . . .

Pause.

Kelly   What?

Leo   Fill it in yourself.

Kelly   Silly what?

Leo   Fill in the blank yourself, you know what you are, I can't be arsed.

Russell   I'm not being funny or anything, but he always a little bit pissed me off –

Zoe/Rachel/Leo   Russell!

Russell   God rest his soul, nothing personal, and thank you for going off to fight for my country, but what I actually meant was, like, a backhand compliment – I mean, Mr Southwall basically rated him as God.

Leo   It's true, he did, / he was . . . like . . .

Russell   And no matter how well you did or what you achieved, Charlie had done it about three years before and better. All them trophies in the cabinet, they're mostly him –

Aimee   Not the hockey, that's mine –

Rachel   Ours.

Aimee   Ours.

Kelly   I'm gonna miss him.

Rachel   Awh. (*Hugging her.*) It's all right, Kelly. Just got to be strong.

Leo   Oy, shut up! Seriously, Kelly.

Kelly   Do one, Leo!

Leo   You didn't know him, he never went out with you, it's all bollocks.

Kelly   He did.

Leo   It's bullshit. I know it is, we were mates, he'd have told me.

Rachel   He might not have done.

Russell   Actually, yeah, if I shagged you, Kelly, I'd probably wanna keep it a secret.

Kelly   Fuck you, Russell –

Russell   Joke!

Kelly   This is nothing to do with you.

Russell   Was a joke, wasn't it, laugh, 'ha ha ha'.

Rachel   Leo, if Kelly says she went out with him, then she went out with him, why would she lie?

Kelly   Why would I lie?

Leo   Right. (*Picks up his bat again.*) I'm going out the window.

Spencer/Rachel/Aimee   Don't!

Leo *moves away, pacing, swinging his bat, towards the desk.*

Leo   Must be another key. (*Pulls at a locked drawer.*) Man, everything's locked in this school, don't they trust people? (*Tugs harder.*)

Rachel (*sarcastic*)   Oh yeah, that's a great idea, Leo, go through her drawer, that won't get us in trouble at all.

Jonathan   I'm really against this, Leo. It's her private belongings.

Leo   Not private – school. And anyway, she's only a supply teacher, supply teachers don't have any privacy.

Russell   Come on, I'll help.

Leo *smashes the drawer a few times with the bat, and with force he and* **Russell** *manage to yank it open.*

Dean   Leo! She'll know!

Leo   All right, Dean, don't piss yourself.

Dean   I'm trying!

Leo *and* **Russell** *root around the drawer.* **Leo** *pulls out a set of small keys.*

Leo   Is these them?

Jonathan   Dunno, could be.

Leo *goes to the window and tries while* **Russell** *roots around the drawer more.*

Spencer   He's not really going to go out the window, is he?

Kelly   No, don't worry, he's just showing off, as always.

Russell   Awh man, look at this. Miss Kirmani's notes. (*Laughs.*) They're all from Wikipedia!

Joanne   What?

Russell   She's just printed a load of stuff off of Wikipedia. Jesus Christ, I could do that, maybe I'll be a teacher. What do they get, like a hundred grand a year?

Jonathan   Supply teachers do.

Russell   Urgh, it's just history and war and things.

Dean (*hands between his legs*)   Oh God, seriously, if she's not coming back in the next ten minutes then we're gonna have to think of something.

Russell (*holding up an empty bottle of Cola*)   Dean, why don't you just go in this?

Dean   I'm not pissing into a bottle.

Russell   Fine, piss into your pants instead then.

Zoe (*with* **Leo** *at the window*)   Have you tried that one?

Leo (*fiddling with the keys*)   Hold on, hold on.

Dean   Shit, all right then, give me the bottle.

Rachel   Urgh, don't, Dean, that's gross.

Dean   No one watch.

Kelly   Dean, trust me, no one's gonna wanna watch, OK?

Dean (*reaching to take the bottle from* **Russell**)   Here.

Russell   Fiver.

Dean   What?

Russell   Five pounds please.

Dean   What?

Russell   Supply–demand, mate.

Dean   You're a bastard, Russell.

Russell   I can see it on Facebook now. 'Dean peed his pants today in Citizenship class.' Stuff of legends, mate. That shit never goes away.

Dean   I'll hold it.

Russell   You sure?

Dean   No.

Russell   Have a think then, come back in a bit.

Dean   All right.

Russell   But it'll have gone up to a tenner by then.

Dean   What?!

Russell   Inflation, mate, recession's a bitch.

Leo   Done it!

He opens the window.

Shanti   Ah, some fresh air at last.

Zoe   Well done.

Leo   Right.

Leo *swings his leg over and sits on the ledge. Some others run over to stop him.*

Jonathan/Russell/Graeme/Joanne/Shanti/Amid   No!

Leo   What?

Amid   It's too high.

Russell   Leo, don't, mate.

Leo   Honestly, I know how to land, land and roll, I've seen it, like on *Call of Duty*. Then I can go find that bitch, get the key off her, come back, and let you out. Simple as.

Russell   We need you for the game on Saturday, if you twist your ankle or break a leg –

Zoe   He's right, Leo, I don't think you should.

Pause, as **Leo** *sits on the ledge, looking down.*

He climbs off the ledge and back into the room. A sense of relief.

He takes hold of his bat and paces again, swinging it.

Leo When she comes back, I'm telling you . . . (*Swinging the bat.*) Making me miss it.

Jonathan Do you . . . do you have *Call of Duty* on Xbox or PS3?

Leo PS3.

Jonathan Me too.

Leo Yeah? Have you completed any of the Special Ops on *Call of Duty – Modern Warfare 2*.

Jonathan I just did the Delta Special Op, completed it on Veteran level.

Leo No fucking way.

Rachel Urgh, boys and their stupid games.

Leo 'S not games, it's good practice.

Rachel For what?

Leo For war. In case we ever have to go.

He pulls an imaginary weapon and points it at **Rachel***'s head, firing it several times.*

Russell Incoming!

Leo Get down!

Russell *mimes tossing a grenade.* **Leo** *rolls on to and off a table, making firing noises as he goes, followed by the noise of a fake explosion.*

Dean My brother showed me *Call of Duty – Black Ops* on his PC. It's a-ma-zing.

Russell I prefer *Halo 3*.

He imitates the character in the game, ducking and firing a weapon.

Leo   Favourite weapon?

Russell   Easy, plasma gun, no question. No, no, no, wait, shotgun! Shotgun. Simple, clean.

Leo   No, man, what about the Magnum, semi-automatic, that shit rips through flesh.

Russell   Oh yeah, yeah, and when you get a headshot it just completely explodes. (*Mimes his head exploding.*)

Graeme   . . . laptop.

Dean   What? Squeak up, Graeme.

Graeme   I've got my laptop.

Dean   Lucky you, so what?

Graeme   The projector. Like what Mr McPherson does in Drama, to watch films. I could connect it to the DV projector and go online. We could maybe watch it online. The repatriation. Project it on to the whiteboard.

Leo   Yeah? Could you?

Russell   Can you do that?

Graeme   Maybe, yeah.

Rachel   Like a cinema.

Leo   Awh man, go on then.

Jonathan   I'll help.

Russell   Finally, clever people are becoming useful at last.

Graeme *starts opening up his laptop as he and* **Jonathan** *begin working on the projector.*

Joanne   It might not be live, will it? The repat.

Jonathan   I bet it is on the BBC News Channel. Rolling twenty-four-hour news, they're always struggling to fill their schedules with something, that's why they love stuff like this.

Leo   And Spencer, you're turning back round and watching it when it's on.

Spencer   I'm not.

Leo   You are.

Spencer   I'm not!

Dean   Spencer, aren't you bored? Jesus.

Spencer   I'm thinking. (*Beat.*) A bit bored, yeah.

Russell   Here, you can read Miss Kirmani's notes, learn something.

He takes some pins and sticks up the sheets from the desk on to the wall in front of **Spencer**'s *face.*

Spencer   Awh, thanks Russell, that's wicked.

Russell   I'll test you later.

Amid   Maybe that's what we should be doing now? Finishing our projects. So that when she comes back –

Zoe   No, forget it, doesn't matter, it's only Citizenship.

Leo   You don't need a grade in Citizenship to be a British citizen, it's bullshit, it's bollocks, man, I hate it. You can't learn that, they can't teach that.

Zoe   And no offence, and no disrespect, but Miss Kirmani isn't exactly the best person to be teaching it, either, is she?

Dean   What do you mean?

Shanti   What 'cause she's not white and English and / born in Wiltshire?

Zoe   That's not being racist, Shanti, that's just saying, she was born in a different country, she said so, that's all I'm saying. She might be from America, for all I care, or Belgium, or . . . you know, I don't know, anywhere. Holland. China, erm –

Russell   France.

Zoe   France. Exactly. I'm just saying what can a teacher *born* in Pakistan teach me about Britain. That's not being racist.

Shanti   India. She's Hindu, like me. Hindu is mainly India, not Pakistan.

Leo   Shanti, chill out, she's just saying she's a wank teacher.

Russell   She is pretty shit.

Amid   She's shit at everything, she's a supply teacher, supply teachers are meant to be shit. That's what they supply: they supply shit.

Rachel   I can't believe how badly she lost it.

Aimee   I don't think she's coming back ever. And it's lunchtime, I'm starving, I am literally starving. The rest of the school are gonna come back after they've seen the coffins go past and they're gonna find *us* dead.

Leo   Oy. Don't.

Aimee   Sorry. But –

Dean   You're not gonna die from starvation in an hour, Aimee.

Rachel (*looking through* **Leo***'s things from his bag*)   Leo, why have you got spray cans in your bag?

Leo   Art.

Rachel   What?

Kelly   Oh-oh, someone was gonna graffiti something, naughty.

Leo   I've got art, Lesson 5. It's an art project.

Kelly   Bollocks. You were gonna spray a wall or something, I know it.

Leo   You don't know – how do you know? You don't.

Kelly   Because I know.

Leo   Psh. You wish you knew me –

Kelly   What?

Leo   You wish you knew me.

Kelly   Urgh, dream on.

Leo (*taking a can*)   I might tag this wall. That'd show Miss Kirmani.

Kelly   Oh, whatever.

Spencer   Don't, Leo.

Kelly   He won't, don't worry.

Leo   A big fuck-off Union Jack. That can be my project. Citizenship. A-star, job done.

He takes the lid off and shakes the can, aims it at the wall . . .

Spencer/Dean/Graeme/Aimee/Rachel   Don't!

Pause. **Leo** *smiles and puts the top back on the can. Paces, swinging . . .*

Amid   What time is it? Do we really think Miss Kirmani won't be back until after lunch?

Rachel   Amid, if we knew that, then . . .

Amid   Well. I may have to pray here.

Leo   You what?

Spencer *starts to count something on the sheets.*

Amid   Noon prayer. *Dhuhr.* If people don't mind.

Jonathan   Of course no one minds, Amid.

Rachel   Spencer, what you counting?

Spencer   The wars.

Rachel   The what?

Spencer   Twelve. We had twelve wars. Britain.

Russell   Uh, I think we might have had a few more than that, Spence.

Jonathan   When does that timeline start from?

Spencer   Er. Oh yeah, 1900.

Russell (*laughs*)   Numpty.

Spencer   All right, twelve since the start of the century, then.

Joanne   Last century.

Spencer   What?

Joanne   That's last century.

Spencer   Whatever, it's still a lot.

Russell   It's not that many. All things considered.

Aimee   All what things considered?

Russell   I dunno, it's a saying, isn't it.

Zoe   Amid?

Amid   Yes.

Zoe   Can I ask you something?

Amid   Yes.

Zoe   Don't take it funnily.

Amid   Don't take it what? What?

Zoe   Does it bother you?

Amid   What?

Zoe   Being the only one?

Amid   The only . . . ?

Zoe   Muslim.

Amid   Uh, there's one or two more of us, actually. I saw some the other day on telly.

Russell (*laughs*)   Yes, Amid. Get in.

Zoe   You know what I mean, in the school.

Amid   No.

Joanne   Yeah, that's only this school, if we were in Reading or London or somewhere, we'd probably be / . . . you know, in the –

Rachel   Why would it bother him, gets special privileges, doesn't he?

Amid   What special privileges?

Rachel   You know. Nothing bad, just saying.

Zoe   Like getting to skip out of some lessons to pray and all that.

Shanti   It is a bit odd when you first come here and there's only like a handful of people who aren't white.

Leo   Well, what do you expect, that's not our fault.

Shanti   No, I know.

Leo   I can't help it that I'm white and I'm not sorry, either.

Shanti   Zoe was asking a question.

Leo   Yeah, to Amid, not you, about being a Muslim, not you.

Amid   Actually, Zoe, getting out of lessons means I just have to work harder, so no, they don't actually feel like privileges, actually.

Rachel   Are you gonna pray now then, Amid, or not?

Amid (*looking around, uncertain*)   In a second.

Shanti   How's your sponsored silence going, Lucy?

Lucy *gives thumbs up*.

Leo   Hey, Lucy –

Leo *jumps up behind her, making a noise, tying to make her jump, which she does a bit.* **Leo** *laughs, carrying on pacing around, swinging his bat.* **Lucy** *scowls.*

Rachel   Don't be a twat, Leo, she's doing really well. Trying to ruin it and make her speak.

Kelly   How long's it been now, Luce?

Rachel   Kelly!

Kelly   What?

Rachel   You're just as bad, stop tricking her.

Kelly   She can hold her fingers up can't she? I'm just asking how long.

Lucy *flashes ten fingers, then another ten . . . then thinks . . . then holds up six fingers.*

Spencer   What's she doing?

Joanne   Holding her fingers up.

Spencer   How many.

Rachel   Twenty-six.

Shanti   Twenty-six hours!

Russell   Well done, Lucy.

Amid   Well done, Lucy.

Kelly   I don't think I've been quiet for twenty-six hours altogether in my whole life.

Leo   Yeah, no shit.

Dean   What's she raising the money for?

Jonathan   Royal British Legion.

Aimee   Well done, Lucy.

Leo   Well done, Lucy. Sorry for being a dickhead, that's brilliant.

Kelly   Well done, Lucy.

Russell   It's the veterans who started the whole lining the High Street thing, wasn't it? When the first coffins went past.

Amid   He used to be the mayor. The man.

Leo   I was out there. The second time it happened. Soon as I heard what was happening, I was out there.

Joanne   My grandad's a veteran.

Aimee   Mine too.

Joanne   He's one of the people with the flags. When they lower them as the coffins pass. Outside the Cross Keys.

Jonathan   Will he be out there now?

Leo   They all will be. We should be. Course he's out there now. Proud.

Joanne   He doesn't like the clapping, though. Goes on about it all the time.

Russell   Why not?

Joanne   He just thinks the clapping is wrong.

Leo   It's not wrong. It's saying thank you.

Joanne   He just thinks there should be silence.

Leo   Jesus Christ, people clap all the time, at everything, things that don't deserve anything, people singing, or doing dancing with a dog or something on *Britain's Got Wankers* and all that. You've got to clap people who are fighting to protect us, they deserve it. Got to.

Aimee   Be better if they just came home alive, though, wouldn't it?

Zoe   What do you mean?

Aimee   Well. You know. (*Slight pause.*) 'Cause they can't . . . you know, they can't hear everyone clapping. Can they? When they're dead . . .

Leo   Doesn't mean we should bring them home, though, Aimee, they're out there fighting to protect us.

Aimee   I'm just saying I wish it could end so they could all come home.

Leo   I don't wish it could end, I want it to go on and on. I want it to go on until I can get out there.

He mimes being a soldier, holding a rifle, ducking and scouting around.

Joanne   Leo, haven't we all had to watch enough coffins go down the High Street?

Rachel   I was in Worcester yesterday visiting my cousin – well, she's not really my cousin, but like my auntie's new husband's – anyway, she's like in her forties, or something, like old anyway, and her nan died the other week and she was saying she was nervous about going in because she'd never seen a coffin before and I was just like, 'Seriously? I'm, like, a kid and I've seen about a hundred, 'cause of living here.'

Leo   Yeah, it's because of seeing them that I wanna go out. So they didn't die for nothing.

Kelly   That doesn't even make any sense, Leo.

Leo   So. You don't make any sense. (*At* **Joanne**.) You don't make any sense. (*At* **Aimee**.) You don't make any sense. So . . .

Aimee   I'm just saying I don't know any more, that's all.

Leo   What don't you know any more?

Aimee   It's just my opinion.

Leo   What's your opinion?

Aimee   I just don't know whether them being out there is protecting us, whether they're actually making a difference or not, I don't know.

Leo   Making a difference?

Russell Oy, OK, let's not start a debate, it'll only end in tears.

Leo Whether or not it's . . . You say that? On the day of a repat, on the day when one of our old pupils from the school flies back in a coffin –

Aimee I'm not saying I'm not grateful –

Leo It sounds pretty ungrateful.

Aimee I'm not saying that I'm ungrateful –

Leo Because it sounds pretty ungrateful.

Russell Leo, mate.

Aimee And it makes me sad when they die, and I'm grateful that they risk their lives, OK, all right, I'm just not sure what the point is any more.

Leo Point is so they don't come over here and blow us up, that's the point.

Aimee I'm –

Leo That's the point, Aimee.

Amid The 7/7 guys were from Leeds.

Leo What?

Amid (*pause*) The 7/7 guys. Who blew up the tubes. They were from this country, they were from Leeds.

Leo And?

Amid And I'm just saying.

Leo What?

Amid I'm just saying.

Leo What are you saying?

Spencer Oy.

Russell All right, chillax, everyone, Jesus.

Amid   And they said that it was Iraq. Why they did it.
Because Britain was in Iraq.

Leo   So.

Spencer (*looking at his sheets*)   Actually, Britain's been in Iraq
before, lots of times. In fact we were the ones that invented it,
kind of. Drew its borders anyway, after the First World War.
Used to be called Meso – . . . Mesop – . . . po-ta-mia. Or
something. And then we invaded in 1991. With the Americans
again. So we've already done this war, once before! Did
anyone know that?

Russell   How would we know that, Spence; we weren't
even born.

Amid   So if we weren't there, there wouldn't have been any
bombs. Is all I'm saying.

Leo   So because we got bombed we should give in?

Amid   No.

Leo   Because we're scared?

Amid   No. I'm just offering up an alternative view. From
yours.

Leo   You don't think we should be there?

Amid   Like when all those images came out with the
Americans abusing the prisoners.

Jonathan   Abu Ghraib.

Kelly   Abu what?

Amid   The prison. Torturing the prisoners in the prison.

Russell (*scrambling on to a table*)   Oh yeah, have you seen that
one with the guy and a blanket over him, stood like that with
electrodes and shit on his fingers like a scarecrow.

He stands on the table, mimicking the image.

Amid   Photos of them stripping them down and being naked and pointing and laughing and getting them to pile on top of each other and touch each other and –

Leo   Yeah, but you just said it, that wasn't us, that was America.

Amid   – so I just don't necessarily think we've made ourselves safer by being there.

Leo   So you don't think we should be there, Amid, right? Am I right?

Amid   In Afghanistan we should maybe be there. Maybe. I don't know.

Leo   We are in Afghanistan, though.

Amid   I don't think we should have been in Iraq.

Leo   Oh?

Jonathan   I don't think we should have been in Iraq.

Leo   Oh. Lots of views. OK.

Kelly   I don't know the difference, sorry.

Leo   Well, this is interesting. This is interesting. On the day that Charlie is flown home, on the day of his repat, and on all those other days on all those other repats, when we've had, what is it now, over a hundred coffins go past us and we all stood and watched that –

Russell   Mate.

Leo   I'm just saying it's interesting, Russell, especially how many of us, as well, have relatives up at Lyneham or based elsewhere, army, navy, RAF, yeah? I'm jut saying it's interesting.

Amid   I can be grateful for the soldiers' sacrifice without agreeing with the reason that politicians sent them in the first place.

Leo   Can I ask you something?

Shanti   Can we all just maybe talk about something else instead?

Leo   You know them Islam4UK people, those people who were gonna march through Bassett in protest?

Amid   I know what you're going to say, don't.

Leo   What?

Spencer   Leo.

Joanne   Leo.

Zoe   No, maybe he should ask it, I'm interested.

Rachel   Zoe.

Amid   Don't.

Leo   Did you agree with them? Did you think they should have been allowed to march through Bassett holding fifty empty coffins?

Amid   Because I'm a Muslim?

Leo   Because of what you just said.

Amid   Because we're all the same?

Leo   Did I say that?

Amid   Because we all believe the same things?

Leo   Did I say that, Amid? I said, 'Do you agree with them?' I was asking, asking a question. Do you agree with them?

Amid   No.

Leo   No?

Amid   No. I'm going to pray now if that's OK.

Leo   (*long pause, indicates the floor*)   Be my guest.

Pause. **Amid** *goes off on his own, and begins raising his hands up, before folding his arms across his chest, and eventually kneeling on the floor . . .*

Amid   (Allahu Akbar . . .)

Leo *continues to pace, swinging his bat. Some silence . . .*

Spencer   Does anyone know who started the First World War? I can't make it out, even from this. We won it though.

The projector flickers on and off, projecting numbers on to the board.

Zoe   Is it working?

Graeme   Erm. Getting there, just . . .

Graeme *and* **Jonathan** *keep fiddling with the wires. Working on the laptop.*

Russell   I remember speaking to Charlie once, in Year 8, he was a prefect, he helped me. Some pricks had stolen my packed lunch box and were taking stuff out. They stamped on my sandwiches and just as they were about to stamp on my Mars bar, Charlie came along and sorted them out, pushed them away and snatched my Mars bar back. I don't even like Mars bars, but that's not the point.

Spencer   I love Mars bars.

Kelly   Awh yeah, me too.

Russell   I prefer a Twix.

Aimee   I like Bounties.

Russell   You're off your tits. Bounties? They're rank.

Shanti   I got an award from him once, for maths. He was Head Boy and he presented it to me in this, like, after-school assembly thing. A certificate. Still got it.

Leo   Remember beating Matravers once, football, three–two, Charlie was captain. I was subbed, second half, left-back, we were like two–one down. What's-his-name's brother, ginger hair, got sent to prison, I chipped it down the line to him, about ten minutes to go and he scored, top right-hand corner, and then about three minutes to go, Charlie got fouled, just outside the box, everyone went forward for the free kick, including me, because it was all-or-nothing type of thing. Charlie takes the kick, and he could have gone for glory, everyone thought he was just going to blast it, swerve it round the defence, doing a Beckham, but he didn't care about glory, Charlie, never did, a team game, wanted the team to win, and instead he did this light little tap, to his right, to ginger thingy, and ginger thingy with a clear view of the goal, blasted it in, three–two, job done. Awesome.

Jonathan I saw his passing-out parade.

Rachel His what?

Jonathan When you're a cadet, after training, before you go off for active duty. Get your green beret.

Leo You saw him?

Jonathan Brother was the same year as him, they went out to Afghanistan together. We were there to watch him, but Charlie was part of it as well. Stood behind him when they marched past.

Leo Awh, that's wicked.

Joanne Your brother's in Afghanistan?

Jonathan Yeah.

Joanne My uncle is.

Graeme Jonathan's in the air cadets.

Leo Are you?

Jonathan Yes.

Leo Do you do all the marching and that shit?

Jonathan Yes.

Leo Awh, that's wicked, show us.

Jonathan Show you what?

Leo Do some marching, show us.

Jonathan   No.

Russell   Yeah, go on, Johnno-boy.

Jonathan   You'll just take the piss.

Zoe   We won't.

Joanne   We won't, Jonathan.

Jonathan   Well, like what, I don't know what you mean.

Leo   When you march past and salute and all that.

Jonathan   What, like this?

He marches into the centre of the classroom, and stands fiercely to attention. Everyone cheers or whoops or goes 'whoow'.

Kelly   Whoow!

Rachel   All right, Jonathan, Jesus.

Russell   Bloody hell, you're like a proper soldier.

Leo   Show me.

Dean   I think a little bit of wee just came out, oh God.

Rachel   I want to do it as well.

Leo *(marching around)*   Is that it, just swinging your arms?

Jonathan   Well, if you're going to do it properly like at the air cadets, you have to start by standing in rows, like this, a line of two, next to each other. Leo, you at the front here, I'll be next to you.

Leo, **Russell**, **Rachel**, **Joanne** *and* **Lucy** *arrange themselves, organised by* **Jonathan**. **Amid** *is still praying in the corner.* **Graeme** *is working on the projector.*

Jonathan   So you swing your right arm forward as you step out with your left leg, keeping your arm really straight, counting one, two, one, two, to that rhythm. OK?

He joins **Leo** *at the front.*

Jonathan   So on my command. 'Quick. March.'

They begin to march around the room. The others watch, occasionally laughing, or clapping. Suddenly the BBC News Channel appears, projected on to the whiteboard from **Graeme***'s laptop. Everyone breaks off and looks.*

The High Street is getting ready for the coffins to pass through, the pavements lined with thousands of people.

Kelly   Oh wow.

Russell   Well done, Graeme, you bloody legend you.

Rachel   Jesus, how many people.

Aimee   That's more than normal.

Russell   Do you reckon?

Shanti   Are his mum and dad there?

Leo   Course they'll be there, idiot.

Spencer   They'll be by the post office, won't they? That's where they normally stand.

Kelly   Nothing's happening yet.

Jonathan   They won't even have left Lyneham yet.

Spencer   What's happening?

Russell   Nothing, get back to your wall.

Joanne   Awh, this is so sad.

Kelly   I'm gonna cry.

Leo   Shut up.

Joanne   I don't want to watch it, it doesn't feel right.

Aimee   Let's not have it on until it happens.

Leo   Keep it on.

Aimee   But the build-up and everything, there's no point, turn it off until they come.

Leo   Keep it on.

Russell (*going to the laptop*)   Let's go on YouTube, watch people falling over or something, that'll cheer us up.

Leo   We don't want cheering up! This isn't about cheering up!

Dean   That's it, I can't wait any more!

He runs to near the desk and grabs a plastic bin, running with it to a corner of the room, and undoing his fly. Everyone screams.

Kelly   Dean, what you doing, you munter?!

Rachel   No way! Don't piss in the bin!

Dean   I can't help it!

Aimee   Waaah!

Shanti   That's disgusting.

Russell   This is hilarious!

Spencer   What's he doing?!

Russell   Pissing in a bin.

Spencer   What?!

Dean *starts to wee, back turned to the class. More screaming and laughing from everyone. On the whiteboard, some new websites come up as* **Russell** *surfs the web on the laptop.*

Joanne   Oh my God!

Aimee   Urgh! What if it leaks.

Kelly   It's gonna smell.

Dean   Shut up, it won't.

Kelly   Aimee, dare you to go have a look.

Aimee   No!

Dean   No, don't!

Russell   Mate, have you thought what you're going to do with it after?

Dean   I've not thought anything except that I need a piss! Just leave me alone, will you, bit of privacy, God's sake.

A quick flash of some very soft porn suddenly gets projected on to the screen – **Russell** *laughs as some of the girls scream and turn away.*

Graeme   Oy, what are you doing?!

Rachel   Russell!

Spencer   What? What is it?! What's that noise?

Graeme   I'll get in trouble!

Leo   Russell!

Graeme   How did that get past the school filter?

Shanti   Russell, I don't want to see that, turn it off.

Leo   JUST TURN IT OFF, RUSSELL! NOW!

Russell *turns it off. The screen goes blank.*

Leo   We're not even meant to be here! We're meant to be out there! Watching Charlie come home and you're just messing around like knobheads.

Russell   All right, Leo, calm down.

Beat. **Leo** *goes to the desk where his spray cans are.*

Leo   Fuck this.

He shakes the cans – a red one and a blue one – and aims them at the wall.

Dean   Leo, don't.

Leo *begins spraying. Everyone watches.*

He sprays the red Cross of St George first. And then blue around it to create the Union Jack. He tosses the cans to one side and stands, assessing his work.

Kelly   Mate, you're a goner.

Leo   What? It's the best citizenship project Miss Kirmani will have ever seen, I bet. I know my flag, I like my flag, I'm proud of my country, A-star in Citizenship, surely? Done.

Russell   Fucking hell, mate, that . . . that's bad.

Spencer   What? What's he painted?

Russell   Mate, that's . . . what you gonna – what are we going to do? When she asks us?

Leo   Tell her.

Amid *finishes praying. He stands and sees the flag.*

Leo   What do you think, Amid? Like it? For Queen and Country?

He salutes, and then starts marching around the room again. Others watch.

Rachel (*looking at the flag*)   We do have the best flag, don't we?

Aimee   You what?

Rachel   I'm just saying. When you look at everyone else's flag, some of them are seriously minging, but ours, I think it's probably one of the best. Ours and America's.

Joanne   Yeah, except you're not really meant to have it around or anything, are you.

Zoe   What do you mean?

Joanne   I mean it . . . it means something, doesn't it. Sometimes. Means . . . you know . . .

Zoe   No.

Joanne   That you might be seen as a bit . . . racist.

Leo   No, what the fuck are you talking about, Joanne? Racist.

Shanti   I know what she means.

Joanne   I just mean that people might *think* you are, because other people have, like . . . what do you call it. Nicked it – hijacked it, that's what I mean.

Shanti   Like the BNP.

Leo   Why is – this is what pisses me off, why is it racist to be proud of where you're from?

Joanne   It's not, but –

Zoe   In America, nearly everyone has a flag in their back gardens, and they salute it like once a day, and everyone thinks they're great and nobody ever says they're racists.

Leo   Exactly, Zoe.

Amid   I think a lot of them are sometimes probably a bit racist.

Zoe   Well . . .

Shanti   It's not racist to be proud to be British because Britain is full of lots of different races, and they can be proud of Britain as well, it's not racist, fine, but I think what Joanne was saying is that when idiots and thugs and skinheads and people have it in their window or tattooed on their arm or whatever, they're normally like BNP or racists or something.

Joanne   Exactly, and I'm just saying that it's a shame, because I like it, I like the flag.

Leo   Fine.

Joanne   I like the colours.

Leo   It's not about the colours.

Dean   There was that guy who stood as a BNP thingy, he lives next to you, Joanne.

Joanne   Not me – Aimee.

Dean   Aimee, then.

Aimee   Yeah, so?

Kelly   Do you go round and have tea with him, Aimee?

Aimee   No, course not, I hardly even know him.

Dean   Does he have a swastika in his living room?

Aimee   I don't know, I hardly know him, just say hello now and again, that's all.

Shanti   You say hello? Why? Why are you nice to him?

Aimee   He's my neighbour, you have to be nice to your neighbour, don't you? Even Hitler was probably nice to his neighbours.

Spencer *(looking at his sheets on the wall)*   Depends what you mean by neighbours; if you mean Poland and Czechoslovakia then, no, he wasn't very nice to his neighbours.

Aimee   It doesn't mean anything, he's just a man, an old man who we say hello to.

The church bells ring in the distance. Everyone turns towards the sound.

Leo   It's starting, it's coming. Oy, put the news back on the thing!

Graeme *turns the footage back on so that it is projected on to the screen. An image of the High Street. Full now. The coffins are starting to arrive.*

Kelly   I've changed my mind, I don't want to see it.

Zoe   Kelly, don't.

Kelly   What? It's too painful for me.

Leo   Shut up, Kelly! Everyone stay quiet!

Rachel   No, I think she's right, I don't want to see it, it's too sad.

Zoe   Well then, just look away.

Leo   No! Everyone watch! The least you can do.

Rachel   I'm just a bit sick of it. This town. It being us all the time. I'll be glad when it ends. I'm sorry –

Kelly   I don't want to see his coffin. I don't –

Graeme   Maybe I should turn it off.

Leo   Graeme, you leave it.

Jonathan   It's Graeme's laptop.

Leo   No. Shut it!

Jonathan   He can do what he wants / with it –

Leo   Oh you two, shut up will you, you pair of gays?

Rachel   Leo!

Aimee   Oy?

Jonathan   What? No.

Leo   Everyone knows what you two are, just no one ever says anything.

Graeme   That's not true.

Rachel   Stop it, Leo! That's really mean.

Leo   Even if you don't know what you are, I can tell, so just shut up and watch.

Jonathan   Leo, that's really not fair, I was only saying –

Leo   Shut up, you homo! All of you! Shut up and watch the screen!

Lucy (*breaking her silence*)   LEO, JUST STOP IT YOU EVIL LITTLE BASTARD!

Everyone gasps.

Rachel   Lucy!

Aimee   You broke your silence.

Lucy   You bully. You hypocrite. You know what I'm talking about.

Russell   Eh?

Kelly   What, what you talking about?

Leo   Nothing. Nothing, Lucy. Get back to being quiet, no one cares.

Lucy   You're such a fucking bully.

Leo   Get back to being quiet, I swear.

Kelly   What you talking about, Lucy?

Lucy   He knows.

Leo   Haven't got a clue.

Lucy   You have.

Leo   I haven't.

Lucy   You have.

Leo   Tell everyone, then, if it's such an amazing secret, tell everyone.

Lucy   You're such a nasty bully.

Leo   Tell everyone.

Lucy   Charlie.

Russell   What?

Kelly   What?

Lucy   He knows.

Kelly   WHAT?!

Lucy   You're such a hypocrite, leave them alone. Leave everyone alone.

Kelly   Him and Charlie what?

Lucy   What I saw. In the changing rooms.

Rachel   What?

Lucy   Year 8.

Aimee   Are you joking?

Lucy   After football.

Russell   What's she talking about?

Lucy   I was walking in to find Mr Hunt, after Hockey. Donna in sixth form needed the first-aid box.

Kelly   What?

Lucy   Charlie kissed Leo.

Russell/Kelly/Spencer/Dean/Rachel/Aimee/ Shanti/Amid   WHAT?!

Lucy   So you're such a hypocrite, Leo. Leave them alone.

Russell   Charlie was gay?

Kelly   No he wasn't! I went out with him.

Dean   He was captain of all the teams, though!

Russell   That doesn't mean you can't be gay, you bell end.

Lucy   It was just one kiss, and Leo pulled away and Charlie said sorry and he said he'd never done anything like that before and Leo said that was OK, it didn't matter, he thought it was funny and they shook hands and that was that and the only reason I'm telling it now is because you shouldn't bully people all the time because we're all growing up and we all have questions and we're all really fucking confused most of the time so don't bully Jonathan or Graeme or anyone and just leave us all alone.

Silence.

I'm going back to being quiet now. If anyone tells anyone I broke the silence I'll rip your teeth out and bite you in the arse with them, OK?

Silence.

Spencer (*still facing the wall*)   We, we drew the borders of a couple of other, erm . . . countries as well. After wars. And that seems to have caused some trouble now and again too, but I think that we meant well. Pakistan in 1947, separating it from India. Huh, like you Shanti, and you Amid –

Kelly   Leo, I can't believe you kissed a boy.

Russell   Oy, a boy kissed him, *once*, there's a difference.

Spencer   And then Israel –

Rachel   Spence! Shut up.

Kelly   What about all those girls over the years. All that 'big man' shit you chat all the time, what's that about, eh?

Zoe   It doesn't mean he's gay, all right? Lucy said Charlie kissed *him*. Right, Luce?

Lucy *points to her mouth to indicate her silence.* **Leo** *goes and stands in front of the whiteboard, watching the news images. The hearse has appeared on the High Street. Some people have started to throw flowers. People start to clap.*

Beat. **Russell** *looks around. He starts to clap. So do the others. Except* **Leo***. Who just stares at the screen.*

They clap, and watch the images of the coffin coming to a stop on the High Street. **Leo** *walks close to the whiteboard. His face almost pressed against it, and the image.*

Leo *turns, grabs his baseball bat, and starts smashing the desk with it. Some of the others scream, others jump out of the way,* **Spencer** *stays facing the wall.*

Leo   WANKERS! ALL OF YOU! DISRESPECTFUL, UNGRATEFUL, IGNORANT WANKERS! Why did you have to ruin it, today! Him coming home! Why did you have to bring that up, Lucy?! He's dead, he's dead, he died protecting and serving you lot, you ungrateful bastards, and then you go and bring up something like that!

Russell   Mate . . .

Everyone stands around the edge of the room, scared. **Leo** *paces, swinging his bat. Stops. He's begun to cry . . .*

He sees **Amid***. He points his bat at him . . .*

Leo   Come here.

Amid *doesn't move.*

Leo   Come here.

Pause. **Amid** *edges in to the centre of the room. Faces* **Leo***. Pause.*

Leo   Get on the floor.

Amid (*pause*)   W . . . what?

Leo   On the floor! Bent over!

Russell   Mate.

Beat. **Leo** *raises up his bat.*

Leo   ON THE FLOOR!

Russell   Leo!

Amid   It's OK! It's . . .

He gets on to his knees. **Aimee**, **Shanti** *and* **Joanne** *have started to cry.*

Leo   Graeme, come here.

Graeme *comes over, nervously.*

Leo   Lie on top of him. Across, like that.

Graeme *stays still.* **Leo** *knocks him in the back with his bat, not too hard, but hard enough . . .*

Leo   On top of him.

Graeme *lies on top of* **Amid***.*

Leo   Shanti.

Shanti *doesn't move.*

Leo   Shanti.

Shanti *comes forward.*

Leo   Lie on top.

Shanti *lies on top of them both.* **Leo** *steps back and takes a picture on his phone.*

He looks around. Points at **Kelly**.

Leo   You.

Kelly *shakes her head.*

Leo   You. You big . . . you . . . fucking . . . sl-slut. You.
COME ON!

Kelly *doesn't move.* **Leo** *raises his bat above her head. She flinches.
She lies on top of the pile. He steps back and takes a photo with his phone.*

Jonathan   Leo, please.

Leo *(turning on him)*   You. You puff. On the table.

Jonathan   What?

Leo   ON THE TABLE NOW, SOLDIER! Quick, march,
quick, march, one, two, one, two!

Jonathan *gets up unsteadily on to the table.*

Leo   Trousers down. You . . . you big . . . gay.

Russell   Leo, mate . . .

Leo *raises his bat to* **Russell** *and he flinches. He swings his bat at*
Jonathan*.*

Leo   TROUSERS DOWN! NOW!

Jonathan *undoes his belt, shaking, and lets his trousers fall down.*
Leo *tosses him up a sports T-shirt from his bag.*

Leo   Put that over your head. Put your arms out.

Jonathan *puts the T-shirt over his head. He slowly raises his arms
out to his side.* **Leo** *takes a picture on his phone. Then another of the
pile of people. Exhausted. Crying. Rubbing his head. Unsure . . .*

Spencer *(still facing the wall)*   And erm . . . course in the
Second World War, I think . . . I think a lot of people forget
that we were the first ones to declare war. On Germany. Not
America or anyone. Or France. Or . . . which, you know, I
think . . . well, that's quite brave. Isn't it? Really. We didn't
want a war, says here, we were still a bit buggered from the last

one. But we saw someone doing something wrong to people. Invading countries that didn't belong to them and doing bad things to the people that lived there. And we thought . . . 'No, that . . . that's not right.' And so we did something about it. And Hitler made us an offer to stay out of it, which would have meant a lot of our grandads and grandmas wouldn't have died and we'd be really powerful, but we still said no. And by the time they got to us, we were like completely alone. And everyone thought we would lose. But we didn't. And then it looks like America came along, and finished it up, and then we owed them a lot of money because we'd been fighting for so long on our own. And that meant we lost our empire and have been shrinking and struggling a bit ever since, never quite the same, but we knew that might happen and yet we still did it. Because we thought we had a responsibility. And I think that . . . you know. That's something that we should be, like, proud of. A bit more. And something that we forget, when all this other stuff is happening. Even when we get things wrong, and make mistakes. That if it wasn't for us. On this island. Then, like, the world and all that, it would be really quite bad right now. Worse than it is. And so . . . you know . . . that's what I've learnt, anyway. That we're better than we think we are. And that we can do better, most of the time. If only we remembered that. So I think we'll be all right, actually . . . you know, in the . . . in the, like, long run. I do. I actually do . . .

Silence.

Leo *lowers his bat slowly. Quivering. Tired . . .*

From the other side of the door, the sound of keys.

The door is unlocked. It starts to open . . .

Blackout.

Bassett

BY JAMES GRAHAM

*Notes on rehearsal and staging, drawn from a workshop
with the writer held at the National Theatre, October 2015*

*From workshops led by James Dacre and Matthew Dunster,
with notes by Sam Pritchard and Abigail Graham*

How James came to write the play

James wrote the play in 2011, inspired in part by his thinking
about the tenth anniversary of the 11 September attacks. He
was struck by the fact that the young performers for whom he
was writing would have been five or six at the time of the
attacks. They hadn't known a world without the 'War on
Terror' and a perpetual background of conflict.

Watching the TV coverage of the repatriations at Royal
Wootton Bassett, James wondered what it might be like to
live in that town and in particular as a teenager. War had
always existed as an abstract or distant thing for him, but it
came to their town every week as the bodies of dead
servicemen and women passed through the streets.

In recalling his own school days, James said that the politics
of war mirrored the politics of the classroom. Young people
want power and control, and they form alliances accordingly.
The play looks at what young people do to gain control, and
what happens when they lose it.

On a series of visits to the town, James spent time at Royal
Wootton Bassett School running workshops with students.
Many of them contributed to characters in the play and
helped him understand how close their lives were to war.
James says that he is often 'moved by plays that put people
under pressure that allows them to discover the worst and
best about themselves. No one ever planned for these coffins
to go through that town but they did. The play is the product
of an extraordinary series of coincidences that converge

on this group of teenagers stuck in that classroom on that particular day.'

The suspense that is created by the time pressure in the play is important and James was inspired by Harold Pinter's ability to show tension and violence without explicit acts of violence onstage.

Structure and story

A central task of any rehearsal process will be to clarify the story the company are telling together. You might spend a few minutes with the actors by asking them to write down the 'stupid story' – a brief and simple synopsis of the narrative and then a few sentences about the impact each person wants the play to have on an audience. You can return to these immediate responses throughout the process, changing and refining them as you get to know the text.

GIVEN CIRCUMSTANCES

It can be really useful to establish what the immediate facts of the situation are at the start of the play and also any circumstances that can be inferred. Questions to ask include:

- What time is it exactly at the start of the action?
- What is the time scale of the play?
- What is the temperature in the classroom?
- What exactly has happened with Miss Kirmani that led to her locking them in?
- How well do the class know Miss Kirmani?
- Are these fourteen students the whole class, or have some people been let go?
- Has the school been allowed the afternoon off for the repatriation?
- How many students are at the school?

It might be useful to note that it is lunchtime and the characters may well be hungry, which will affect their behaviour. It could be helpful to create an offstage soundscape to alert the audience to the fact it is lunchtime – perhaps the hustle and bustle of other students leaving the building?

Time is a very important given circumstance in this play. The students want to be part of an outside event, and time is running out. Finding a way to foreground the importance of time in your production could be useful. Help the actors to remain aware of the countdown; as every beat of the play passes and characters remain locked in the room, they are closer to missing the parade. This will help the stakes of the play to develop at their own pace.

THE INCITING INCIDENT

What happened just before the action of the play begins?

The question of what happened before the play begins is an important one. Characters were in a Citizenship class. Spencer has been standing in the corner facing the wall since before the action of the play begins. What might the class have done for the teacher to lock the door on the day of the parade? It is interesting to note that none of the characters question why she locked them in, or call her unreasonable – which could suggest that their behaviour was unacceptable and was not the action of a teacher who was ill equipped to deal with teenagers.

As a director you will need to find a reason for all of them to be standing up. This incident is the rocket fuel that powers the onstage action.

You could set up an improvisation with the cast to really investigate what happened that led Miss Kirmani to lock them in. The locking of the door is an extraordinary event and has to feed into your understanding of the play and allow it to begin with the right energy.

BREAKING DOWN THE TEXT

The play operates as one very long act – around 45 minutes of continuous uninterrupted stage action. This represents a directing challenge not only in terms of pacing and structuring the action, but also in scheduling and planning rehearsals. One way of doing this is to break the text down into units and events.

There are lots of ways of defining an event, unit or beat. Each director uses these tools in slightly different ways. Some rough definitions might be:

EVENT Something happening onstage that affects the behaviour of every character in the room. This could be a line or a piece of action, but it is helpful to be precise about exactly what the event is. An example of an event:

> *They all stop and listen. The sound of a plane flying over.*
>
> **Jonathan**   It's coming in to Lyneham.

Here, it is the sound of the plane that changes the students' behaviour rather than Jonathan's line. It can be useful to work through the script, marking events in with the performers as above. In some moments you may need to be flexible about what the exact event is, allowing a decision to change or become clearer as you work.

UNITS   The action onstage that falls between two events. This will often address one particular key subject or relationship, but may be made up of several plot points.

BEAT   A smaller section within a unit, this might be a brief exchange or an event that affects the behaviour of a few characters but not of everyone.

In working through the text to identify units and events, each unit should be given a TITLE and SUBTITLE. The title should be a short label or reference point for the company to use in rehearsal. The subtitle should then allow you to define clearly with the company everything that happens in the unit and what story needs to be told. Here is an example of how this might look on the page:

> **Amid** (*looking out the window*)   Look. At the bottom of the drive. EVENT

A few of the other pupils scramble and join **Amid** *at the window.*

Spencer   What? What is it?

Amid   They've already started stopping the traffic.

Spencer   Who?

Shanti   Police.

Joanne   Already? That's early.

Jonathan   It's because it's busier today. Because of Charlie.

TITLE: 'Traffic'

SUBTITLE: *A unit in which Amid realises the traffic has been stopped. Joanne suggests it's quite early and Jonathan suggests it's busier today because of Charlie.*

Leo *holds his head, and groans.*   EVENT

These subtitles may seem long and specific, but composing them will allow you and your company to define a clear idea of what story is being told and a sense of what the focus is onstage at any given moment. With fourteen characters present throughout, this will be particularly useful.

As a process, uniting can be time consuming and it may be something for directors to do as part of their preparation, or a process to go through with the company on a specific section of the text. However, it is a good way to structure conversation around the text and to build a collective understanding of the narrative.

Exercises for use in rehearsals

WARM-UPS

As actors remain onstage throughout the play, they will need a high level of focus and will need to be acutely aware of what is going on around them. It is therefore useful to develop warm-ups and games that encourage group awareness and active listening. Call-and-response games could be useful, where instructions are given and then reversed, or rhythm games where everyone has to clap, tap, and stamp at the same time. You can create a seven-beat rhythm, and once everyone is in sync you can give the instruction to miss out crucial beats. This focuses the group and encourages them to work together.

SEVENTEEN QUESTIONS AND STORYBOARDING

As a pre-rehearsal exercise, answer these questions instinctively. You could then revisit the questions during rehearsals to remind yourself of the direction you want to head in and to ensure that you can make informed and clear choices with your actors.

1 What feels real in the play?
2 What don't you believe?
3 What can you see most of in the space?
4 What's the thing you can see second most of in the space?
5 What do you see third most of in the space?
6 What would you love to do with this play you think you wouldn't dare to do?
7 What film genre is this play?
8 Who is the lead character?
9 What is the play about?
10 In three words, what is the play about?
11 In one word, what is the play about?
12 What is the strongest image in the play?
13 What pressure does the offstage, outside world put on the play?
14 What do you think of when you think of Royal Wootton Bassett?
15 What is the main event of the play?
16 Who are the four main offstage characters?
17 Write down two important questions I should have asked.

You could also draw the twelve most important images as a way of storyboarding the play, and have them in your mind when you are staging the play. Even if you end up creating something completely different, it can be helpful to have a visual starting point, particularly if you have limited rehearsal time.

READ-THROUGH

When beginning work on the play it can be useful to do a line-by-line read-through in a circle. You might ask each person to read just one line of dialogue or stage direction rather than reading their own character. This allows everyone in the group to engage with the story and takes the edge off any nerves involved in the first rehearsal. It is a democratic approach in which everyone is responsible for the narrative and also allows the director to gauge the pace of the play. This could be useful with a text that often moves at a ferocious speed, particularly at the start.

THE WORLD OF THE PLAY

Being as specific as possible, pull out all the facts of the environment from the script. The workshop participants identified the following:

- The play is set in a second-floor classroom of a modern secondary school in Royal Wootton Bassett. The door of the classroom can be locked from the outside and the door opens inwards.
- The classroom has one window, which looks out on to the school driveway. Beyond the driveway there is a set of traffic lights and a high street. This high street is where the coffins of dead soldiers are paraded.
- Royal Wootton Bassett is a small suburban town with a Tudor high street. At one end of the high street is an army base. Once a week the bodies of dead soldiers are brought back to base. James Graham referred to the town as 'a passageway where things happen'.
- The town is mainly working class and lower middle class.

Matthew suggested that, where possible, groups take a trip to Royal Wootton Bassett. If this is not possible, he suggested asking the cast to find images of the town, school and so on to share in rehearsals.

IMPROVISE THE TEXT USING EVENTS

Once you have broken the text into units with a sense of the key beats in each, it can be useful to improvise the action of each unit without using the exact words from the text. This allows performers to take ownership of the story, discover the impulse behind their characters' actions and to actively engage those characters who might not be speaking in each unit. Giving the actors a strict time limit also helps to make this effective.

TEXT AND SUBTEXT

During scene rehearsals, you might ask actors to speak their actual intention or the subtext beneath the line before saying it. This can quickly give structure and colour to the text and ensure actors are playing an intention with each line. It's useful to encourage them to make these as active as possible rather than more general thoughts.

STREAM OF CONSCIOUSNESS

You might run a section of the text but ask one character to speak every beat of their internal stream of consciousness out loud. This could be a particularly good way of animating and engaging those characters who are silent for long periods, like Spencer and Lucy, helping to establish their body language and reactions to events.

WANTS AND NEEDS

If you are struggling to work out what a character wants in a particular moment, you could look at what they want overall (their 'super-objective'), and it will help you to see what their smaller wants are – and vice versa.

To illustrate this, the participants looked at Leo's smaller 'wants'. It is very clear that Leo wants to get out of the classroom and go to the parade at the top of the play; the emptying of his bag on to the table to get out the rounders bat but choosing not to smash the window is a clear cry for attention; On page 178 he is trying to get the group to turn against Miss Kirmani so as to recruit them to his point of view. By asking the question 'And then what?' with each new discovery, you can get closer to the driving force behind these actions. The participants arrived at the decision that Leo's super-objective could be to gain power and control over his own destiny.

Another way of working out what a character wants is to look at their obstacles. For example, Leo has a lot of unanswered questions, and therefore he wants answers.

The participants investigated why Spencer does not move from his place of punishment in the corner and wondered if his super-objective could be that he wants to be good; he is bored with being the naughty one. The awareness of this 'want' can inform his actions.

ACTIONING/PAINTING COLOURS

Actioning the text involves asking the actors to decide on a transitive verb or action for each line or thought. The verb needs to have a specific target, an aim to change another person's behaviour. This process can be used throughout or in sections, as it is time consuming. Putting a range of verbs on the wall might also be a way of offering your actors choices and helping to speed up the process.

You might run a section with actors stating the verbs and then without. You can then ask performers to change the intensity with which they play the actions, painting them boldly (*in oils*), more softly (*in watercolour*) or in between (*in acrylic*) and finally in the silent-movie version without words. You then have a palette with which to colour the texture of particular moments in the action. This may be particularly useful in a play where the intensity and stakes switch quite suddenly.

BIG COMPANY ONSTAGE

Having fourteen people onstage at all times represents a particular challenge. For James Graham there is no significance to that number, except that each character represents a particular perspective on the events. He says that it's important 'that everything is sort of public in the play, each character's decision to speak or not to speak in each moment is an active rather than a passive choice'.

You might begin to enliven the staging by exploring an *animating activity* for each character. Are they someone who is doodling, texting, teasing, eating or getting on with homework? Giving each character a personal prop or deciding on a 'physical gesture' can also tell us something about who they are.

There's a risk that too much going on in the background can be distracting. Each director will have to balance and moderate this with their company, setting activity against the focus of the story. Ask yourself, would an alien understand the gist of this moment without speaking the language?

You might decide to start by fixing the staging for key moments by building tableaux or images for these moments with the actors. It will also be useful in staging to establish early on whose territory is where and at what points the students take over or engage with the teacher's space and desk.

Finally, pace and tension are important tools when delivering a story with a large group of actors. James Dacre talked about the stepping-stones that different moments provide in order to reach 'the extremity of the events at the end of the play' and referenced Edward Bond's idea that the audience should always be wondering where 'the gun' is in the room. Moments such as Leo revealing the bat, Zoe questioning Amid about his faith and the flag being spray-painted on the wall are examples. You might choose to mark these moments with the company on a scale of tension from one to ten, helping them see where it rises and falls.

Themes

A useful exercise is to ask your company to write down what the play is about in three words, then just choosing one word.

For the workshop participants, it felt like war was a central theme – both inside the classroom and outside. Inside. the students are fighting for power and control, analysing the different codes of behaviour that people live by (e.g. praying, training to go and kill people), and battling with the inner turmoil of being a teenager. Outside, the war is being paraded through Royal Wootton Bassett. Put simply, war is conflict and conflict is drama – when X wants something from Y and Y does not want to give it to them.

THE MILITARY AND REPATRIATIONS

Britain's military involvement in Afghanistan and Iraq and the loss of lives in those conflicts sit at the heart of the play. In any group of young people working on the text there are likely to be connections to conflict – whether through family, grandparents or friends – that are worth discussing.

It is significant that James Graham's characters are in Year 11, on the cusp of becoming sixteen, and able to join up and fight themselves. Individual actors might want to decide whether their character has considered this or how they feel about the idea of serving. As a group or individually you might do some research into the process of signing up to the army.

It will be important for you and the company to have a strong sense of how the repatriation ceremonies at Royal Wootton Bassett worked from footage or news reports at the time. Coffins were driven through the town on their way from RAF Lyneham to the John Radcliffe Hospital in Oxford from 2007 onwards. The public element to these events was spontaneous rather than organised, a result of the British Legion and the people of the town starting to line the streets every time it happened.

NATIONALITY, RACE AND IDENTITY

Much of James's writing engages with British politics, big national issues and questions of identity. Often he will take a place, person or group of people and use them as an allegory for Britain or for a particular moment in time. In *Bassett*, the class of students in all their diversity of opinion, gender and race might be seen as reflective of the British population as a whole. In particular Leo, whose name may be an echo of the British lion, could be read as a symbol for a modern Britain struggling with its military role and identity in the world.

It will be useful to explore what each character feels about the idea of being British and how they relate to the diversity of their community in terms of race and sexuality. You might also ask performers to think about how their character's attitudes change. James points out that the play asks 'how the events in this 45 minutes will permanently change the individuals in this room'.

FROM 2011 TO 2016

The play was written in 2011, a time difference that will be significant both for your actors and your audience. Repatriations through Royal Wootton Bassett ended in September 2011. As a result, audiences may be less familiar with the process than they were in 2011. It will be important to ensure that the storytelling around the details of repatriation is absolutely clear. This might make a case for ensuring that the audience see the projected images of the parade that Graeme screens.

You and your company must decide how strictly you will set the production in 2011. Is it specific to that moment in British history, or can we imagine that we're in the present day? James's general feeling is that in theatre 'the more specific you are about time and place, the more universal you can sometimes be in the story you are telling'.

OTHER POSSIBLE THEMES

- Grief: they are grieving for Charlie.
- Sex and suppressing sexual desire.
- Growing up; power.
- Faith, love, pride.
- Human rights: they have just been learning about this in their Citizenship class.
- Ceremony: part of what makes Royal Wootton Bassett special is its ceremony of parading the dead soldiers through the street, codes of behaviour – military and religious.
- Citizenship, fighting for survival and coming of age.

It can be useful to regularly discuss with the cast what the play is about and you may find that the answer changes as the process progresses.

Characters and characterisation

Characters are revealed by how they behave. For example, Leo carries a baseball bat, and yet does not smash in the window. Spencer has been told to stand facing the wall by the teacher and even when his classmates tell him he can turn round he does not.

While Leo is a major character, this is an ensemble piece. It is important that each character is worked on in as much detail as possible, especially those who do not say very much, because having a vivid inner life will help to keep the actors present, grounded and truthful.

When thinking of the characters, James Graham suggested it is helpful to remember that they are all trying to survive the jungle of the classroom. Who they form alliances with is all about survival.

Read the play looking for specific pieces of information about each character. For example, we learn that Kelly is dressed more provocatively than usual. Why might this be? We also learn that she does not live in Everleigh Road (where Leo

lives), and would not want to go near there. What might be
the reason for this?

It is useful to remember that the audience are joining these
characters sixteen years into their journeys. Back-story is the
fuel of the present action of the play. Leo, in particular, has
several explosive moments and your production has to earn
them. The actor playing Leo needs to understand his
background and where his anger comes from. Could his
hidden feelings about his sexuality contribute to his anger?
There is a great deal of pressure on him – especially when
you consider what is special about that day (Charlie's dead
body is coming back from war) and the kiss that he shared
with Charlie.

Sex is important to all the characters – they are on the cusp
of becoming adults and sex is a 'hot topic'. It is important not
to hide from this because the cast are young.

There are several offstage characters that are very important
to get to know and bring into your rehearsal process where
possible. First, the young people's parents, and their core
beliefs about the war have an immeasurable influence on how
these young people think and behave. Then there are Amy's
BNP neighbour, Rachel's brother and granddad, Jonathan's
brother, Joanne's granddad and Miss Kirmani. She is a
supply teacher, but the things they say about her suggest this
is not the first time she has worked with the group, as her
behaviour has taken them by surprise. Her nationality might
also be an interesting factor to think about.

CHARLIE

Charlie is perhaps the most significant offstage character in
the play. You might choose to build a picture of who he was
together with the company so that he is a strong and clear
reference point for the group. Individual members of the
company might also have their own private details about
their character's relationship with Charlie that make
remembering him very active. There is a sense in the play

that James has left this character quite open, perhaps for each audience member to imagine their own version of who he was.

CHARACTER RELATIONSHIPS

Each character might have certain roles within the class dynamic – class clown, leader, follower, teacher's pet, antagonist, peacekeeper, provocateur and so on. Which character fits into which role?

These two exercises can help clarify relationships for the actors:

- Stand in a circle and ask everyone to say how well they know each other, and then how much they trust each other – you could do this in secret on paper first – ranking how well they know each person and how well they trust them from one to ten – and then have them give feedback to the group. Another way of approaching this exercise is to do it actively – ask them to sit next to whom they feel they know best and then next to whom they trust the most.
- Ask the cast to line up in order of status and then the status they would like to have – you could do this exercise after every major event in the play to explore how the status shifts and changes between events.

Casting

For those companies tackling the challenge of staging the play without the requisite numbers of girls and boys, there are some key relationships to preserve:

- *Leo* and *Dean* feel like the characters whose masculinity is most important.
- It feels significant that *Jonathan* and *Graeme* are the same gender.
- It also feels important that *Kelly* is a girl and that she is a different gender from *Leo*.
- A female *Spencer* feels like a possibility.

- It may be useful to note some of the alliances that gender creates (such as *Leo* and *Russell*'s bond).

For James Graham, the truth of what the actors are playing is always more significant than what we are seeing. It is more important that the actors playing Amid and Shanti play the difference in their background from the group than that actors of the exact ethnicity are cast. The play tells us who these people are. Similarly, even if there are age differences within the company as long as they are playing the same age with confidence that should be clear for an audience.

Having a company that is larger or smaller than fourteen may present more difficulties. Each character represents a distinct and important perspective. It might prove problematic to have actors onstage who don't speak and to make that choice feel active for each of them. Any decisions about splitting roles or changing the casting need to be tested with your group in practice.

If holding auditions, it could be useful to audition the cast in small groups to see who works well with whom – after all, they are all on stage together the whole time so this is crucial.

Production, staging and design

ENVIRONMENT

With a play that takes place entirely in one location, it is important that the company have a strong, shared sense of what this environment is like. For the characters, the environment is their prison and their war ground. Building a picture of the classroom will be a vital part of the design process. In addition to the previous facts about the world of the play, you might also work together to gather a list of things you can infer. These include:

- Whose classroom is this and what subject is taught in it?
- What kind of mood or feeling should the environment evoke?
- What's on the walls?

- What time of year is it?
- What's the temperature/weather?
- Whose territory is where in the room?
- What can you see outside the window (sports field, road, etc.)?
- How much is British history/culture a physical presence in the room?
- What kind of school are we in (new-build, academy, old comprehensive)?
- What are the essential objects needed onstage to tell the story?
- Whose point of view do we see the room from (students, teacher's, no one's)?

James's play is set in a very specific real location – a school that actually exists in a particular town. You will have to decide how far to observe the real details of that location – how much to research and reference the actual details of Royal Wootton Bassett School, its uniform, buildings, size and so on.

CONFIGURATION

James wrote the play without any particular configuration in mind and it could be staged end-on, in-the-round, in thrust or traverse. You may even choose to reverse your staging halfway through! An important thing to remember in both design and configuration is that everyone is onstage the whole time.

There is a real challenge in moving fourteen characters through a space in-the-round, particularly with the audience on the same level. It will be important to think about how you use aisles to open up moments and have characters sitting or standing in order to ensure the audience aren't looking through bodies. This configuration may enhance the sense that the characters are trapped here.

Working end-on gives you an ability to focus on particular moments or individuals by pulling them downstage and to reduce focus on individuals when they are seated or upstage.

SPENCER

Spencer's position onstage is a choice that will be dictated in part by your configuration. In-the-round or with Spencer facing the fourth wall, his reactions will be very available to an audience and may mediate our relationship with the action. If he faces upstage or against a wall, we have to work more actively to imagine and engage with him. There is a real dramatic tension about whether he will turn around and the actor may create a more engaged relationship with the wall. James emphasised that it is an active choice to remain there for the character. He may be moving, stealing glances or struggling – there are many ways to enliven that relationship.

WINDOWS/DOORS

Where to put these key features onstage represents crucial choices. They will be defined by how you want to stage the moments that focus on these landmarks (e.g. the initial realisation that the door has been locked). The second-floor window provides a constant reminder of escape, thus increasing the onstage tension. Characters are desperate to be outside and with every minute that passes the stakes get higher. If you haven't got a physical door or window it may be useful to locate them on the downstage (fourth) wall, depending on your configuration.

COSTUME AND PROPS

The big costume question is whether there is a uniform at the school that the students share. This might help with the claustrophobic feeling of the environment and the heat of the room, with jumpers being removed over the course of the action. It might be useful for the company if the uniform isn't too similar to any one they themselves wear.

Actors should create their characters' own version of the uniform. Are they scruffy or neat, do they wear wrist-bands or jewellery, do they have different ties, shoes and school bags?

James pointed out that it was important for him that it is a rounders bat Leo has in his bag. It is an object that brings a subtle sense of threat into the room that then grows as events escalate until it is used as a real weapon at the end of the play.

ACCENTS AND SLANG

The play is written with Wiltshire accent and speech patterns in mind, but the dialogue works in any accent. There is a softness to the accent and a use of flat 'a's that might be useful for those companies intending to replicate it. However, if it can't be done well it risks becoming a distraction.

James also suggests that the specificity of words like 'minging' is useful in capturing this very teenage world and substitutions should be avoided.

PHONES

In 2011 mobile phones were much less common in the classroom than they are now. They also represent a particular plotting challenge. If they exist in the classroom, why do the students not call someone to let them out? Does their presence ruin the sense that there's no communication with the outside world? If you are going to use them, it is worth assessing whether they are a distracting detail and an obstacle between the audience and the story.

PROJECTION AND SENSITIVE CONTENT

For James Graham, the most important thing about everything that appears on the projector is the effect it has on characters in the room. In the case of the footage from the repatriation, that moment brings the reality of what is going on outside into the classroom. The 'soft porn' Russell flashes up on to the screen is a glitch in the action that makes bigger themes of sexuality a presence in the room and brings something disruptive into the space.

It is the dramatic purpose of these moments that is key to bear in mind whilst deciding whether or not to show projections to the audience. Sometimes the bond between actors and invisible footage can be powerful or you may also make the choice that seeing the coffins adds a sense of the external reality and explains the process of repatriation.

Similarly, the moment when Jonathan is forced to pull down his trousers is key in terms of its impact rather than the specific actions. For James, this moment is about shame, humiliation and Leo's control. It can be a difficult moment to approach with a company of young people, but if you work towards creating a rehearsal room that is supportive and sensitive, you can encourage your actors to take the same risks as the characters and play the moment with sensitivity and conviction. There is no wrong response from an audience – nervous laughter can be a sign of real discomfort. For companies who are worried about this moment, there may be ways of placing and lighting it that will help in tackling it sensitively.

SPRAY PAINT

Companies concerned about the difficulty of repeating Leo's spray-painting of the flag asked about its significance. For James, the image of fourteen teenagers looking at their flag is a powerful and important one. Like the bat, it brings subtextual issues (in this case about nationality) into the room in a physical form. It is also important that Leo's actions leave a permanent mark in the room and on his future.

Style and Technique

PUNCTUATION

James uses punctuation as a tool to signal the intent or thought in particular lines. An *ellipsis* is often a pause in which a character is searching for a thought. A *dash* often indicates a switch to a new idea and a *semi-colon* can suggest a stumble or qualification in the thought.

NATURALISM

For James, the emotional truth of the action onstage is more important than questions of style. We have to invest in the emotional life of these characters. He says, 'Sometimes simplicity is key in making the story about these fourteen human beings.'

The swear words are important to the way these characters express themselves, so please work to keep them in.

Suggested reference

Wootton Bassett – The Town that Remembers, documentary, BBC TV, June 2011 (available on YouTube).

I'm Spilling
My Heart Out Here

by Stacey Gregg

The oldest and strongest emotion of mankind
is fear, and the oldest and strongest kind of fear
is fear of the unknown.

H. P. Lovecraft

My life is like a movie and I do my own stunts.

Lil Wayne

A group of mates start falling apart when a new boy enters their midst, shifting allegiances and sparking rumours. But what's real and what's not? And what are you meant to do when a strange epidemic strikes and no one seems to find it weird?

Age suitability: 15+

Cast size
Nine named characters:
five girls, four boys

Stacey Gregg is a writer for theatre and screen, and a performer. She is currently in residence with Clean Break and under commission from the Royal Court and the Abbey in Dublin. Writing for theatre includes: *Perve*, *Shibboleth* (co-commissioned for the Goethe-Institut Berlin) and *Josephine K and the Algorithms* at the Abbey, Dublin; *Perve* at Théâtre La Licorne, Montreal, and Galway Cúirt Festival; *Lagan* at Ovalhouse; *Override* at Watford Palace; and *Jackie's Taxi* for NI Opera at The MAC, Belfast. Screen credits include: *Spoof or Die* (Channel 4); *Raw* (RTÉ); and *The Frankenstein Chronicles* (ITV2/Sky Encore). She is currently working on a series for the BBC and has a feature film in development, *Here Before*, for Rooks Nest Entertainment. Credits as performer: *Moth* at the Bush; *Cheer up Kessy* for The MAC/Outburst; and *Everything Between Us* for Project Arts. She is recipient of the Brian Friel Guthrie Fellowship, the Stewart Parker Award and is a MacDowell fellow.

Characters

Karen, *fifteen*
Wilson, *sixteen*
Alexa, *sixteen*
Sean, *sixteen*
Dom, *fifteen*
Osh, *fifteen*
Sweep, *fifteen*
Ciaran, *twelve*
Jody, *fifteen*

Location
A small town.

Notes
This is an evocation of a time when it is hard to tell the difference between reality and illusion, hard to guess at the repercussions or stakes involved. A time when most of us are accidentally sharing untruths, being messy, just wanting to be okay.

This is an invitation to explore expressivist stage pictures and metaphor. We are resisting trying to represent the 'reality' of a world that it is not representable in onstage drama. We are interrupting the illusion of 'reality' in theatre.

As much mess as the production allows, stylised, multi-coloured, outrageous or otherwise. It is an accumulation of impossible things.

Dialogue
A foward slash (/) in the text indicates overlapping dialogue, which should generally go at a quick pace. Pace and energy are supremely important.

Scene One

A group has gathered around **Alexa**, *fizzing in anticipation. She is taking off her cardigan. They talk over each other, viscous, never still.*

Dom   Do it.

Sweep   Stand still, Alexa.

Dom   Now you have to breathe –

Osh   In and out, in and out really –

Jody   Like you're hyperventilating –

Dom   Yeah, like you're about to dive.

Alexa *breathes in and out exaggeratedly.*

Osh   You've got to concentrate, Alexa.

Sweep   You've got to breathe in and out for sixty seconds.

Dom   Is it sixty seconds?

Sweep   Yeah, it's sixty seconds – who's timing?

Wilson   I'm timing.

Karen   Yeah, you've got a stopwatch on your phone, you do it.

Jody   Ohmygod.

Wilson   Okay, I'm timing, are you breathing?

Osh   Deeper – like – (*He demonstrates.*)

Jody   Yeah, that's how they did it online –

Karen   Like having a baby.

Sweep   Did you see it?

Jody   No. but I heard.

Osh   Yeah. I saw it.

Jody   It's like when they do blessings at church.

Sweep   Only your freaky fundy church.

Jody   Its not fundy.

Karen   She's going a funny –

Osh   She's meant to go a funny colour.

Dom   How long's that?

Wilson   Nearly forty seconds.

Karen   Looks like she's gonna puke.

Dom   No she doesn't, right babe?

Jody   Ohmygod –

Osh   Ohmygod, it's mad.

Jody   This is mad.

Osh   It totally works.

Dom   Its amazing.

Osh   And after, you feel amazing.

Jody   I heard it was like / being stoned –

Dom   Being stoned, yeah! I heard that.

Osh   It's totally like being stoned.

Dom   How would you know, titchy balls?

Wilson   FIFTY-THREE.

Karen   Keep breathing.

Wilson   Ready?

Dom   Someone needs to shove her in the chest –

Jody   Really hard.

Dom   Someone shove her or it won't work!

Osh   Who's doing it?

Wilson   I'm timing, its fifty-six seconds –

Jody   You have to do it now or it won't work!

Dom   You do it –

Jody   You do it –

Osh   You do it, she's your girlfriend, Dom –

Karen   I'm not doing it.

Dom   Who's done it before?

Karen   You said you saw them do it.

Jody   Yeah but –

Dom   You flippin do it!

Alexa   Somebody do it!

All   Do it! Do it! Do it! Do it! DO IT! DO IT!

Wilson   SIXTY . . .

Jody   Do it, chicken!

WHAM. Someone pushes **Alexa** *hard in the chest and holds her against the wall She drops like a stone, in a dead faint.*

A moment of silence.

Whoops, shouts, buzz, high-fives. Two of the girls roll her over and fan her. Everyone's phones are out, a sea of arms taking photos and videos.

Scene Two

Outside a café. **Wilson** *and* **Karen** *slurping Cokes.*

Wilson *is charismatic, boyish, laptop open on her knee.* **Karen** *taps her heels, impatient. She is most people's mate: witty, mildly alternative.*

Karen   Did Alexa really pass out?

Wilson   What?

Karen   Alexa.

Wilson   Dunno.

Karen   It was so cool she did that.

Wilson   Or did she fake it?

Karen   Dunno.

They slurp on their Cokes in unison.

I can never tell if things are real or fake.

They slurp on their Cokes in unison.

I heard Alexa's entire leg fell off once. Just dropped off. Genuinely. Just like that.

Wilson *taps on her laptop.*

Wilson   I'm so nearly in.

Karen   What're you doing?

Wilson   Hacking the school intranet, so . . .

Karen   Really? Shut up, that's mad.

She examines a split end.

Kkkhh, what's taking Jody so long? Maybe she's haggling him up.

Wilson   That never works with CreepyMartin.

Karen   Does. Sweep did it.

Wilson   Did she?

Karen   Got him up to two hundred.

Wilson   Rubbish – highest ever was Alexa and she's hot, he would've like offered the clothes off his back for her.

Karen   Maybe.

Wilson   What'd you get again?

Karen   Hundred and forty.

Wilson   Oh yeah, that's right. Reasonable. You can hold your head high. Fair amount of money to offer a minor for sex.

Karen   Oi.

Wilson   What?

Karen   Thought I might get one-fifty.

Wilson   Well, you don't want to look like Alexa, even if that is what he goes for.

Karen   Suppose.

Wilson   And the best I got was 'Are you a boy?' and a tap water. So . . . Oh – I'm in! YES. (*Typing.*)

Karen   What's it say? Can you access our reports?

Jody *appears, prim, triumphantly waving a fresh bottle of Coke.*

Karen   Owp – here she coooomes . . .

Wilson   Well?

Jody (*commiserating*)   One-ten?

Jody   Nope.

Karen   One-thirty?

Jody   Nope – hundred and thirty-fiiiive.

Karen   Hi fiiiiive.

Wilson   Nice one.

Jody   What age is CreepyMartin anyway?

Karen   Don't know. Forty? Fifty?

Wilson   Thought he was in his thirties.

Karen   You got your free Coke out of him . . .

Jody   Two, baby.

Karen   Then our job here is done.

Wilson He's so ridiculous.

Jody Diet. One for me, one for Alexa.

Karen Alexa?

Wilson Like when will he learn? No one falls for it.

Jody Yeah, cos he's rank and we're not stupid.

Karen I didn't know you were with Alexa.

Wilson Wonder how many Cokes CreepyMartin's bought pretty girls over the years.

Jody I wasn't. She was just there and I don't know crashed my party.

Wilson Millions.

Karen Flipping Alexa.

Wilson Alexa gets in on everything.

Karen Thunder-stealer.

Wilson Thunder-thief.

Karen Sounds like a superhero name. (*Hero voice.*) Thunder Thief!

Wilson What would you be?

Karen Average Boobs. Super Average Boobs.

Wilson Flippin rubbish superhero.

Jody Did Alexa really pass out?

Karen Dunno.

Jody It was so cool she did that.

Wilson Or did she fake it?

Jody Dunno. She's so reckless.

Karen Looked fake.

Jody How can you tell?

Karen Typical. Either way.

Wilson Said she was out cold.

Jody Yeah, she said her life passed before her eyes.

Wilson Yeah, she also said she's booking a B&B for Dom's sixteenth so they can get it on, so . . .

They slurp their Cokes in unison. This is juicy and disturbing.

Karen Everyone's sayin they've been going out for ever and they haven't done it. Everyone's obsessed with their sex life.

Wilson Everyone's obsessed in general – obsexed. I blame TV. And a lack of local amenities. Boredom leads to babies.

Jody I believe her. She's cool. She chain smokes.

Wilson/Karen Pfft/Meh.

Jody The other day she was like 'Hey any of you girls want some milk, we had too much so I just brought the bottle out.' She's so cool she didn't even care how it looked.

Karen She was holding a bottle of milk? Like an actual pint?

Jody Just on the street. It was mad.

Wilson I don't care how *I* look . . .

Jody Yeah but you're . . .

She indicates **Wilson***'s look.*

Wilson Thanks.

Jody Don't you want to look cute, Wilson?

Wilson I am.

Jody I mean. Like. Sexy.

Wilson   Not if it means 'Please put your man-face on me,' no.

Jody   Don't you ever wear Sunday clothes even?

Wilson   Are you from the 1950s?

Jody   You're so lucky you don't have to worry about looking hot. Sad you'll probs burn in hell. Want the rest of this, Karen?

Karen   Not want it?

Jody   My mum says Diet makes you more fat. It's a trick. Then I'll never get a boyfriend and die on benefits and loveless.

A beep.

All three whip out their phones as they go, fingers a frenzy of networking.

Scene Three

Ciaran *and* **Karen** *in cycling helmets, bicycles, mooching home.*

Ciaran   Can we get chips, Karen?

Karen   No.

Ciaran   Karen.

Karen   What?

Ciaran   Can we get chips?

Karen   No.

Ciaran   Okay.

Karen?

Karen   What?

Ciaran   What's a BJ, Karen?

Karen (*spluttering*)   Uh, look, doesn't that cloud look like a burger?

Ciaran   Yeah. But what's a BJ? Have you had one?

Karen   You shouldn't know about them. It's rude and Mum'll kill you for asking . . .

Ciaran (*thoughtful*)   Oh.

Karen   In Year7 we were still making treasure maps out of pasta. Don't kids do that any more? What happened to childhood?

Ciaran   The internet.

Osh and **Sean** *wander across,* **Sean** *carrying a football and wearing headphones.* **Karen** *whips off her helmet, fluffs up her hair.*

Ciaran   I'm tellin Mum you take off your helmet to look cool.

Karen   They should invent a helmet that goes over your entire face and then never let you out – Oh HI! What's up?

Osh (*rapid*)   Sean's new. Just moved here. We're meeting Alexa. She's amazing. Did you see her faint? That was crazy. She's got a modelling job till five. But she said we're gonna hang out so we're meeting up with her. After. Her house is massive. Like a castle.

Karen   Cool. Um. Going to youth club later?

Ciaran (*mimics, flirty*)   'Going to youth club later?'

Osh   Youth club is where fun goes to die.

Sweep, *the scary make-uppy girl, has joined them, munching a sausage roll, swinging an arm round* **Karen**.

Sweep   Hi, Tiny.

Osh   Shuddup, Sweep.

Sweep   I've got an urgent message for Karen.

Karen   O God, what?

Sweep   New boy is so far out of your league he's in another dimension.

Karen   Sweep –

Sweep   Are you hot for him?

Karen   My twelve-year-old brother is here.

Ciaran   Hi.

Sweep   He needs to learn.

Ciaran *nods earnestly.*

Sweep   Everyone, Karen has the hots for Sean HUBBA HUBBA. (*Orgasmically.*) H-h-h-HOT!

Sean   Mega.

They look at him.

Sweep   What?

Sean   N – nothing.

Osh   Sean, we hang out with Alexa, we can't hang out with her. Anyway she's weird and hangs out with Wilson the freaky girlboy. (*To* **Sweep**.) And why d'you call me 'Tiny'? Is that what people think? Cos if that's what people think, you should say. You should just let me know. Is that what people say? You should just tell me if it is. I mean it's not like I'm insecure. I'm not insecure, do you think I'm insecure? Cos / I'm not. So . . .

Sweep   Osh, shut up.

Osh   Fine.

He puts his phone down his pants and experimentally takes a snap.

Sweep   Karen! Your little heart eyes are bugging outta your head.

Karen   No they're not. Heart eyes. No they're not –

Sweep   Put them back in!

Karen   I've got normal eyes. Completely normal non-heart eyes.

Sweep   Hey, has your little geek-in-my-pocket fixed my laptop yet?

Karen   Don't know.

Sweep   If I miss any assignments cos of Wilson, you'll miss your vagina once I've kicked it out your mouth into space. Bye.

She goes, shoving past **Ciaran**, *whose mouth hangs open after her.*

Karen (*to* **Ciaran**)   Don't worry, she'll be dead one day. Choke to death on a bag of Hula Hoops hopefully.

Beep. **Karen** *frowns at her phone.*

Karen   Osh. Did you just Snapchat a photo of your – ?

Osh   NO.

Karen   Looks like you.

Osh   NO. Shut up.

Ciaran *studies the image too. Then studies* **Osh**.

Osh   As if – I mean – (*Shriller.*) You wouldn't even know what a – what it looks like . . .

Sean *takes a look too.*

Osh (*small*)   Does it look okay?

Karen   Yeah. It's nice.

Ciaran (*agreeing*)   Looks like a face.

Osh   Okay. You can tell people it's nice.

Sean   Its mega. Really MEGA.

The lights flicker. They react, studying **Sean**, *who shrinks back with his football.*

Karen   Did he just say MEGA?

Sean   Yeah.

Osh   C'mon, Sean, we're supposed to be meeting Alexa.

Sean   Mega. Mega.

Karen   But Alexa was just at CreepyMartin's.

Osh   No she's not, she's modelling.

Karen   No she's not, I just saw her getting Cokes off CreepyMartin.

Ciaran   Who?

Karen   This weird guy at the café – he gives girls free Cokes.

Osh   Again? But she was there yesterday.

Ciaran   Can I get a free Coke?

Karen   Are you pretty?

Ciaran   Yes?

Karen   No. Are you a girl? Then no. Stay away from CreepyMartin.

They split their separate ways.

Scene Four

Karen *and* **Wilson** *in gym kits.* **Wilson** *in a fetching boy's ensemble. They peer through the gym window with toy binoculars.*

Wilson   Poor Sweep. PE is cruel. That should be on the Wildlife channel.

Karen   Y'know she didn't start wombchunks till she was fourteen.

Wilson   That. Is. Disgusting.

Karen And when they did come it was only one every four months and then WHOOOSH! True story.

Wilson *sips from a novelty coffee flask.*

Wilson Think we'll get caught?

Karen I've got a new excuse. Ready?

Wilson Go.

Karen Nosebleed. Doesn't sound as done as period pain – anyway, Miss Farnam memorises last time you said it and keeps a diary to catch you out instead of having an actual life. It's sad.

Wilson She is so so sad.

Karen Adults are complete saddo sell-outs. All they do is talk about boring things and pretend it's interesting. Makes me feel CRAZY. I mean, all growing up is is getting better at *lying* 'YES I LOVE' that boring thing it's SO INTERESTING and suddenly you're considered 'mature' – if you just lie OH YES PLEASE, let's watch a million pukey romcoms – relationships boringness internet dating pathetic Bridget Jones' – I WANT TO KILL MYSELF, WHO CARES ANYWAY?

She slurps her coffee dramatically.

Wilson So what's the deal with you and Seanywaunywoo woo?

Karen Nothing.

Wilson Don't lie. How long have I known you?

Karen For ever.

Wilson Well, he's well outside your Venn diagram and he's hanging out with Alexa.

Karen Jealous?

Wilson No way José. Just reckon if you want to lose it don't lose it to a douche.

Karen   I'm scared of making love.

Wilson   'Sex', Karen. You're sixteen.

Karen   It's not gonna happen till I'm twenty-three. I did a quiz and that's what it predicted. You know what's weird? Sean says 'mega'.

Wilson   People say it.

Karen   Yeah, but it reminded me of Scott. Remember Scott That Died?

Wilson   Scott That Died at the funfair?

Karen   Yeah Majesto's. That's ironic – 'fun' fair. Not so 'fun'. Huh? '*Fun*fair' –

Wilson   Yeah, I get it.

Karen   Sweep took pictures

Wilson   I was nearly on the news, you could see the back of my head.

Karen   The funeral was awful.

Wilson   Did you go?

Karen   No, but I saw the pictures.

Wilson   They were fakes.

Karen   They were real. Anyway. Sean is just like Scott That Died. And I swear the lights flicker when he sneezes. It's one hundred per cent spooky.

Wilson   You talked to him?

Karen   Not really.

Wilson   You didn't talk to him.

Karen   I was looking – I saw him. I was watching him.

Wilson   What, like a spy? You're the spooky one, Karen.

Karen   He seems nice.

Wilson   Wow.

Karen   What?

Wilson   You *like* him.

Karen *peers through the binoculars at the gym.*

Karen   Can you look up Sean when you finally hack the school's records?

Wilson   Kkkhhhh, you are so underwhelming, Karen. I bring you riches and you ask for rubbish. IT'S SO BORING HERE, this town's started to intermarry. The novelty'll wear off, and he'll be just another dick with a football. Cannot believe you think he's cool. The world implodes, Karen. We fundamentally can't exist together. Like oil and water, like cheese and pineapple. I question your moral compass. He hangs out with a gang who call themselves the 'A Team'. Without irony.

Karen   Why do you care?

Wilson   I don't! I don't even care. Just thought, y'know, you and me, don't run with the herd.

Karen   His hair is so *conditioned* it floats. I think he could be my first.

Wilson   I can't see you let me just clean the vomit from my eyes.

Karen   Ciaran was asking sex questions. Since when did little kids become sexually aware?

Wilson   I was.

Karen *briefly contemplates* **Wilson**, *who looks back at her through the binoculars.*

Karen   Did you always know?

Wilson   What?

Karen   You know. That you're a g.a.y.

Wilson   Yep. PS, Sean's a douche.

Karen   Do you know what a douche is?

Wilson   No.

Karen   Should Google it.

Wilson   Are you gonna ask him out?

Scene Five

The church hall, because it's wet outside and there's nowhere else. **Jody** *is mixing a bowl of gunk.*

Alexa *passes with a big bag of crisps, stopping to take in* **Wilson**. **Alexa** *smiles, glorious.*

Alexa (*genuine mystification*)   Why is your hair weird?

They watch as she exits accompanied by the sound of angels.

Jody   Alexa walks like she's gliding. It's cos she's modelling and everything. Posture. She has a walk. And your hair is weird.

Wilson   Is this avocado?

Jody   Yeah, it's always in skin creams. (*Airy.*) You doubt, like Thomas the Apostle.

Karen   Noticed how much money Alexa's been throwing around? She's like buying people lunch and stuff. Dom said she actually booked that B&B for his birthday so they could do it.

Wilson   Where's she getting the coins from?

Jody   Says her dad gives her it.

Wilson   Nope, her dad's a massive skinflint. Remember her thirteenth? We all went to the cinema and had to buy our own popcorn?! That was insane.

Jody *pastes green muck on* **Wilson**'*s face.*

Wilson Jody –

Jody Haven't you ever used face-mask?

Wilson Hello, have you met me? I spent primary school figuring out I wasn't actually a boy.

Jody Yeah. The tomboy thing is something you grow out of though, maybe.

Wilson Yeah, into a fully-grown trouser-suit wearing gay.

Jody *looks shy.*

Wilson You still don't believe me?

Jody No, I do. I was thinking about what you said. Did you really think you were a boy?

Wilson Wished it so much and then I just decided to ignore the fact I wasn't till I had to deal with it.

Jody Didn't you think that was weird?

Wilson No. Cos I always felt like that – so it would be weird not to. AaaaAAAHH – my face . . . my face is hot . . . AAAAAAAHHHHH, WHAT IS IT?

Karen Yo, what's wrong with her –

Wilson *claws at her face, removing the gunk. They watch, interested.*

Wilson Ohmygod, my face! Get it off! It's on fire!

Jody Wow, I've never heard her make that noise.

Karen Like a squirrel in a blender.

Jody Think her face is melting?

Karen What if she's disfigured?

Jody She'll be our cool gay disfigured friend.

Karen Disfigurement is way cooler than gay.

Jody Hey, talking of disfigurement did you hear about Sean?

Karen   What?

Jody   That new boy you fancy. Had like a full-on heart transplant.

Karen   No way.

Jody   Yeah, and everyone's saying Sean is just like Scott That Died.

Karen   Are they?

Jody   Yeah, everyone's said it.

Karen   Like when he says 'mega'?

Jody (*portentous*)   And did you *see* the *hat* he's wearing? (*Calling.*) Dom! Didn't you hang around with Scott That Died?

Osh, *carrying badminton rackets, and* **Dom**, *carrying a rucksack, approach.*

Osh   Yeah, Scott that was on The Fury, the ride that was advertised somewhat ominously with a Grim Reaper, and something went wrong.

Dom   Why're you guys hangin out at youth club? Come to the park for my birthday.

Jody   It's raining.

Dom   I've got fireworks and booze.

Jody   This place has radiators and snacks!

Osh   Didn't Scott go flying out of the ride and hit the like metal –

Dom   His head nearly came right off.

Osh   That's what happened, though his head was hanging off –

Dom   Like a swingball –

Jody   And that new boy Sean is *just like him.*

Wilson   So?

Jody   No – Sean, the one Karen fancies, had like a heart *transplant*. Don't you get it?

Osh *nibbles at the bowl of face-mask.*

Osh   Haven't you guys heard of cellular memory?

Wilson   I've heard of it – works like homeopathy or some wank.

Dom   It's not wank, actually, my dad did a course in homeopathy

Sweep   Can someone tell me what you lot are on about?

Osh   Cellular memory – when people donate organs, and the person who gets the new organ starts like acting different or remembering things they couldn't know, and like – scientists and stuff think it's cos there are cells that still have the memory of the dead person in them.

Sweep   Still don't get it.

Osh   OhmyGOD, so for example person A is scared of water and then they die and their heart gets transplanted into Mr B who used to be a diver and when he wakes up he is suddenly terrified of water.

Dom   Yeah, I saw it on a documentary, it's true.

Karen   Wait, so everyone thinks Sean is Scott That Died?

They're huddled round now. Maybe lightning flashes, thunder.

Jody   He was in the queue for tuckshop and he's wearing literally the most identical hat to what Scott always wore.

Osh   Scott dies horribly and has his organs donated. Sean receives a heart and it's Scott's. Karen said he says 'mega'.

Jody   I mean WHO says 'mega'?

Osh   That is incontrovertible EVIDENCE.

Wilson   That you're an idiot.

Osh   We should have a seance, contact Scott!

Jody   We can't, we're in a church

Osh   A church *hall*, and it's just youth club, no one would mind.

Sean   Hi.

Alexa *and* **Sean** *have appeared on the corner of the clique. The group jump, gawk up at him.* **Sean** *is wearing the hat.*

The lights flicker.

Osh   WoooooooOO.

Jody   I am so freaked out right now actually.

Alexa   What're you talking about?

Jody   His eyes are kind of dead.

Dom (*mock-medium voice*)   Scoooott are you *iiiin there*? . . . Hey Sean, how are you?

Sean   Um. Mega.

Excitement swells, meaningful looks are exchanged. **Sean** *looks puzzled.*

Dom   Sean, show us the scar.

Alexa   What?

Osh   Yeah

Sweep   He doesn't have the heart!

A groan. **Sean** *looks uneasy.*

Alexa   Guys, don't –

Karen   That's awful

Sweep   We just wanna peep

Wilson   It's obviously just rumours –

Osh   Sean?

Alexa   Seriously? You don't have to, Sean.

Sean *sighs, adjusts his top.*

The scar runs down the middle of his chest. It is very real.

A ripple of guilt.

Osh   Wow –

Dom   Respect –

Jody   That is massive –

Osh   Does it still hurt?

Jody   You'll never be able to model, does that upset you?

Sweep   But it looks hot.

Jody   Scars are super-hot.

Something slips out of his chest and on to the floor. A gasp.

Phones are out, taking photos.

All   WOOoooooOOW / EEeeewwWW / UuurrrggggG

Karen   Oh my God! Is it *beating*?

Osh   Hate when your insides fall out

Dom   Sean. Mate. You dropped something.

Sean   Give me it –

Alexa   Give him it.

Osh *nudges it with his toe.*

Sweep   Cringe. That is SO WEIRD!

Sean *snatches it back off them.*

Dom   Don't take it bad

Sweep   Yeah, Sean, don't take it to heart.

Jody   Tt, so rude, Sweep –

Sweep   I didn't even mean it seriously. Ohmygod it literally slipped out.

Jody   You did it again!

Osh   We were only messin, Sean.

Dom   Yeah, jokes.

Alexa   Urg, you're all rubbish. Why would you do that?

Sean *leaves, followed by* **Alexa**.

Dom   Was that real?

Osh   Come on, he was playing up.

Dom   Attention-seeker or what – whose guts just fall out?

Wilson   It was his heart.

Jody   And why was he wearing that hat then?

Dom   Alexa gave him that hat.

Sweep   Alexa gave Sean the Scott hat?

Wilson   Why would she do that?

Sweep   To stage a drama she could be in the middle of, obviously.

Wilson   I hate Alexa.

Karen   You're just guilty cos you humiliated him.

Jody   Cannot believe Alexa gave him that hat.

Dom   You know she puts on a stutter to sound cute?

Karen   Aren't you scared she'll hear you?

Dom   I dumped her.

Jody   *Why?* Can't believe you broke up with Alexa. Omygod if I don't get a boyfriend soon I am literally going to die.

Wilson   B&B never worked out then?

Dom   Shuddup. How'd you know about the B&B?

Osh   Well, you know where she got all that money from, don't you?

Jody   What, the B&B money?

Osh   Yeah, Dom and Alexa had this blazing row and eventually she just started chucking things and said she got the money off CreepyMartin.

Jody   WHAT?

It hangs in the air.

Karen   What do you mean?

Dom   Jesus, Osh.

They process.

Jody   But no one does it.

Karen   No one actually *does* it. Do they?

Dom *wanders off.*

Sweep   She must've got a lot of money.

Osh   No apparently it was only eighty quid.

Sweep   What?

Wilson   For real?

Stunned silence.

Jody   Is it a joke?

Karen   No.

Jody   For Cokes?

Karen   For money.

Wilson   Really though?

More stunned silence.

Dom   *Come on*, idiots, I'm goin to the park!

Jody   Oh my goodness he's inviting *me*! I'll get Alexa.

Osh   Nah. Don't bother.

They grab their things and follow him.

Scene Six

Later. The park.

Sweep *holds* **Jody** *by the hair.* **Jody** *doesn't do much but hang there.* **Sweep** *occasionally swigs from a litre of cider with her free hand.*

Sweep You're great.

We're not that different.

I mean I just say stuff. To speak in your language, Jodes, I bet even Jesus just said stuff. Didn't he curse that fig tree? I mean it's not even fig season and the idiot curses it cos it doesn't have any figs – surely that's just like me?

Believe it or not, Jodes, I'm a virgin. Just like Mary.

Don't tell anyone. Or I'll break your bloody legs. Cos I mean, Mum had me at seventeen, how stupid does everyone think I am?

I am pretty upstanding, actually. An upstanding human. Me and Dom promised never to tell anyone. But we. Got to third base.

Then he started crying.

Just played the PS3 for a few hours. I'm pretty *conservative*.

You're a good listener. Wrote a poem last Tuesday.

She shakes **Jody** *testily by the hair as the others arrive with drinks.*

Osh I feel sorry for her. No one actually does it with CreepyMartin, that's the like rule. I mean, no one actually *does* it at all, right? She is such an attention-seeker. I heard she did a gangbang.

Dom You do not *do* a gangbang you have one –

Osh Like a party –

Sweep A gangbang party.

Osh I gangbang, you gangbang, he she gingbongs –

Jody *comes around momentarily to contribute.*

Jody SHE HAS GINGBONGS AND SHE MADE SEAN WEAR THE DEAD SCOTT HAT.

And she's gone again. They look from each other to **Jody**'s *inert form.*

Karen Did she know those pineapple ones were alcoholic?

Sweep Oh crap. Let's get her home.

Dom What if her parents answer?

Sweep They'll pray for us, it'll be heartwarming.

Osh We can dump her in the drive.

Sweep They have a caravan up the drive, we can put her in there till she sleeps it off.

Muttering and improvising, they carry her off. **Karen** *hangs back with* **Sean**.

Karen Sean? – Uh – ever been to Nancy's? They do amazing hot chocolates.

I was gonna go. This weekend. If you want – Just cos, they're amazing. Really, um, chocolately. And stuff.

Like crack.

But uh. Chocolatey. Not drugs.

Sean Mega. Uh – super mega. Yeah.

He jogs off.

Karen *does a triumphant fist pump.*

Karen Yeah MEGA! Exactly. Um, bye. Ciao. Hasta la pasta. Till hot chocotime!

She does a triumphant little dance, but –

Wilson You didn't wait for me.

Karen Oh – I forgot.

Wilson We always meet.

Karen I was – busy –

Wilson   Doesn't matter. (*Awkward.*) Hey, listen, I found stuff on the school intranet. Stuff about Alexa, you know when she was off –

Karen   I'm kind of over that –

Wilson   No, it's –

Karen   What're you doing poking around people's records?

Wilson   You asked me to.

Karen   Do you do everything I ask?

Wilson   No. But it said Alexa was –

Karen   God, stop going on about her.

Wilson   What? I'm not –

Karen   You are. I get it you don't like Sean. You only went on there to find crap on him – prove a point.

Wilson   No, it's not – it's Alexa –

Karen   Do you fancy her or something?

Wilson (*taken aback*)   What?

Karen   Wilson, it's not fair. You're holding me back. Don't see why you hate the idea of me and Sean so much. Maybe it's 'cause you want it too – secretly – have everyone think how successful you are, even parents. The way our parents even look at – the ones who always have boyfriends and – I don't understand what's so wrong with wanting people to think I'm lucky or cool – look at *me* like that for once. Why can't I have that and be friends with you too? Why do I have to flipping choose? Don't you want to be *normal*?

Wilson   You're drunk. On one blue WKD.

Karen   Yeah, well, you have a stupid lezzy lez crush on me so –

Wilson   Yeah well. You get on like you know everything but you don't know anything, you don't even know anything even though you think you do, know everything, but you don't / know anything –

Karen I'm SICK of your / mood.

Wilson I'm SICK of your piney piney Seany face. What, do you love him or something?

Karen What would you know about love?

A beat.

Wilson Know what – you've been a bit of a bitch lately.

Karen *I* have?

Wilson Here –

She throws something at **Karen***.*

Wilson I FIXED YOUR STUPID WANGY BINOCULARS

Karen *catches them, and hurls them back with force that surprises both of them.* **Wilson** *shoves* **Karen***, who grabs her.*

And they properly fight.

Wilson *pulls away.* **Karen** *double-takes at her.* **Wilson** *looks down. Touches her chest.*

Sticky. She's –

Karen You're – leaking

Wilson No I'm not.

Karen *looks at her own heart. It is also leaking.*

Wilson Just stay out of my face.

She pushes past.

Karen *picks something up.*

Karen Wilson – you dropped your – heart.

Scene Seven

The street.

Sweep *eyeballing* **Ciaran**. *Some moments.*

Sweep   Okay. Go.

She lets **Ciaran** *touch her boob, just once, one little scrunch. He immediately snatches back his hand as though burnt.*

Ciaran (*husky*)   Thank you.

They are kind of like my mum's but smaller.

This is the best day of my life.

He sticks out a hand, earnest, and she shakes it.

Sweep   You're cute. I'm confused. Maybe I'll wait for you.

Ciaran *darts away, holding back tears.*

Dom   Sweep.

She turns startled, acts casual.

Seen Alexa?

Sweep   Nope. Hasn't been to school in a week.

Dom *scuffs for a second, troubled.*

Dom   Do people know about her mum and everything now?

Sweep   Dunno.

Dom   This is crap. Everyone's being crap.

Sweep   Need a plaster on that. You're leaving a trail.

Dom *rubs at a splodge seeping through his chest.*

Dom   Keeps doing that.

Sweep   Here.

She hands him a tissue. He dabs it.

Dom   Police were round, askin questions. It's really real. Her dad flipped.

Sweep   I was totally co-operative and then they were like 'Do you know what grooming is?' and I was like, get out of my house A-holes. Or that's what I said in my head.

Dom   Is that . . . ?

She hasn't answered the phone all week. She used to tell me everything.

Pause.

Sweep   Thanks for not – telling anyone. About us.

Dom   What?

Sweep   That I didn't want to do the you-know. (*Mimes sex.*) With you.

And I. (*Mimes crying.*)

Dom   Oh, yeah. Course.

Sweep *puts an arm round* **Dom**.

Sweep   You're a much better boyfriend for Alexa. I was a crap girlfriend.

Dom (*gentle*)   You were okay. You were sweet. Especially that time you set my shoes on fire.

Sweep   It was just one shoe.

Osh *and* **Jody** *arrive, dishevelled.* **Jody** *is sniffling.*

Jody   I've just been bawled out by the police and then teachers and then my parents again.

Osh   She is such a fantasist.

Jody   You can't trust her – I woke up in my CARAVAN.

Osh   She rides anything that moves.

Jody   I stayed over at her house once and she sleeps without jammybottoms. No jammybottoms at all.

Sweep   Breezy.

Jody   The police were talking to CreepyMartin, my parents freaked — I had to lie and say he just *gave* us the Cokes. And *then* Wilson starts just like coming apart in blobs – right in the middle of Physics – the teacher does not even blink.

Osh   Yeah, she slips on a bit of Wilson –

Jody   Think it was her lower intestine –

Osh   She just goes like 'Good gracious – er, turn to page 65'.

Alexa *appears. She is leaking. She's a mess.*

She approaches, carrying a big bag of crisps. No one looks directly at her.

Alexa   Guys. Look. I didn't – I didn't mean –

I don't know why this started happening. Guys?

I think I lost a lung around here. Has anyone seen it? What's with the vibe?

Umm. Anyone fancy a maize-based snack?

Osh *eggs her.*

The others fan out around her, encircling her like at the beginning.

Osh   Next she'll be pretending to faint.

Jody   Would you ever wash your hair?!

Sweep   Back off, Jodes –

Alexa   I don't understand why you're being like this!

Sweep   Everyone needs to do a sun salutation or something.

Osh *pelts another egg. A shout goes up.* **Wilson** *is suddenly there. They yell and improvise over each other –*

Wilson   Oi – who threw it?

Osh   Slapper!

Alexa   Dominic?

Jody   JEZABEL. WHORE. SLUT.

Wilson   Back off.

Alexa   Dom, wait –

Wilson   STOP – stop it –

Dom   Guys –

Alexa *drops like a stone.*

They stand there for some moments.

Sweep   Is this her thing now? Should we call someone?

Scene Eight

Sean *and* **Karen**. *A phone between them plays some tinny ballad, adding to the general crapness.*

Karen   This is lovely. Lovely view. Lovely pylons. (*Quieter.*) Not awkward at all.

They kiss. It is unsuccessful. Bumpy. **Karen** *pulls back, disappointed, and sighs.*

Sean   So rude.

Karen   It speaks.

Sean   Like you'd notice.

Karen   Did I miss something?

Sean   Thought you were okay. You pretend to like me – but you didn't do anything when they were being crappy to me at youth club.

Karen   Yeah, well, why'd you pretend to be a dead boy?

Sean   I didn't – just, didn't say I *wasn't*.

Karen   Yeah, well, why'd you say 'mega' all the time?

Sean   I'm nervous okay! I'm a nervous kinda guy. It just kept coming out! Anyway – you're the one using me – kissing my face.

Karen   Yeah, that's tough.

She kisses him.

Sean   You did it again!

Karen   You kissed back!

Sean   Didn't want to be rude!

Karen   Wilson totally had your number. Said you were a dick the moment she saw you.

Sean   Nice. Welcoming. To your stupid town.

Karen   You don't get to say what's nice, you lied about some dead boy. You probably never even . . .

She has stopped herself.

Sean   What? Probably never *what*?

Karen *looks away.*

Sean *unbuttons his shirt.*

He takes **Karen**'s *hand, pushes it inside his chest.*

Sean   On the waiting list for months. Intensive care. Might come as a surprise but I don't really like to talk about it. (*Of his heart.*) They bruised it. It keeps falling out. Only Alexa understood.

Karen   It's warm. It's like a planet. In my hand. I feel everything.

Everything you're feeling. It's. It's too much.

Sean   You just want to be part of Alexa and Dom and all, too. Just want to be in the whatever. Group.

Karen   Sorry.

She withdraws her hand.

Sean   It's okay.

Sometimes I just want to sleep through till I'm eighteen.

Karen *reaches into a stained pocket. Pulls out another heart.*

Sean Collecting them?

Karen Wilson's.

They consider it.

Sean Weird.

Karen Yeah.

Sean Does this happen a lot here?

Karen Don't think so.

Sean Saw a kid carrying her ears around in a Sainsbury's bag, and you think *I'm* the weird one?

Karen Yeah.

Sean I like Wilson. You should give it back to her.

Karen . . .

Sean What?

Karen She hates me now.

Sean Yeah right. No she doesn't. Go and fix it, doughnut brain.

Karen Yeah?

Sean Yeah.

Karen Yeah.

They pull each other up and go.

Scene Nine

Karen *finds* **Wilson** *screwing Pritt Sticks until the gluey bit drops out.*

They have stains around their hearts, and are wounded and bruised. **Wilson** *offers* **Karen** *a stick.*

Karen *gratefully accepts, and plops down next to her. They twist their gluesticks thoughtfully.*

Karen   Maybe it's just a girl crush –

Wilson   I know.

In the movie of your life you're the girl who gets the guy.

Sometimes I am too. Dream of this blokey bloke with a sensible windbreaker and we have a collie-spaniel cross and everything is so easy.

And I wake up and remember – oh, I don't fancy boys. So . . .

Karen   Not you, me. My crush. On you.

Wilson *frowns.*

Wilson   Well. Even if it is just –

Karen   Don't.

Wilson   Well. Let me know when you find the answers.

Karen *takes out her own heart. Squeezes it.*

Karen   Suppose I'll have to follow Clare Balding on social media. I will always hate really gay-looking shoes though, so –

She kisses **Wilson**. *It is short, but certain.* **Karen** *smiles.*

Gives **Wilson** *her heart.* **Wilson** *studies it, their stains.*

Karen *takes out* **Wilson**'*s heart.*

Karen   I've got yours.

They consider their weird little messy hearts.

Is this supposed to happen?

Wilson   Is it normal, do y'think?

Karen   Should we tell someone? I'll Google it. Maybe it's trending.

She starts to search, but her phone beeps.

Kkkkhh, if this is Osh's knob again – Alexa.

Wilson   She's sent loads.

Karen   This one's different . . .

Wilson   Think it's real?

Karen   Don't think it's a joke. How can you tell what's real?

Wilson   Did you know her mum's sick?

Karen   No.

Wilson   Read it in her notes. Remember Alexa was off school – she wasn't in Antigua. She was in hospital. Her mum is like Sean. Maybe that's why they hang out. Cos she understands.

Karen (*of the text*)   She's saying she's at your house.

Wilson   *What?*

Scene Ten

Alexa, *battered and unkempt, drops like a stone. Around her, her bits and pieces tumble across the floor. Her heart. Maybe her stomach. Her lungs.*

Maybe she is inside out. Alone. Aloneness.

Alexa (*to us*)   Weird – I –

Try to clean off – the egg – go to my phone to – No one to call, really.

Go a bit blank.

Send a message, to everyone.

Just says 'Help'.

Next thing, heart just blops out – like flipping lying – on the floor – next to me.

Like, relief.

Jody said – if I went to CreepyMartin, he'd give me money, and Dom wouldn't break up with me then.

Don't, feel much.

Keep doing things — tryin to feel something. Feelin
everything – nothing – everything – it's – and I'm like this
scream in my head but only I hear it –

Wilson *and* **Karen** *burst in.*

Wilson   She putting it on?

Karen   She'll be okay.

Wilson   How can you tell?

Karen   Dad used to do this. Alexa?

Karen *sits* **Alexa** *up.*

Wilson   Alexa – Hey, Alexa, it's us – Wilson. And Karen.

Alexa   Hey.

Wilson *scoops up an organ.*

Wilson   You alright? Want us to call your dad?

Karen   We'll tell him we're just watching TV, eating ice
cream.

Alexa   I didn't, uh, know where to go. (*Self-conscious.*) Your
mum let me in.

Wilson (*joking*)   You've messed up my floor.

Alexa   Sorry!

Karen   No, we're joking.

Alexa   Oh.

Thanks.

Wilson   What for?

Alexa   For – (*Grateful.*) Answering my text.

Wilson   Look, I know about – your mum. Sorry.

Alexa   She's sick.

Wilson   We didn't know.

Alexa   When I went to. Uh, the café. To *him*. I didn't mean to.

Wilson   I know.

Karen   Dom's outside. Sweep brought him. Says he's sorry. I mean, everyone'll calm down. And. It'll be okay, Alexa.

Alexa   It's like – even – like when I was talking to – *him* – and then it was happening . . . kept thinking, it's not real.

None of it's real. I'm outside it.

But then, suddenly, it is.

She takes in **Wilson**.

Wilson   What?

Alexa   Just. You seem so. Sorted

Karen   It's her disguise.

Alexa   What?

Wilson   Just decided it's funnier to find myself funny than, you know, upsetting.

Alexa   I never find myself funny.

Wilson   You aren't.

They sit next to **Alexa**, *battle-spattered, wrecked.*

Karen   You OK?

Alexa   Yeah. (*She eyes* **Wilson** *and* **Karen**'s *battle wounds.*) You guys?

Karen   Yeah.

Wilson   Yeah.

Alexa   Um. Do we have to talk to each other in school? If we see each other in the corridor and stuff?

Wilson   Too much of a good thing –

Alexa   – can kill it, yeah.

Wilson   We can talk to each other in our twenties.

Want to text your dad?

She offers her phone. **Alexa** *takes it and texts as* **Karen** *and* **Wilson** *pop the rest of the bits in a bag.*

Karten   Ew.

Wilson   Ew.

Alexa   Oh, thanks.

Wilson   Think that's all of it.

Alexa   Missed a bit there. And there. And there.

Karen *hands* **Alexa** *the bag.*

Alexa   Oh, thanks.

Wilson   Think that's all of it.

Karen   Can we just watch something till Alexa's dad comes?

Wilson   Yeah, course.

She flips open her laptop as **Dom** *appears, sheepish.*

Dom   Hey.

All   Hey / Hey Dom.

Dom   Brought some. Um. Ice cream. Gone a bit melty.

He joins them all, on the couch maybe, next to **Alexa***, and they gather round the laptop.*

Dom   You okay?

Alexa   Dad's on his way.

Dom   Cool.

A knock from offstage.

Wilson   YEAH, MUM? (*Listens.*)

NO JUST ME AND KAREN. (*Weird.*) AND ALEXA. (*Weirder.*) AND DOM.

All   Hi Mrs Wilsoooonnnn/ Hellooo!

Wilson   Mum says 'Crisps or juice?'

All   NO THANKS! / I'M OKAY THANKS, MRS WILSON / YES PLEEEASE.

Wilson *goes for the ice cream.*

They yawn, one after another. A Mexican yawn. They dab mess off each other.

Karen   Seen this one?

Alexa   Yeah, this one's good.

Dom   Yeah, it's hilarious. I love horror.

Karen   Think it's real?

Alexa   It's a reality show

Dom   But fiction.

Wilson   What?

Alexa   It's real. But it isn't really real.

Karen   I can never tell.

Dom   Doesn't matter, s'pose.

Wilson   Thank God for TV. Nothing happens here.

*A phone rings. They all check if it's theirs. It's **Karen**'s.*

Karen   Hi, Mum . . .

Okay, can you pick me up?

No, nothing really – just ate ice cream, watched TV. Yeah.

Okay, see you soon, love you too.

They watch TV and eat ice cream. They look pretty happy.

I'm Spilling My Heart Out Here

BY STACEY GREGG

*Notes on rehearsal and staging drawn from a workshop
with the writer held at the National Theatre, October 2015*

*From a workshop led by Richard Twyman,
with notes by Rosy Banham*

How Stacey came to write the play

Stacey explained that the gesture of the play is, in part, to
evoke the sense of enormity that is so often attached to
everyday occurrences for teenagers. Passing disagreements
and fleeting fancies can seem monumental; there is a feeling
that everything in a teenager's life is somehow stretched and
heightened beyond its objective reality. This is reflected in the
style of the piece, which careers into an abstracted or magical
place where emotional turbulence is manifested in the literal
spillage of organs onstage. The result is mess: emotional and
physical mess, both of which go some way to communicating
the messy time of life that is adolescence.

For Stacey, it is important that in spite of this mess – or
perhaps because of it – the characters in the play will come
out the other end and, as the end of the text suggests, start
another day. There is a joy and a hope in their collective
capacity to pull through, and there is electricity in the depth
of feeling that they experience along the way.

Approaching the play

Stacey described the play as an invitation to young people to
take ownership and feel liberated by its non-naturalistic form.
She wanted to give them the chance to explore issues around
adolescence in a way that is neither restrictive nor prescriptive.
As a result, there is no onus on directors or companies to 'get
it right' in their approach.

Richard offered participants a series of text-based tasks that
can be carried out either prior to rehearsals or alongside. In

working through these exercises, participants can expect to come to a more detailed knowledge and understanding of the script, while beginning to identify what their personal response and approach might look like.

TITLING SCENES

On a basic level, titling a scene can help a director and their company of actors to get away from the traditional and somewhat clinical numbering of scenes, which offers no clue as to the contents or feel of the material contained therein. Richard offered a selection of titling options, the use of which allowed participants to describe and imagine the scenes of the play in new and unexpected ways.

The group were asked to create titles which:

- Denoted what happens in the scene in the most literal and basic terms (e.g. Scene One: *A teenage group of friends experiment with a technique to reach a natural high which they found on the internet*).

- Described what happens using the metaphor of weather (e.g. Scene One: *High-pressure wind and rain is relentless until we're inside the eye of the storm and then the lightning strikes*).

- Expressed the action as a twitter hashtag (e.g. Scene One: *#youdoitchicken*).

- Viewed the scene through a particular character's eyes (e.g. Scene One: *Karen hesitates in joining in with the group and their excitement*).

These titles can crystallise a focus for the scene or indeed offer a new 'way in' when exploring the text in rehearsals. For example, if you gave a company of young actors the weather-based title listed above for Scene One, they might well begin to understand something more of the *feel* or *atmosphere* you wanted to achieve. Titling scenes can happen in advance of rehearsals or be carried out with your actors – the act of titling can afford the company a sense of ownership over the material, and can also serve as an easy rehearsal room shorthand ('Let's look at #youdoitchicken this afternoon').

IDENTIFYING EVENTS

An event is a major turning point in a scene; a moment when something changes for every single character onstage. Some scenes might contain one clear central event. Others might contain several. In either case, through identifying events, a director can begin to understand the shape of a scene, and subsequently consider how best to present that shape to an audience. Richard suggested that articulating events through our changing stage pictures can be a powerful tool in the move from page to stage, allowing audiences to see psychological shifts play out physically in front of them.

As a group, we discussed what might constitute the central event in Scene One. Several offers were made: the moment that Alexa is pushed; the moment that Alexa faints; the moment of silence following the faint; and the group's decision to take photographs on their phones. We acknowledged that identifying events is a subjective act, and that directors' productions may well vary according to where their chosen events fall in the text. Once selected, however, events should be 'looked after'; they might be moments that directors choose to spend more time staging and honing with actors.

WHO DRIVES?

Identifying which character 'drives' a scene is another helpful tool in preparing for rehearsals. If you had to identify one character who is driving Scene One, who would that be? What is your first instinct after hearing the scene read aloud? Members of the group suggested that either Dom or Jody might be driving this particular scene. We tested our instincts by subsequently reading *only* the lines spoken by those characters:

All of Dom's lines in Scene One:

    Do it
    Now you have to breathe
    Yeah like you're about to dive

Is it sixty seconds?
How long's that?
No she doesn't, right babe?
It's amazing
Being stoned yeah! I heard that
How would you know, titchy balls?
Someone needs to shove her in the chest
Someone shove her or it won't work!
You do it
Who's done it before?
You flippin do it!

All of Jody's lines in Scene One:

Like you're hyperventilating
Ohmygod
Yeah that's how they did it online
No but I heard
It's like when they do blessings at church
It's not fundy
Ohmygod
This is mad
I heard it was like being stoned
Really hard
You have to do it now or it won't work
You do it
Yeah but –

When you hear their contributions to the scene in isolation, what impressions do you get of their roles? On hearing all of Dom's lines, participants were struck by the number of questions he asks ('Is it sixty seconds?', 'No she doesn't, right babe?', etc.). While our instincts suggested that Dom might be the driving force behind the scene, his repeated questioning could nod towards a level of uncertainty, nervousness or passivity that lingers behind his dominant front. We learn from Jody's lines that she would like to seem well researched and clued up on the 'fainting' process; she is keen to appear an authority on the matter at hand. She is excitable ('Ohmygod', 'This is mad') and quick to shut others down ('No but I heard', 'It's not fundy'). She might well be a contender for the scene's driver.

Once you have identified the 'driver', how might you choose to reflect or represent this in performance? For example, you might decide to give status to the 'driver' through their positioning within broader stage pictures; through the ways in which other onstage characters respond to them; through a particular physicality or vocal quality; or through a considered costume choice. As with identification of events, this is not an objective task, and there is no 'right' or 'wrong' answer. Different choices will inevitably result in different emphases and dynamics within the scene, and directors may wish to experiment with different 'drivers' in rehearsals.

FACTS AND QUESTIONS

Richard explained that he tends to compile lists of the facts and questions that are associated with each scene prior to rehearsing with actors. A fact is anything that is unarguably true and a question is anything that we cannot be sure about and must therefore phrase as a question. Facts will help directorial choices – they are the non-negotiables that must be acknowledged and in some way adhered to – while questions will guide directors towards further decisions they will need to make, devising answers through inference or imagination.

Participants drew up lists of facts and questions attached to Scene One of *I'm Spilling My Heart Out Here*:

Facts

  Alexa is taking off her cardigan
  There is a group who are gathered round
  Alexa is not standing still
  Alexa breathes in and out exaggeratedly

Wilson is timing
Wilson has a stopwatch on her phone
Jody has heard about someone who watched a video of
    this process online
Jody has been to church
Sweep is not a member of Jody's church
Dom is Alexa's boyfriend
There is a moment of silence

Questions

Why is Alexa taking off her cardigan?
Where does the scene take place?
How did this particular group come together?
Was this event prearranged or spontaneous?
Why are the group never still?
In what way is Alexa moving?
What is Dom's experience of diving?
Why does Alexa breathe in and out exaggeratedly? Is she
    consciously overdramatising or not?
Has Osh seen the video Jody mentions?
Is Jody religious?
Have any of them ever been stoned before?
Has anyone here carried out this process before?
Who in the group pushes Alexa against the wall?
What sort of wall is Alexa pushed against? Is it indoor/
    outdoor?
Does Alexa genuinely faint or is it an act?
Which two girls roll her over and what do they fan her with?
Who is whooping, buzzing, shouting and giving high fives?
    Are all of them doing it, or just some of them?
How does each character celebrate?

Participants were encouraged to carry out the same list-
making process for each scene, placing the facts and questions
derived from each one opposite the relevant pages in their
script. In rehearsals, they will then be able to see clearly those

facts which can be offered up as concrete notes to actors, and those questions which they might attempt to tackle either with their acting company or through independent decision-making. For example, there are several possible answers to the question 'Why is Alexa taking off her cardigan?' It may be that taking off an outer layer is part of the ritual that they are about to carry out as a group. Or it may be that she feels nervous, hot and flustered by being surrounded and therefore takes off her cardigan. Or she may take it off with a certain performed gravitas to attract the attention and admiration of the group. The options are endless, but being aware of the questions is the first step towards answering them.

Characters and characterisation

CHARACTER LISTS

Choose a character in the play and create two lists of quotations from the text:

* Anything the character says about themselves
* Anything said about the character by other characters

Participants began to compile these lists in small groups. Two examples are listed below.

Things Alexa says about herself:

> No one to call really.
>
> Don't, feel much.
>
> Keep doing things – tryin to feel something. Feelin everything – nothing – everything – it's – and I'm like this scream in my head but only I hear it – can't seem to be scared. Till, well, now.
>
> Kept thinking, it's not real. None of it's real. I'm outside it.
>
> I never find myself funny.

Things other characters say about Alexa:

> Did Alexa really pass out?
>
> It was so cool she did that.

Or did she fake it?

She's hot.

Well, you don't want to look like Alexa, even if that is
what he goes for.

She was just there and I don't know crashed my party.

Flipping Alexa.

Alexa gets in on everything.

Thunder stealer.

Thunder thief.

Did Alexa really pass out?

She's so reckless.

She said her life passed before her eyes.

Yeah she also said she's booking a B&B for Dom's
sixteenth so they can get it on, so . . .

She's cool. She chain smokes.

She's so cool she didn't even care how it looked.

She's amazing. Did you see her faint? That was crazy.

She's got a modelling job till five. Her house is massive.
Like a castle.

Things Wilson says about herself:

And the best I got [from CreepyMartin] was 'Are you a
boy?' and a tap water.

I don't care how I look . . .

Yes. [I always knew that I was gay]

I spent primary school figuring out I wasn't actually a boy.

Wished [I was a boy] so much then I just decided to ignore
the fact I wasn't till I had to deal with it.

In the movie of your life you're the girl who gets the guy.
Sometimes I am too. Dream of this blokey bloke with
a sensible windbreaker and we have a collie-spaniel
cross and everything is so easy. And I wake up and
remember – oh I don't fancy boys.

Just decided it's funnier to find yourself funny that you
know upsetting.

[I don't want to look sexy] if it means 'please put your
man-face on me', no.

Things other characters say about Wilson:

Don't you want to look cute, Wilson? Like. Sexy.

You're so lucky you don't have to worry about looking hot.
Sad you'll probs burn in hell.

Little geek-in-my-pocket.

The tomboy thing is something you grow out of though,
maybe.

Yeah well you have a stupid lezzy lez crush on me so –

You seem so. Sorted.

Reading these lists back, we can begin to build a stronger idea
of who these characters are. There is, for example, a wide
gulf between what Alexa says about herself and what others
say about her. She is seen as attractive, popular and assured,
but she concedes that she often feels something close to
numbness. As a point of comparison, others might view
Wilson as odd, but what she says about herself reveals a
certain level of self-reflection, emotional intelligence and
maturity beyond her years. These lists can help directors
and actors to access various areas of character – from basic
details that surround physical appearance to more complex
psychological depths.

CHARACTER BODY MAPS

Participants were each given a human-sized sheet of paper.
In pairs, participants took it in turns to lie on their sheet of
paper, while their partner drew an outline around their body.
Once the outlines were completed, participants wrote the
name of the character they were interested in exploring at the
top of their paper.

Participants were asked to come up with three words that
capture the essence of their character. For example, Sweep
might be aggressive, arrogant and vulnerable. Richard

stressed that these words can absolutely contain contradictions that exist within the character – humans can be both arrogant and vulnerable, stubborn and uncertain, generous and jealous (most often, the one exists to cover or hide the other). Actors were then asked to write each word on a different part of the body where it most 'lives' or fits. Aggression might therefore be written on the hands (if Sweep's fists are always at the ready to spring into a fight), arrogance might find its place on the chest (a puffed-out chest creates a sense of don't-mess-with-me-bravado), while vulnerability might exist in the stomach (where nervousness ties itself in knots and childlike openness persists). There is no 'right' or 'wrong' in this exercise – it is entirely up to the actor to place the word where it feels most alive and where it sets off the most interesting chains of thought and feeling for them.

Participants were then asked to think about a time when their character was at their happiest. This time doesn't necessarily have to fall within the script – it could be a memory that the actor has created, inspired by what he or she knows about the character. They were told to place this memory on the character's body – either as a short sentence or a picture. The actor playing Wilson might, for example, place a memory of self-acceptance – of a time when she came to celebrate who she was – over her heart.

The same process was carried out again, but this time with a memory of shame. The actor playing Karen might have a shameful memory of experiencing romantic or sexual feelings towards Wilson (prior to the action of the play), which she could place around her genitalia.

Finally, participants were asked to identify what their characters most feared and what their characters most wanted in life, and similarly place both of those discoveries on to the body.

Participants were subsequently asked to walk around the room as the character for whom they had drawn up a body map. Richard gradually introduced elements from the exercise, reminding participants of their character's memories, wants and fears, and asking them to consider how these factors affected their physicality and gait as they moved about the space. A scale of one to ten was adopted as shorthand for the difference between subtle naturalism (1) and heightened buffoonery (10). This exercise can be helpful in getting away from teenage stereotypes and moving towards nuanced, specific physical characterisations. Moreover, in a text which depicts a group of teenage friends, this exercise can be useful in differentiating between characters, providing a distinct energy, rhythm and pace for each actor.

Exercises for use in rehearsals

POINTS OF CONCENTRATION

A point of concentration offers actors something to focus on throughout an exchange or a scene as a whole. It can serve as a useful tool in preventing young people from 'switching off' when they don't have lines. The group experimented with different points of concentration for the characters in Scene One. First, actors were asked to play the scene 'cold' – without a point of concentration. Then they were asked to run the scene again, focusing this time on the idea that the teacher might walk through the door at any moment. The group subsequently suggested alternative points of concentration: a desire to impress another member of the group; a desire to 'top' the character who had the line before; a fixation on Wilson's stopwatch; a hyperawareness of location (e.g. the school library or, conversely, the school's playing fields). Each of these points of concentration will inevitably offer the scene a different tone and quality. Ultimately, directors should aim to give each character in the scene a different point of concentration to produce a varied scene picture and a focused company of actors.

STATUS LADDER

Ten sheets of A4 paper numbered 1 to 10 were laid out in a line across the space. Actors were asked to position themselves along the 'status ladder' according to where they felt their character began Scene Five, with 1 representing the vulnerability, self-consciousness or insecurity associated with very low status, while 10 represented the confidence, superiority or arrogance associated with very high status. Actors were told they could move up and down the status ladder as the scene played out, according to whether they felt their status was rising or falling in relation to the other characters.

The exercise revealed those moments when a group of characters were vying for the 'top spot' in a status battle (for example, when Osh, Wilson and Dom discuss cellular memory, each wanting to prove their superior knowledge to the others, those characters all placed themselves around the 9 or 10 mark in the ladder). It was also interesting to note that the actor playing Karen descended to rung 1 at the moment that Osh and Dom entered the scene, and subsequently stayed silent for some time.

Richard suggested that identifying the pecking order of characters in this way can give you important clues as to how to create the physical life of the scene in performance. Do you want to highlight the vulnerability of a certain character by isolating them from the group onstage? Do you want to suggest the power of another character by placing the rest of the group around them? The exercise can also help young actors who are prone to physical aimlessness – to 'wandering' in the space when unsure of what to do. Status shifts can guide actors as to when they might have justification to move in accordance with their feelings of power and control (or lack thereof).

ATTRACTION AND REPULSION

A circle of chairs was arranged in the centre of the space, with at least double the number of chairs as there were participants in the exercise. Actors were asked to occupy chairs in the circle and very simply play Scene Five, moving between chairs according to which characters they felt attracted to or repelled from at any given point. After an initial run of the scene in the circle, Richard encouraged participants to make bolder choices about who they wanted to be near and who they wanted to be far from.

As characters moved around the chairs in the circle during the second scene run, the formation and dispersal of cliques within the scene became more obvious, as spectating participants watched teenage allegiances form through physical proximity and enmities develop through physical distance across the circle. Karen and Jody, for example, temporarily sat beside one another as they reflected not altogether kindly on Wilson's response to the face cream. When Sean entered, a group gathered across the circle from him, coming together to grill and analyse him.

THE SPILLING OF GUTS

One of the key challenges in staging *I'm Spilling My Heart Out Here* comes in the form of stage directions like this:

> **Alexa**, *battered and unkempt, drops like a stone. Around her, her bits and pieces tumble across the floor. Her heart. Maybe her stomach. Her lungs. Maybe she is inside out.*

Richard asked participants to stage this moment in small groups, according to several different sets of rules. First participants were asked to stage it as literally as they could. Next, they were asked to create a version that involved every single person onstage. Then, they were encouraged to approach the stage direction using only sound; then, using only one prop that is recycled or in some way changed throughout the course of the action; then, using the entirety of the rehearsal room.

Rules or limitations can often free up the imagination, as paradoxical as that might first appear. In responding to the tasks set, participants experimented with using people as organs, with using fabric as malleable and changing body parts, with using squelching sounds and graphic mime.

Staging fights

Professional fight director Brett Yount worked with the group in developing a range of options for staging the moment that Alexa is pushed and passes out, as well as the fight between Karen and Wilson.

Before engaging in practical work, however, Brett stressed that the style of your fights and stage violence must match up with the broader style you have adopted across the production as a whole. If, for example, your performances are heightened, then you may well want moments of violence to play into that same exaggerated or stylised approach. If, however, your production is entirely naturalistic, you would probably choose to adopt naturalism when staging fights. Of course, you could deliberately decide to swing between presentational styles – just make sure that this is a conscious choice and one that you can justify.

Brett explained that a non-contact strike is made up of five elements: an action which is clearly seen; a reaction of appropriate size and direction; a sound (most often created by a 'knap', a sound created by an actor that mimics the sound of a blow); accomplished timing (the action, reaction and sound need to happen at the same time); and the illusion of contact (which is often dictated by performers' positioning onstage).

Participants were encouraged to keep fights as short as possible. The more you give performers to do the less likely they are to get all of it right, and the more likely the audience are to 'see through' tricks or become desensitised to the violence in front of them. Brett also recommended getting the set designer involved in conversations around onstage violence at the earliest possible opportunity, because the set may well need to facilitate a safe stage fight. For example, if you need part of the set to be solid and stable so that it can be used – for example, the wall in Scene One that Alexa is pushed up against – then this needs to be communicated at the earliest stage to your set designer.

In staging the moment that Alexa is pushed, Brett demonstrated how the actor playing Alexa should, despite appearances to an audience, retain a level of control. She could put her leg against a wall before she 'hits' it to guide her as to how near she is. In staging the fight between Wilson and Karen, ensure that you find safe ways of showing the pulling of hair, scratching and slapping. If at any point an actor is not comfortable, they should find an alternative way through the fight.

Style

Stacey encouraged participants to set up a clear 'world' at the beginning of their productions and make sure that this world remains consistent throughout. She asked participants to consider how they might set up a style at the start of the play that justifies or enables the subsequent abstraction and spillage of organs. The danger is that these elements might jar with what has come before, arriving, as they do, halfway into the play. Stacey validated mess, colour and freedom in the staging of the piece, reiterating her belief that the play invites young people to invent beyond the known, tried-and-tested realms of naturalism.

Language

Stacey affirmed that the language is intentionally heightened. It is not based on an existing dialect; rather, it is Stacey's own brand of made-up slang specific to the particular group of characters that she has created. Stacey encouraged directors to explore this language with their casts and to search for ways to help young people to own it and enjoy it. If there is a word here or there that an actor is finding problematic – difficult to get their mouth around, or to understand – then Stacey would advocate the odd change to the text, but for the most part she would suggest that companies try to find ways of justifying and relishing the peculiarity of the language in the play.

Casting

Stacey suggested that divvying up lines to create additional
characters in the group of friends might dilute or confuse the
dynamics written into the text. Similarly, reassigning genders
to characters might also detract from the female-led nature of
the piece. However, there are various ways in which additional
actors could be used to support the action of the play. What
might a chorus look like and how might it function? Could
a large company create movement sequences in scene
transitions to reflect and communicate the play's central
preoccupations – e.g. adolescent relationships, sexual identity,
slavery to technology?

Suggested reference

Stacey referred to the films of John Hughes, which she
watched as a child, and which influenced the writing of the
play.

Gargantua
by Carl Grose

When Mr and Mrs Mungus have a baby it isn't the bouncing blue-eyed boy they were hoping for. After a two-and-a-half-year pregnancy, Mini Mungus gives birth to a monster – one with an accelerated growth rate and an insatiable appetite for anything that moves (including joggers). But when sinister military scientists become intent on cloning an army of giant babies from the giant, he breaks his chains and escapes. The world can only watch in horror as he embarks on learning how to walk and rampant destruction. Who will stop this freak of nature? Who will decide his tragic fate? And who, more importantly, will change his nappy?

Age suitability: any age

Cast size
many named characters,
plus ensemble, plus songs

Carl Grose's plays include *Grand Guignol*, *Superstition Mountain*, *49 Donkeys Hanged*, *The 13 Midnight Challenges of Angelus Diablo*, *Gargantua* and *Horse Piss for Blood*. For the past twenty years he has worked with the internationally acclaimed Kneehigh Theatre as both actor and writer. Writing for Kneehigh includes *Tristan and Yseult*, *The Bacchae*, *Blast!*, *Cymbeline*, *Hansel and Gretel*, *The Wild Bride* and, most recently, *Dead Dog in a Suitcase* (and other love songs) – a new version of *The Beggar's Opera*. Grose has also written for Spymonkey, the National Theatre of Wales, Told by an Idiot, and BBC TV and radio. He is currently writing new plays for the RSC, the National Theatre, and the Drum Theatre, Plymouth.

Characters

Gargantua, *aka Hugh Mungus*
Mini Mungus, *his mum*
Marcus Mungus, *his dad*

Prime Minister, *Dave*
Pippa Wellard, *Deputy Prime Minister*
Jeff Creams, *Treasury*
Robin Wilt, *Junior Minister*
General Rex Malahyde, *an American Army General*
Professor Julian Swan, *Head of Janus Technologies*

Sally Butters, *a TV news reporter*
Arnie, *her cameraman*

Regina Buxley, *local businesswoman*
Lionel Buxley, *her husband*

Dr Lucky
Nurse 1
Nurse 2

Gazette, *local reporter*
Morning News, *local reporter*
The Bugle, *local reporter*

Agent Allbright
Agent Starkhammer
Agent Blackstone

The Voice of the Door

People of Skankton Marsh
**The Three Good Women
    of Skankton**
Sandy, *the hairdresser*
Skankton Girl

Skankton Boy
Constable Yapp
Preacher Pike
Headmistress Gunning
Brian Uber, *record producer*
Grannies Wintz, Curdle
    and **Hawkhumph**

Chorus
Citizens
Midwives
Hardhats
Soldiers
Nappy-Wearing Zealots

And featuring
The Dummysuckers,
    a rock band

Darkness.

In the distance, an ominous sound:

Boom . . .

Smoke hangs thick. Civilians slowly pick themselves up from the rubble.

The sound, closer, more frequent now:

Boom . . .

TV news reporter **Sally Butters** *appears from the shadows.*

Sally   Hear that?

Boom.

Sally   Arnie? We keep filming. No matter what happens, we stand our ground and we keep filming. We'll cover this story to the end. Or my name isn't Sally Butters, TV news personality of the year. 2010. How's the hair?

Arnie, *her cameraman, gives her a thumbs-up.*

Sally (*to camera*)   As you can see from the devastation around me, the monster tore through this street only moments ago . . . People nearby pick themselves up from the rubble, shell-shocked, unsure of what has just hit them.

Boom.

We understand that the military will engage the creature and bring it down at all costs but so far we've seen nothing –

BOOM.

That was close.

BOOM!

He's coming back.

BOOM!!

Arnie, he's coming back!

Everything moves in slow motion. Jaws drop in utter disbelief.

BOOM!!!

Bodies shake –

BOOM!!!!

With the intensifying –

BOOOM!!!!!

Vibrations.

Necks craning, they all look up and point at the sight before them.

Sally   He's here!

Everyone   Run!

The crowd scatter in all directions to reveal a two-hundred-foot giant baby.

This is **Gargantua** *(aka Hugh Mungus).*

He brings his foot down hard with an earth-shattering –

BOOOOOOOOOOMMMMMMM!!!!!!!

Gargantua *(a monstrous echoing roar)*   Gaaaa-gaaaa-goooo-gooooo!

Tiny Sally   Keep filming, Arnie! Keep film—

Gargantua *crushes her underfoot like a grape.*

Tiny Arnie   SALLY!

Gargantua   Haaaaa-haaaaa-haaaaaa!

A band, **The Dummysuckers***, rock out:*

Singer
  Gargantua! Gargantua!
  You can try and outrun him but you won't get far!
  There's nothin' but to bow before his giant might
  Cus man, this baby knows just how to win a fight!
  Gargantua! Gargantua!

Army General *(through megaphone)*   Open fire! Open fire!

Machine guns and heavy artillery let rip.

Singer
> Armour-piercing bullets land like flakes of snow!
> Those laser-guided missiles dunno where to go!
> So this is how it ends? Well it just might be!
> Armageddon all thanks to a big baby!
> Gargantua! Gargantua!
> You can try and outrun him but you won't get far!

Twisting metal, explosions, buildings collapsing.

The **Chorus** *run for their lives, scattering in all directions.*

Singer
> And what of those who lead us? Well, they've all jumped
>   ship!
> So much for politicians shooting from the hip!
> We're left holdin' the baby – the baby from hell!
> Will mankind survive? Guess only time will tell!
> Gargantua! Gargantua!
> Gaa! Gaa! Gaa! Gaa! Goo! Goo! Goo!
> Gargantua!

Gargantua, *in glorious slow motion, towering amidst smoke and fire, cries out a gurgling howl of triumph.*

Suddenly, everything stops.

Plummy English Voice   Prime Minister? Prime Minister, are you alright?

Wellard   Prime Minister!

The **Prime Minister** *sits bolt upright.*

Prime Minister   Who's cooking onions?!

We're in an ante-chamber under 10 Downing Street.

At the back is a large metal door. To the side of it, a numbered control panel in the classic style.

Standing over the **Prime Minister** *are members of his cabinet –* **Jeff Creams** (*Treasury*), **Pippa Wellard** (*Deputy Prime Minister*) *and* **Robin Wilt** (*Junior Minister*). *There is also*

General Rex Malahyde (*of Texas*) *and* **Professor Julian Swan** (*of Janus Technologies*).

They all look concerned.

Wilt   He's alive!

Creams   Well, that's something.

Malahyde   What's all this 'onions' talk?

Wellard   I have no idea.

Prime Minister   Where am I?

Wilt   You took a knock, sir. Gently does it.

Prime Minister (*to* **Wilt**)   Doris? Is that you?

Wilt   It's Wilt, sir? Junior Minister. But I can be Doris if you want me to be . . . ?

Wellard   Wilt? Concentrate.

Creams   We need the entry code, sir. And we need it now.

Prime Minister   Yes . . . of course . . . but . . . *Who's* cooking onions?

Malahyde   No one's cookin' onions! Goddammit! What the hell is he talking about? Swan? You're a man of science. Enlighten us!

Swan (*steps forward*)   I believe the Prime Minister has suffered what is commonly known as . . . a mind melt.

Everyone   A mind melt?

Wilt   Think I had one of those in the canteen earlier.

Swan   The undue stress he's been under these past seven days has finally taken its toll. That, and *concussion*.

They all look to **Wellard**, *who blows on her knuckles.*

Creams   But only *he* knows the entry code to get us through that door and safely underground before the nuclear missiles launch in –

Everyone (*they all look at their watches*)   Twenty-nine minutes!

Wellard   Yes. But he also has the power to call the launch off!

Swan   Let's not start this all over again.

Wellard   He should never have authorised a nuclear strike!

Malahyde   But he did.

Wellard   Only because you made him, Malahyde!

Wilt   He's the Prime Minister. He has a mind of his own.

Swan   Except when it's melted.

Malahyde   He had no choice but to retaliate what with that nappy-wearing fiend runnin' around up there!

Creams   The countdown's begun, Pippa. It can't be stopped.

Wellard   It can be stopped, Jeff. All he has to do is make the call. (*She has a mobile.*) And we don't have to obliterate the whole damn country to stop Gargantua! Prime Minister? I beg you. Make the call.

*The **Prime Minister** looks at **Wellard**.*

Creams   Prime Minister? You must remember the entry code!

*The **Prime Minister** looks at **Creams**. He then blows a raspberry and slaps his hands together like a seal.*

Swan   The Prime Minister has gone bye-byes.

Prime Minister (*to **Wilt***)   It's so lovely to see you again, Doris.

Creams   It's finally happened. Loco in the coconut.

Wellard   Can't we bring him round? Snap him out of it? Jog his memory?

Malahyde   I'll jog his goddamn memory –

Malahyde *hauls the* **Prime Minister** *to his feet and goes to slap him.*

Swan   Not that way, General Malahyde. His brain is in a state of flux. We must coerce his neural pathways back into operation *gently*.

Creams   How?

Swan   Remind him. Remind him of the past seven days, in as much detail as you can stand.

Creams   And then he'll remember the entry code?

Wellard   And then he'll stop the missile launch?

Wilt   And then he'll stop calling me Doris?

Swan   We can only hope.

Wellard   Prime Minister? Listen very carefully. We're going to tell you about what happened over these seven days . . .

Prime Minister   Why? What's happened? Anything I should know about?

They all look to each other. None of them quite knows how to start. They take a deep breath and –

We crash back in time – seven days earlier.

Sally *and* **Arnie**, *seven days before we saw them last, are filming.*

Sally (*to camera*)   I'm here in the quiet village of Skankton Marsh. 'Where?' you might ask. Well, you'll be hard pressed to find it on any map, that's for sure. But today, all that is about to change. Because today sees the grand opening of the town's formidable new mega-mall, a vast construction more than two years in the making. And the visionary behind this monster is local businesswoman and mayonnaise magnate, Regina Buxley –

Enter **Regina Buxley** *before a crowd of Skankton Marshians.*

Regina   Hello, good people of Skankton Marsh! That's right. You know me. Reg Buxley. Go on. Take a look at that mega-mall! Massive in't it? It's the biggest in the world by three cubic centimetres! Eat that, America! Any questions? Yes, the *Skankton Evening Gazette*?

Gazette   Mrs Buxley, critics of the mega-mall say you've ruined an area of outstanding natural beauty?

Regina   You're telling me this palace of glass and steel in't as impressive as some rare breed of duck? Ruined it? Improved it, more like! Next question. Yes, Peter.

Morning News   Hello, Reg. Got to ask. Does Skankton Marsh really need a forty-nine-screen cinema complex given that there are only forty-eight people living in the village?

Regina   Everybody gets a screen, Peter – you can't say fairer than that! Next?

Bugle   The *Skankton Bugle*. Mrs Buxley, where will the customers park?

Regina   Have you not seen? There's a multi-storey out back so big it'll make you want to puke! Listen up. Regina Buxley does not do things by halves. This masterpiece behind me took vision. And time. And craploads of money. But 'ere it is. Done. Dusted. And dropped right on your bloody doorstep.

A frail man with a neck brace and crutches stands beside her – **Lionel**.

Regina   Now, before I ask my beloved husband Lionel here to cut the ribbon, I just want to say . . . those of you that fight your way to the front get a free jar of my delicious Buxley's Traditional Homemade Mayonnaise. One free jar on first dibs – and that's just a taster of the great things to come. So get in, spend your money and enjoy yourselves! This is my legacy to you. Scissors at the ready, Lionel. And so, without further ado, I now declare the Skankton Marsh Mega –

From the crowd, someone groans.

Nutter in the crowd. They'll be pleased to know the mall's got
its own insane asylum. Oh, I've thought of everythin', me.
Scissors, Lionel.

Lionel *does his damnedest to ready the scissors and balance on his
crutches.*

Regina   I now declare this mega –

Another groan. The crowd parts to reveal **Marcus** *and* **Mini
Mungus**, *a young couple very much in love.* **Mini** *is twenty-two
months pregnant, and massive. She groans again and starts puffing.*

Regina   Could you keep it down, love? I'm trying to open a
mega-mall 'ere.

Marcus   Mini? Are you alright?

Mini   No, Marcus. I'm not. It's the baby . . .

Marcus   Eh?

Mini   I think . . . I think . . . I think it's on its way!

Sally (*smelling a story*)   Arnie? Shoot.

Arnie *films* **Mini**.

Mini   My waters are about to break . . . it's coming . . . it's
coming . . . look out, love!

The Dummysuckers *kick off as* **Mini**'s *waters break* –

Singer
All of a sudden there's a tidal wave!
Tell the lifeguard there's many lives to save!
All of a sudden now the waters rise!
This shock tsunami took us by surprise!

Mini *blasts the bystanders with a high-pressure force. The people of
Skankton float underwater.*

Singer
Someone call Noah, say we need his ark!
This amniotic fluid gush is quite a lark!

This girl's birth water is unstoppable!
Somebody get her to a hospital!

Mini *spins in on a gurney puffing and panting, her enormous belly bulging and rippling.* **Marcus** *holds her hand.*

Nurse One   How are the contractions?

Nurse Two   Like earthquakes!

Mini   Oooooooooohhhhh, here comes another!

Everything shakes and rattles.

Nurses One *and* **Two**   Dr Lucky?

Dr Lucky *bursts through a pair of swing doors. He hands his glass of Scotch to* **Nurse One** *and his bag of golf clubs to* **Nurse Two**.

Dr Lucky   Yowza! Is that for real?

Nurse One   Patient's name is Mini Mungus.

Nurse Two   Patient is very very very very pregnant.

Dr Lucky   How overdue is she?

Nurse One *and* **Two**   Two years?

Dr Lucky   Two years?! Leaping lizards! That's a world record for longest pregnancy of all time! Gown me.

The two **Nurses** *dress him in green surgeon gown, mask and cap, rubber gloves.*

Dr Lucky   Is the husband/partner/lover/donor here?

Nurse One   Right there.

Dr Lucky   Where?

Nurse Two   He's the one holding her hand, Doctor.

Dr Lucky   *That's* the father? He looks like a kitchen utensil. What's your name, son?

Marcus   Marcus. Marcus Mungus.

Dr Lucky   Well, Marcus Marcus Mungus, today you and your wife are in luck. Because I'm Dr Lucky.

Marcus   That puts my mind at ease.

Dr Lucky   Ultimately, it's just a name. It doesn't give me superpowers, son. But it does give me edge, and sometimes that edge is all the difference you need.

Marcus   Will she be alright, Doctor?

Dr Lucky   Do you love her, boy?

Marcus   More than anything!

Dr Lucky   Then why the hell didn't you bring her in after nine months? How could you let it get so big?

Marcus   She just . . . held it in.

Dr Lucky   She doesn't want the child?

Marcus   Oh, she does! She's just not keen on giving birth is all.

Dr Lucky   She's going to want her pelvic floor back at some point. Stay here, Marcus. And don't touch my golf clubs. (*Returns to* **Mini**.) Nurse. Close the door. Let's give this woman some dignity. She's about to give birth, for God's sakes! Now then, Mini, let's get this baby out, shall we?

He roughly hoiks her legs up in the air.

Mini   I don't want to give birth, Doctor.

Dr Lucky   Why ever not? It's the most natural thing on earth! Nurse, give her lots of drugs!

Nurse Two *jabs* **Mini** *with a large syringe.*

Mini   No, I . . . Ooooooooo . . .

Dr Lucky   Better, eh? What you're feeling is drugs. Delicious, pain-killing *drugs*. Forceps!

Nurse One *hands him forceps.*

Mini   Mmmmmmmmmm . . . (*Starts singing a song.*)

Dr Lucky   Now let's have a looky see. My, he is a big one.
(*To* **Nurses**.) Hit her again. This is going to hurt.

Nurse Two *jabs her again.*

Mini   Ooooo, yes! That's lovely! More . . . more . . .

Dr Lucky   Plunger!

Marcus   Plunger?

Nurse One *hands* **Dr Lucky** *a plunger.*

Nurse One   Oh my God! Is that its *head*? That's its *head*!

Marcus *stares at her in horror.*

Dr Lucky   Damn. Too bloody big! Can't squeeze the skull
through the pelvis. I didn't want to do this but . . . I'm going
in!

Nurse One *and* **Two**   You're going *in*?!

Marcus   He's going 'in'?!

Dr Lucky   It's what's commonly known as the Heineken
Manoeuvre or the Kronenberg Technique. One of the two.
I forget which. I'll see if I can't push the thing out from the
back. Wish me luck, ladies. I may be some time.

He climbs head-first up into **Mini**.

Mini   What's going on . . . ?

Nurse One   Relax, Mrs Mungus. Doctor's just performing
an impossibly dangerous birthing technique on you. Nothing
to worry about.

Mini (*stoned*)   Okay . . .

Nurse One   Look! It's coming!

Nurse   He's doing it! He's doing it!

An arm suddenly bursts out from **Mini**'s *groin.*

Nurse One   Shit a brick!

Nurse Two (*to* **Marcus**)   We're gonna need a hand here, dude.

Nurse One   Push, Mrs Mungus! Push!

Nurse Two   Pull, Mr Mungus! Pull!

Mini *wails.*

Nurse One   What a day to be understaffed!

Nurse Two   We're understaffed every day!

Nurse Two (*at the top of her lungs*)   Auxiliaries!

Midwives   Push . . . (pull).
Push . . . (pull).
Push . . . (pull).

Singer
  Now comes the seminal moment in our story
  When he is born unto us in all his glory
  The prodigal son turns to greet the dawn
  Gargantua, the monstrous one . . .

Mini *screams. So does* **Marcus**.

Suddenly, POP!

Singer
  . . . is born!

Revealed in **Mini***'s arms is a huge, man-sized baby.*

Midwives   Sweet merciful God!

Nurse One   It's . . .

Nurse Two   It's . . .

Mini   A little baby boy!

Midwives   Little? He's fudging *enormous*!

Mini   I'm going to call him Hugh. Hugh Mungus.

Marcus   Well done, love. You did it.

Mini   *We* did it. (*Thinks, then.*) No. Actually, you're right.
I did it.

Nurse One   Shall I cut the umbilical cord?

She holds aloft a large pair of rusty shears.

Nurse Two   Before you do, could we have Dr Lucky back?

Mini   Yes, of course. Why? Where is he?

Dr Lucky (*emerging from* **Mini**)   Good work, everyone! It
seems the delivery was a complete success!

He's handed back his Scotch and downs it. **Marcus** *faints.*

Three Good Women of Skankton *sit and have their hair done
by* **Sandy**, *who hovers and sculpts.*

Good Woman One   Is he as big as they say?

Good Woman Two   Bigger!

Good Woman Three   How did he get so big?

Good Woman One   Who knows? It's Nature's way!

Good Woman Two   What happens when he grows?

Good Woman Three   The cost of new clothes, they ain't
cheap!

Good Woman One   Mini Mungus – mother of a modern
miracle!

Good Woman Two   Or a monstrous abomination.

Good Woman Three   Either way, it beats traipsing round
that mega-mall all day.

Regina *staggers in, distraught.* **Lionel** *hobbles beside her.*

Regina   I shan't forget this, Lionel. The day my dream was
eclipsed by a bloody great baby. I shan't forget, and I shan't
forgive. But in the meantime . . . I think I just want to go
home.

She opens a jar of mayonnaise and spoons a wodge into her mouth.

Sally (*to camera*)   So it seems Skankton Marsh has had a busy day. A day where the world's biggest mall was overshadowed by the world's biggest baby.

Arnie *gives the thumbs-up, lowers the camera.*

Sally   Arnie. We shouldn't leave. I smell Nobel Peace Prize for Journalism all over this sucker! Let's go see what the word on the street is.

Arnie *throws his camera on to a series of pacey vox pops:*

Skankton Girl   I just love little Hugh. I just want to wear nappies and hang out.

Then on to:

Skankton Boy   My girlfriend told me I was a big baby – I took it as a compliment, you know?

And so forth:

Constable Yapp   I saw them leave the hospital. Lashed him to the back of Wilf Canker's pick-up truck. It was quite something!

Sandy the Hairdresser   He's cute. Huge. But cute.

Preacher Pike   When something like this happens it happens for a reason . . .

Headmistress Gunning   I look forward to welcoming the boy to Skankton Primary. But he better mind his head. We have low ceilings.

Grannie Wintz   I'd give anything to nibble on his pudgy leg.

Grannie Curdle   It's the flesh, you see? Old women love baby flesh.

Grannie Hawkhumph   Well, there's certainly enough flesh to go round on this one.

Grannies (*imagining nibbling*)   Mmmmm . . .

Preacher Pike   There are lots of visitors pouring in from all over. I suppose Skankton Marsh is like Bethlehem, isn't it? But without the camels.

Brian Uber (*record producer*)   It's refreshing to see an icon who's created such a stir who isn't connected to the music industry, yeah? Who isn't a movie star, yeah? Or some overpaid sports personality, who is just pure individuality. Yeah?

Sally   Might we hear a hit single from the Giant Baby some time soon?

Brian Uber   We've got him gurgling in the studio on Monday. It's gonna be *big*.

Preacher Pike   I might be speaking too soon but . . . this Gargantua could be the new messiah!

Swan   The specimen's physiology is fascinating. He seems possessed of an accelerated growth rate quite unlike anything I've ever seen. Hello, I'm Professor Julian Swan, head of Janus Technologies –

Malahyde   This *enfant terrible* is a walking ten-man army. If he *could* walk, that is. Right now, I believe he's just at the crawlin' stage. When the world goes to hell, I want this drooling Gargantua on our side!

Sally   Prime Minister, one last thing. What's your view on Hugh Mungus?

Prime Minister   He'd get my vote, Sally!

The **Prime Minister** *winks.*

Sally   So there we have it. Even the Prime Minister has gone gaa-gaa for Gargantua.

Mini *shoos the final stragglers out of the garden.*

Mini   Alright! That's enough! Show's over! Come back tomorrer! Visiting hours two till four. It's his feeding time now. Thank you. Bye, bye!

Gargantua *sits there like Buddha, now the size of a house.* **Marcus** *is up a ladder feeding the ravenous* **Gargantua** *with a bucket.*

Marcus   Open wide, Hugh! Here comes a choo-choo train! Come on. Open up! Nice, look, mmmmm. Daddy likes it! Lovely cabbage purée!

Gargantua *opens his mouth.* **Marcus** *pours the bucket down his throat.*

Marcus   Good boy! More?

Gargantua (*flapping his arms excitedly*)   Maaaaahhhhhhh!!

Marcus *climbs down the ladder and fetches another bucket.*

Mini (*fondling a pair of woollen booties*)   It's a shame nothing I knitted him fits.

Marcus   He's a growing lad, aren't ya, Hugh?

Mini   You can say that again. Gor, he puts it away, doesn't he?

Marcus   He's like his mother in that respect.

Mini   Cheeky.

Marcus   Sling us another bucket, love.

Mini   There are no more.

Marcus   Check the cement mixer. I made up a fifty-cabbage batch.

Mini   It's empty, Marcus. He's had it all.

Marcus   And he's drunk the milk lorry dry!

Gargantua   Waaaaaaaaaaahhhhhhhhhh!!!!

The sound is deafening.

Mini   There, there, Hugh. Come on, you've had your fill for today.

She climbs up the ladder and sings:

> Hush little baby don't say a word
> Mummy's gonna buy you a mockingbird . . .

Gargantua *instantly falls asleep.*

Mini   Look at our boy, Marcus . . .

Mini *and* **Marcus** *look at their boy, look to each other, smile, then collapse with exhaustion.*

Meanwhile, in a secret laboratory . . .

Swan   General Malahyde. Welcome to Janus Industries.

Malahyde   I appreciate the invite. Always wondered what you boys got up to down here, Swan.

Swan   Can you guess why I asked you here to my . . . secret underground laboratory?

Malahyde   Would a freakishly oversized baby have anything to do with it?

Swan (*smiles*)   Do you remember what we once discovered about each other that time on the shores of Lake Geneva?

Malahyde   Indeed I do. That we both have tattoos in unusual places.

Swan   No, no, the *other* thing we discovered about each other.

Malahyde   That we share a common ambition?

Swan   Bingo.

Malahyde   We knew that with our combined talents, we could control the world if we wanted.

Swan   Precisely. My brains. Your brawn. And our place in history sealed for ever.

Malahyde   It was an impossible dream, Professor!

Swan   Not so impossible now, my friend.

Malahyde   The baby?

Swan   Yes, General. The baby.

Malahyde   Okay, So. Whadda ya need from me?

*Back to the **Munguses'** house.*

*From nowhere, three **Sinister Agents** appear. They wear shades and black suits. They are **Agents Allbright**, **Starkhammer** and **Blackstone**.*

Agents   Mr and Mrs Mungus?

Marcus *and* **Mini** *(waking up)*   Yes?

Allbright   May we have a moment of your time?

Mini   Marcus, I've just got him off. Tell 'em to go away.

Marcus   Listen, lads, it's been a long day and we –

Allbright   Oh, we're not salesman.

They all flash their badges.

Blackstone   Agent Blackstone.

Starkhammer   Agent Starkhammer.

Allbright   Agent Allbright.

Starkhammer   Please. This really won't take a second.

Blackstone   We'll jump straight to the point.

Allbright   The thing is, Mr and Mrs Mungus, the world is hanging by a thread.

Starkhammer   If the thread snaps, somebody needs to catch it.

Blackstone   And that somebody is your boy.

Mini   Who are you people?

Marcus   It's obvious, love. They're from the government.

Allbright   Ha.

Starkhammer   Ha.

Blackstone   Haa.

Allbright   Not the government, Mr Mungus.

Starkhammer   A higher power than that.

Blackstone   Who we work for is classified information.

Allbright   That's right. We're so top secret, even *we* don't know we're here.

Starkhammer   The fact that we're even talking to you is . . . (*Thinks.*) Wait. Even we don't know we're here?

Blackstone (*getting confused*)   It . . . I what know he means but . . . we're here because Janus Technologies –

Starkhammer   Shh! Don't say the name of the top secret organisation that we aren't supposed to work for, you spoon!

Blackstone (*to the* **Munguses**)   Forget you heard that. Wipe it. (*Clicks his fingers like Derren Brown.*) Wiped. Waitrose! We work for . . . Waitrose!

Marcus   You're . . . Ocado Men?

Blackstone   No! Look, let's just cut to the chase –

Agents   We need your baby.

Mini   What? Hang on a minute -

The **Agents** *all hear something in their earpieces and vanish as –*

Regina *enters with* **Lionel**, *on crutches. They stand before the* **Munguses**.

Regina   How do. You know me. Regina Buxley. Mega-mall *constructeur extraordinaire*!

Mini   We certainly do, Mrs Buxley.

Marcus   We buy your mayonnaise.

Mini   When we can afford it.

Regina   This frail piece of work is my husband, Lionel.
Don't shake his hand. His bones are like glass!

Lionel *looks on pathetically.*

Regina   So. You're the proud couple, eh? Got your hands
full though, eh? Look at it! Bloody great thing, in't it!

Mini   It's a 'he', actually. His name's Hugh.

Regina   Oh! Oh, yes! Very good! Hugh!

Marcus   Have you got any children, Mrs Buxley?

Regina (*re* **Lionel**)   What, with this cup of weak piss?
Hardly. You keep your baby in the front garden then?

Mini   We couldn't get him through the door.

Regina   What do you do when it rains?

Marcus   We've got a tarpaulin, and plenty of plastic sacks.

Regina   What do you feed him on?

Mini   Odds and sods. He's only three days old, so he's not
that fussy.

Regina (*sniffs a bucket*)   Cabbage purée from a bucket?

Marcus   I can assure you everything's been properly
sterilised.

Regina   I'm not Social Services, son. You don't have to
justify anything to me. Feed him rat poison for all I care.

Mini   I beg your pardon.

Gargantua *stirs, yawns, stretches.*

Regina   There he is. My nemesis.

She squares up to **Gargantua**.

Gargantua   Maaaa-maaaaaa-mooooo-mahhhhhh . . .

Regina (*quietly*)   Don't you 'maaaaa-maaaaa-mooooo-maahhh' me. You stole my fire yesterday, son. I've been constructing that mega-mall for as long as you've been gestating. It's cost me a lotta dollar and I need to see some comeback. Now after what you did it's fair to say I could take an aggressive stance against ya. But I won't.

Gargantua   Oooooh?

Regina   No. So consider yerself blessed. Cus Regina Buxley is one loco bitch you do *not* want to mess with.

Gargantua   Goooooooooo!

Regina (*back to* **Mini** *and* **Marcus**)   Good. I think an understanding has been reached. I've got a proposition for ya, Mum and Dad. I want the Big Feller 'ere to open my mega-mall.

Mini *and* **Marcus**   Hugh?

Regina   The mall is the biggest of its kind on the planet. So's this leviathan. We could be rivals. However, I am offering the chance to join forces and become partners.

The **Agents** *appear from hiding places and watch intently.*

Marcus   Oh, Regina! That'd be wonderful!

Mini   No it wouldn't, Marcus. She's saying our Hugh becomes an advert for the Skankton Marsh Mega-Mall!

Marcus   Are ya?

Regina   I am.

Marcus   She is.

Mini   I know.

Marcus   But Mini –

Mini   I don't want Hugh advertising someone's business.

Regina   Just think of him as a living blimp!

Mini   Excuse me! My son is not a living blimp!

Regina   That's as maybe, sweetheart. But times are hard.
Ten ton o' cabbage a day starts to add up. How long can you
poor struggling sods keep the boy fed? You don't look like
you're made of money.

Mini   You're right. We're not. But it's the principle of the
thing.

Marcus   Mini, love, it could help us out.

Mini   Marcus!

Gargantua   Mmmmmaaaaaahhhhhhh!!

Marcus   Alright, son, I know you're hungry.

Regina   It's simple business sense. I keep you in enough
cabbages and milk to last a bloody lifetime, and your son
advertises my mall. Tit for tat. Come on, people. Don't throw
the baby out with the bathwater.

Mini   Look, Mrs Buxley –

Regina   Regina, please. Or better still, Reg. I know it's a
little masculine but my father was a Reginald, and it makes me
feel close to him, God rest his soul. He was a real man. Not
like my Lionel over there. Oh, yes. I know what the townsfolk
say – that Regina Buxley's more of a man than 'er husband
ever was.

During this, **Lionel** *has shuffled round to see* **Gargantua**. *All of a*
sudden, **Gargantua** *scoops up* **Lionel** *and eats him.*

Marcus *and* **Mini** *see this but cannot speak.* **Regina**, *her back to*
the scene, is oblivious.

Regina   Let 'em gas. Lionel is a funny sort. But his heart's in
the right place, and when you want him you always know he'll
be right where yoooooooooou –

She turns around but all that remains are **Lionel**'s *crutches lying*
scattered right where he was standing.

Gargantua *burps.*

Mini   Hugh!

Regina   Did your son just eat my Lionel?

Marcus   Mrs Buxley, I don't know what to say . . .

Regina (*as she picks up the crutches*)   That grotesque cannibalising freak! He swallowed my husband whole!

Marcus   Oh no, he bit Lionel's head off first. It would've been quick, Mrs Buxley.

Mini   Marcus!

Regina   Quick it may have been! But that does not change the fact that your child is a people-eater!

Marcus   Please, Mrs Buxley, if there's anything we can do . . .

Regina   Oh, there is! Your son. My mega-mall. The grand opening. This weekend. Say *no* and I'll have that baby thrown in jail for murder-eatin!

Gargantua   Ooooooooooooooo.

Regina   I'll be in touch.

She exits.

Pause.

Mini   Hugh, that was a very, very bad thing to do!

Gargantua   Waaaaahhhhhhhh!!

Mini   Are you just going to stand there gawping, Marcus? Tell him off or something!

Marcus   He was just hungry was all.

Mini   She's right, ya know. We haven't got the money to feed him. Not at the rate he eats. And he's just going to get bigger and bigger. He'll be too big for the garden in a few days. Then what'll we do?

Marcus   We'll manage, Min. We wouldn't have got him otherwise. He's our special boy.

Agents *appear again.*

Allbright   Oh, he's so much more than that, Mr and Mrs Mungus.

Mini   Not you again.

Starkhammer   That's why we've come to take him off your hands, Mr and Mrs Mungus.

Marcus   Over my dead body.

Blackstone   We knew you'd say that, Mr Mungus.

Mini   Then you've wasted a trip! Be off with ya!

Agents   Mr and Mrs Mungus . . .

Allbright   That's such a mouthful.

Starkhammer   Mr and Mrs Mungus? To save time, may we call you 'the Mungi' to save time?

Mini *and* **Marcus**   Eh?

Blackstone   The Mungi is much better.

Allbright   It's better, it's *quicker*.

Starkhammer   So, the Mungi?

Mini *and* **Marcus**   Yes?

Blackstone   We hereby inform you that we are requisitioning your child.

Mini   No!

Allbright   He will be taken to a secret but secure environment –

Starkhammer   Where, we assure you, he will be very well looked after.

Marcus   We look after him here!

Blackstone   I think we all know that's not true.

Allbright   He just gobbled up an old man. Who knows who's next?

Mini   You aren't taking him!

Marcus   Please! He's our son!

Starkhammer   I know this must be hard but trust us – it's for the common good.

A deep bass rumble, like thunder, rattles the land.

Allbright   What's that sound?

Marcus   It's his stomach. He's hungry . . . again . . .

Mini   But we've nothing left . . .

Blackstone   Where he's going, he'll get the parenting people like you could never hope to provide.

Mini *and* **Marcus** *look to each other and realise that the* **Agents** *are right.*

Mini   Could we come and visit . . . ?

Starkhammer   Of course. You can see him whenever you like.

Blackstone   Here. Take this card.

Allbright   Call this number. One of our guys will collect you, day or night.

Starkhammer   Easy-peazy. So, what's your decision, the Mungi?

The **Mungi** *both nod.*

Blackstone   Sign here.

They sign a form.

Allbright *(whispers into his cufflink)*   That's a good-to-go.

The sound of helicopters approaching eventually drowns everything out. A team of hardhats encircle the area (JANUS TECH *stencilled on* *the backs of their day-glo jackets) and flag the 'copters down around* **Gargantua**.

Confused and disturbed, he starts to cry and reaches out for his mum and dad.

Mini *and* **Marcus** *can't watch as* **Gargantua** *is lifted to the sky. The helicopters' downdraft sends everything into a whirl.*

Mini *and* **Marcus** *are left holding each other as the sound of helicopters fades.*

Mini   Oh Marcus, what have we done?

Sally (*to camera*)   Hugh Mungus-mania continues to spread across the globe, but it's here in Skankton Marsh where the phenomenon is in full effect. Behind me, hit rock band The Dummysuckers are performing their number-one smash 'Potty Trained'!

The Dummysuckers *perform their hit before a seething mosh pit.*

Song
    I'm only happy in a nappy!
    I go so dotty on my potty!
    If I do something rather naughty!
    You better smack me on the botty!

And that's all we need of that song, because we suddenly find ourselves in –

A vast underground silo.

Gargantua *howls and struggles against his restraints. He's now the size of a church.*

Professor Julian Swan *addresses the audience.*

Swan   Ladies and gentlemen, I, Professor Julian Swan, head of Janus Technologies, have a vision of the future. Picture, if you will, this unique creature, cloned! Picture, if you will, an army of giant super-babies! The ultimate biological weapon! Ladies and gentlemen, I give you . . . Project Gargantua!

A burst of applause.

Wellard (*stands*)   I'm sorry, Professor Swan, but this is completely unethical! He's just a baby.

Swan   He is an anomaly of nature, perhaps the most wondrous we have ever seen! And his potential must be harnessed!

Wellard   Exploited, you mean?

Malahyde   We live in a fragile world, Ms Wellard. Don't you want our country protected?

Wellard   By an army of giant babies?

Swan   They would be controlled, trained, placed on our country's borders –

Malahyde   Or dropped into war zones. The Cute Factor alone would stun the enemy into submission.

Swan   This is the next revolutionary step in passive-aggressive warfare tactics.

Wellard   How many millions have you sold the genetic patent for, Professor Swan?

Swan   Ms Wellard, please –

Wellard   How many *billions*?

Malahyde   You're embarrassing yourself, missy. Now sit down.

Wellard   No, General Malahyde, I won't. Prime Minister, I move to block this insane motion –

Prime Minister   Sit down, Pippa.

Wellard   You aren't seriously considering this?

Prime Minister   I said. Sit. Down.

Wellard, *stunned, sits.*

Prime Minister   What's the next step, Professor?

Swan   Bone-marrow extraction, as well as blood typing, biopsy and skin-tissue samples –

Wellard (*to* **Gargantua**)   You poor baby.

Swan   Then we can get the cloning under way. We just need the go-ahead, Prime Minister.

Malahyde   The thumbs-up from the Main Man.

Swan   The good ole government-funded 'green-light'.

Malahyde   The A-OK from the Big Kahuna himself. You, Dave. *You.*

Prime Minister   You have it. Do our country proud, Professor.

Swan   We'll do our best, Prime Minister. Let us begin the extraction process at once! Prepare the drills!

Wellard   Monsters!

Sally (*to camera*)   But where is the world's favourite giant baby? His sudden and conspicuous absence from Skankton Marsh is taking its toll on everyone.

Arnie *turns the camera to citizens of Skankton Marsh. They cry like babies.* **Headmistress Gunning** *runs through popping dummies in their mouths. They suck contentedly.*

Sally   His parents were unavailable for comment.

Marcus (*on mobile*)   Yes, hello, I'm ringing about my son, Hugh? Hugh Mungus? No, it's not a joke. That's his name. We wanted to see him. Oh. Right. I see. Thank you.

He hangs up.

The card those agents gave us . . . it's for Dave's Pizza Delivery.

Mini (*cradling his feeding bucket*)   They tricked us. We've lost him. We've lost everything.

Enter **Regina** *from nowhere.*

Regina   Howdy, Munguses!

Mini *and* **Marcus**   'Lo Regina.

Regina   Where's the star of the show? The mall opens
tomorrer. Now where is he? I want to get him painted up to
look like an enormous jar of mayonnaise –

Mini   He's gone, Reg. They took him.

Regina   Who took him?

Marcus   A sinister trio of agents from Janus Technologies.

Regina   They took our baby against our wishes?

Mini   What do we do, Regina?

Regina   We get him back, love. We get him back.

Silo.

Gargantua *howls inconsolably. A dozen* **Soldiers** *surround and
guard him.*

Soldier 1   Poor thing's been crying all night.

Soldier 2   I'm not surprised after all it's been through.

Soldier 3   I know what used to soothe me. A nice lullaby.

Soldier 4   Go on, then. Somebody sing to him.

Soldier 5   Timothy, you've got the voice of an angel.

Soldier 6   No I haven't.

Soldiers   You have. Sing to him.

Soldier 6
   Hush little baby don't say a word
   Momma's gonna buy you a mockingbird . . .

Soldier 2 *joins in.*

   And if that mockingbird don't sing
   Momma's gonna buy you a diamond ring

And more join in. **Gargantua** *calms.*

   And if that diamond ring turns brass
   Momma's gonna buy you a looking glass . . .

Gargantua *is asleep.*

Soldier 1   Nice work, lads. Nice work.

Elsewhere in the silo:

Swan *(holds aloft a small glowing test tube)*   Extraction was a success! We have everything we need, General Malahyde.

Malahyde   Giant baby DNA. Who the hell woulda thunk it?

Prime Minister *(appearing from shadows)*   This is a momentous day, gentlemen.

Swan   It is indeed, David.

Prime Minister   To our chapter in history!

All   To our chapter in history.

Gargantua *farts, blowing several* **Soldiers** *across the floor.*

Malahyde   Sweet mother of God! Open the air vents!

Outside, there is a crowd of **Gargantua***-worshipping* **Zealots** *all dressed as babies. In nappies, in bonnets, you name it. At the head of the pack are* **Mini**, **Marcus** *and* **Regina**.

Zealots   Free the Baby! Free the Baby! Free the Baby!

Sally *(to camera)*   I'm standing outside the secret laboratories of Janus Technologies where, it is alleged, the giant baby Gargantua is being held captive. There are literally thousands of groupies, admirers, self-declared Hugh-worshippers, who have all caught wind of his whereab – *(Smells* **Gargantua***'s fart.)* Ye gods! Who let one go? Arnie, was that you?

Mini   No! That's my Hugh! He's let off a distress signal! He's definitely in there, Reg! A mother knows!

Regina   Right! Babies? Storm the silo! Charge!

Sally *(to camera)*   Gargantua worshippers are scaling the walls of the compound, tearing down fences –

Silo.

Swan, **Malahyde** *and the* **Prime Minister** *all laugh maniacally, then suddenly stop.*

Swan   Hush. What's that noise?

Wellard (*running in*)   I tipped off the media to our whereabouts. It's the sound of your chapter in history going down the toilet. Gentlemen.

Soldier   Babies! Incoming!

Nappy-wearing **Zealots** *storm the space.*

Soldiers *flee.*

Gargantua *gurgles with delight as the* **Zealots** *bow to him.*

Zealots   Hugh . . . Hugh . . . Hugh . . .

Sally (*to camera*)   The swarming masses are overpowering military might! In fact, the soldiers are actually throwing down their rifles and donning nappies! The liberation of Gargantua has begun!

Gargantua *breaks his chains and stands triumphantly on two wobbly legs.*

In run **Mini** *and* **Marcus**.

Tiny Mini   There he is! There's our boy!

Tiny Marcus   My, he's grown!

Tiny Mini   Look Marcus! He's standing!

Gargantua *scoops them up in his hand.* **Mini** *and* **Marcus** *turn 'tiny' in the baby's massive hand.*

Tiny Mini   Hello, darling!

Tiny Marcus   We missed you, Hugh!

Gargantua   Mmmmmm . . .

Tiny Mini   He's trying to say something!

Gargantua   Mmmmmmmeeeee . . .

Tiny Marcus   His first word! His first word!

Gargantua   Mmmm-mega malll . . .

Regina   That's my boy! Right. Let's get back to Skankton Marsh and get it bloody open! Onward!

Swan   Stop! This specimen is the property of Janus Technologies!

Gargantua *eyes* **Swan**, *heaves, then projectile vomits all over him.*

Sally (*to camera*)   And yes, the giant baby has covered Professor Julian Swan in a biblical flood of thick milky baby puke!

Swan (*dripping*)   Noooooooo!!

Malahyde   That's a bad boy! Bring him down!

Soldier   Sir?

Malahyde   He's outta control! Tazer the brute! A thousand volts!

Soldier   I don't think I can, General.

Malahyde   What is your problem, soldier?

Soldier   I've grown rather fond of the fella. (*Punching the air.*) Free the baby! Free the baby!

Sally (*to camera*)   Hugh seems to be hitting his troublesome tantrum phase, and I think I know why! Yes, I . . . I can see it! His first tooth!

Tiny Mini   Oh Marcus! Can you see it protruding through his gums?

Tiny Marcus   Of course I can see it, love! It's the size of a blinking bus!

Gargantua *reveals a huge single top tooth.*

Mini *and* **Marcus**   Oh, Hugh!

Gargantua *turns his attention to* **Malahyde**.

Malahyde   What the hell is he doing now?

Swan   He's torn a hole in the waste container!

Malahyde   Is that bad?

Swan   It's worse than bad. It's where we dispose of his soiled nappies.

Malahyde   Oh. Shit.

Gargantua *throws down disgusting, soiled nappies, dropping them like giant pancakes on to the* **Tiny Soldiers** *below.*

Swan *gets splattered. Again.*

Everyone   Phhhhhooooorrrrrr!!

The world cheers.

Sally   He seems to be forging a path through the maelstrom with his mother and father in the palm of his hand!

KER-RASHHHHH!!

And he's out through the wall, and off into the night!

Regina (*as she leaves*)   Never mess with us Skankton Marshians! Now Hugh, to the Mega Mall!

Malahyde   Son of a gun. He got away. Nobody gets away from General Malahyde! There's a monster on the loose, men. He's a threat to civilisation as we know it! Hit him with everything we've got.

Soldier   But, sir, he's just a baby.

Malahyde   Must I do everything myself? Mobilise all units! Ground-to-air! Air-to-air! Go! Go! Go!

Two hundred **Soldiers** *run past* **Malahyde**.

Back at Skankton Marsh:

Gargantua *sets down his* **Tiny Mum** *and* **Dad** *on the roof of the Mega Mall.*

Tiny Mini   We're so proud of you, Hugh.

Tiny Marcus   We're so sorry we ever gave you up.

Tiny Mini   We've got you back.

Tiny Marcus   And we'll never let you go again!

Tiny Regina   I now declare the Skankton Marsh Mega-Mall well and truly ohhh −

Malahyde (*in silo*)   Launch missiles!

WOOOOOSSSSSSSSSHHHHH!!!!! (*Missiles.*)

Regina   − Bugger.

Mini *and* **Marcus** *see the missiles approaching, headed directly for them. They look to* **Gargantua**. **Gargantua** *sees what's about to happen.*

Gargantua   Mamma? Dadda . . . ?

Mini *and* **Marcus**   He said our −

KAAAAA-BOOOOOMMMMM!

Mini *and* **Marcus Mungus** *are no more!*

Malahyde   You vaporised the parents, you knuckle-heads!

Sally   That's not good.

Gargantua (*beat, then*)   WAAAHHHHHHHHHH!

Regina   Steady now, young man! I know you're angry, but − you mind my beloved Mega-Mall!

Gargantua *swats* **Regina** *like a fly, and roars with rage.*

He goes wild, and tears the mall apart.

Sally (*to camera*)   He's ripping through the mall. Pounding with his fists. Buckling metal. Shattering glass. Decimating the place flat. And who could blame him?

Gargantua *destroys everything he sees in glorious slow motion.*

Skankton Boy   What's he doing? He's destroying everything!

Preacher Pike   He's no messiah! He's the spawn of the Devil!

Sandy the Hairdresser   Minister! Run for your lives!

Grannies *(really slow)*   Mmmmmmmmmm . . .

Gargantua *scoops them up, chews them and spits them out.*

Soldiers   He's eating the OAPS, sir.

Malahyde   Open fire! Open fire!

10 Downing Street.

The **Prime Minister** *and his cabinet (* **Wellard**, **Creams**, **Wilt**) *watch on in horror.*

Wellard   Congratulations, Dave. You're in the history books *now*.

Wilt   He's tearing up the world.

Creams   He's not a happy bunny.

Enter **Malahyde** *and* **Swan**.

Swan   Prime Minister? I regret to inform you that Project Gargantua has suffered a temporary setback.

Malahyde   Setback? That creature's destroyed half the country! And he don't show no sign of quittin'!

Creams   Oh God, he's headed straight for us.

Wellard   Of course he is. We blew up his mum and dad! What do you expect?

Creams   We should get below ground and hide. For a really long time.

Prime Minister   There's a secret bunker below Downing Street. Only I know the entry code.

Wilt   Punch the buttons, sir!

Wellard   I'll punch you in a minute.

Malahyde   Sure, sure. We could all bury our heads in the sand like silky boy said. Or . . . we could stand up to the beast and stop it in its tracks good and proper.

Wellard   I thought you'd hit him with everything you've got.

Malahyde   Not yet. I still got an ace up my sleeve. I say we get out the Big Guns. I say we go *nuclear*.

Everyone falls silent.

Prime Minister   That is the last possible option, General Malahyde.

Malahyde   It's the *only* option, Prime Minister. This little terror is hell-bent and will stop at nothing. He'll keep eating and growing and walking all over us with those oversized tootsie of his unless –

Wellard   Unless we nuke him and take half the northern hemisphere with us?

Malahyde   The decision is yours, Prime Minister.

Everything shakes.

Wilt/Creams   He's almost here!

Prime Minister   So be it. Bring out the Big Guns, General Malahyde.

Malahyde   Yes, sir.

Wellard   You utter fool.

Prime Minister   It had to be done, Pippa.

Wellard   Yeah? Well, so does this.

*She decks the **Prime Minister** out cold.*

Wellard   Been wanting to do that for years.

Creams   But we need him for the entry code!

Wellard   Oh, arse.

Echoing the image from the first scene, standing amidst smoke and fire, **Gargantua** *howls to the heavens.*

Back to the ante-chamber. Back to the present.

The group are exhausted in the telling of this epic story.

Wellard (*at top speed*)   So. You give the go-ahead for a nuclear strike. I crack you one. You collapse clean away. Prime Minister? Prime Minister! You wake up. Who's cooking onions? You've lost your memory! Mind melt! Forgotten the entry code along with the past seven days! We replay the whole flippin' event. The birth of Gargantua. The secret cloning plan. The giant baby's DNA extracted. The people revolt. All-out war! The baby escapes! Raahh! We attack! Booshh! We kill his parents. (Sorry!) He goes on the rampage! Bang! Crash! Impossible to stop! Stop! Prime Minister has no other choice! (Stop me!) Launch missiles. Entry code! Moral dilemma? Die with the masses or save our privileged skins? (Umm.) Into the safe-house! Please somebody! (I can't stop!) Missiles! Dick. Boof! Prime Minister? You come around! Hmm! Onions? Lost your memory! The missiles! The code! Ah! Oo! Replay the past seven days! Again! And again! And again! And . . . Prime Minister, the missiles launch in thirty seconds. Does any of this ring any bells?

Prime Minister   You . . . hit me . . . Pippa?

Swan   The entry code, man? Do you remember it?

Prime Minister   I don't deserve the safe-house after all I've done . . .

Creams   Then just give us the code and you can stay here.

Prime Minister   None of us deserve it. We've brought this catastrophe upon ourselves.

Wellard   Speak for yourself!

Malahyde   Missiles launch in twelve seconds.

Creams   What's the bloody number, Dave?

Prime Minister (*quietly*)   Who's cooking onions?

Everyone groans with despair.

Prime Minister   You know, one of my first memories was of an old lady named Doris. She used to cook onions every

Thursday night. Fry them up. She was our neighbour. Lovely woman. So kind. I remember that smell as if it were yesterday.

Wilt   So it was *Doris* who was cooking the onions!

Swan   I'm glad we got that cleared up.

Prime Minister   And, I'll never forget, she lived at Number 49.

The **Prime Minister** *punches in the numbers on the control panel.*

Prime Minister   Forty-nine.

And again.

Forty-nine.

And again.

Beat. Ping.

Voice   Access to safe-house granted.

They all sigh with relief.

Prime Minister   Funny . . . the things you remember as a child. Poor Hugh Mungus . . . Shame he had to die. Oh well. Come on everyone. To the safe-house!

He looks at them all, then opens the door to reveal –

A huge eyeball peering in at them.

The Dummysuckers *kick in:*

Singer   GARGANTUA!

Everyone screams. **Garantua** *emits a deafening roar. They slam the door closed.*

Boom! Boom! Boom! BOOM!

The door explodes inwards. They all fall back.

Singer   GARGANTUA!

Gargantua*'s huge hand reaches in and grabs the* **Prime Minister**, *crushing him in his grip.*

Singer
    You can try and outrun him
    But you won't get far!

Gargantua *eats and squashes everyone except for* **Wellard**.

Wellard (*quietly*)   Ten . . . nine . . . eight . . . seven . . . six . . . five . . . four . . .

Gargantua *draws* **Wellard** *into the unending darkness of his gigantic mouth –*

Wellard   Three . . . two . . . one . . . Boom.

Darkness.

Gargantua

BY CARL GROSE

*Notes on rehearsal and staging drawn from a workshop
with the writer held at the National Theatre, October 2015*

*From workshops led by Adele Thomas and Melly Still,
with notes by Stella Odunlami and Olly Hawes*

How Carl came to write the play

'The play is a combination of ideas. I really liked the title
Gargantua, and I liked the idea of Rabelais's original story –
I hadn't actually read it – but liked the idea of the story! I
thought I would like to write something you don't see much
in Connections – I wanted to ask companies to do something
quite impossible, challenging, ridiculous, a play that had stage
directions that make you go 'What?!' – I was just looking for
an excuse to do a monster movie on stage really!

'In terms of other inspirations there's a tonne of stuff – *Rocky
Horror*, *The Simpsons*, comic books, B-movies – and hopefully,
companies performing the play can look to them, but then
find their own style.

'I'm very interested in farce as well – and pace is an absolutely
key aspect of the play – it's really high octane. For example,
the scene with the community of villagers works best when it's
pacy and light – almost throwaway. The characters in that
scene are expositional, and if you linger on anything too
much the scene doesn't work. Scale, precision, clarity and
transitions are all important factors to consider.

'And the idea for the band? I just really wanted to have one
in there! After writing the first draft I was toying with taking
the band out – but then I realised that the band gives the play
an epic thing – and that's why it's there. How the band is
used is up to individual directors – they could be present
throughout or just present when there are songs in the script.
In the end you have to trust what you like – everyone's shows
are their own.

'The play is meant to be naughty, there's lots of naughty stuff in there, and it's all there for a reason – and that includes the swearwords. If you absolutely need to take those out then that's what you've got to do – but remember, they are there for a reason.'

Approaching the play

In discussions concerning how best to approach the play, four key areas of consideration were identified:

1 The sense of scale – how can changing scale be utilised to tell the story?

2 How can the anarchy that exists within the play be embraced rather then embellished? The characters are heightened for a reason – but if they go too far, the story will get lost.

3 Pace is hugely important. It might be useful to set yourself a running time of fifty minutes, because the dialogue works best when it's performed with pace.

4 How do the songs inform the overall language of the production?

Themes

- consumerism and capitalism
- warfare
- pregnancy and labour
- corruption
- urban sprawl
- commodification, of nature in particular
- greed
- mass hysteria
- celebrity culture and false idols
- the impact of media
- advancements in technology and science
- the government versus the people
- xenophobia
- the arms trade and nuclear weapons

Structure

When exploring how to utilise the structure of the play, it will be useful for a director to identify the key dramatic event in each scene – the moment on which each scene hinges. This will be what guides you in your storytelling and what you should focus your scenes around. It may not be the 'biggest' event, but rather a 'smaller' one that changes the course of the action – for example, the moment when Mini and Marcus decide to give Hugh away. It will be important to keep the sense of peril alive in every scene. In order to do this, you will need to know what the stakes are. For example, in this scene Gargantua's liberation is at stake; the audience should be asking 'Will Gargantua be liberated?'

It is also useful to consider what drives the narrative of the whole play. The majority of the play is actually framed as the retelling of the story of the events leading up to the Prime Minister falling unconscious. Within that story the drama drives towards the question: will the Prime Minister push the button to engage the nuclear warheads? Once that issue has been resolved the play hinges on whether the Prime Minister will remember the code to the safe house, and then what the fate of Gargantua – and the rest of the human race – will be. Finding a way to ensure the audience know the difference between the 'present' and the story that has taken place over the past seven days.

Characters and characterisation

The play is mostly populated by heightened comic characters, but it is crucial the story is not lost in absurdity – finding a balance between the play's farcical nature and its narrative is essential.

In order to do this it is vital to recognise that characters speak and act in order to try to achieve something, so to identify what it is they want or are trying to achieve is of primary importance; how they behave (with a silly voice or an imbecilic walk, for example) is of secondary importance.

These characters are entertainingly unusual, weird, preposterous and farcical – but critically, they themselves believe they are normal, and if they are too colourful, too inventive, we will lose the story – and so directors must always come back to making sure they are telling the story – to communicate to the audience the desire or need the characters have.

In comparison to the other characters, Wellard and Mr and Mrs Mungus, are normal – and their normality heightens the abnormal nature of everyone else. More than that, these characters represent us – the audience. They are the everyman characters, our representatives in a crazy world, and so we need to really care what happens to them. However bonkers the rest of the play is, we must still feel sadness when Hugh is taken from his parents, and shock when Mr and Mrs Mungus are killed. Another potentially unexpected moment of poignancy could be the soldier singing the lullaby. This moment works if the audience truly believe the soldier feels sorry for the baby, really wants to soothe him and genuinely tries to sing the song in a calming way.

In order to get to grips with their characters, it is important that performers understand the *story* of the play. This can be difficult when rehearsing with young performers at school or in a youth theatre, when scheduling can be erratic and there can be much time pressure. In order to achieve this understanding, directors may consider, at the start of each rehearsal, running the play from the beginning up to the point they arrived at during the previous rehearsal. This may feel messy and dispiriting but over time the performers will tune in to the arc of the story they are collectively telling; they will begin to enjoy the pace and rhythm of the writing and the twists and turns of the characters.

Finding the musical heart of the play

The play is anarchic and full of energy and invention. Carl expressed the importance of connecting and integrating the function of the band, The Dummysuckers, to the rest of the play.

He stressed that he did not want to impose any style on the piece by setting a specific genre for the band. They are key to the piece and it might be useful to use them as a starting point and allow the decisions that are made about the band to inform the rest of the play.

It is also important to understand that anyone can access the role of The Dummysuckers, regardless of their musical aptitude. While there are specific songs written into the play, there is also a whole sound world just waiting to be unearthed.

Adele's version of the play would see The Dummysuckers as a surfabilly/rockabilly band.

Think about your cast. What types of musical references are relevant to them? What references do they have that fit the energy and pace of the play: blues, punk, rock and roll, gospel? This has no correlation to any musical proficiency. Decide on your band and you can build the world of the play around that.

Production, staging and design

The play presents a huge staging challenge because it requires productions to present objects that exist on vastly different scales. There are numerous ways a company can respond to this challenge. It may be useful to consider all the theatrical tools you have at your disposal: performers' physicality and voices, use of space, light, sound, music, set, props, costume. The solutions to problems posed by the text may come from unlikely sources. For example, during our workshop the scene that was meant to take place in a 'vast underground silo' was brilliantly and simply created by the performers speaking as if their voices were echoing, and we often found that there was as much – if not more – impact in communicating the size and effect of Gargantua through the way others responded to him as opposed to trying to create the gigantic baby itself. It also became clear that as well as the challenge of the different scales as such, shifting from one scale to another presents another set of challenges, and doing so will require both a lot of practice and planning. But remember that these challenges also represent fantastic theatrical opportunities – this is a play that pushes theatre makers to be bold and innovative.

Productions of this play could be (not necessarily should be) very messy. It will be important for directors and any creative and production team they are working with to find solutions to creating this mess safely and reliably, and only if it supports and serves rather than muddles the story. In this regard, rehearsals are a chance to test and explore different solutions in a controlled environment.

Three questions will be important here: does this solution work theatrically (does it create the intended effect)? Is this solution manageable (will we be able to re-create it in performance conditions)? And is it safe? For example, if you're using, say, watermelon as a substitute for blood and guts, you might ask yourself: Does this actually look like blood and guts? Can we afford enough watermelons? Will we have time to clean the mess up? And can we ensure that it won't create a slippery surface that would be hazardous in later scenes?

It will also be important to ensure rehearsal conditions are the same as performance conditions – for example, if you're using a band throughout the play and that means having lots of electrical leads on stage, it will be important to introduce these leads into rehearsals early on to make sure that the leads and any choreography you develop can co-exist safely and effectively.

CARL: 'If there's a particular convention, frame or "palette", e.g. food or baby toy, really stick to it.'

MELLY: 'Sometimes if you set yourself rules/parameters it gives you a framework within which you can be creative without the risk of going bonkers and confusing the audience with too many ideas.'

ADELE: 'It can be liberating – and you don't need a huge budget to do it.'

MELLY: 'There is a wonderful magic in using the same props in various ways for different events; and sometimes you have to go off piste with your thinking.'.

Style and technique

It is important for a director to remember what inspired Carl when he was writing the play. He counts Rabelais's original story of the same name, comic books and cartoons as influences, but it is most akin to a thriller/horror B-movie full of gore, grotesquery and terror. It is worth bearing in mind that, as in all good horrors, it is often what we leave out that scares us most: tickle the audience's imagination by all means but don't be afraid to leave a lot for them to imagine. Nothing is as vivid as what we produce in the mind's eye.

The play has many different scenes and settings, and in terms of establishing the style and performance language of a production, moving between those scenes and settings is as important as the scenes themselves. The scene changes need to paint the picture of the story – the audience need to know straight away that the new characters entering are, for example, baby-eating old ladies, or a group of soldiers. Even in the scene changes it is possible to make the telling of story the priority, to keep asking 'Are we telling the story?' and to utilise them to ensure you are doing so.

Exercises for use in rehearsals

Below are a number of exercises that focus on work that can be done with your cast early on in the rehearsal process. The exercises are directly linked to the text and are designed to help performers develop an understanding of the play, a sense of ensemble and of their own individual characters, and to enable directors to discover and build the world of the play and the style of the production. They echo the tone and style of the play, and the way the group behave and work with one another can be referenced when rehearsing the scenes of the play – or even used as a way of devising the scenes themselves.

CHANGEABLE GREETINGS . . .

Melly asked the group to walk around the space trying to keep a sense of equal space between each performer, as if you have eyes in the back of your heads and bodies, always alert to everyone in the room. Once this was established she asked that 'When you walk past, someone wink.'

Then after some winking introductions she instructed the group to 'stop, shake hands and introduce yourselves to each other – even if you know each other already'. Once the group had spent a little time doing that, Melly asked them to introduce themselves to each other, but this time 'a bit too enthusiastically'. Then 'as if they were at a funeral', and finally 'as if they know the person they're saying hello to is having an affair with their partner'.

The activity is a great way for a group to warm up: it creates a lot of noise and energy in the room (without asking directly for those things to occur) and allows people to have individual moments with other members of the ensemble and start acting and being playful with one another in a low pressure situation.

PASSING ENERGY AROUND A CIRCLE

Adele asked the participants to choose a line from the play that they thought was most important and to form a circle. Each person then passed their line on to the person standing next to them with as much energy as possible, the aim being to avoid any gaps or drops in energy between lines. This then graduated into lines being passed across the circle with an invitation to play with the level of energy and intention. This exercise is a useful way of beginning to identify some of the key moments in the play and get a sense of just how high the stakes are right from the very first line. Maintaining this level and pace of energy can be difficult but is vital in the world of the play.

WALKING AS AN ENSEMBLE

Melly asked the group to walk around the room – trying to fill it evenly, leaving no space unfilled. She then established a scale, from 0 for standing completely still and 10 for walking (not running) as quickly as possible. Initially Melly asked the group to all move at the same number on the scale – moving up or down the scale consecutively (4 . . . 5 . . . 6 . . . etc.), or jumping numbers (4 . . . 8 . . . 3 . . . 10 . . . etc.), then she asked people to move at different rates by getting anyone whose name begins with A to walk at 4, anyone whose name begins with B to walk at 8, anyone whose name begins with C to walk at 2, and so on.

Returning to the group all walking at the same number, Melly then challenged the group to all stop at the same time, and then, once they've managed that, to all start walking at the same time, at the same number: 2.

This activity is good for getting the group working and moving together as an ensemble. It asks participants to focus on their own task (walking at the pace they need to walk) but also to be very aware of the fellow performers (by walking at the same pace, ensure they're walking at the right pace, or trying to stop and start at the same time). It is also useful for a director to observe the impact that can be made simply by asking the ensemble to walk at the same or different paces, and feed the imagination about what else they might be able to do.

GROUP MORPHING

Melly split the ensemble into groups of four or five and gave them ten seconds to make a cow giving birth (without any humans involved), with everyone in the group being involved. Once the cows have been giving birth for a while – perhaps half a minute – make a giant insect that moves. Once that's happened the insects have to become aggressive, then terrified, then morph – over a count of six – into a troop of soldiers marching, then standing to attention, then morphing into a barbershop quartet, then into a gaggle of gossips, then an army of ants working together, which, after a time are squashed by a human foot – resulting not in their deaths, but rather in their severely hampered attempts to continue working (Melly structured each morph by counting to six and then saying 'action').

This activity asks the group to start working together to develop scenes that are drawn from or echo the play. In asking the group to morph from one image to the next the inclination to think –which can, so often, obstruct creativity – is removed with the group having simply to work physically with one another, respond to instructions and organically morph from one being to the next with as much clarity as possible. It is worth asking the groups to observe each other and give feedback (no criticism) about what has most clearly and in the simplest way communicated (to the audience) a party of protesters, a gaggle of gossips and so on.

GARGANTUA'S IMPACT . . .

Melly asked the group to lie on the floor and to imagine that they are experiencing an earthquake. Whenever the ground shakes (Melly bashing the piano in the corner) maintaining balance is almost impossible. Now the floor is tipping towards one corner, now to the opposite . . .

This activity begins to explore how to communicate to an audience the scale of Hugh (Gargantua) through the impact he has on others. Melly suggested looking at YouTube videos of people experiencing earthquakes, and asked participants to think about differentiating between the different impact Hugh has on others as he gets bigger throughout the play and does different things. What is the impact when he walks? Breathes? Cries? Farts? Roars? Might it be useful to employ wind machines/fans/megaphones? One of the most effective devices employed by one of the groups was cowering under a ladder and jolting violently every time they 'felt' a giant footstep.

VOCAL WARM-UPS

Melly asked the group to keep walking and warm up their voices by repeating the following sounds formed phonetically from the alphabet as they do:

'Aah buh kuh duh', then 'eh fuh guh huh'.

She asked the group to repeat this, but now making the sounds clearer and crisper:

'Aah Buh Kuh Duh', 'Eh Fuh Guh Huh'.

Keep going through the alphabet in this way:

'Eee [I], Juh, Kuh, Luh.'

'Muh, Nuh, Oh [as in the sound at the beginning of 'otter' as opposed to 'open'], Puh.'

'Cuh [Q], Ruh, Suh, Tuh.'

'Ooo [U], Vee, Wook(y)Zee [WXYZ].'

Repeat the whole alphabet again, this time quicker, louder and with more precision – the idea being to get quicker without losing any of the vocal quality. This is a simple vocal warm-up that anyone can do to warm up the mouth, jaw and tongue.

TONGUE-TWISTERS

There are numerous tongue-twisters you can use, but we chose the following:

Fuzzy Wuzzy was a bear
Fuzzy Wuzzy had no hair
So Fuzzy Wuzzy wasn't fuzzy was he

Henry had a little hen
Her name was Henrietta
Henrietta laid no eggs
So Henry ate her.

Saying a line, the group repeats it, then everyone says the whole twister together – usually repeating several times – more slowly, more precisely, hitting the consonants and really opening the mouth, and then quicker – but retaining the quality and precision of the sound, finding 'air' between each word (e.g. between 'wasn't' and 'fuzzy' instead of compounding the words into 'wozzenfuzzy').

To make the most of tongue-twisters it is important to be as precise as possible and to really stretch the mouth and the other vocal apparatus

Melly noted that *Gargantua* is a play that really relishes language, so the more thoroughly directors can get their companies to warm up vocally – enjoying and getting really good at tongue-twisters – the more the language is going to come alive in their performances

PASS THE BATON

Take any object that can easily be grabbed from someone's hands – like an empty bottle of water. (Ideally the object should have some sort of relevance to the play – for example, for this play it might be the prop used to represent the nuclear strike button.) Ask the actors to stand in a tight circle and perform their lines. Whenever their character speaks the performer must grasp the object in order to say the lines (and the previous performer must allow them to – indeed the object must be readily offered and taken).

This is an activity that facilitates listening, communication with one another and an understanding of pace. It also allows performers to get a strong sense of why their character speaks at the moment they do speak; it challenges them to find a reason, to get a sense of imperative without slowing down. It's called 'Pass the Baton' because it recalls relay racing where there is no hiccup in flow. For this play, where the sense of urgency increases throughout, it could be a great way to enable the performers to grasp the raising of the stakes.

AN EARLY RUN-THROUGH EXERCISE

Melly split the group into four or five and assigned each group four scenes from the play, one from the beginning, two from the middle and one from the end.

There was an enormous table of props – ranging from simple objects like cardboard boxes, sheets and paper (that could be used to represent a variety of things or perform a variety of roles/functions), to various food items (including watermelon, the flesh of which works as convincing blood and guts on stage!), to items of clothing (wigs, aprons, lab coats, sunglasses), and other erroneous items – cheese graters, cup holders, footballs, coat hangers – as well as larger items of the set – a ladder, various tables and chairs and a clothes rail.

The groups were given a little over an hour to devise and rehearse each of their assigned scenes, and were encouraged to be creative as possible in their staging, use as many props as they pleased, and play with a sense of scale. They were also asked to think about precision, pace, clarity and transitions in their work.

At the end of the hour the groups positioned themselves in a large circle and ran the entire play from start to finish, without stopping – each group taking it in turn to perform the scenes they had been assigned and ready to take over from the previous scene without any break.

Working in this way was advantageous for two main reasons. First, it compelled people to play – to work together quickly, to make things, to say yes, and to avoid sitting around talking, procrastinating and, essentially, thinking too much (often the scourge of many devising processes). Second, it gave the group an immediate and shared sense of the play as a whole, something live and acted out to which everyone could refer afterwards, thus enabling our discussions to be rooted in things that actually happened and that we all saw, as opposed to what form the action of the play might take in theory.

Musical exercises for use in rehearsal

The following exercises are useful in exploring how sound and music can be used in your storytelling. Use whatever instruments and objects you have at your disposal. (The workshop used: a microphone, drum-kit, fans, amp, guitars, rattles, maracas, piano, afoxi, melodica, keyboard, claves, bells and drumsticks.

MINING THE PLAY FOR SOUND

As a whole group, read through the play together, section by section, with each person reading one line. Make sure to include all stage directions and finish at the next full stop. Ask the group to keep the energy and the pace of the action in mind.

After each section, ask actors to comment on what they had noticed about the sound world and to list any sounds that are present in the script, or that they might hear. For example, the workshop group read the first two pages, up to Sally's line 'He's here', and their sounds included: vibrations, bodies shaking, people picking themselves up from the floor, rubble falling, sounds of Hugh as he returns to the same spot, the tremors of the earth.

MUSICAL GRANDMOTHER

- Nominate one person to be the walker.
- Using any of the objects and instruments available, each group has ten minutes to devise a short sequence to music that includes:
  1 The walker moving forwards.
  2 A monster action/gesture.
  3 A surprise.

Below are some of the things that the participants found useful when doing the exercise.

THE VOICE   is a beautifully simple tool that can be used for generating music and sound. A simple hum or other sound made with the voice can be a great for scoring moments. If the band only use their voices, this could possibly allow them to become more involved in the action of the story as they are not restricted by instruments.

THE MICROPHONE   is extremely versatile. It is great for creating close-range sounds, and for amplifying interesting vocal noises. It is also mobile and can be used all over the stage, which allows for the exploration of exciting possibilities between the source of the sound and the action taking place. It also encourages the use of objects to generate sounds, which is great in moving away from the idea of musical excellence and further into the exploration of how to build a world of sound.

REPETITION OF A SONIC MOTIF   is both a great way for creating and building tension and also for demonstrating the personality of a character. If a certain sound is repeated each time that a character appears onstage you can very simply and effectively signpost to the audience who they are watching. This could be particularly useful with a small cast where actors are doubling up frequently.

USING JUST ONE INSTRUMENT   is a great way to come up with very inventive solutions. If you are using a drum kit, why not interrogate every part of the kit and explore the full range of sounds that you are able to elicit from it? What can each cymbal do? Can they be incorporated into the action? Showing the inner workings of the play and how the sound is being made is interesting to watch and again allows for the band to be part of the action. The instruments may become parts of the set, furniture, or even puppets, all of which aid in the telling of the story.

CREATING THE BAND AND SCORING THE PLAY

Ask each group (say of five) to choose a genre and a sound to explore, and have a go at building a band! In thirty minutes, devise a proposed soundscape and world for the first two pages of the script, using the instruments in the room. Be disciplined and rigorous in the exploration of the instruments used. Can you manipulate one instrument in such a way as to allow it to explore the full range of possibilities afforded by that one choice? Keep your palette simple and do not overcrowd with sound/music for the sake of it.

For example, the soundscape could all be generated vocally by a band speaking gibberish or screaming, or they could be playing baby instruments and rattles. Whatever theme emerges from this exploration can help generate ideas for the musical theme and the tone of the production. The key thing is to ensure that everyone is part of the same world.

Things that worked particularly well within the workshop included:

Using the instruments as part of the set
A piano was set in the space, from behind which the band emerged while telling the story. It was played traditionally and more experimentally in response to the tension and fear that was felt onstage by the characters. It was also wheeled around the space, framing and reframing the action in different ways. Is there a version where the whole play takes place around, on top and below a piano?!

Building instrumentation out of everyday objects
The use of commonly found objects such as a bin, a table and some claves showed how easy it was to generate sound. Is there a version of the play that is set in an office and the story told through the use of office supplies?

Microphone
The stage directions are vital in framing the story. A microphone could be used by a narrator (a member of the band?) to speak the stage directions. All other sounds could be generated by the actors around the microphone. Could there be a radio play version that is played out onstage?

This exercise is useful in opening out the endless possibilities and choices available, and in revealing that clear ideas and simple palettes can yield some great imaginative responses.

Song
Ask the groups to use the lyrics on page 328 and decide on a genre of music. Write a version of this song that matches their

chosen genre. This is an easy and playful exercise that requires energy and attitude – the musical aptitude of the group is not important.

Suggested references, reading and viewing list

To explore the possibilities of how you can create sound effects in unconventional ways, you may consider researching Foley artists. Lots of examples of Foley art in action can be found on YouTube.

Adele showed a series of filmic references that she felt would be useful sources for explaining the style and world of the play. The sheer size of Hugh Mungus in relation to the other citizens, the pace and the epic scale of the action all sit within the world of 1950s B-movies. The participants were invited to offer their views on what they found useful in the clips that were shown, as a source for inspiration in their own productions. Below is some of their feedback.

Godzilla (1954):

- The representation of scale/contrast between the tiny figurine – clichéd and recognisable images that are part of a shared visual language.
- Jump-cutting shots; the exterior destruction versus the shots of characters in interior locations.
- Simplicity of the mechanics that work because the actors believe in it.
- Gendered stereotypes of the screaming female against the stoic straight-faced males.
- The declamatory style of acting and the melodrama it creates.
- Jump-cutting between the action and commentary
- The use of sound effects – bombs and sirens – that help to maintain a constant tension and feeling of threat

Godzilla was the clearest example, but useful motifs found in other filmic references that the participants briefly explored included:

Mars Attacks, 1996   A Technicolor version of a B-movie.

Cat Women of the Moon, 1953   The use of a voiceover for narration is something that could be considered.

Plan 9 from Outer Space, 1959   Music used effectively to build tension throughout the last scene.

Dr Strangelove, 1964   The repetitive use of simple drum patterns to build tension and the drama of silence. The manipulation of volume to evoke an emotional response.

The Beach Girls and the Monster, 1965   The use of a band in the film is one possible iteration of The Dummysuckers.

Children of Killers
by Katori Hall

The president of Rwanda is releasing the killers. Years after the Tutsi genocide, the perpetrators begin to trickle back into the countryside to be reunited with their villages. A trio of friends, born during the genocide's bloody aftermath, prepare to meet the men who gave them life. But as the homecoming day draws closer the young men are haunted by the sins of their fathers. Who can you become when violence is your inheritance?

Age suitability: 15+

Cast size
eight named characters:
three girls, five boys, plus chorus

Katori Hall is a writer and performer. Her plays include: *The Mountaintop* (2010 Olivier Award for Best New Play), which ran on Broadway in 2011 starring Angela Bassett and Samuel L. Jackson (for the past two theatrical seasons, the play has been one of the most produced plays in America), *Hurt Village* (2011 Susan Smith Blackburn Prize), *Children of Killers*, *Hoodoo Love*, *Remembrance*, *Saturday Night/Sunday Morning*, *WHADDABLOODCLOT!!!*, *Our Lady of Kibeho*, *Pussy Valley* and *The Blood Quilt*. Her plays have been presented on six continents, and she is currently under commission to write a new play for the National Theatre. Additional awards include the Lark Play Development Center Playwrights of New York (PoNY) Fellowship, the ARENA Stage American Voices New Play Residency, the Kate Neal Kinley Fellowship, two Lecomte du Nouy Prizes from Lincoln Center, the Fellowship of Southern Writers Bryan Family Award in Drama, a NYFA Fellowship, the Lorraine Hansberry Playwriting Award, the Columbia University John Jay Award for Distinguished Professional Achievement, Audelco Award for Playwright of the Year, the National Black Theatre August Wilson Playwriting Award, the Otto Rene Castillo Award for Political Theatre and the Otis Guernsey New Voices Playwriting Award.

Characters

Vincent, *eighteen years old, son of 'The Butcher'*

Innocent, *fifteen to eighteen years old, the peacemaker of the group*

Bosco, *fifteen to eighteen years old, charming and energetic, yet carries the seed of extremist hatred in his heart*

Mama, *Vincent's mother*

Vincent Snr

Félicité, *five to fourteen (very flexible with age), Vincent's young sister*

Esperance, *nineteen to twenty years old, a survivor of the 1994 genocide, the elder sister of Emmanuel*

Emmanuel, *fifteen years old, called 'a child of bad memories'* (enfant mauvais souvenir), *a product of rape, is slowly dying of AIDS*

The Guhahamuka, *the silenced (can be played with as few as three or as many as ten)*

Setting

Rwanda. Yesterday.

Notes

Guhahamuka: the point of speaking where words cease to exist. It is where breath refuses to make syllables amounting to silence and emotion instead.

(/) indicates overlapping of dialogue

(−) indicates an interruption

Scene One

A field in a rural village. A fútbol *game. A group of boys playing barefoot.*

Innocent   Pass it! Pass it!

Bosco   Pass the bloody ball, Vincent!

Vincent   No! Hell, no!

Innocent   But you always get to score!

Vincent   This is World Cup, yo!

Bosco   The best players always pass! They know how to attack together.

Vincent   No, they don't. They take it to the goal.

Bosco   Bloody hell, just pass the bloody ball!

Vincent   Vincent the Invincible never passes!

He kicks the ball past the invisible goalie. He scores. He dances around and around in jubilation.

Bosco   Awww, meean. You only score 'cause we don't have a goalie.

Innocent (*out of breath*)   I am too-too tired.

He falls out on the grass.

Vincent   Get up! Get up! Get up, Innocent. We not finished yet!

(*Raps.*) *We gonna rock this field, like a niggah shoot to kill.*

Innocent ⎫   Oh, my God.

Vincent ⎭   (*Raps.*) *Rock it like a soldier and like no niggah will.*

Bosco   Been watching too many rap videos on YouTube?

Innocent   He thinks he's the Jay-Z of Africa.

Bosco   You think Jay-Z will ever come to Rwanda?

Innocent   Why would he need to come to here? He already has his Beyoncé. When will I get me my Beyoncé?

Vincent   When you get a new face!

Bosco   Ohhhh!

Innocent   Wha, wha! What are you talking about? I have a beautiful face.

He stands there showing his face in profile.

I could model. Rwanda's Next Top Model, yo.

Vincent   Modelling's for girls.

Innocent   That is what you think. I will be the next Djimon Honsou. Look at that face. Look at these abs. Could cut a diamond.

They laugh.

Bosco   Innocent, quit your dreaming and pass the bloody ball!

Innocent *passes it to* **Bosco**. **Bosco** *does a quick loop or figure of eight around the other boys.*

Vincent   Oh, look at that! He's on his World Cup grind!

Bosco   Next time the World Cup comes back to Africa, I'll be ready.

Vincent   You think you can bob and weave as good as me?

He lunges towards him and tries to swipe the ball away. **Bosco** *quickly dodges him.*

Bosco   Nope, better!

Innocent   Ahh ha ha ha ha! He schooled you. He schooled you.

Bosco   What'd you learn, Vincent, huh? What'd you learn?

He is running towards the other end of the field.

Look at the way I make love to this ball. Look how she do what I say? This ball's my bitch!

Innocent   He's been practising.

Vincent   I can see that.

Bosco   I'm World Cup bound!

Vincent   World Cup, my ass!

Bosco   World Cup, oh! I'll be ready for it next time. When they come back to Africa I'm gonna be World Cup, yo!

He scores. He plays to his imaginary audience.

(*Making crowd sounds.*)   Ahhhhhhhhh! Ahhhhhhh!

He takes a bow. Then realises that he's stepped into a pile of cow dung.

Awww, meeeean. Meeeen. Meeeen!

The other boys laugh.

Vincent   They say it is good luck to step in the shit of a cow.

Bosco   Who say this?

Vincent   The ancestors.

Bosco   Eh-eh! They never know what the hell they are talking about. (*He continues to inspect his feet.*) Meeeen. Meeeen!

Innocent   Whoever's cow made that was loved.

Bosco   Now I got to pick this shit out from between my toes. This is bloody disgusting.

Innocent   Be happy that you don't have to pick it out of your teeth.

Vincent *takes the ball and bounces it on his knees. The boys continue laughing.*

Vincent (*with a start*)   Eh-eh, what time is it?

Bosco *reaches into his pocket and pulls out an iPhone.* **Vincent** *runs to get something out of his backpack.*

Innocent   Ehhh – where did you get that iPhone?

Vincent   Knowing you, you must have stolen it.

Bosco   Ay, I'm not no pickpocket!

Innocent   Then how'd you get it?

Bosco   I took it out of that American's backpack. At the cabaret.

Innocent   So how you no pickpocket?

Bosco   I didn't pick it out his pocket, I picked it out his *bag*. Differences, my friend Innocent. Differences.

Innocent   You are a consummate thief.

Bosco   Well, a young man has to be good at something.

Vincent   'Cause you're certainly not good at *fútbol*.

He has taken out his transistor radio and is trying to get it to work.

Innocent (*playing with the ball*)   Vincent, we still have a score to settle!

Vincent   Time to hear the news.

Bosco   Ah, the 'old man' is trying to hear the news.

Vincent   Call me an 'old man' one more time, and I'll beat you like an old man should.

Bosco   Awwww, / meeeeen.

Innocent   You can't get the news out here. You can never get the radio to work up here.

For a moment the channel clears. A Beyoncé song pours through the speakers. **Bosco** *and* **Innocent** *start to grind it out.*

Bosco   Even in the most remote hills of Rwanda there is Beyoncé.

Innocent *starts to sing the song, but another song riding on the wind catches his attention. The village is wailing.* **Vincent** *turns off the radio.*

Bosco   Eh-eh, why you / turn it off!

Vincent   Shhh, be quiet, yo.

Bosco   Wha, wha? Ah-ah!

There is singing coming from way off. Way off deep in the valley.

Why in the bloody hell are they singing?

Innocent   I don't know.

Bosco   What is it?

Innocent   If you would just quit your yapping for just a few seconds maybe we could hear.

Vincent   The song. Sounds familiar.

Bosco   It's the –

Vincent (*interrupting sharply*)   Shhhh . . . Listen!

The village continues to sing. A deep wail. Beat.

Innocent *and* **Vincent** *look at each other.*

Innocent   Could it be –

Bosco   True?

Vincent   I thought I would never hear that song.

Innocent   Never thought I'd hear it in my lifetime.

Bosco   It's the song of . . .

Vincent *and* **Innocent**   Machete season.

Emmanuel (*off*)   I got MTN credit! Orange credit! Credit! Credit!

A young boy, **Emmanuel**, *is selling cell-phone credit. He is wearing a bright yellow jacket. He is of similar age to the young boys, but much* *slighter. He has the sickness. He is out of breath from his climb to the top of the hill.*

Bosco } Eh-eh! Emmanuel! It true?

Innocent } Emmanuel!

Emmanuel   That what they say. The village is celebrating. We all heard it on the radio.

Innocent   We didn't.

Bosco   Your radio's for shit, Vincent.

Vincent   Fuck off, Bosco.

Bosco (*laughing*)   I gotta call my mama. Emmanuel, I need a SIM card.

Vincent   iPhone take MTN SIM?

Bosco   I got it unlocked, yo.

Vincent   *Butter!*

Emmanuel   A thousand francs for a SIM. But for you, Bosco, I'll take fifteen hundred.

Bosco   Eh-eh! That not no steal.

Emmanuel   I know you got it.

Bosco   Eleven hundred.

Emmanuel   Thirteen hundred.

Bosco (*fast*)   Twelve fifty.

Emmanuel (*fast*)   Thirteen hundred.

Bosco (*faster*)   Twelve fifty-one.

Emmanuel (*even faster*)   Thirteen fifty!

Bosco *sucks his teeth and fishes for the francs. The wailing in the village gets louder.*

Bosco   You should be the president of Uganda as slick as you are.

He hands **Emmanuel** *the francs from his pocket.*

Innocent   My mama used to sing this when she rocked me to sleep. I was only this high. 'When they come home this will be riding on the wind.'

He sings the song, he knows it well . . .

Isn't it the most beautiful song you ever heard, Vincent?

Vincent *is visibly shaking.*

Emmanuel   The President just announced it. They start the release on Friday.

Innocent   Friday?

Vincent   So soon?

Emmanuel   So soon. (*Acknowledging him.*) Vincent.

Vincent   Emmanuel. How's your sister?

Emmanuel   Esperance is cool.

Bosco *rolls his eyes.*

Bosco   What are you going to do when you meet your papa, Innocent?

Innocent   Man, I don't know. Maybe I'll –

Bosco   Hug him?

Innocent   No, I will let my sisters hug him. That is for the girls to do.

Bosco   Maybe you'll –

Innocent   Bring him out a Primus beer!

Bosco   Mama said that was my papa's favourite. Primus.

Innocent   Rwanda's favourite beer.

Vincent   It's Rwanda's *only* beer.

Innocent   Well, my auntie will make a jerrycan of banana beer to celebrate.

Bosco   Well, I'm coming over there!

Innocent   I can't believe it. I can't believe they are coming home!

Bosco   Our papas are finally coming home.

Innocent   No longer will we have to run the streets hungry.

Bosco   Or steal potatoes from other people's fields.

Innocent   Or raise our young brothers.

Bosco   Or give our sisters away at weddings.

Innocent   Or be the men of the house.

Emmanuel (*wryly*)   The killers are coming home.

Beat.

Bosco   Ah-ah, why you call them that? They're not that.

Innocent   Well, technically –

Bosco   Technically they *are* that, but you didn't have to *call* them that.

Emmanuel   Well, I'm a blunt boy.

Bosco   Blunt?

Emmanuel   I'm just saying.

Bosco   You're not *saying* anything –

Innocent (*interrupting*)   How many of them did your father kill, Bosco?

Bosco (*proudly puffing out his chest*)   They say my father killed 678.

The Boys (*without* **Vincent**)   *Whoa*!

Innocent   Well, they say *my* father killed 752.

The Boys (*without* **Vincent**)   *Whoa*!

Bosco   Well, no one has anything on Vincent's father. Isn't that right, Vincent?

Vincent (*weakly smiling, head bowed*)   That's what they say.

Bosco   Known around here for killing the most Tutsi. More than any Hutu man. That's who Vincent was named after.

Emmanuel   Really?

Bosco   Vincent the Invincible!

Innocent   Vincent the Invincible, Junior!

Bosco   Ah, oh!

Innocent   They say his father was so cold that he once made a man chop his own children to bits.

Bosco   They say he killed more than forty men in a single night.

Innocent   They say a man begged him to be shot with a bullet. But his father was soooo cold he chopped him to bits with the machete anyway.

Innocent *and* **Bosco**   Ooooo!

Bosco   No, no, no. Top this. They say, they say, *they say* he chopped off the head of a Tutsi woman and then made her children play *fútbol* with it.

He bounces the ball into the air playfully. They all stand there imagining . . .

Innocent   Man, really, that's too *too* cold. Cold as ice. Cold as ice.

Emmanuel   So, you're the son of 'The Butcher'?

Beat. Head still bowed, **Vincent** *has grown remarkably uncomfortable.*

Vincent   Yeah, that's what they say.

Innocent *and* **Bosco** *look to* **Vincent** *with great pride,* **Emmanuel** *with great fear – and* **Vincent** *to himself with great shame.*

Bosco   Emmanuel, who is your father?

Silence. **Emmanuel** *looks around.*

Emmanuel   I don't have one.

Innocent   We all have a father.

Bosco   Yeah, we all have a father.

Emmanuel   I have no father.

Bosco   Impossible.

Emmanuel   Why is that impossible?

Bosco   It's biologically impossible for you *not* to have one.

Emmanuel   How do you know?

Bosco   'Cause I know about it. I read it in a book I stole.

Innocent ⎫   Goodness, gracious.

Vincent ⎬   Bosco!

Bosco   Wha? Wha? Nobody else was using it. I had to read up for the big moment.

Innocent   I've already had my big moment –

Bosco   Liar!

Innocent   I have. She said I was good!

Bosco   Liar!

Innocent   Whatever, Bosco.

Bosco   Go to bloody hell!

Innocent   No, you go! Come on, Emmanuel. Tell us who your father is.

Emmanuel   Like I said before, I have no father.

Bosco   As a seed you were spit out of the sword of life. Only a man can spit you out of his sword. (*He gestures.*)

Innocent   Bosco, did you read that biology book correctly?

Emmanuel   I have no father. My mother told me that I was conceived like Jesus.

Beat.

Innocent   Like Jesus?

Emmanuel   Yes, so help me God. I am a miracle child. Conceived during the genocide. Amongst the destruction and death, God blessed her with life, me, 'Immaculate Emmanuel'. I am the result of a 'virgin conception'.

Innocent *and* **Bosco** *take a look at each other.*

Bosco (*smiling*)   You?

Emmanuel   That's what she said. I am directly from God.

Bosco   Well, I certainly didn't read about that in no biology book.

Emmanuel   You should have stolen a Bible, then you'd know.

Bosco *takes a step towards* **Emmanuel.** **Innocent** *put his hand on* **Bosco**'s *chest.*

Innocent   Well, his mother's name *is* Mary.

Bosco *and* **Innocent** *laugh, while* **Vincent** *grows increasingly uncomfortable.*

Vincent   Leave him alone.

Bosco   So you think your mother was a virgin when she had you?

Emmanuel   Of course not. Esperance was born of man, but I, *I* was born of God. Like Jesus. I am a child of God.

Bosco (*laughing*)   Aren't we all.

Emmanuel   Not in the way you mean. I am special. I don't need a father.

Innocent   Nooo, I think I know your father.

Emmanuel   Yes, my father is God.

Bosco   No, I think your father is Claude.

Innocent   Or Alphonse

Bosco   His father could be Jean-Pierre.

Emmanuel } I was born like Jesus.

Innocent } Or Vianney.

Emmanuel } I have no father.

Bosco } Or François.

Innocent } Or Olivier.

Bosco } Or Jonas.

Innocent } Or Gazazi, his brother!

Vincent } Leave him alone.

Emmanuel   That's what my mother said! 'Immaculate Emmanuel!' That's who I am.

He runs away downhill as fast as his legs will carry him. **Bosco** *and* **Innocent** *throw something at him.*

Vincent   LEAVE HIM ALONE!

Bosco *and* **Innocent** *look after him and laugh.*

Innocent   Immaculate conception? That was a good one, eh?

Bosco   There is nothing immaculate about that poor boy. He skinny.

Innocent   That what the sickness do, yo. Disappear you.

Bosco   That's what his mama died of, too.

Innocent   Yeah . . .

Bosco   His mother wasn't no virgin. More like a whore. Can you believe he believed that story she told him? What a shame he doesn't know who his father is.

Vincent   Well, his father might be yours.

They both stop chuckling.

Bosco   Wha? Eh?

Vincent   Maybe Emmanuel is your little brother.

Bosco   Impossible.

Vincent   You're so busy trying to name his father, you forgot to put yours in the mix.

Innocent   Hey . . .

Bosco   That's not . . . fair.

Innocent   Heeey!

Bosco   My father would never have done *that*. He did other things, but he would never ever do *that*.

Vincent   Why not?

Bosco   Because I *know* him.

Vincent   Oh, do you?

Bosco   Yes, I *know* my father wouldn't do that.

Vincent   Don't be so sure.

Innocent   Hey, guys, let's stop.

Bosco   Are you calling my father *that*?

Vincent   How else do you think Emmanuel came to be? He is a miracle child alright, but not that kind of miracle.

Bosco   My papa did not rape Mary. My papa did not do that. Plus they say – eh, eh – Emmanuel got the sickness. My papa don't got the AIDS. They made the men with the AIDS rape the women. My papa don't got the AIDS.

Innocent   How you know?

Bosco   Does your papa got the AIDS?

Innocent   Hell, no.

Bosco   Well, my papa don't either. My papa didn't have to force no women to be with him.

Vincent   Well, that's not what I heard.

Bosco   Well, there's a difference between what you hear and what you know. And, 'old man', why are you bringing up all this anyway? All this old shit! It's just rumours. Those down in the village don't know our papas. We do!

Vincent   We've never even met our fathers, Bosco. None of us! You don't *know* him.

Bosco   I know my father.

Vincent   Yeah, and what do you know about him?

Bosco *stands there in silence.*

Vincent   Emmanuel's right. They're killers.

Innocent   Look, the government made them do it.

Vincent   Do you really believe that, Innocent?

Innocent   That's what they said. That's what they said happened.

Vincent   Come on, Innocent. Think for yourself.

Innocent   Vincent, what's gotten into you?

Vincent   Do you really think that the government put a machete in your father's hand?

Bosco   That's what they said. So that's what we have to believe.

Innocent   Hey, that is what they are teaching in the schools?

Vincent   What if your papa just had it in him, just had it in him, and he wanted to go kill those women, those children –

Bosco   Ah-ah! My papa didn't kill no kids, *yours* did!

Vincent   The question is, do you know that *yours* did?

Bosco *stares at his friend. Beat.*

Bosco   I'm going home.

Innocent   Bosco –

Bosco *begins to trudge down the hill. He sharply turns.*

Bosco   Innocent, you coming?

Innocent *looks back to* **Vincent** *who stares back at him.*

Innocent (*foraging up a smile*)   Hey, guys, they're coming home. There's so much to celebrate. So much to be happy about . . .

Vincent   Yeah. They're coming home. No longer will we be the men of the house.

Innocent *follows* **Bosco** *down towards the bottom of the hill.*

Scene Two

Night time. **Vincent** *is lying in his bed. He is tossing and turning. A worn ball rolls from one side of the room. He continues to sleep. A little girl emerges from the corner. She has on a slip. It is horribly distressed, caked with dried blood and vomit. She plays with the ball. She would have been a pro* fútbol *player. Would have been . . .*

Another girl comes from the other corner. Her clothes, too, are caked with blood.

Guhahamuka 1 *laughing.*

Guhahamuka 2   Shhhh! He's sleeping.

A young boy emerges from the shadows.

Guhahamuka 3   Not peacefully though.

Guhahamuka 1 *laughing.*

Guhahamuka 2   Why does she laugh so much?

Guhahamuka 3   Because they cut off her tongue.

Guhahamuka 1 *laughing.*

Guhahamuka 2   You're gonna wake him.

Guhahamuka 1 *laughing.*

Guhahamuka 2   Stop!

Guhahamuka 3   Be quiet both of you. Let's go to work.

The Guhahamuka *take their positions.*

Guhahamuka 1 *laughing.*

Guhahamuka 2 *and* **3** *(raps)*   *We are the gahahamuka.*

Guhahamuka 1 *laughing.*

Guhahamuka 2 *and* **3** *(raps)*   *We are the gahahamuka. Here to tell the tale if only you would listen.*

Guhahamuka 3   Listen.

Guhahamuka 1 *laughing.*

The young boy – **Guhahamuka 3** *– raises a machete above his head. He is about to take a slice. He raises the machete and with all his might he goes for* **Vincent***'s head.*

Félicité *(offstage)*   Vincent . . . Vincent . . .

Vincent *shoots straight up. He looks around himself.* **The Guhahamuka** *have vanished. His eyes adjust to the dark and he finally sees* **Félicité** *standing at the edge of the bed.*

Vincent   Why are you standing up there laughing at me?

Félicité   I'm not laughing at you.

Vincent   Yes, you were. I just heard you.

Félicité   It wasn't me, Vincent, I swear.

Vincent   What do you want?

Félicité   I need to take a piss.

Vincent   Piss in the bucket, Félicité.

Félicité   Unh, unh. I hate how it smells in the morning.

Vincent   So what you really have to do is go take a shit?

Beat.

Félicité   Guilty.

Vincent *sighs. He pulls the covers back and hops out of bed. Laughter rides on the wind.*

Vincent   What was that?

Félicité   What was what?

Vincent   That?

Félicité   What?

Vincent   That? Did you hear that?

Félicité   I didn't hear anything.

Vincent   Laughter.

Félicité *listens.*

Félicité   Maybe that was Mama.

Vincent   No, Mama doesn't laugh at night; she cries.

Crying and laughter ride the wind.

Shh! Listen, there it goes again.

Félicité *is shifting in her pants.*

Félicité   Vincent, I have to go shit. Bad!

Vincent   Alright. Alright.

Vincent *takes* **Félicité**'s *hand and they walk out of the hut into the darkness of the night. Out of the shadows one of* **The Guhahamuka** *emerges. The ball she was holding has now been replaced with a skull.*

Scene Three

Next morning. The kitchen hut. **Vincent** *and his little sister,* **Félicité**, *around ten years old, sit at the table.* **Vincent** *is tuning in his transistor radio.* **Mama** *stands at the stove, cooking.*

Radio   The President's prisoner release programme is well under way. A wave of prisoners has been released from Gingkoro Prison in southwestern Rwanda.

Félicité   That's near us, Mama!

Mama   Shhh, Félicité!

Radio   Many prisoners have completed the national rehabilitation programme and are coming home. (*Voice of the President:*) 'The past is over and the future is now. Rwanda can only walk into the future with all of her children. We can co-exist peacefully in this society as neighbours. Gone are the days of the Hutu and Tutsi. In this Rwanda, the new Rwanda, we are one.'

Félicité *heads towards the stove.*

Mama   Eh, eh! Why you goin' for seconds?

Félicité   I'm a growing girl. Mama, let me eat.

Mama   Eh, eh, eh! We have to save that for later.

Vincent   Félicité always has to have seconds.

Félicité   Because Félicité is never satisfied.

Mama (*laughing*)   Yes, indeed that is true.

Vincent   I swear you have a tapeworm.

Félicité *sticks her tongue out at her brother.*

Félicité   Mama, can I please have seconds?

Mama   Eh! Eh!

Félicité   Mama, pleeeease . . .

Beat. **Mama** *sighs.*

Mama   Fine. But make sure you leave a little in the pot for the gods. Always have to have a little bit left over for them.

Félicité   Thank you, Mama!

Mama   Leave some for Vincent.

Vincent   Ugh, ugh, I don't want.

Mama   What, boy, you gotta eat. You don't want to look like a Tutsi now, do you?

Vincent *goes over to the stove. He fills his bowl with more porridge.*

Mama   Where are Innocent and Bosco? I do not hear those knotty-headed boys wrestling outside your window. I wonder why they are late.

Vincent   I – I – I told them I'd meet them down the road.

Mama   Good. Those two boys give me headaches.

She sits down at the kitchen table and pulls out a tube of red lipstick. Her hands shake, but she applies it gingerly on to her pursed lips.

Félicité   Ooo, Mama! Why are you putting that on?

Mama   Mind your business, child.

Félicité   Can I put it on?

Mama   You don't need to practise.

Félicité   Practise what?

Mama   Being pretty. Because you already are. Unfortunately, your mama is out of practice.

Vincent   And who are you practising for?

Beat.

Mama   You know, Vincent.

Vincent   No, I don't know.

Mama   Don't be so silly, Vincent.

She picks up the rusted machete and continues applying the red lipstick.

Vincent   That stuff makes you look like a –

Mama   Vincent, you are not too *old* to get slapped.

Félicité *giggles.* **Vincent** *sulks at the table.* **Mama** *finishes her application. She looks up.*

Mama   How do I look? Do you think your papa will like this?

Vincent   If he likes a woman as beautiful as you, then indeed he will like this new look of yours.

Mama   I haven't worn red lipstick since . . . Almost forgot I had it.

She holds it close to her chest.

Félicité   Can I wear some, Mama?

She stares at herself in the machete. She smiles at herself approvingly.

Mama   Red was always his favourite colour.

Félicité *goes over to kiss her* **Mama** *on the lips.*

Félicité   There! I got some on my lips, too.

Félicité *looks at herself in the machete.*

Mama   Little girl, go by the bucket and wash that off your lips! And wash that millet from your hands while you're at it!

Félicité   Aww, meen.

Mama   Sa-sa! (*Clapping her hands.*) Child, and remember you are not too *young* to be slapped.

Félicité *trudges to the bucket in the corner.* **Mama** *continues to stare at herself in the shine of the machete.*

Vincent   What will he say about her? About Félicité?

Mama   Why, boy, what do you mean?

Vincent   Don't you think he's gonna be mad?

Mama (*laughing*)   What's he got to be mad about? I ploughed this land and made it bigger and better. When he left we had one cow, now we have three. We have a well on our land now, and why, my Vincent? I do think that it is because of me.

Vincent   And me.

Mama   Yes, so you pulled your weight, too. We had to. We all had to. Life goes on. Félicité is an example that life goes on.

Vincent   Yes, life goes on, but aren't you scared of him? What he will say –

Mama   Why would I be scared of your father? He is gentle as water rolling down a hill.

Vincent   He will know that you were not faithful –

She slaps him hard across the face.

Mama   What is 'faithful' when you are hungry? What is 'faithful' when you need somewhere to sleep? What is 'faithful' when someone must pay your school fees? I didn't hear you complaining about my 'faithfulness' then.

Vincent   I was a boy then; I'm a man now.

Mama   Let's see how much of a man you'll be when your papa comes home.

Félicité *stares at them from across the kitchen table.*

Mama   Time to go to work.

She looks back into the machete, admiring her face.

Scene Four

Bosco *is waiting by the well. He has a machete in his hand. He is about to start work out in the fields. A* **Guhahamuka** *runs by him.*

Guhahamuka 1 *laughing.*

Bosco *jumps.*

Bosco   Who's there?

Guhahamuka 1 *laughing.*

Bosco   What the bloody hell . . .

He lifts up his machete, hovering in a batting position.

Hey, Innocent, quit playing games.

Guhahamuka 1 *laughing.*

Bosco   Stop it, now. I'm not playing with you.

A ball is kicked towards him. He ducks. He runs to pick it up.

Guhahamuka 1 *laughing.*

Bosco   Innocent! Stop playing you bloody –

Bosco *takes a look at the soccer ball. It is covered with blood. He drops it. And stares at his hands. He runs to the water pump to wash his hands. He keeps washing and washing and washing and washing and washing.* **Bosco** *turns around –*

Bosco   Aaaaahhhhh!

Innocent   Aaaaahhhhh!

Bosco   Why you playing around like that? You're always playing round!

Innocent   What you talking about? I called your name. You didn't hear me?

Bosco   When?

Innocent   Just then!

Bosco   Why you throw that ball at me, man?

Innocent   What ball?

Bosco *looks to where the ball was. It's gone.*

Bosco   Right –

Innocent   Where?

Bosco   It was. Just. Right . . . there.

Innocent   You going coo-coo.

Bosco *looks to his hands. He holds them up. They are no longer red.*

Bosco   Must have been staring at the sun too long.

Innocent   Something.

Bosco   Seeing things . . .

Innocent   You think he's mad we didn't stop by? To pick him up?

Bosco   Who cares.

Innocent   He's never been that way before. I wonder what's gotten into him.

Bosco   'Old man' just about had a heart attack.

Innocent   He's only a few years older than us.

Bosco   So what? He still bloody old.

Innocent   Why you always saying 'bloody'?

Bosco *pauses and takes a look at his hands.*

Bosco   It's every Rwandan's duty as newly minted members of the British Commonwealth to use the curse words of our fellow brethren.

Innocent   I rather say 'fuck' like the Americans.

Bosco   Bloody. Fuck. Whatever. You'd think he'd be happy. Our papas coming home, and there he goes bringing up all that – that history –

Innocent   Just think, twenty years ago we all would have been speaking French.

Bosco   French bloody sucks. I will thank the President every day for changing the national language to English.

Innocent   Why?

Bosco   So I can get me an American wife.

Innocent   Don't no American wanna marry you.

Bosco   An American see this fine African specimen, and she will keel over in delight and wanna make her a fine African-American.

They laugh. One of **The Guhahamuka** *runs behind them in the brush.*

Guhahamuka 1 *laughing.*

Bosco *jumps.*

Bosco   Innocent, did you see that?

Innocent   See what?

Bosco   There it is again. I saw something. Like . . . like . . . like a kid.

Innocent   You need to get out of the sun.

The Guhahamuka *runs past them again.*

Guhahamuka 1 *laughing.*

Bosco   There it is again. I know I heard something. Laughing. Something laughing . . .

Innocent (*he points*)   Maybe it's her, but I don't know what she got to laugh about.

A beautiful teenage girl walks down the hill. She balances a yellow jerrycan full of water on her head. She bears the marks of a survivor. Scars decorate her arms like bracelets. There is one that cuts across her head. (She may only have one arm.) But the slices of the machete were not able to cut her beauty away from her. She pauses when she sees the boys. She wonders whether or not she should continue. She decides to walk forward . . . carefully.

Bosco   Oooo, my God, it's hot.

He fans himself. **Innocent** *laughs.*

Innocent   Can we have some water?

She does not speak to them. They rib each other.

Bosco   We know you have a voice. A very pretty voice. That's what they say.

Innocent   Yeah, that's what they say.

Bosco   Don't be scared of us. We not gonna hurt you.

Innocent   At least *I'm* not.

She proceeds slowly.

Bosco   You wanna see my new phone?

Innocent   She don't wanna see that thing.

Bosco   I bet she do. Don't you want to see it?

She ignores them.

Innocent   *Inyenzi*, don't you hear us talking to you?

She whirls around and faces them.

Esperance   Do not call me that. That is not my name. You know my name is Esperance. Not *cockroach*.

Bosco   That's what we used to call you. During the war. That's what you are.

Innocent   Yeah, that's what you are.

Esperance   Have you looked in the mirror lately?

Innocent   Ooooo!

Bosco   She's a tough Tutsi. Haven't seen one of those before.

Innocent   She won't be so tough in a minute.

Esperance   You don't scare me.

Bosco   Oh, we don't?

He goes up to her and pushes the jerrycan from her head. As it falls water splatters all over the ground.

Ooops!

Esperance *picks up the jerrycan and throws the rest of the water at* **Bosco**.

Esperance   Leave me alone!

Innocent   Look! Look at her! The Tutsi who fights back!

Bosco   Hey, you got my iPhone wet! Grab her! Grab her!

Innocent *grabs* **Esperance**.

Esperance   Stop it! Stop it! Let go of me!

Esperance ⎫   Let go of me! Let GO!

Bosco ⎭   You got my iPhone wet!

He comes up to her and points his finger in her face.

Bosco   When my father comes home you better run. He will finish. He will finish what he started.

Esperance   Well, tell him to come. I may only have one arm, but the other can wield a machete just as wildly as any other man.

Bosco *raises his hand, but, suddenly, out of nowhere,* **Vincent** *barrels down the hill. He tackles* **Bosco** *to the ground.*

Bosco ⎫   What the bloody hell you doing?

Vincent ⎭   Get off of her!

Vincent *then rushes to* **Innocent**, *who has* **Esperance** *in his grip.*

Vincent   Let her go!

Innocent *is no match for the bigger* **Vincent** *and quickly lets her go.*

Esperance *takes off running down the hill away from the young men, leaving her jerrycan behind.*

Bosco   What you do that for, Vincent?

His nose is bloody.

Innocent   We were only playing.

Vincent   Playing?

Bosco   It was a joke. She was laughing. See, she was laughing.

Vincent   She was not laughing.

Innocent   Yes, she was.

Vincent   She was scared out of her mind. What were you trying to do to her?

Innocent   Nothing.

Vincent *pushes up close to* **Bosco**, *fire streaming from his eyes.*

Vincent   What were you trying to do to her?

Innocent   I said NOTHING!

Bosco   Why do you care so much about them, about her?

Vincent   I don't.

Bosco   You act like you love her.

Vincent   Fuck you!

Bosco   Is that it? Is it that you love the *inyenzi*? You a cockroach lover? Well, I tell you one thing, they don't love us. They would kill us Hutus if they could. Round us all up. They're out for revenge.

Vincent   That's not true.

Bosco   Remember how the Tutsi kids used to taunt us in primary. Huh, Vincent?

Innocent   They looked down on us.

Bosco   Because they had better clothes than us. Because everyone felt sorry for them. Everyone was giving them everything. 'Oh, the poor little orphans, they have no parents. Oh, the poor Tutsis.' Well, what about us, Vincent? What about us?

Innocent   They locked our papas away. Making *us* orphans.

Bosco   Called us children of killers.

Vincent   Well, can you blame them?

Bosco   We didn't do anything to them, Vincent! And we are the ones being punished.

Innocent   It's *inyenzi* like her that need to be punished.

Vincent   Punished for what?

Bosco   In case you don't remember, she is the main reason our fathers are behind bars. She is the one that pointed them out. At the trial?

Vincent   I don't believe that.

Bosco   Well, you better. My mother said that it was Esperance who pointed. She pointed her little finger and then my father was gone. Our fathers. Gone. If it wasn't for her . . . You know, all my life I've had to teach myself how to be a man. How to shave my beard. How to take a piss. How to hoe. How to sharpen a machete. How to chop firewood for the stove. How to make love to a woman. How to . . . She took my father away from me, Vincent. From *us*!

Vincent   She was just a child.

Bosco   *I wasn't even born!* I didn't even get to meet my father, Vincent. Not once. I've always wondered, do I have his nose? Do I have his hands? Do I have his moles? Do I have . . . I don't even know how he looks, Vincent. I don't even have one memory of him. I never got the chance. Because of her. Because of her little finger. Well, I wish they hadda chopped off her other hand.

Vincent ⎫   Are you hearing what you are saying?

Innocent ⎭   Hey, buddy, calm down. Calm down.

Bosco (*near tears*)   She was wrong. She was wrong. She was wrong. She was wrong. She was wrong. She was wrong.

Suddenly, the village begins to wail. They are singing the 'machete song'. There is a beat of the drum. A celebratory chant. It is louder and more aggressive than before. The young men stare at each other.

Innocent   They're here. Oh, my God, they're here.

Bosco   My papa . . . My papa's home.

He takes off running down the hill.

Innocent, you coming or what?

Innocent   I'll meet you. I'll meet you down there.

Bosco (*from the distance*)   Hurry! Hurry!

He is gone.

Innocent   We weren't going to do anything to her, Vincent.

Vincent   People can get carried away.

Innocent   It wasn't like that.

Vincent   Yeah, that's what they say.

Innocent   I feel sorry for you.

Vincent   Yeah, well. I feel sorry for him.

Innocent   Why?

Vincent   Because he's just like his father.

Innocent   Well, you're nothing like yours.

He runs after his friend.

Vincent *picks up the jerrycan that* **Esperance** *left behind.*

Scene Five

The village is wailing the machete song.

Esperance *carries a basket of purple flowers. She sprinkles them on a soft patch of grass. She kneels down. While she speaks* **The Guhahamuka** *surround her and lay hands on her. To give her strength.*

Esperance   You told me that this day would never come.
You promised me. When you were in the hospice you said
that the worst was over. 'Don't worry, I am the last victim of
the genocide.' I remember you saying. 'I am the last.' You
hear that song? That sweet song that rings of murder? They
are coming home. They are coming home to finish what they
started. They can kill you fast, or they can kill you slow, but
at the end of the day they still kill you. They killed you slowly.
So slowly. I don't know why you wouldn't tell me. I knew.
I knew you had the sickness, Mama. I knew you took those
pills. But then you got worse. You got worse, Mama. Who
knew that Death would take so long, toying with you,
torturing you? You would have thought the rape would be
enough, but Death came right along to screw you until your
dying day. Filling your lungs until you could not breathe.
Ripping your skin with sores. Who knew one would rather
die at the stroke of the machete than of the slow tick-tock of
the AIDS clock. Our little Emmanuel is . . . getting worse.
We try to get the money together every month, you know, for
his medicine . . . he's selling credit in the streets, I'm weaving
baskets and selling them by the roadside, it's barely enough . . .
I don't know what I'll do without him. If he goes then . . .
what am I going to do? I'll be the only one left. The only
one left of our family. They are singing in the streets. In
the cabarets. They are coming home. My neighbours, my
killers . . . I feel like I'm back beneath the dead bodies again.
I'm back to being smothered beneath the weight of the dead.
When they found me, they thought I was gone. Blood, blood
everywhere. Somehow I survived, but, Mama, I'm tired.
I don't think I can be a survivor any more.

Suddenly she can see **The Guhahamuka**. *They sing her a sweet
song that is a sharp contrast to the machete song. She is strengthened for
a moment and she sings along, and briefly the victims drown the machete
song out.* **Vincent** *emerges from the forest, carrying the jerrycan. He
watches her for a spell until she finishes her song.*

Vincent   Is this where your family is buried?

Esperance *looks up. Beat.* **The Guhahamuka** *have disappeared.*

Esperance   No, just my mother. I don't know where the rest are buried. Some say the mass grave up on the hill. Some say the mass grave down the hill. I do not know.

She begins to lift herself off the ground.

Vincent   Do you need any help up?

Esperance   No, I can do it on my own.

With one arm, she has trouble getting herself up.

Vincent   Here, let me help you.

Esperance   Look, I said I was fine.

Vincent   I just want to help.

Esperance   I don't need your help.

Vincent   Please let me help –

She takes a stumble. He catches her. He steadies her.

Esperance   Thank you.

Vincent   You're welcome.

Esperance   I guess you want another thank you for before.

Vincent   No, I don't want anything from you.

She looks him up and down cautiously.

Esperance   Why aren't you down there with them? Singing.

Vincent   I'm not a good singer. You are, though. A beautiful singer.

Esperance   How long were you standing there?

Vincent   Just enough to be blessed by your concert.

She looks down and blushes. She notices the jerrycan in his hand.

Esperance   You filled my jerrycan for me.

Vincent   Yeah. Can I get a 'thank you' for that, too?

Esperance *smiles.*

Vincent   Lips like the sun, teeth like the stars.

Esperance *blushes. No one has told her that she's pretty before.*

Esperance   Thank you.

Vincent   You're welcome.

Beat. They hear the machete song in the distance.

Esperance   Are you happy your father is coming back?

Vincent   Yes.

Esperance   What are you going to say to him when you see him?

Vincent   I haven't thought about it.

Esperance   Come on, you have to have thought about it. You've had a whole lifetime to think about it.

Vincent   Really, I haven't thought about it.

Esperance   Think. If there was one thing you wanted to say, wanted to ask, what would it be?

Vincent (*without thinking*)   How does it feel to be like God?

Esperance *stares at him.*

Vincent   Sometimes I wonder. I wonder when he had the time . . . As he was roaming the countryside killing and maiming, taking an arm here, a nose there, a life here, a life there, he had enough time to give me life.

Esperance   Perhaps he wanted to put something into the world because he was so busy taking so much out.

Vincent   I understand the hatred in your heart.

Esperance   The hatred in my heart?

Vincent   Yes, I understand why you hate me.

Esperance   Why would I hate *you*?

Vincent   I'm Hutu.

Esperance   It's not that simple, Vincent.

Vincent   But – I want you to hate me.

Esperance   I'll never hate you, Vincent.

Vincent   Why not?

Esperance   Because you didn't do anything.

He looks at her softly. He takes in the scars adorning her body like tattoos. She stands there and lets him see them. Lets him see her. He takes his hand and slowly traces his finger along her past.

Vincent   Who gave you these?

Esperance   Your father.

The Guhahamuka *stand in silence and witness.*

Vincent   I'm sorry.

Esperance   You are not who I want to hear sorry from.

Vincent   But I –

Esperance   You should go now. Go and meet your father. Go meet him now.

Vincent   I'm scared.

Esperance   But you are Vincent the Invincible, are you not?

Vincent *begins to walk away, she looks after him. He looks back.*

Vincent   Thank you, Esperance.

Esperance   You're welcome, Vincent.

She picks up the jerrycan and places it on her head and walks away.

Scene Six

A figure in a dark hoodie writes something on a wall. **The Guhahamuka** *stand there as witnesses. The machete song is getting louder and louder.*

Guhahamuka 1 *laughing.*

Guhahamuka 2   It is starting again.

Guhahamuka 3   He will be sorry.

Guhahamuka 2   A soul like that knows no contrition.

Guhahamuka 1 *laughing.*

Guhahamuka 2   He knows not what he does.

Guhahamuka 3   He knows exactly what he does.

Guhahamuka 1 *crying/laughing.*

Guhahamuka 2   Shhhh, don't cry. Don't cry, sisi.

Guhahamuka 1 *crying.*

Guhahamuka 2   Look, they've upset her.

Guhahamuka 3   It's upsetting. They haven't learned.

Scene Seven

Esperance *has arrived at her hut, her jerrycan delicately balanced on her head. She stands there looking up at her hut. It says 'Kill the cockroaches' across one side. Horrifying graffiti. She looks wildly about.*

Esperance   Emmanuel! Emmanuel! Are you in there?

Emmanuel *walks out of the hut with sleep in his eye.*

Esperance   Oh, my God. Thank God. Thank God you are alive. They didn't do anything to you, did they?

Emmanuel   No, no, what are you talking about?

Esperance *points.* **Emmanuel** *takes it all in. Silence. He looks at his sister.*

Emmanuel   What are we going to do?

Esperance *stands staring at the writing on the wall.*

Emmanuel *wobbles back inside the hut.*

Esperance *quickly takes the jerrycan full of water and heaves it at the wall. The water makes a splash against the stone. The words begin to slide like blood down the wall. She washes the hatred away.*

The machete song grows louder and louder until –

Scene Eight

Bright neon lights. Disco. **Innocent** *and* **Bosco** *are at the outdoor cabaret.* **Innocent** *is dancing, but* **Bosco** *is downing a beer in the corner.*

Innocent   This is cause for a celebration! A celebration, I say! Everyone raise your beer. Raise your beers! Our papas have come home!

He runs up to **Vincent** *and gives him a huge hug. They walk through the cabaret together.*

Vincent   Where are they?

Innocent   At home, getting washed up. They're on their way to the cabaret.

Vincent *notices* **Bosco** *in the corner.*

Vincent   I need to apologise to him.

Innocent   Hey, Vincent. Bosco's a bit –

Vincent   Tipsy? I can see that.

Innocent   Nooo. It's not just that.

Vincent   I know I've been acting crazy these past few days. I just want to –

Innocent   His father wasn't on the bus from the prison.

Beat.

Vincent   What, what do you mean? They said everyone from the village was coming home.

Innocent   That's what they said, but – bu—

Vincent   What happened?

Innocent   Something about him not expressing 'contrition'. Kept him. He got ten more years, they say.

Vincent   Why didn't he say he was sorry?

Innocent   I don't think he was.

Beat.

Vincent   Well, what about yours?

Innocent   Butter! The man is butter, yo! I see where I get this handsome face from.

He turns to show off his profile.

Rwanda's Next Top Model!

Vincent   You so silly.

Innocent   I know, man! This stuff make me silly. The papas are home! THE PAPAS ARE HOME!

He takes a huge celebratory swig from his beer.

Vincent   Innocent, did you see my papa?

Innocent   Yeah. I did.

Vincent *begins to shake.*

Innocent   You alright, Vincent?

Vincent   It just all of a sudden got a little chilly. Rainy season must be on its way.

Innocent   Rainy season would be a bit early if it's on its way.

Vincent   Maybe it is early. How did he look?

Innocent *gives him a look; he understands.*

Innocent   I don't think he's coming to the party tonight.

Vincent   I'ma go say 'hey' to Bosco, then head on home.

Innocent   Bosco's naturally . . . you know.

Vincent   Let me go talk to him.

Innocent   Just talk to him soft though. Talk to him soft.

Vincent *walks up to* **Bosco** *at the bar.* **Innocent** *watches carefully from the corner.*

Bosco (*to the bartender*)   Hey, can I get another Primus?

Vincent   I heard.

Bosco   What you hear?

Vincent   I'm sorry, man.

Bosco   No matter. He's a man. He stood by his values. What more could you ask for?

Vincent   Still, I'm sorry, man.

Bosco   Well, he's stubborn. I guess I see where I get it from.

Vincent   Like father, like son.

Bosco *pauses, his Primus in mid-air.*

Bosco   Yeah, like father, like son. Saw your father though – sa-sa . . .

Esperance *enters.*

Bosco   Well, look at that. The cockroach has joined us for the party.

Esperance *looks around the cabaret. The disco lights spin around the silence. Fire coming out of her eyes. As the following scene continues, one by one* **The Guhahamuka** *emerge from the shadows. Witnesses of the past, witnesses of the present. Everyone is oblivious to them though.*

Esperance   Who is the coward? Huh? I say, who is the coward in this room?

Bosco   So sad. She's gone crazy.

Esperance   You answer my anger in silence, eh? You cowards. You cowards. I spit at your feet.

She spits – the absolutely most horrible thing you can do in this culture.

I spit at you. If you wanna finish your work, then you do it. You DO IT!! But you do it in the light. I dare you to do it in the light!

Innocent *sweeps in and grabs* **Esperance**.

Innocent   You better leave before they come.

Esperance   They can come. I am waiting for them. I am waiting for them. I refuse. I refuse to leave.

Innocent   You need to leave, Esperance.

Esperance   I will not be leaving. Not before you show your face. Who did it? Who did it?

Bosco *begins laughing in the corner.*

Bosco   The Tutsi has gone mad. Look at her cockroach antennas shaking back and forth.

Esperance   So this is a joke to you, Bosco?

Bosco   You have gone mad. You are mad to be here. Get out before something happens to you.

Esperance   What will happen? Coward. You – you – you orphan!

Bosco   Vincent, you get her out of here before she says something she will regret.

Esperance   I will never regret anything. Never. Do not step one foot near my hut, Bosco! Or the anger of my ancestors will rain down upon this land. Step one foot near me and Emmanuel and I will kill you.

Bosco   Bitch, I don't know what you are talking about.

Esperance   You do! You were there tonight. You're so stupid you couldn't even spell cockroaches right.

Bosco   Can someone please tell me what the bloody hell she is talking about?

Esperance   He came to my hut!

Vincent   Calm down, Esperance. Slow down.

Guhahamuka 1   *laughing.*

Vincent *pulls* **Esperance** *outside. The others quickly follow.*

Bosco *can hear the laughter in his brain. The hollow echoes of the spirits. The reminder of the past.*

Esperance   He threatened me. Outside of my hut. I saw. I saw it. 'Kill the cockroaches.' Just like they used to say. It is a threat pure and simple.

Bosco   I didn't step anywhere near your hut, Esperance. I wouldn't step on Tutsi ground. It is evil.

Guhahamuka 1 *laughing.*

Bosco *grabs his head.*

Esperance   You step on Tutsi ground when you want to steal some potatoes to eat. You just take, take, take! Well, I refuse to let you take anything from me any more.

Bosco   Hush up, Esperance.

Guhahamuka 2   Hush up, Esperance.

Guhahamuka 3   Be silent.

Vincent   Yes, be quiet, Esperance.

Esperance   I will not be silent any more.

Guhahamuka 1 *crying laughter.*

Esperance   My back is already bent from carrying water from the well. You will not bend my back any more.

Guhahamuka 2 ⎫   Please, Esperance.

Vincent ⎭   Please, Esperance.

Bosco *holds his head.*

Bosco   Shut your mouth, Esperance, before I shut it up for you.

Guhahamuka 1 ⎫   *laughing.*

Esperance (*laughing*) ⎭   Are you that big and bold to threaten me out in the open like that?

Bosco   Stop the laughing. Stop laughing at me.

Esperance (*turning to everyone*) ⎫   Will you all just let him threaten me like that?

Guhahamuka 1 ⎭   *laughing.*

Guhahamuka 2 ⎫   His threats are promises.

Bosco ⎬   I do not make threats, Esperance, I make promises. Believe me, a threat that passes from my lips will be an order that is completed.

Esperance *goes up to* **Bosco** *and pushes him with her one arm.*

Bosco   Go home, Esperance.

Esperance   You think you can scare me? Well, I will not be scared. I will not! Your father did not scare me. And he is right where he belongs. Where I was.

Guhahamuka 2   In the bottom of the pit –

Guhahamuka 3   With a bloody lump –

Guhahamuka 1 *laughing.*

Bosco (*warning her*)   Esperance . . .

Esperance   Swimming amongst the piss.

Guhahamuka 1   *crying.*

Guhahamuka 2 *and* **Guhahamuka 3**   And shit.

Esperance   Alone. With dead bodies being piled on top. And stones being thrown down.

Guhahamuka 1   *laughing.*

Esperance   I hope he rots alone . . .

Guhahamuka 1   *laughing.*

Vincent   Shhhh, Esperance . . .

Esperance   At the bottom of that jail where he belongs.

Beat. **The Guhahamuka** *tremble at her hatred.*

Bosco *lunges at her.*

Bosco   I will finish you! I will finish you off! I will finish you!

Vincent   Bosco, GET OFF OF HER!

But **Bosco** *is on top of her. Choking her with his bare hands.*

Guhahamuka 1 *crying.*

Guhahamuka 2   When will they learn?

Innocent   She's not worth it!

Guhahamuka 3   When will they stop?

Guhahamuka 2   It has begun again.

Vincent   LET HER GO!

Guhahamuka 3   Breathe, Esperance. Do not come to the other side. We are lost −

Guhahamuka 2   Floating in the piss −

Guhahamuka 3   And the shit −

Guhahamuka 2   Thrown into mass graves −

Guhahamuka 3   We are lost.

Guhahamuka 1 *crying and laughing and crying.*

The Guhahamuka *cry. The dead cannot help. They can only watch. Those that are alive could help, but they choose not to. They choose only to look on as history repeats itself. But* **Vincent** *does the unthinkable – he does something. He pushes* **Bosco** *off* **Esperance**. **Bosco** *lies on the ground.* **Vincent** *picks up a heavy stone. He towers over his friend.*

Bosco   Eh-eh! What are you doing?

Vincent   Stop.

The Guhahamuka   Stop.

Bosco   Whose side are you on?

Vincent   Stop.

The Guhahamuka   Stop.

Bosco   Are you sure your father was a Hutu?

Vincent   Stop.

The Guhahamuka   Stop.

Innocent   Put that down, Vincent.

Vincent   I'm tired of this.

The Guhahamuka   Stop.

Vincent   I'm tired of you.

Innocent   Put that down.

Bosco   What are you doing?

Vincent   I'm doing something. I'm doing something.

He raises the stone to his chest.

The Guhahamuka   Stop.

Innocent   Vincent, stop! Don't do it! He didn't do anything.

Vincent   He'll continue to terrorise her.

Innocent   Stop it!

The Guhahamuka   Stop.

Vincent   Did you do it, Bosco? Did you?

The Guhahamuka   Stop.

Bosco   Vincent! Vincent! Vincent!

The Guhahamuka   Stop. Stop. Stop.

Bosco *is backing into the corner, crawling away. He is in a vulnerable position.*

Bosco   What, now we are to kill each other? Other Hutus? But we are brothers, Vincent! We are brothers!

The Guhahamuka   Stop.

Innocent   It wasn't him.

Vincent *closes his eyes.*

Bosco   Vincent . . .

Vincent *lifts the stone above his head and –*

Blackout.

Scene Nine

In the darkness. The sound of water pouring on to the ground.

Vincent *is outside his hut. He is washing his hands at the pump. He is washing his hands. Washing his hands. Washing his hands.*

The hut door opens. **Mama** *stands at the door.*

Mama   Vincent . . . Vincent! Are you out there?

Vincent   Yeah. I'm out here, Mama.

Mama   Well, what are you waiting on, Vincent? Come on inside.

Vincent *walks through the door. His shirt is splattered with blood.*

Mama   You look like you've been slaughtering cows for the feast.

Vincent   I have.

He stands there and for the first time in his life he sees the man who fathered him.

Vincent Snr, *a withered man, sits at the table. Eating porridge. He is stooped over the bowl. He looks up. He has the face of the young* **Guhahamuka 3**.

Mama   Vincent, there he is. Your son.

Vincent Snr *stares at his son for the longest time. He stares. He does not get up from the table. Then he looks down again and begins eating.*

Vincent Snr   He's mine alright. Has my eyes. This one on the other hand . . .

He indicates **Félicité**. **Mama** *becomes nervous.*

Mama   Go in the back, Félicité.

Félicité   Why do I have to −

Mama   I said GO!

Félicité *takes her plate from the table. Not a child of 'The Butcher', she is forced to eat in the corner of the kitchen.* **Vincent Jr** *sits down and joins his father and mother at the kitchen table. He begins to eat. He eats with his left hand, the same as his father. They are mirror images of each other. The same.*

They sit and eat their dinner in silence and silence and silence.

Children of Killers

BY KATORI HALL

*Notes on rehearsal and staging drawn from a workshop
with the writer held at the National Theatre, October 2015*

*From a workshop led by Maria Aberg,
with notes by Miranda Cromwell*

How Katori came to write the play

A pilgrimage in 2009 took Katori to Rwanda and moved her
from writing for herself to writing for the world. It changed
her life. At a memorial site, a guide told them a story where
children were forced to play football with their mother's head.
They visited the church and then went to an association
where survivors and perpetrators were trying to live together.

A friendly-looking man with a vivacious shirt and a broad
smile went to shake a woman's hand. The woman did not
want to shake his hand but when she became aware tourists
were watching her, she did. As it transpired, this man had
murdered the woman's family. Katori was later seated next to
this man and was surprised that even though he was a killer
she could still like him. She found him to be charismatic and
charming and questions remained with her. How easily had
he been able to go back into society? What scars have been left?

'That was the beginning of the story. Being there after such
an intense amount of horror, it is astounding how fast this
country has moved forwards and in doing so it has left
questions about this community, our nation and our world.'

Guhahamuka means breathlessness because emotion has caught
you up. Their presence in the play is about silence. The
silence in Rwanda is so loud. There is an eerie feeling of
things left unsaid.'

Approaching the play

To begin with Maria suggested a method for analysing the
text.

- Break down the scenes into smaller chunks, creating a break when there is a significant change in subject or when a new character enters.
- Give each section a title by naming it after the most important thing that happens in that scene.
- Establish what you think each character wants in each scene. Think about making the intentions active and playable but more complex than they immediately appear.

For example, Scene One (first section):

Title: 'Hearing the call'.

Key event: the machete song is heard. It signifies the papas coming home.

Intentions: Innocent wants to show off. Bosco wants to maintain his authority. Vincent wants to . . . and so on.

Themes of the play

- Coming of age.
- The aftermath of genocide.
- Cycles of violence.
- Forgiveness and revenge.
- Sexual violence as a tool in war.

Katori: 'At the core it is a play about overcoming.'

Maria suggests approaching the physiological themes in the play that could make it relatable to your young people. Ask questions that have a universal and personal connection. For example, what does it mean to be a man?

Structure

The timeline of the play happens over a day, a night and another day. The genocide began on 6 April 1994 and the killing went on for a hundred days. The play was set originally in 2011, as a time nearly now. Katori thinks now that in 2015 it should be a time just recently past.

Timelines could be done for all the characters to better understand their ages and relationships between each other. Vincent is the oldest of the boys and was conceived at the beginning of the genocide, which means he is two years older than Bosco or Innocent.

Language

In terms of pronunciation and meaning, Katori clarified some of the words below, but was clear to state, 'You don't have to impose the accents but consider the natural rhythms and speech patterns.'

Sa-sa   as used by the mother is sharper. more authoritative

Ah-ah   No

Eh eh   Surprise or for real

Meeeen   American-sounding 'man'

Butter   Awesome

Félicité   Felicitay

Guhahamuka   Goo-ha-ha-moo-ka, breathlessness, silence

Inyenzi   Cockroach

Hutu   Hootwo

Tutsi   Tootsi

Primus   Preemus

Fuck off   *Tumbavu* (East African slang word, sounds as spelt)

Djïmon Honsou   a famous and handsome male model

Note: the French helped the *Interahamwe* (Hutu extremists) with the Rwandan genocide so they got rid of the French language.

The participants discussed the East African interjections that were short sounds rather than full words. The basic rule with these is: if they were to be words, what would they be? The task is to work out the intention, and remember that the change in pitch is different with each one and important. A few examples from pages 367 to 369:

Bosco   Eh-eh (whatever)

Vincent   Eh-eh (stop/pause)

Innocent   Ehh (hey)

Bosco   Eh-eh (WTF?!)

Note that when characters' lines are bracketed on the page they speak simultaneously.

Some challenges for directors

- Painting a visual picture with the words, to get a sense of duality in the production.

- How to make it relevant and meaningful for the whole diverse group?

- How to justify the curse words? How to prepare an audience in advance for the curse words?

- Doing justice to a real-life story, how to get a young company to understand the gravity of the story?

- Making sure a company understands the research and makes the connection to what is happening onstage.

- Capturing the truth of the spirit and essence of the piece.

- Making the casting work with different gender combinations.

- With an all-white cast, how to get into the research and understanding?

- 1994 is very recent to us but how do we get the next generation thinking about its influence on their lives today?

- How to mark the changes in atmosphere?

- Making the characters' back stories really clear.

- The set changes; how to create the set on a minimal budget?

- How to fully bring to life the music and movement opportunities?

Characters and characterisation.

- List all the facts about the character.
- List all the questions you have.
- Define what they need to achieve in the play.
- What do they do to achieve it?
- What is at stake if they don't get what they want?
- Write a list of everything each character says about themselves?
- Write a list of everything that other characters say about them?

This is what the participants came up with for the key characters in the play, which could be helpful as a starting point for further discussion.

EMMANUEL

Facts

He is fourteen.

He is a businessman.

He has the sickness.

He has a sibling.

Questions

Who is his dad?

How old was he when his mum died?

Does he know he is the son of the rapist?

What does he say about himself? He is the Son of God.

What do others say about him? He is a child of rape.

What does he want? Respect.

To affirm he is the Son of God.

To be accepted.

To earn enough money to pay for his medicine.

What happens if he doesn't get it? He will die.

What does he do to achieve it? Insists he is the Son of God.

ESPERANCE

Facts

Her mother has died of AIDS.

She is not afraid.

She is pretty.

Her brother will die.

Her name means hope in French.

She has a relationship with the spirits.

She is courageous and fights to be heard.

She has one arm.

Questions

What is her relationship with the other people in her village?

How big is the village?

How closely do they know each other?

Why is she so convinced it was Bosco who painted the graffiti?

When did her mother die?

Did she testify against the killers?

Who and where is her father?

What does she say about herself? She is not *inyenzi*.

What do others say about her? She is daring.

She is beautiful.

She is *inyenzi*.

What does she want? She wants be able to breathe.

To fight back.

To get an apology.

To not be seen as a survivor of the genocide.

To not be ashamed.

To represent other survivors.

To keep her brother alive.

What happens if she doesn't get it? Her brother will die.

What does she do to achieve it? She holds the individual responsible.

BOSCO

Facts

Fourteen to fifteen years old.

He attacks Esperance twice.

He's influenced by American culture.

He was bullied at school.

He has a beard.

He drinks.

His father isn't released from prison.

He sees ghosts.

He doesn't know his father.

Questions

What happens to him?

Is Emmanuel his brother?

What would have happened if his father did arrive?

How does he feel when his dad doesn't come back?

What does he say about himself? Like father like son.

He is going to be famous.

What do others say about him? He is like his father.

What does he want? He wants his actions to be justifiable.

He wants to know his father.

What happens if he doesn't get it? It will affect his whole identity.

What does he do to achieve it? He embodies his father.

MAMA

Facts

A Hutu.

Married to 'The Butcher', a notorious killer.

She has two children, one is her husband's and one isn't.

She cries at night.

She ploughs the field.

Questions

Was she a sex worker?

Does she still love her husband?

What does she say about herself? She did what she had to survive.

What do others say about her?

What does she want? To be able to provide for her family.

To keep her children alive.

For her choices to be understood.

What happens if she doesn't get it? She could be rejected and lose everything she has worked for.

What does she do to achieve it? She sent Félicité away from the table.

Casting

Katori is very open to non-traditional casting; the play can work with an all-white cast, an all-female/male cast and racially mixed casts. However, she urges directors using diverse casts to understand the implications of certain casting choices for an audience. For example, to cast young black men in all of the Hutu roles and a young white woman in the role of Esperance, a Tutsi, might inadvertently perpetuate a stereotype. Casting white actors as Hutus (e.g. Vincent's mother, Bosco) would allow the audience to dismiss race as a signifier of identity, which is one of the issues the play seeks to deconstruct.

In addition, she would suggest that it is important to see some physical embodiment of Esperance's disability; you need to find a physical vocabulary to demonstrate the physical disability.

Production, staging and design

Maria split the group into three and gave them each some design tasks to consider. Below is what they came up with:

1   *As many different ways as you can to design the production using only light, candlelight, shadow play, etc.*

You could use light to dictate space; the field needs to feel big and the inside to feel small. Fluorescent tubes could physically mark out space. The chorus could be half lit; shadows, gauze and backlight for shadow puppetry could be used to give the Guhahamuka chorus a presence throughout. You could use red light for blood and the sunset, or flickering lights to manifest tension. Maria suggested you could consider projection and video or you could only use practical lights operated by the chorus.

2   *As many different ways to use colour. What can different colours mean? How can they impact on the design?*

You could use sand, or mud, cracked paint, bamboo, corrugated iron for a rugged, earthy aesthetic. You could use red more subtly with the football, the door, to symbolise anger, death and blood. Colours and choice of material could be used to represent differences in the character – for example, football shirts and batik print. Could you integrate the audience and place them inside the play somehow? Maria recalled *Stoning Mary*, a production by debbie tucker green, which used a mud-cracked floor that was bright blue. Katori noted that purple is the colour of mourning. Many memorials had purple signs but recently they decided to shift to grey.

3   *As many different ways to use sound and music, choir, singing, sound design.*

You could use silence to create a profound space that enables emotion to live. How do you make silence very strong? A heartbeat and heavy breathing could be used in order to break the silence. A heartbeat could be created by the footballs. Play and children playing could be at the root of the sound, perhaps using nursery rhymes. You could change the lyrics of the rhymes and ask the young people to write them. You could research the true meanings of songs – but be careful about what religious or spiritual connotations there are in the music. Percussive instruments, rainmakers, drums and/or body percussion could be used to dictate the tempo of the scenes. Distorted sounds could reflect the burden of the psychological effects. French colonial sounds or French nursery rhymes could be used as a theme for all your sound. You could use whispers of death, rape and persecution: sound as memories. The chorus could spread out among the audience, passing rumours and creating soundscapes; people could come to whisper sounds in the audience. The radio could be used throughout as a theatrical device and/or microphones and distorted voices.

4   *As many different ways to use only one object per scene; they could be abstractly related.*

This group noticed the significance of mirrors and reflections within the text. They established the following objects as having significance in each scene:

SCENE 1   Radio

SCENE 2   Machete

SCENE 3   Lipstick

SCENE 4   Jerrycan

SCENE 5   Flowers

SCENE 6   Aerosol to see the words temporarily

A word on the music

Katori: 'This play has now become the past. The music used for the killing was real music and they changed the working songs, with different lyrics. You cannot find this music and it would be wrong to authenticate it and use it. Write your own music or your own lyrics. You could translate different songs into the language. You can go for it and experiment. The really crucial thing is that it is a good song; the machete song is catchy, beautiful and celebratory. There is an irony with this music, that people's music unintentionally became a beat to the genocide.'

Maria: 'Making up your own songs may bring it closer to home and help bring it closer to your own experience.'

Exercises for use in rehearsals

Ask the cast to answer these questions about each of the characters:

Work is . . .

Boys are . . .

Girls are . . .

The future is . . .

The past is . . .

Violence is . . .

Dreams are . . .

I am . . .

Below is what the group came up with. Your company might find completely different answers.

BOSCO

Work is in the fields.

Boys are men of the house.

Girls are difficult to understand.

The future is mine for the taking.

The past is black.

Violence is power and control.

Dreams are achievable.

I am unapologetic.

MAMA

Work is pulling your weight.

Boys are never too old to get slapped.

Girls are problematic.
The future is uncertain.
The past is done.
Violence is inevitable.
Dreams are necessary.
I am a survivor.

EMMANUEL

Work is something I need to be alive.
Boys are cruel.
Girls are nurturing people I can trust.
The future is whatever I can make.
The past is black.
Violence is what I was born into/is the sickness.
Dreams are something I can't have.
I am the Son of God.

ESPERANCE

Work is necessary to survive.

Boys are always thinking that they are mine.

Girls are resilient.

The future is shaped by our past.

The past is something I'll never forget.

Violence is what I was born into.

Dreams are all we have.

I am not going to be the victim.

Style and technique

Maria: 'It is important to engage the audience's imagination within this play.'

How to represent the Guhahamuka is an interesting challenge. How do you represent absent people?

There is flexibility around how the chorus could be represented onstage; there could be moments of magic realism where the soccer ball is a skull, or perhaps it all happens in the imagination of the audience. It does not have to be literal but there should be a reflection of heightened moments.

What is the scale between walking dead or ghostly apparitions? Perhaps the key to this is not making them too different from the other characters in the play. Maria suggested them stepping into paint and leaving footprints. They could ritualistically set up the space and frame it, to demonstrate that the past is constantly shaping the present. You could use UV paint or water to differentiate them from the other characters.

You could play with backlight and gauze to see the chorus only at certain points. You could use your iPhone to create short projections to aid scene changes. Or you could have actors whispering over the PA system. You could use children's possessions and clothes.

Katori: 'In Kigali in a church they took all the clothes of the dead bodies and left them in the space. In another space I also saw bodies laid out that are preserved in lime.'

Could they be omnipresent and always in the audience?

How do you portray the moments of violence?

- Bosco and Innocent at the well.
- Esperance and Bosco at the well.
- Mama slapping Vincent.
- Bosco and Vincent at the end.

You could really play with the build-up to the fight and replace the action with distraction on an inanimate object. So you create separation to achieve an act of aggression.

You could use physical theatre to represent the act of violence with the Guhahamuka. Or use sound with the chorus to take over the actual act of violence. You could have the audience only see the impulse moments of the fight by having it spill into the chorus. You could use shadow play to allude to the violence or sound to imagine what is happening.

Some further key questions to consider

Was Vincent right at the end?

'He was right to protect her but not to kill him. He is using the same rationale as the previous killer's. He is trying to destroy his father; in his actions he completes a cycle of violence. His father would have started by killing one person.'

How does one separate an act of protection from the act of destruction? War, for example.

'The thing that happens at the end of the play has to be contained from the beginning. Maybe it's his own fear; he is trying to destroy the spark of violence by using violence.'

How do we move on from our past histories?

On page 391, is Innocent speaking for Bosco?

Katori: 'Yes they both were participating in the struggle with Esperance.'

What should we not do?

Katori: 'Just make sure you say the words and don't reorder the scenes.'

How do you know what are the right choices?

Katori: 'Everything is in the execution, nothing is wrong, be inspired by your young people. Make work that is like the work you want to see.'

What is the situation now in Rwanda?

Katori: 'I speak to people in Rwanda when I visit and for many the feelings haven't changed; some of the victims of the genocide still want their family's murderers to pay. But President Kagame came in and stopped the genocide and drove the Hutu extremists out. There is a saying in Rwanda, though, that still waters go deep. There is an undercurrent of animosity because there are so many people who went free. People admitted some crimes but not all. The progress of the country is built on the back of the victims in the society. I don't know what will happen in the future.'

Maria questioned how to balance accessing the sheer brutality of the genocide with the responsibility to protect young people. What content will be most helpful and appropriate for them?

Katori: 'The film *Shooting Dogs* does not shy away from the graphic details; however, there is an easier access into this film as it is told from a young person's perspective. You have to be honest and not shy away from the truth. But enjoy the humour in the play and allow them to be kids so that when the violence comes into the piece, you get the humanity, comedy and tragedy lying side by side. There has to be games and playfulness.'

Maria suggested finding someone who can come in to speak to the cast in the rehearsal room. To answer questions and share their stories whether it is from this genocide or something else that is more relevant to them.

Maria suggested a research task for the young people to find:

- Three portraits of people that relate to the play.
- Three pieces of music.
- Three facts about the genocide.

It could be useful to create a timeline of events between the genocide and when the play takes place alongside that of the timeline of the characters.

Katori suggested creating a dramaturgy board to help the audience with their connection to the play, inviting them to understand the story in the larger political context. It is useful for them not only to be told this story but also why it happened. This board could be set front of house to be seen by the audience after the play ends. Maria suggested creating the board with the students to cement the information with purpose.

Suggested references, reading and viewing

Like all genocides, the 1994 Rwandan genocide was very complex, so start with a few comprehensive books and films and share the material with your group.

Katori outlined a basic history to touch on the complexities of the issues: 'Three tribes: Twa, Hutu farmers, Tutsi cattle herders. The Germans were the first colonisers. The Belgians decided that the 14 per cent Tutsi populace would be the ruling class over the Hutus. The colonisers came and said these people are better than others.'

Note the different factions of Twa, Hutu and Tutsi have imposed differences. They share the same religion, the same cultural practices. Hutu were farmers and the Tutsi were cattle herders. The only perceived differences were physical traits – being tall or having bigger noses – and those in time proved to be meaningless. There are many tales of tall Hutu men being mistaken for Tutsi and killed during the genocide.

Below is Katori's essential list for further reference:

BOOKS   If you read nothing else then please read *Genocide: My Stolen Rwanda* by Révérien Rurangwa.

The Antelope's Strategy and *Machete Season* by Jean Hatzfeld.

We Wish to Inform You that Tomorrow We Will Be Killed with Our Families by Phil Gourevitch.

INTERNET: www.hrw.org/reports/1999/rwanda/

FILM: If you watch nothing else then please watch:

Kinyarwanda, dir. Alrick Brown, 2011.

My Neighbour, My Killer, dir. Anne Aghion, 2009.

Sometimes in April, dir. Raoul Peck, 2005.

Shooting Dogs, dir. Michael Caton-Jones. 2007.

Take Away
by Jackie Kay

Take Away tells the story of a town which is in the grip of onions – everyone is doing what they can to get their fix. Darcus, a travelling poet, turns up and offers to rid the town of the onions with his rhymes, for a small fee. A poetic ensemble piece about a community who pay the price for refusing to keep their promise.

Age suitability: any age

Cast size
many named characters, plus chorus

Jackie Kay is a novelist and poet, and has written extensively for stage and TV. *The Adoption Papers* (Bloodaxe) won the Forward Prize, a Saltire prize and a Scottish Arts Council Prize. *Fiere*, her most recent collection of poems, was shortlisted for the COSTA Award. Her novel *Trumpet* won the Guardian Fiction Award and was shortlisted for the IMPAC award. *Red Dust Road* (Picador) won the Scottish Book of the Year Award and the London Book Award, and was shortlisted for the PEN Ackerley Prize. She was awarded an MBE in 2006, and made a fellow of the Royal Society of Literature in 2002. Her book of stories *Wish I Was Here* won the Decibel British Book Award. Jackie Kay's children's book *Red Cherry Red* (Bloomsbury) won the Clype Award. Her most recent plays include *Manchester Lines* (produced by Manchester Library Theatre) and *The New Maw Broon Monologues* (produced by Glasgay). Her most recent book, *Reality Reality*, is a collection of stories and she is currently working on her new novel, *Bystander*. She is Chancellor of the University of Salford and Professor of Creative Writing at Newcastle University.

Note on the set

The set should give the idea of a part of a city. There should be a river running across the set. There should be a takeaway with an upstairs and downstairs. There should be several corners or doors for people's different homes. There should be a table for the town council's Onion Commission.

Note on the onions

Onions could be used imaginatively: onion street lamps, onions rolling across the stage, perhaps an onion tree.

If it is possible the Onion Pushers should cycle across the stage with strings of onions hanging from their handlebars.

The onions in the play are metaphors for what is potentially dangerous and destructive in our society: drugs, addictions, obsessions, sadness, depression, violence . . .

It would be good to use real onions, bearing in mind that they are also symbols.

Characters

Darcus, *tap-dancing poet, male or female*
Kimberley, *works in the takeaway*
David, *Kimberley's big brother, works in the takeaway*
Mitzi, *Kimberley's mother, works in the kitchen downstairs*

Tyrese, *young angry man*
Ruth, *Tyrese's girlfriend*
Jatinder, *Ruth's mother*

Kirk, *onion addict*
Mohammed, *Kirk's friend*

Kenneth, *oddball loner*

Eve, *young woman*
Ivy, *Eve's best friend*

Town, *a very mixed bunch of young people, that later on, in the last scene, become the parents*

Onion Pushers, *dressed in clothes of many brown layers. People who sell onions on bicycles and have long strings of onions hanging over their handlebars. They wear French berets and sell the onions, door to door. They can speak in a French accent*

Onion Commission, *two people, could be more:*
Mr McDonald
Mrs Morrison
(*Could also be Mr and Mr or Mrs and Mrs*)

If Darcus is female, please amend script accordingly

Scene One

Place: a Chinese and Indian takeaway, with a Chinese menu and an Indian menu, in the city.

Time: Bitter Friday night in winter.

What's happening? All the young people are out in shirts with no coats. There are **Onion Pushers** *on street corners, everywhere.*

Darcus *is tap-dancing towards the city from a long way off.*

He has plans to make the city a better place.

He is going to get rid of the onions in the East End.

Darcus (*tap-dancing as he talks and looking at his watch*)
  The river nice. I hear tell about it, now.
  The river pretty in the city
  plenty fishy in there, flipping and flashing
  their tales in that tea-brown water.
  The river snakes its dark coil
  round the city, you can see it everywhere
  you look, a sparkle of the river's glitter.
  The river always busy heading someplace.
  Never lazy, never slowing down a pace.
  Boats sail down the river.
  Children skip flat stones
  one, two, three, four,
  like a promise, like good news coming.
  The flat stone, like a little girl
  skipping to school
  in her smart black shoes,
  a little shipping girl singing
  her sad onion rhyme.

A **Dancing Girl** *dances around* **Darcus** *singing:*

Dancing Girl
  Cry baby cry,
  Watch the onion fry.

Cry baby cry,
Someone's going to die.

Darcus
I feel attracted to this city:
a wide deep river, a frisky West End
a busy bustling shopping street
and the best takeaway
in the country. Of course I is not forgetting
this city's big onion problem in the East End.
That's where I am heading.
I am going to do something.

The **Town** *is standing in a long queue outside the takeaway. They are trying to pretend they aren't cold.*

Chorus of Cooks
Tandoori, peshwari, dopiaza,
Vindaloo, masala, jalfrezi,
Naaaaaaaaaaaaaaaaaaaaan.

Aloo gobi, tarka dhal, mutter paneer,
Sweet and sour, chop suey, chow mein
Naaaaaaaaaaaaaaaaaaaaan.

Goat curry, stewed chicken, plantain,
Rice and peas, hot pepper sauce, please,
Naaaaaaaaaaaaaaaaaaaaan.

Pierogi, Halushi, kielbasa
Lasagne, pizza, risotto,
Naaaaaaaaaaaaaaaaaaaaan.

Roti, chapati, popadom,
Prawn cracker, dim sum, dumpling,
Paper dosa, egg fried rice, noodles,
Naaaaaaaaaaaaaaaaaaaaan.

No dirty knives, no dirty hands, no dirty boards, no dirty
woks. Clean pots. Clean cooker. All above board. No germs,
we are all so very hygienic. Very good meal. Good takeaway.
Good carry-out. Best in the country. Have a taste. Treat

yourself. We're good. Yes, yes. We are very very delicious.
Come in. Come in and have some tandoori, peshwari,
dopiaza . . .

Continue with previous chorus for as long or as short as seems right.

*People are jostling with each other to try and get forward in the queue.
Two **Onion Pushers** walk up and down the queue trying to tempt
people to buy onions.*

Kenneth   I was before you.

Tyrese   No you weren't, you liar.

Ruth   Don't get involved, Tyrese.

Kenneth   Shift or I'll shift you.

Tyrese   Funny guy!

Ruth   Ignore him, he's a complete nutter.

Town (*circling the queue*)
  The biggest problem in this city is the onion rings.
  This city can't control the atrocious onion rings.
  Mountains of onions on the main streets.
  Onions sprouting from the city walls.
  Onions snoozing on double-decker buses,
  Onion pushers inside our offices,
  hanging around outside schools.
  Onion pushers with their long strings
  Cycling down the narrow lanes,
  Onions rolling on the football fields,
  Onions bumping around the town hall
  Onions on church pews:
  People are even praying for onions.
  Kids stealing from their mother's purses
  To get their onion fixes!
  Unmarked onion vans in side streets.
  Onions in bathrooms at parties.
  Onions downloaded on the internet.
  They don't know who is responsible.

Nobody knows who is responsible.
Nobody knows who is to blame.
Nobody has a name.
They are all anonymous, faceless,
Hooded, masked.
It's a crying shame.

The onions are killing our confidence.
They've got the city police on it.
It's a case of red alert.
Everyone has been told to be vigilant, you bet.
And yet . . . yet . . . yet –
So far not one single person
Has been done for onion possession.

Darcus *is dancing towards the long queue. The two* **Onion Pushers** *hold out some bags of onions. They run alongside* **Darcus** *holding out the bags.*

Onion Pushers   Five pounds a bag, cut-price onions, Terrific, wonderful, fantastic onions! Without onions there would be no cuisine. Dream the onion dream. All recipes begin with the chopping of the onion. *Bien sûr.* For sure, for sure.

Darcus
A man in the south told me
about the city in the east
with the big onion culture.
I'm attracted to a place
with a bad problem
like a bunion on a toe.
Darcus is your man, I said.
Then took off for the city.
(*To the* **Onion Pushers**.)
Not for me, thank you.

Darcus *pushes the* **Pushers** *and they both fall down. Their onions roll everywhere. They look perplexed and shocked.*

Onion Pushers   Did you see that? Did you see that? We're having him. Who does the man think he is? Who is he? He's a stranger. We'll catch him later

Onion Johnnies   My goodness. Did you see that man?

Inside the takeaway: **David** *and* **Kimberley** *are taking the orders.*

Kenneth   How did you decide chicken chow mein would be Number 23? Why didn't you make chicken chow mein Number 27? That's my birthday. 27 November. Chow mein is my favourite. Why did you make Number 27 sweet and sour pork? I don't like sweet and sour pork. Why don't you switch the numbers? Twenty-three is the date my mum died. I don't like Number 23. Can't you switch the numbers, big man?

Tyrese   Hurry up!

Ruth   Tyrese! I don't want you getting in more fights. Please.

Tyrese (*to* **Ruth**)   Shut it!

David (*speaking non-fluent English*)   We can't switch number. (*Gently.*) We got menus printed. You say 27 and we bring Number 23? No problem.

Kenneth (*angry*)   You think that helps?

Tyrese   There's a big long queue here! Come on! Come on!

Kenneth   Why not? Is it a lot to ask? I'm falling apart here.

He stomps off.

Ruth (*quietly*)   You've got to feel sorry for that man.

Kimberley   What's eating him?

Tyrese   He's barking, barking.

David   Number 23 is eating him.

Ruth   My favourite is mushroom chop suey. My favourite number is nine. But mushroom chop suey is not Number 9. That's life. We can't all go about getting our favourite numbers on our favourite meals.

Kirk (*to* **Mohammed**)   What are you having? I'm having chicken Madras and pilau rice.

Mohammed   You always have the same.

Kirk   That's the point about takeaways, to always have the same. It's comforting.

Mohammed   You never needed comforts before you started on the onions.

Kirk   I didn't realise the beauty of the same thing, again and again.

Mohammed   Kirk, I think you've become a bit strange.

Kirk   No I haven't. I'm just the same bloke eating the same curry on a typical Friday night.

Kenneth (*turning back*)   Why can't we? It's only a small thing to ask. I mean, I'm not asking to win the bloody lottery. (*To* **Tyrese**.) What did you call me?

David   No trouble. We don't want trouble in here.

Tyrese   I'm not making any trouble. He's the one you should be talking to.

Kimberley (*to* **Kenneth**)   Tell me your order and stop this nonsense.

Kenneth (*quickly*)   Chicken chow mein and a can of Coke.

Kimberley   Chicken chow mein and a can of Coke. Take a seat, please.

David   What wrong with me?

Kimberley   You give in too much. You need to be strict with a silly man like that one there.

David Shhhh!

Kimberley He isn't frightening me. I've got more things to be frightened of than a man who doesn't like Number 23.

Darcus *is tap-dancing outside the takeaway*

The chorus made up of town people can take a line each.

Town
    The onion problem is a problem
    For the whole of society.
    The dogs don't like the onions
    When they turn up in their bowls.
    The teachers don't like the onions
    When they roll into schools.
    The women don't like the onions
    Spoiling their conversations
    The policemen don't like the onions
    At the end of their truncheons.
    The footballers dislike the onion penalty.
    The basketball players hate it when
    The onion hoops the loop.
    The snooker players don't
    Like the onions socking the pockets,
    The electrician and the optician don't like the onions
    In the sockets
    The doctors don't like the onions
    On the end of their stethoscopes.
    The astrologers don't like it when onions
    Forecast the horoscopes.

    The whole society cannot cope with
    The invasion of the onion, its scope
    Its ubiquity, its viral tendencies.
    These are terrible times we are living in.

Darcus
    Many old people have cited onions the biggest of their fears.
    All the city people hate the onions when they are reduced
        to tears.

The big worry is those who have fallen in love with the
    onion
Those who are addicted to ripping off its brown skin
Till they get to their pearl moon, eating, eating
The whole onion raw like you'd eat an apple and ting
Those whose breath stinks of onion, bitter in the morning,
Who go to sleep dreaming onion dreams, rings and
    rings, never ending,
Those who believe the moon is an onion.
Those who wake up in the morning weeping and crying.
Take an onion. Peel it. Look at its many layers.
Can you comprehend the problem
The oniony East End is facing?

Darcus *dances past the* **Dancing Girl**

Dancing Girl
    Cry baby cry,
    Watch the onion fry.
    Cry baby cry,
    Someone's going to die.

Scene Two

David *goes outside to try to clear the onions away. Many onions roll
around on the street. Some have lost their skins. It is slippery. He tries to
sweep his street clean.*

David   What you think you doing?

Onion Pushers   We're selling onions. *Oui, oui*, precisely.
Bien sûr.

David   Not outside my shop. Leave my shop alone!

Onion Pushers   Or else? Are you threatening us?

David   I call police!

Onion Pushers   Call the police! There's plenty onions in the police. You can try but don't be surprised if you find yourselves under investigation with the Inland Revenue, for instance. Just saying!

Is it possible to be amicable? To have a place for everybody, no?

David   I'm telling you last time. Last warning!

Onion Pushers (*sarcastically*)   Ooooh we're very frightened. We are. We freely admit. *Nous avons peur.*

Town
    We've seen deaths on the streets
    Sights we wish we hadn't seen,
    Wherever we've gone, wherever we've been,
    We've seen how rival onion rings operate
    We've seen people frightened to co-operate
    And every investigation evaporate
    There is no stopping them,
    They have no shame.
    Once this was a good city.
    Terrible pity, terrible pity.

Mohammed *and* **Kirk** *are outside in the street under the onion street lamps. As they talk, the* **Onion Pushers** *dance around them in a circle faster and faster, like their conversation.*

Mohammed   Don't buy the onions!

Kirk   I want some onions.

Mohammed   No, don't buy the onions. They are bad for you.

Kirk   I need onions.

Mohammed   You don't need onions! Don't be silly. How can somebody need an onion?

Kirk   I do need onions. If I can't have onions, I feel depressed. I've got no purpose. Nothing to look forward to. Friday night is boring without onions.

Mohammed   Yeah, but you're starting to eat onions every night of the week.

Kirk   No I'm not. Only have them for a treat.

Mohammed   No you don't. I've seen you. Sometimes, three, four, five whole onions a night.

Kirk   Thing is, I can't sleep without my onions. I can't get to sleep. If I could get to sleep, I wouldn't take them any more. I'd give them up.

Mohammed   That's pathetic.

Kirk   Come on. Go on. Have a bag, it won't do you any harm. I've never had flu since I started taking them. They're good for you.

The **Onion Pushers** *approach* **Mohammed** *and* **Kirk**.

Onion Pushers   We're selling this batch off cheap. Five bags for a quid.

Kirk   Cool! Five bags, pal.

Onion Pushers   They're hot. Watch your back.

Kirk (*rips the brown skin off quickly and munches into it raw*) Ahhh! Nothing like it. Nothing like it. Have some –

He offers a bag to **Mohammed**, *who takes an apple out of his pocket and munches it as* **Kirk** *munches the onion.*

Mohammed   I couldn't, mate. It revolts me. You stink. Look at you. Check you out! You're crying.

Kirk (*crying*)   I'm not crying.

Mohammed   You are, what's this?

Mohammed *touches* **Kirk**'s *tears.*

Kirk   My eyes are a bit watery that's all, no problem.

He has a big sneezing fit.

Mohammed   You need help. This is so sick it's not true.

Kirk *blows his nose.*

Kirk (*transforming*)   Chill out. Hey! You should try this. Nothing like it. Raw's the best. Some people fry them and roast them and shit, but I like them raw. Nippy. Hot. Bitter. Pure white-hot heat.

Mohammed   How long for? How long before the onion rings take over? How long before we've got no choice at all.

Kirk   You're talking nonsense. That's just panic talking.

Mohammed   Not from what I've been hearing. Not from the word on the street.

Kirk   What? What are you on about?

Mohammed   I heard the onion pushers are planning to close the takeaways down. They are working on a big attack right now. That's what I've been hearing.

Kirk   Why would they want to do that?

Mohammed   So that they can sell more onions, obviously.

Kirk   Are you on something? You're talking mad.

Mohammed   Me mad? I'm just eating an apple here. It's you on the onions. Kirk, can you not see yourself? You've changed. All you care about is knowing your onions. They are going to destroy you. I'm your mate. I'm concerned for you.

Kirk   Look at the fucking moon up there. It is one big onion. Look at the stars, they are bright little chopped onions. Look at the night sky, Mohammed. It is sparkling. The stars are fizzing and frying in the sky. Look at my skin, it's translucent. I can almost see through myself, you know. I'm a many-layered guy, Mohammed. The world's a complex place. If I didn't eat these onions, I wouldn't see its beauty or its complexity.

He has another sneezing fit.

Mohammed   You're talking garbage. That's the onions talking. You are off your onions. Look at the state of you! Why can't you see it?

Kirk   I know my onions. I'm a guy who *knows* his onions! All you care about is the superficial, Mohammed. What is a little bit of sneezing, a little allergical reaction, to understanding the meaning of life?

Mohammed   Which is?

Kirk   Life is complicated.

Mohammed   Is that it?

Kirk   And some other stuff. I forget. Listen to the moon singing. Isn't that beautiful? Smell the stars. Sniff the night's sweat. That's the meaning of life. Live in it, Mohammed. In this moment right now with your friend Kirk. I love you, Mohammed.

Mohammed   I told you. This isn't you any more. This is the onions talking.

Kirk   No, it's not. It's the truth. The onions peel away the bullshit till you get to the truth. This is the truth, Mohammed. (*Sneezes again.*) You are the best mate an oniony guy could have.

The **Dancing Girl** *dances past them in the dark.*

Dancing Girl
    Cry baby cry,
    Watch the onion fry.
    Cry baby cry,
    Someone's going to die.

Scene Three

Downstairs in the takeaway's kitchen. **Mitzi** *is cooking in the woks fast and putting the meals in takeaway boxes.*

The **Town** *run round the stage collecting the meals and taking them to* **David** *upstairs. The* **Town** *could give some meals out to the audience.*

Kimberley (*crying*)   I'm fed up working here, being stuck down here half the day and stuck up there half the night with all these mad people out there. I'm fed up getting my skin burnt with fat from the woks when my friends are watching *Breaking Bad* and nobody else is working. I don't know if I'll ever fit in properly when I spend so much time down here. I'm tired at school from working down here till midnight. I'm falling asleep in my lessons.

Mitzi   Nothing we can do. Don't worry about fitting-in thing. Who care? When we get enough money, we go back.

Kimberley   I don't want to go back. How can I go back when I've never been there?

Mitzi   You are from there!

Kimberley   I am from here.

Mitzi   You can't forget yourself.

Kimberley   I can't remember myself.

Town (*suddenly freezing into statues*)   Remember. Forget. Remember. Forget. Remember. Forget. Remember. Forget. Forget. Remember. Forget. Remember. Forget. Remember.

Mitzi   You are confuse.

Kimberley   I was born here, Mum.

Mitzi   You are from there not here.

Town (*rushing around again*)   Here-there, here-there, here-there. There-here, there-here, there-here.

Kimberley   My brother is getting in a state up there. He can't take the orders without getting into a fight with some mad person in the queue.

Mitzi   Dear Kimberley. Always worry. Always think family. Don't worry. Everything okay. Your brother okay. Your father okay. (*Laughing.*) Everybody okay.

Kimberley   But I do worry. I have a bad feeling about our shop. There is a strange atmosphere out there tonight.

Mitzi   Friday night. Always busy Friday night. Always drunk people, crazy people Friday night. Hospital busy Saturday morning because of Friday night. Don't worry, my girl.

Town (*dancing*)   Friday night in the city. Disco dancing. Pub-crawling. Boys and girls snogging. Boys drinking. Girls drinking. Everybody dancing. Friday night, Alright, alright. Everybody's out on a Friday night.

Kimberley   Why don't I believe you? Why don't I feel reassured?

Mitzi   Have some dumpling. I just made them. Nice and fresh. Have some green tea. Relax. Sit down a minute.

Kimberley   I can't, we've got a massive queue up there. I better get back upstairs.

Mitzi   You are a good girl, Kimberley.

Kimberley   I'm not. I have bad thoughts. I can feel a nosebleed coming on again.

Mitzi   Ask David to call in somebody.

Kimberley   Joy gen.

Mitzi   See you later.

Town (*whispering*)   Good girl, bad girl, good girl, bad girl, good, bad, good, bad, good, good, good.

Kimberley *cries all the way up the stairs.* **Town** *follows her up.*

Kimberley (*to herself*)   I can't seem to stop this weeping all the time. I can't stop the feeling of sadness. My heart is heavy. A sad feeling across my chest. Time is so slow in here. We can't take away time.

Town (*slowly*)   Tick tock tick tock tick tock tick tock tick tock . . .

Scene Four

Kenneth *on his own in a corner, ordering onions in a neat row.*

He cuts the top of each onion and sniffs along a line of onions.

Kenneth   I used to like when I was a little fellow playing with an abacus and arranging the colours. And then I liked those puzzles where you had to arrange the numbers in squares. And then I liked those cube things where you had to get a whole side of yellow and a whole side of red. I was good at all that. And my mum used to buy me lots of those metal puzzles and I was good at those too. And then my mum died. She just died. And I'm not good at anything now. I'm good at peeling and playing onions. That's what I'm good at.

Obsessively, he plays with the onions, rearranging them into different configurations.

I liked that girl in the takeaway tonight. She got me to say what I wanted, not like the guy. She had something nice about her. Not like him. He was a fool. But she was nice. If I see her on her own, I'm going to ask her if she'll go out with me. My mum said if I had friends I would be happy and I said she was my friend and she said she wasn't enough and then she died and she defo wasn't enough! Maybe that girl would like me. Maybe she'd like my onions.

I never had many special friends. Some people don't. I was always a bit of a loner, a bit of a freak, a bit of an anorak. Just when I try and do something normal, I spoil it, at the last minute, and say something weird. I can't help myself. I know when I'm going to do it, like you know when you're going to fall and then you fall anyway. You can't stop yourself. It's something to do with gravity.

Scene Five

Eve *and* **Ivy** *leave the takeaway with their order and walk down the street. Enter* **Onion Pushers**.

Onion Pushers   Do you want some of this?

Eve   No, I'm not interested

Onion Pushers   Come on, you haven't tried them raw, have you? They are pure.

Eve   We don't want any. We're going home.

Ivy   I'm a bit tempted –

Eve   Shhhh!

Eve *and* **Ivy** *walk on.* **Onion Pushers** *follow them and circle around them.*

Onion Pushers
  Try the edible rounded bulb.
  Munch the concentric close coats.
  Taste the powerful pungent flavour.
  Sniff the strong smell.
  Underneath one ring, another ring,
  Underneath that ring, another ring.
  Crunch the edible rounded bulb eaten since early times.

Ivy   It won't harm us to try the once. It's Friday night. I'm bored.

Eve   No, Ivy, don't be silly. You can't even trust these guys. They might be rotten onions. You don't even know where they got them.

Ivy   Eve! I'll be able to tell if they're rotten.

Eve   How?

Ivy   I'd smell, of course.

Eve   You're mad, leave me out of it.

Onion Pushers   We're selling them cheap. It's a bargain.

An onion hung in a room will ward away disease. Put an onion under your pillow and dream of your lover-to-be.

If you can't decide which lover to pick, then scratch the name of both men of two potentials on two separate onions, leave them in a warm place, whichever sprouts first will tell you the strongest love!

Ivy (*suddenly excited*)   Give me a bag!

Eve   Ivy!

Ivy   You're such a girl. Grow up!

Eve   You think it's grown-up to do this?

Ivy   Oh come on, Eve, just this once. You heard him! They're amazing!

Ivy *buys a bag from the* **Onion Pushers**. **Ivy** *and* **Eve** *walk off quickly, looking behind them, for home.*

Ivy   Smell that! Somebody's frying onions. Ahhh. Nothing like that smell. Please let me have onions for my tea.

Eve   It used to be such a nice innocent thing, eating onions on hamburgers, on sausages. It's all changed now. It's not the same. Nothing is innocent any more, not even onions. Don't you see, Ivy? You shouldn't have bought them. Throw them away quick! Before it is too late.

Ivy   You've gotta be joking! What do you take me for? I've just paid good money for these.

Eve   I've got a bad feeling, a bad omen.

Ivy You and your silly omens! You are the most superstitious girl I know. Come on. Let's get back to my place and try these.

Scene Six

In the takeaway, downstairs.

Mitzi I have something to tell you two. Your father and I are going home and we are going to leave you to run the take-away. We trust you. Soon you big enough to go away from school.

Kimberley I don't want to leave school. I'm only fifteen.

Mitzi Soon, you will.

Kimberley I want to go to university.

Mitzi There are things we all want to do. I am a good artist. I never paint. In China I paint. Here no time. No time to have life. I miss my people. Miss speaking my tongue. This country no country for a Chinese woman to grow old.

Takeaway look after you.

David It's okay by me.

Kimberley Well, it's not by me! Look at the queue tonight. We can hardly manage never mind without you and Dad.

Mitzi We'll get more help.

Kimberley I wish I had my own life.

Mitzi Everyone wishes they have own life. Everyone have responsibilities. Too many onions in this city. I started to dream them at night. Time to go back.

Onion Pushers *enter and start to peel off their layers, very slowly in a dreamlike trance-dance.*

Mitzi   In my dream I peel off layers of my skin. Down to my own bone. When I got to my heart, I pulled it out. I ate my own heart. (*Starts weeping.*)

David   Ma. Don't be silly, It only dream. We don't do onions. They are selling them on the black market, but Kimberley and I don't buy them.

Mitzi   No, thank God.

Kimberley   We still get affected by them, I'm sure that's the reason we weep.

David   You can't blame us for them

Mitzi   I don't blame you. I just say I want home. I don't like dream. I am old woman. Tired. I want to spend last days in China. Sad without China. Not myself here. I look in mirror, I am surprise at myself. I look wrinkled. I wonder what has happened my life?

Kimberley   You chose to come over here! You can't come and leave us.

Mitzi   You come back too when the takeaway makes enough money.

David   Our mother deserve this. She work hard.

Kimberley   It will be me that does all the work while you go out to Chinese film and Chinese gambling. I will be making the money and you will be spending it.

David   Rubbish. I don't gamble.

Mitzi   No, he doesn't gamble. He only like mahjong.

Kimberley   I don't think it's selfish of me to want to go to university.

Mitzi   You are a girl.

Kimberley   Yes? And? So?

David   Don't talk like that to your mother.

Kimberley   I feel trapped.

Mitzi   Don't be silly. You save, you come back home. No problem.

Kimberley   I can't speak Cantonese properly any more, or Mandarin.

Mitzi   Don't worry. You learn fast.

Kimberley   Somebody has just come in. I'll go and take the order.

She runs up to the order counter.

Mitzi   She has never been easy, never easy child. Always argue and complain.

David   She be okay. I look after her

*Enter **Kenneth** into the **takeaway**.*

Kenneth   Number 27 please.

Kimberley   Chicken chow mein?

Kenneth (*clearly pleased that she has remembered he doesn't like number 23*)   Yes, thank you.

Kimberley   Anything else?

Kenneth   A can of Coke, please.

Kimberley   You okay now?

Kenneth   I think about you.

Kimberley   You think about me?

Kenneth   Yes, yes I do.

Kimberley (*laughing*)   What do you think about?

Kenneth   I just think about you

Kimberley   What about me?

Kenneth   Your eyes.

He jumps up and sits on the counter. Several onions roll into the takeaway. An onion light comes down from the sky.

Kimberley   You are a bit strange

Kenneth   I know. I've always been odd.

Kimberley   Why are you strange?

Kenneth   I don't know. Would you like to? I mean would you consider . . . Oh, never mind

Kimberley (*gently*)   What? What?

Kenneth   Would you like to go out with a strange guy?

Kimberley   Depends on the guy.

Kenneth   I mean me. Would you go out with me?

Kimberley   Go out where?

Kenneth   I don't know. I know! A surprise. When is your night off? I will come and take you out for a surprise somewhere.

Kimberley   I'll try and get off tomorrow. You won't forget.

Kenneth   How could I forget when you have those eyes?

Kimberley (*laughing*)   I like strange guys.

Kenneth   Why?

Kimberley   Because you are too strange to be boring.

Kenneth   Thank you very much.

Scene Seven

Ivy *and* **Eve** *are in a private space.*

Ivy *gets four of the onions, peels them with a small knife. She cuts the name 'Sam' into one and the name 'Alex' into the other.*

Ivy   Sam. Alex. Now, who do you fancy? Who is it between? You like that guy Tyrese, don't you, that Ruth goes out with?

Eve   No way. You don't know anything. No I don't!

Ivy   Who then? Come on, this is fun.

Eve   Put Mohammed and –

Ivy   Mohammed! You're joking!

Eve   I'm not doing this.

Ivy   Okay, okay, okay, Mohammed and . . .?

Eve   Am not saying.

Ivy   Write a name

Eve (*blurts out*)   Sam!

Ivy   I didn't know you knew any boys called Sam.

Eve   I don't.

Ivy   We'll leave these ones here and whichever sprouts first, that will be our men.

She peels the last onion, then cuts it into a quarter.

Eve   I told you. I don't want anything to do with this.

Ivy   Everybody does it.

Eve   I'm not everybody.

Ivy   Yes you are everybody. There are no individuals any more, Eve, get real. We are all everybody. That's it – end of story.

Eve   I don't agree with that.

Ivy   Listen to you! You don't agree. It's not about whether silly little Miss Eve Rain agrees or does not agree. Don't you see? Aw, stop it. I'm doing this.

She sets a match to a quarter of the onion, then she eats it.

I'm telling you, Eve. It's delicious. You should try it.

Eve   Why?

Ivy   Because you are my friend. And if you don't try it we won't be the same any more. Don't you see, Evie, we'll be different and we won't be close or anything.

Eve   Stop it, you're frightening me. We are close!

Ivy   Not if I've tried onions and you haven't tried onions.

Eve   Oh, all right then, just this once.

Ivy   Excellent! Excellent news.

She lights a match and roasts **Eve** *a quarter.* **Eve** *takes it from her slowly and is scared to eat it.*

Ivy   Go on! It won't bite.

Eve *takes the onion and eats it.*

Ivy *(starts laughing hysterically)*   It's good, isn't it! It makes you feel so good. What did I do before, I wonder, to make me feel this good? Do you remember when we were little we were happy with playing hopscotch! Hopscotch. *(She is laughing till the tears pour down her cheeks.)* Is that sad?

Eve *slumps immediately and her eyes glaze over.*

Enter the **Town** *on tiptoes; they walk around* **Eve**. *They whisper.*

Town
　　Here goes another one. Whose will is done?
　　Here goes another one. Who bit the sun?
　　Here goes another one. What was her name?
　　Here goes another one. All for a game.

Ivy *(still laughing hysterically)*   Do you remember how we used to like to wear the same clothes and we'd get our mothers to buy us the same things! Aw, those red shoes! Remember them with the buckles! Those tights with the giraffes down them from Sock Shop! Fancy wearing giraffes on your legs! You should wear giraffes on your neck if you're going to wear giraffes. (*Killing herself laughing.*) Oh God, that's funny. Do you get it, Evie? Giraffes on your neck?

Do you remember how we used to walk to school hand in hand and that big girl Anne Kerr always wanted to come between us? She always wanted you, Evie, as her best friend, but I wouldn't let her. Cheeky cow, trying to steal my pal! Why did she want to steal you, Evie, Evie, Evie?

The **Dancing Girl** *enters and dances round* **Eve**.

Dancing Girl
    Cry baby cry,
    Watch the onion fry.
    Cry baby cry,
    Someone's going to die.

Ivy *suddenly notices that* **Eve** *isn't responding at all. She panics. She starts to shake her.*

Ivy   Eve! Stop messing around. This isn't funny. Evie! Come on. Don't do this to me. Come on, Eve! Wake up. Wake up, Eve. Oh God, oh God, oh God. What have I done?

She rushes around clearing all the onions up from her corner, shoving them in the bin, or hiding them. Then she picks up the phone and dials 999.

(*Screaming.*) A girl here has collapsed! Quick! You've gotta send an ambulance!

Scene Eight

Meeting of the special **Onion Commission**. **Darcus** *is tap-dancing towards them.*

Mr McDonald   We've got to wise up tae the fact. We've a real problem here. And it's no going away. It's getting worse. I was down in the East End yesterday and I saw onions everywhere. Children as young as eight with onions in their pockets. It's no joke. I saw them selling them outside the Chinese carry-out. If we don't rack our brains tae tackle this problem, it's going take over our whole city. Already Councillor Jones has told me there have been five hundred onion-related attacks with people suffering severe onion reactions. The breath of our people stinks by and large. The biggest problem is nobody seems to know how they are getting into the city. Some just roll in on their own. Others have people selling them. We don't know where they get them from.

Mrs Morrison   That's what I've been saying for the past two years. I warned of this ages ago. What we need now is not talk. We've had enough bloody talk and bloody commissions and special meetings and executive councils. *Enough!* What we really need to do is put our minds to this and think of a solution. We need to act not talk. What is that saying? Actions speak louder than words? Let's think now.

They sit in silence, racking their brains. **Darcus** *tap-dances around them.*

Mr McDonald   If only we could just get rid of them altogether. If we could get some vast net and scoop them all up and throw them into the sea.

Mrs Morrison   You wish. It's not that easy.

At that moment, they suddenly look up and notice **Darcus***, wearing a long coat, smiling. He stretches his hand out and shakes with* **Mr McDonald** *and* **Mrs Morrison***.*

Darcus
  I hope you won't mind me barging in on your meeting.
  It's only that I couldn't help but overhear the problems
      you are facing.
  I have come to offer a solution.
  I have ways and means of ridding your city of onions.
  People call me Darcus.
  I is the man with the promise.
  I have been around this whole country

Checking out dis, checking out that.
Any place with a problem, Darcus is your man.
If you pay me just one bar, a thousand quid,
In other words, you can kiss goodbye
To the culture of the onion
And welcome a new civilisation.

Mrs Morrison   A thousand pounds! We'd pay you fifty
thousand pounds.

Mr McDonald   Or fifty bar, as you'd say, since you come
from afar.

Darcus
No, no, no. I insist. One bar is plenty.
Darcus is not the man to take advantage.
Darcus will not exploit the situation,
Your onions are causing worry for the whole nation.
One bar, let's shake on it.
By tomorrow morning your city will be glorious.
Darcus will be victorious. You watch. You wait.
You will see. Believe me. Darcus is your man.
Darcus is the only man to solve the situation.

He dances out into the street and sings in scales, holding his hands on his mouth.

Darcus   Ai and Ai, Ai and Ai, Ai and Ai, Ai and Ai –

The **Dancing Girl** *comes on again, dancing, almost taunting* **Darcus***. She sings her song.*

Dancing Girl
Cry baby cry,
Watch the onion fry.
Cry baby cry,
Someone's going to die.

Scene Nine

*The **Dancing Girl** follows **Darcus**, dancing along behind him.*

Town
> Into the street the dancing man stepped
> Smiling a wide smile
> His eyes lit up, clapping his hands,
> Tapping his feet, singing his strange little song,
> Come along, come along.

Darcus
> Come all ye onions joyful and triumphant
> Come all ye onions to the promised land.

Town
> Into the night, the dancing man stepped
> Wearing his long bright coat,
> His dark black hat, clapping his hands
> Tapping his feet, singing his odd little song,
> Come along, come along.

Darcus
> Come, all ye onions, joyful and triumphant
> Come, all ye onions, to the promised land.

*The entire cast dance around the stage, following **Darcus**. They catch the onions and throw them from one to another to **Darcus**, who puts them in a big brown sack and carries them on his back to the river.*

Town
> And suddenly out they came
> from the cupboards and pans
> from the trees and the fridges
> from the earth and the land:
> the onions from France,
> the onions from England,
> brown and white and gleaming onions
> following the dancing man,
> rolling and skidding and sliding along,
> with the man singing his odd little song.

Darcus

Come, all ye onions, joyful and triumphant
Come, all ye onions, to the promised land.

Town

The weeping and the stinking onions,
the sneezing and the smarting onions.
The bulbous and the pungent onions,
the Welsh onions, the wild onions.

They left the cupboards and the jars
the salad bowls and the frying pans
the window sills and the chopping boards
the vegetable racks and the bicycles.

Darcus

Come, all ye onions, joyful and triumphant
Come, all ye onions, to the promised land.

Town

Dozens and dozens of long strings of onions,
solitary spring onions, scallions, shallots,
pickled onions, long green leeks, garlic.
Red onions, white onions, fried onions, sybies.
Roast onions, onions in their brown skin,
bare naked onions, onions in bulbs,
onions from French onion soup,
gay onions, straight onions,
onions from onion bread.
Every onion that had ever led an ordinary life
rolled along, following the man and his song
all the way to the river bed
the onions hurried along.

Darcus

Come, all ye onions, joyful and triumphant
Come, all ye onions, to the promised land.

He rolls around on the floor, forward rolls, picking up all the onions.

Town
> You should have seen the East Enders
> running around, ringing their bells,
> poking out those onions with long poles
> till every last onion had left the East End
> and floated on the river.

Darcus *stands by the river, throwing in one onion in at a time.*

Darcus
> Watch the onions float along the river
> like lily pads in a pond.
> Watch the onions bob along waves
> like buoys in the sea.
> See the onions appear on the water
> like small white boulders.
> Notice the onions catch the light
> like crystal balls.
> Wait for the onions to tell the future
> like pearls of wisdom.
>
> The onions are leaving the city
> small white fishing boats going out to sea,
> down where the river leads to the estuary,
> where the sea will open its big mouth
> and gargle those onions down.
>
> One day the sea will taste of onions, not salt.
> The sea's waves will froth with onion juice, not spume.
> One day the sea will sweep every last memory
> of onion away.
> Onion ships out at sea.
>
> So watch the onions ride on the sea's galloping back.
> Up, down, up down, up down, and away, away, away.
> The onions are leaving this town.

Town (*gathering around the river*)
> No more bitter breath
> No more iffy kisses
> No more salty tears

No more coughs and sneezes
No more danger, no more violence
No more sudden attacks
No more disappearances.
The brave East End is safe again.
Come and join the celebration.

There is a street-party atmosphere, music, drums, fireworks. **Ruth** *and*
Tyrese *dance happily.* **Kenneth** *arrives at the takeaway to take*
Kimberley *out.* **Jatinder** *is dancing with* **Mitzi**. **Kirk** *and*
Mohammed *are engrossed in conversation. There could be a short*
improvised conversation between each grouping, showing how the onion-
going has made them happy. **Kimberley** *is laughing.*

Only **Ivy** *is not happy, sitting in a corner with* **Eve** *lying at her feet.*

Mr McDonald *and* **Mrs Morrison** *toast themselves.*

Scene Eleven

Darcus *dances through the middle of the celebrations, splitting the*
crowd. He approaches the **Onion Commission**.

Darcus   First, if you please, my thousand pounds!

Mr McDonald   A thousand pounds! I don't think so. Who
said anything about a thousand pounds? Do you realise that
would cost the council a significant part of next year's budget
which could go towards better things?

Darcus   What is better than ridding the town of onions?

Mrs Morrison   The council has some entertaining to do.
We have celebrities coming to the East End. We'll need that
money for Prosecco! For canapés!

Darcus   We agreed one thousand pounds. We shook hands
on it.

Mr McDonald   In your dreams! We're happy to give you
something to eat and drink. Throw in fifty quid. But to be
frank, we never ever said one thousand pounds. Have you got

a screw loose? Anyway, the deed is done. The onions are gone. Pity, but there's not a lot you can do about it. If you heard us say one thousand pounds, what you've done is take a joke seriously. This has been a hard year. Fifty quid maximum. Take it or leave it.

Darcus   Don't muck me about! Or you'll regret it.

Mrs Morrison   How dare you threaten us? See, this is the problem with you people. One second sweet, the next second aggressive.

Darcus   A deal is a deal. A promise, a promise.

Mr McDonald   Look, take your idle threats and get out. There's the door! You don't scare us. You're all talk. The onions have gone. You can't exactly swim in the river collecting them all up again. Moan as much as you like. Fifty quid, top!

Town
   Once again the dancing man took to the streets,
   with a hey hippity hop and a bee bippity bop.
   And he cried out three long notes.
   His voice sweetened the air.
   His notes enchanted the atmosphere.
   It seemed like no time at all
   before all the young people gathered outside the hall
   and followed the dancing man

Kirk, **Mohammed**, **Ivy**, **Eve** (*as a ghost*), **Kimberley**, **David**, **Ruth** *and* **Tyrese** *follow* **Darcus**. **Kenneth** *tries to catch up but gets left behind.*

Town
   Down the street, up that one, and down another,
   left, left, right, left, right, right.
   His hands clapping, his feet tapping
   singing his strange little song.
   Out came the East End youth
   with a curl in the hair and a gold tooth,

Jiving and break-dancing and skimming along
following the music from the dancing man's song,
listening to his big sounds, getting in the groove,
slip-sliding along with the song.

Mr McDonald *and* **Mrs Morrison**, **Jatinder** *and* **Mitzi**
stand still as statues, unable to move.

Town

All the adults froze to the spot
Watching their children skip on by.
Not a single adult could move her foot
To follow the dancing man's cry.

Ruth and Tyrese and Kimberley went by
happy as the day is long,
Kirk and Mohammed followed
the dancing man's song
Eve and Ivy, friends to the last,
Held hands on the way to the river bed.
Only Kenneth couldn't keep up.
Only Kenneth missed out on the water party:
the waves and the spume and the white horses,
the surge and the gush and the rush,
the combers breaking, the surf spraying.
It was Kenneth who did not hear
the incredible music of the deep blue sea:
the babble and bubble, the burble and gurgle.
Kenneth missed the choppy party
in the river that leads to the sea
where the dancing man took the youth that day.

All the young people fall into the sea.

It was a day of cross-currents
of whirlpool and maelstrom.
It was the day when the waves surged and rushed and
    gushed
and all of the youth shrieked and swallowed and
    swallowed and swallowed too much, too much.

This is the ebb and flow.
This is the life we know.
This is the flow and flux
These are the facts.
A promise is a promise.

The dancing man took our children.
The dancing man took our children.
The dancing man took our children
 away, away, away, away out to sea.

Jatinder, Mitzi, Kenneth, Onion Commission *and* **Onion Pushers** *form a circle holding hands. They all scream at the same time. A long, Munch-like silent scream into the dark.*

Kenneth Just when I had fallen in love, my love was taken away. Just when I'd got up the courage. We were going to be meeting that day, Kimberley and I.

I was trying to work out if I should kiss her on the first date or leave it to the second. I knew what I was going to wear. She was beautiful, Kimberley. She made me feel normal. She made me like myself. Now I don't feel normal any more. I'm back to Kenneth the sad loser. I can feel myself unravelling, like a long piece of string.

But Kimberley wouldn't like that. She wouldn't like me falling to pieces. I know she wouldn't. Maybe it's enough that I was nearly loved.

Scene Eleven

Mitzi I can't go back now.

The **Town** *now represent the parents. They come forward and each person utters a different line. The lines to be spoken by* **Mitzi** *are in italics. They are at turns sad, angry, defiant, hopeless, full of regret.*

Mitzi *I have to stay here, here where I lost my children.*

Now the only connection I have to them is this bit of the sea.

There are so many things I never managed to say.

Where am I from? I am from the place where my children died.

What did it matter?

What was it all about?

I wish we'd never bothered about the onions.

I wish I'd never got angry.
I wish we'd left it all alone.
Now look what we've done. We've rid our whole town of its young people. The place is dead. There is no music.

I can't go back. I need to be here where I lost my children.

I'd like the fights again.

I'd like to hear them arguing.

I'd like to see them hanging around the street corners, smoking and joking.

I'd love one to kick a football through my window.

I'd give anything for one to rip my fence off.

I need one to curse and swear at me.

I'd die for one to steal my purse. Go on, take it!

I crave a massive mobile phone bill. I want a what's app voice msg, a tumblr photo. (*Could add here more things that you think annoy your parents that they might end up missing.*)

I'm desperate for the hot water to run out. I want a messy house. I want wet towels on the floor.

I want all the biscuits eaten immediately. Eat them! I want the homework undone.

I can't ever go back. I need to stay here where my children are. You never know one day they might rise out of the sea and come looking for me.

I want somebody to say, 'Where's my book? Where's my shoe? Where's my jacket?' I want them back! Now! I need the young people back. I'll never moan about them again. I'll never complain. I promise. I want the silly jokes: 'What's App Mum?'

I didn't know I was born. I didn't know I was living.

I will love them. I will love life, please.

Just bring them back, dancing man.

Altogether   BRING THEM BACK!

Darcus
>The river nice. I hear tell about it, now.
>The river pretty in the city
>plenty fishy in there, flipping and flashing
>their tails in that tea-brown water.
>
>The river snakes its dark coil
>round the city, you can see it everywhere
>you look, a sparkle of the river's glitter.
>The river always busy heading someplace.
>Never lazy, never slows down a pace.

The End.

Take Away

BY JACKIE KAY

*Notes on rehearsal and staging drawn from a workshop
held at the National Theatre, October 2015*

*From a workshop led by Sarah Brigham,
voice exercises led by Gary Horner, with notes by Phil Sheppard*

Exercises for group, chorus and ensemble work

WARM-UP STRETCHES

Stretch up tall on tiptoes, arms directly above your head, fingers pointing towards the sky, then flop down from the waist with one big exhalation of breath. With knees bent, swing at the waist to bring your sternum over your left knee, then over the right knee.

Still flopped over at the waist, walk your hands forward and then backwards between your feet. Slowly stand up straight. Now lift your shoulders up and down and gently rotate round and round. Lower your head to your chest and *gently* roll your head from side to side with the jaw relaxed.

Isolate the ribcage and move gently from side to side, moving the pelvis round and round. Point and flex the feet, lift the knee and circle the lower leg, then still with toes pointed describe a figure eight in the air.

Try and make your face as *big* as possible (think *pumpkin face*). Accompany this with a big physical gesture and a big vocal sound. Now do the same with a 'small' face (*raisin face*) body and sound. Now try combining a big face with a small body and a small face with a big body.

*

These exercises are useful in encouraging a company to have fun and be silly and *play*, in getting a group's energy levels up and in allowing individuals to relax and lose some inhibitions.

INTRODUCTORY GAMES

- Everyone stands in a circle and taps the person to their left on the shoulder and asks a series of questions all starting with 'Excuse me, excuse me, excuse me . . . ' The questions asked by the participants were: 'What is your name?', 'Where are you from?' and 'What is the age of the company you are working with?' As this exercise is in a circle everyone is required to ask the questions and listen to the answer of the person to their left as well as answering the questions that will be asked by the person to their right. Share the information about the person to their left with the rest of the group.

- Everyone walks in the space and greets as many people as they can, shaking hands and saying hello. Then try tapping as many people as you can on the shoulder, and running away; then tap as many people as you can on the foot; then grab them around the knees and beg for forgiveness: 'I'm sorry, I'm sorry, I'm sorry!'

- Shake someone's hand and then move on to shaking someone else's hand, all the time in contact with at least one other person: 'crowd swimming'. Then, standing opposite a partner, touch hand to hand, or touch foot to foot, a finger to a finger, knee to a knee and if the leader calls 'Person to person' everyone runs to the middle of the room and cries 'I need a friend!', then finds themselves another partner with whom to continue the exercise. The exercise can become more complicated, and intimate by calling out more difficult points of contact: finger to head, nose to shoulder, knee to hip, etc. With all the instructions being accumulative, once a point of contact is made it needs to be maintained and then others are added, until balance, gravity or decorum end the game.

- Establish a clear repeatable physical sequence: stamp both feet STAMP STAMP; then clap both thighs THIGHS THIGHS; then tap your belly twice BELLY BELLY, then clap your hands just once (the eighth beat is silent) CLAP. Repeat the sequence with everyone working together, now try keeping the rhythm going with everyone walking around the room. Now try taking out the CLAP in the sequence but having a silence where the CLAP would go; add the CLAP back in and now take out BELLY BELLY, but keeping a silence where that action went previously; try the same with THIGHS THIGHS and STAMP STAMP; now try taking out THIGHS THIGHS and CLAP, then taking out BELLY BELLY and STAMP STAMP. This is a great exercise for group concentration.

* In a circle everyone tries to perform a simple sharp physical action simultaneously. In the workshop this was a simple knee-bend, both arms outstretched with palms facing outwards and a loud sudden 'HA!' sound. Have your leader count down 3, 2, 1 and then everyone aims to do the 'HA!' action together at exactly the same time. Now try taking out the countdown and see if everyone can do it in unison. Then try it walking around the space, initially with a 3, 2, 1 countdown and then without. Now try it with a partner; try and make the 'HA!' action simultaneously but no one should be leading or conducting the timing of the pairings. Now try it back to back and make the 'HA!' more difficult (and tiring) by adding in a half-turn; see if you can jump, 'HA!' and land at precisely the same time. What other actions or sounds could you make other than 'HA!'?

* Everyone stands in a circle and 'passes' a single clap around the circle: how fast can it go round? Then imagine an invisible cannonball is rolling around the circle over which everyone needs to jump or step; a collective acknowledgement of the speed of the cannon ball is important. Now see if you can send the clap one way around the circle and the cannonball the other way; vary the tempo of the claps and the jumps; see if you can start and complete the actions simultaneously; add in other physical actions or more claps or cannonballs.

• Everyone in the circle is allocated a number. In sequence
  everyone asks, 'I'm number one, where's number two?'
  Number two would then answer and say 'I'm number
  two, where's number three?' and so on until everyone
  knows who is after them numerically in the sequence.
  Then, using a small ball, each person throws it to the
  person they have just identified as following them in the
  sequence. To make sure everyone is paying attention, ask
  the participants to point to who they received the ball
  from and whom they threw it to. Now try to get the ball
  moving as swiftly and efficiently as possible; eye contact
  before throwing is essential. More and more balls can be
  added in, everyone needs to be ready, open and alert,
  focused and ensuring eye contact. If the ball is dropped it
  doesn't matter; just pick it up and move on to the next
  task, just as an actor would be expected to do if a cue or
  line were missed onstage.

Try the ball game in smaller groups, then at a given signal
change the direction of the ball by throwing it to the person
you initially received it from; try doing this walking around
the space, keeping the ball flowing and changing direction;
now challenge the group's focus and concentration by
allowing them to dispense with the sequence and throw the
ball to anyone in their group, but the ball and the group must
keep moving. You could evolve this by giving the group
additional instructions, maybe speaking a speech together,
telling a story, going over obstacles, putting on costumes or
completing a practical group task.

VOICE WARM-UPS

Imagine you are smearing something sweet and gooey all over
your face (jam, honey, cream, chocolate sauce), and rub it all
over; then, just using your lips and without using voice. blow
out your lips and try to cover the person opposite you in the
goo. Then blow your lips out with voice (like you're cold,
'Brrrr'). Next, thinking how delicious the cream/jam/chocolate
sauce combo is, try a bright strong 'Mmmm' sound – try and

create a strong buzzing on the lips. Then open this out into an 'Aaaah' sound. Then try the different sounds as a sequence (unvoiced lips-voiced lips-mmm-ahh). To combine strong nasal and vowels sounds, try saying 'My, oh my!' – happily, aggressively, like you're flirting, but always with a focus on the lips and getting the sound forward and out; try and cross the circle with your voice, don't hold the voice in.

A-CAPPELLA POP SONG – SMALL GROUPS

In groups, the participants chose a song, with only their voices as different instruments. Using no words, they rehearsed and then performed their songs. For this exercise to be successful everyone needs to throw themselves in and see what happens; the exercise really needs to be evolved through the doing and not too much discussion. Encourage groups to be as playful and creative as possible in how they choose to present their songs.

A-CAPPELLA OVERTURE – WHOLE GROUP

Everyone stands in a circle and three types of sound are discussed: *beat/tempo* (percussion; a repeatable, not too complex foundation over which the other sounds will layer); *a drone* (a sustained noise); and *a melody* (don't use the melody from a song you know but make it up on the spot, and also try to avoid words/lyrics, as gobbledygook is preferable).

Now with one person standing in the middle as *conductor* and starting with one person making a beat, everyone adds in either another beat, a drone or a melody, which one of these three being decided by the conductor. Once all the group has added in a sound and the music is established, the conductor can play around with making different parts of the orchestra quieter and louder, taking an element out and adding them back in. Perhaps you could play around with speed and tempo, perhaps getting the group moving around the space.

Perhaps you could use the 'Using the senses' exercise below as a starting point for the music: what tone and sounds might

be appropriate for a piece of music entitled 'Metallic Grey'?
How would this sound different to ones called 'Bright Yellow'
or 'Brilliant White'?

VOICE PAINTING

Stand your company all facing a wall (ideally blank or at least
uncluttered); everyone really needs to be able to see the whole
wall so stand them a good few metres back. This wall will be
their canvas.

Initially the canvas needs to be *primed*; this is to be done with
breath only, no voices yet, just the movement of air, so don't
engage the larynx. Everyone should imagine they are gently
whitewashing the canvas clean and clear in readiness for the
colours. They should try to cover the whole canvas/wall and
also use their whole bodies in the effort, not just their neck
and head.

The next instruction is for them to start painting the background
of this picture: A LARGE HORIZON. Everyone should close their
eyes, visualise the picture and then go about adding a bit more
colour, but being encouraged to stay off-voice, just breath.

The next layer is BIG BLUE WAVES, adding colour but
again off-voice so there might be lots of unvoiced fricatives
(*f*, *sh*, *s*, *h*).

The next image is A GREAT RED SHIP and then A TALL
BLACK MAST, all still off-voice and using the whole body.

Then add SEAGULLS FLYING ALL AROUND; now the actors
can use their voices as the picture gets more detailed.

The final addition is THE SUN BURNS BRIGHT IN THE SKY.
Encourage bright and vibrant noise, shifts in tone, vowel
sounds and 'colour'.

Go back through the sequence of images and add more form
and body to each layer. Then trying speaking and opening
out only the vowel sounds in each phrase, A WIDE HORIZON,
BIG BLUE WAVES, etc., still using the whole body to help
express the quality of each added detail. Now try speaking

only the consonants; how is that different, is it the same 'feeling'? Now speak the whole of each line, remembering the work done on the consonants and vowels.

This exercise can help to 'free up' the voice, allowing actors to become aware of the full range and flexibility of their voices and to discover that words can have a shape and form as well as a sound. Using the wall as a 'target' can also really help with projection.

(As a creative coda to this exercise, ask the group to discuss with a partner where the sailors were in their 'painting'.)

VOICE INTO TEXT

A copy of the Town's speech beginning with 'The biggest problem in this city . . . ' (pages 433–4) was cut up and with each word on a separate piece of paper the speech was scattered around the room. The group moved in the space and picked up a word, which they then pictured, whispered, spoke only the vowels and then fully vocalised along with a physical action. The participants were all urged to project their sound and intention: 'Don't keep it inside your body – get it out. Don't keep it to yourself.'

IDEAS FOR CREATING ENVIRONMENTS

The group worked on images and tempo rhythm for creating a scene that suggested a city. The group were given a series of instructions: STOP, START, DART (move swiftly and suddenly), STALK (choose someone, and don't let them realise you are watching/pursuing them closely) and FOLLOW. Accompanied by atmospheric music the participants shifted from one mode to another, switching from motion to moments of stasis, from observation to activity. The group then tried the same exercise only taking tiny steps, then on all fours. What other variations might be helpful? Sarah then called out evocative images to which the group reacted and added more detail to their activities: 'The sky is dark, you are surrounded by tall buildings, it's hot and humid . . . '

Don't rush these exercises and take note of what emerges – there may be images and elements of staging you could develop further; consider dividing your group into two so that one half can observe the other and give feedback on interesting things they observed. Try different kinds of music and sound under the exercise and see what changes.

Now standing with a partner (it could be in groups of three) shake hands and freeze. This is your first image. Now, alternating in sequence, each actor should take up a new position but try and keep one point of physical contact with their partner and freeze momentarily to form a brief tableau and then move on. It's important not to plan these moves; don't aim for or pre-empt some kind of effect or narrative but let the body go first and see what happens. As before, maybe try dividing the company into two groups so one group can observe.

Now create the tableaux without the instruction to be in physical contact; the actors can be as far away from their partner(s) as they want. As the exercise develops encourage the actors to use things in the room: doors, chairs, curtains and so on.

To extend this exercise further, encourage the actors to add themselves into the tableaux of other groups, but make sure they are 'adding' and augmenting, and not interrupting or choreographing others.

Add the efforts of STOP, GO, DART, STALK, FOLLOW back in. Encourage your actors always to be in activity, physically and mentally, and not resting. You can't plan this exercise; you don't know what other people are going to do and the environment is always changing. Try this with different pieces of music with changes of mood and tempo and compare the responses.

IMPROVISED CHORUS

Using the Town's speech (pages 433–4), the group was divided into two and positioned at opposite ends of the studio. Each group then began to work through a part of the speech with the intention of achieving some consolidation of their group's different voices without planning or rehearsal – a *voice jam*. Initially the participants had different tempos and varying rhythms of speaking, making the text difficult to follow, and it took a few attempts to find a synthesis that suggested a single, shared 'voice'. Listening is essential for this exercise.

The group then divided into four smaller choruses, each being allocated a small section (about six lines) of the Town's speech. This time the participants were given a few minutes to rehearse who was going to say what and also to play around with possible physicalisations of the imagery in the verse. Everyone was encouraged to develop their ideas by *doing*, to experiment and investigate by trying things out ad lib and see what evolves. The groups were also advised not to have a leader.

Through the exercise senses of collective identity emerged in the different groups: one group was likened to members of the Women's Institute, another to a bunch of schoolkids, another to the local constabulary.

The whole group then came together, compressed the playing space so everyone was clumped together, and each group performed their section of the Town speech in turn for an invisible audience. Initially, only the group speaking were allowed to move, applying the STOP, START, DART, STALK and FOLLOW rules. Then, after a run-through, particular words and actions were identified as being moments when the whole group could speak or move; for example, everyone stressed and reacted to the words *onions* and *pushers* and the verbs *bumping* and *praying* were given clear physical actions.

Use these exercises to see what your company can come up with through *doing* and not sitting, chatting and planning. This will allow the development to come organically and collectively, with the task of direction becoming more that of observing and selection rather than the responsibility to come up with the ideas.

ENVIRONMENTS WITH ONIONS

Everyone was given an onion and in small groups challenged to create tableaux, images and objects using their bodies *and* the onions. In groups of three everyone built a bus, then in groups of five a dark city street, in groups of six a takeaway restaurant, in even larger groups a river. Now take out the onions and try creating these images just using bodies, then take out the bodies and try it with just the onions. What images evolve? Could you use these as a setting for your scenes?

MOVEMENT AND TEXT

In groups of four, each was given a number. Number One was then asked to complete one of the following moves: either a MOVE AROUND, a PASS BY or a MOVE THROUGH the other members of their group; then Numbers Two, Three and Four. Then Number One again, and so on until the group had eight rehearsed moves, the ninth and final move being everyone returning to their starting positions.

These movement sequences were tried out with different types of music that effected the tempo, rhythm and energy of the movement. The groups were all encouraged to know exactly where their audience was and to try and exaggerate their movements. The next task was to try the sequence imagining you were a waiter carrying a large heavy tray laden with food, and on pain of a P45 you must not drop or spill anything!

Each group was then allocated a verse from the Chorus of Cooks on page 000. Starting with everyone speaking the whole verse together and then with each participant taking one menu item, which they spoke along with their move. The last word 'Naaaaaaaaaaaaaaaaaaaaan' was spoken by the whole group as a finale as they returned to their original positions.

The world of the play

The participants were all asked to choose one word that they thought described the play in some way. Here is a list of the contributions:

- Choral, lyrical, curious, parable, deep, layered, imagery, moral, fragility, tenseness, choice, society, loss, physical, trial, friendship, community, short-sightedness, pace, justice, desperation, pressure, melancholy, doomed, piper, hope, fairy story and discontent.

Considering all the suggestions made, everyone was then asked to close their eyes and visualise one image or scene from the play and picture the characters involved, being certain about whether it is inside or outside, cold or warm, bright or dark, sunlight or artificial light, a big space or small space. Is it breezy and open or heavy and claustrophobic? When the environment was clearly 'painted' in the participants' minds, they were asked to place a single onion into their image and then asked to describe this scene to someone else. Images that were shared included:

- Five cooks doing labour-intensive, hot, sweaty work in a frantic steam-filled kitchen. A single onion rolls across the kitchen floor unnoticed.

- A complete ensemble standing outside a takeaway at night, giants overlooking them and the whole scene lit by a single onion-shaped street lamp.

Discuss your company's images and see how they might be realised and put on stage.

The participants were then asked if they could ask any of the characters in the play a question, what it would be? Here are some of the questions:

- I'd ask Kimberley why she doesn't leave, why she puts up with it all.

- I'd ask the Dancing Girl if she was real.

- I'd ask Darcus if he suspected the final outcome.

- I'd ask Mitzi why she wants to leave he kids.

These and similar lines of questioning can be helpful in making sure a company understands the play and has been paying attention to the details in the story. Encourage your actors to speak out if there's anything they don't understand.

Using the senses in creating a world

The participants were put in small groups and asked to discuss the following. Their responses are also included below, but a different group might give completely different answers.

If this play was a colour, what colour would it be?
Autumnal browns, metallic steel grey, sepia, concrete grey, amber.

If it were a taste what would it be?
Cinnamon, spicy, bitter, an aftertaste, sweet and sour, rusty cutlery, just-off milk – okay for tea but not cereal.

If it were a smell what would it be?
Burnt sugar, pollution, yesterday's stale takeaway, burnt oil, an old chip pan, ashes from a bonfire.

How might the suggestions for colour, taste and smell influence your design ideas for set or costume?

If it were a sound what would it be?
A silent scream, white noise, crashing pots and pans, water dripping, a klaxon, a kettle whistle, the buzzing of a failing light bulb.

If it were a texture what would it be?
Velcro, rough dry stone, silk, slime, grease on corduroy, crisps, uneven slate.

How might these suggestions for sound and texture be used to create a soundscape or music for your production? Could your musical score be composed not for conventional instruments but for an orchestra of these different sounds?

It Snows

by Bryony Lavery, Steven Hoggett & Scott Graham

Same old story. Boy doesn't meet Girl. Girl doesn't meet Boy. Threatened by terrifying Lads' Gang. Threatened by awe-inspiring Girls' Gang. Mum and Dad have declared war . . . against each other. Weird neighbour in the building opposite. Usual ordinary gloominess. Then, one day, it snows. Everything changes.

Age suitability: any age

Cast size
Many named characters,
plus ensemble, physical piece

Bryony Lavery's plays include *Her Aching Heart* (Pink Paper Play of the Year 1992) and *A Wedding Story* (2000). *Frozen*, commissioned by Birmingham Rep, won the TMA Best Play Award and the Eileen Anderson Central Television Award, and was produced on Broadway where it was nominated for four Tony Awards. She also wrote *Stockholm*, with Frantic Assembly, which won the Wolff-Whiting Award for Best Play of 2008. Recent work includes *Beautiful Burnout* for the National Theatre of Scotland and Frantic Assembly, which received a Fringe First at Edinburgh; *The Believers* with Frantic Assembly at Theatre Royal Plymouth and the Tricycle; *Kursk* with Sound&Fury at the Young Vic and Sydney Opera House; *Thursday* at the Adelaide Festival; *Queen Coal* at the Studio, Sheffield; *101 Dalmatians* for Chichester; an adaptation of *Tales of the City/ More Tales of the City* by Armistead Maupin for BBC Radio 4; and *Treasure Island* at the National Theatre. Forthcoming work includes stage adaptations of *Brideshead Revisited* for York Theatre Royal; *The Lovely Bones* for Birmingham Rep; and a new work, *SLIME*, for Banff Canada/Cape Farewell. She is an honorary Doctor of Arts at De Montfort University, an Associate Artist at Birmingham Rep and a Fellow of the Royal Society of Literature.

Characters

Cameron Huntley, *our hero*
Caitlin Amoretti, *our heroine (pronounced 'Catlin')*
Weird Girl, *our mystery*
Delisha, *Caitlin's best friend*
Tamara, *Delisha's best friend*
Marlee Holmes-Spalding, *the poshest, richest girl around*
Weird Girl's Brother, *another mystery*

Then there are various groups:

Everybody: *this is everybody: do it all together or share it out or what seems right to you; make it real*

Lads: *these include Mr Trouble, Mr Cool, Mr Not Cool, Mr Runner, Mr Rubber: find the name that suits the physical character you are*

Girls: *these include Ms Dizzy, Ms Perfect, Ms Trouble, Ms Big Trouble, Ms Thing, Ms Glam: likewise, find the name that suits the physical character you've made*

Mums: *ditto*

Dads: *ditto*

Members of the Community: *Businessmen/women, Old-Age Pensioners, Milkmen, Postmen, Gritters, Sanders, etc.*

It Snows is a physical piece.
No videos to be used.
Only Caitlin does mime.

Where Everybody speaks, be amazing with the sound delivery of the text, whether speaking together or dividing it up. It is the language of its streets and should be both realistic and gorgeous.

Scene One

We are in a not-very-beautiful place of buildings and streets and windows.

Cameron *is there with a complicated box.*

Cameron
It's finger-freezing-nose-running-bollocking-nut-nipping cold.
It's not Christmas
It's just after.

He starts to open the box . . .

Because my birthday is on Boxing Day every year
Everybody
Even my mogging *mum* forgets my birthday
So because she feels mega-guilty
in the January sales she always feels she's
gotta buy me a *top* gift . . .

Box is open.

This year
It's

He takes out . . .

a digital camera.
(*Very unimpressed.*) Right. That says 'I love you'.

Drops the box on the ground. Points the camera at us.

Stay still

He takes a photograph of us.

Got it.
Round here though there's not much to make a great picture.

He photographs the box on the ground.

Stay still
Got it.

There's a weird girl living in the building opposite.

The **Weird Girl** *stands with her back to her window.*

She mostly looks back into her room. Which is weird. Right?
Sometimes   she looks out of the window

Pause.

Come on . . .

Then she turns to look out.

He positions his camera.

Stay still

She does.

He photographs her.

Got it.

She turns back to the room. Vanishes.

Otherwise
There's just streets
Streets
Streets
Buildings
Buildings
Buildings
School
Saturda job.
Streets
Streets
Streets.

The **Lads** *appear. Amazingly.*

Oh
And yeah
Some Lads
That like to threaten you on a daily basis.

Lads *come and threaten.*

Lads
Oi!

And behaviour . . .

Yo!
No!

Caitlin
Particularly if you're called Cameron Huntley . . .

Lads
Yo!
Cuntley!

Cameron
Huntley
Cameron *Huntley*.

Lads
What we said!

Cuntley!

And they threaten a bit more.
They take the box, put it on his head as a nice hat.
They take his camera, photograph him in positions of pain.

Yo
Yo
Yo

Stick the camera somewhere inaccessible to him.

Yo!

Then turn and vanish.
Cameron *takes off his box hat.*
Retrieves his inaccessible camera as . . .

Cameron
You get spots.
Your body goes weird on you.

Girls ignore you.
Especially Caitlin Amoretti.

The **Girls***, including* **Caitlin Amoretti***, prom on.*

Cameron *points his camera.*

Girls
Do What?
Don't Think So!

Caitlin
Stay still

Girls
Cameron Huntley?
Do What?
Don't Think So!
Get Him!

The **Girls** *do something unspeakable to* **Cameron***.* **Caitlin**
Amoretti *watches.*

Girls
What's in the box, Cameron?
Is it your willy?

Cameron
See?
You wonder if you can vanish.

He tries.

Girls
Go Girlz!
Say What?
Don't Mess With!
Coming, Amoretti?

Caitlin
Staying   might   stay

The **Girls** *prom off.*

Caitlin
>Nothing much happens round here.
>School
>School
>School
>You do Theatre Studies.
>You learn stuff like   Mime

She does some mime.

>Movement

She does some movement.

>You learn useful theatrical terms like . . .
>'Lights up.' 'Lights down.'
>'Blackout.'

The lights may obey her here and throughout . . .

>Upstage downstage stage right stage left – wings
>Exit right – exit left – find your light.

Possibly, though, the light finds her . . .

>You learn acting o-that-this-too-too-solid-flesh-would-melt
>Doesn't count for little butterballs when you come out and

Lads
>Oi!
>Yo!

And behaviour . . .

Caitlin
>Boys like Cameron Huntley just ignore you . . .
>While the others . . .

Lads
>Oo!
>Yo!
>Twatlin Amoretti

Caitlin

Caitlin Amoretti.

Lads

What we said
Twatlin.

And they do something unspeakable to **Caitlin** . . .

Cameron

You discover you're not much of a hero
You go in.

He goes in.

Caitlin

It's so cold your tits are embarrassing in a white school
shirt.

Lads

Look at Caitlin Amoretti's titties!

Caitlin

You use *acting* to protect yourself and hide your all-
enveloping shame

Pointing desperately . . .

Oh no! *Look!*
That's not *the Old Bill* coming this way is it . . .?
With *the drugs-sniffer dog*?

Lads *magically, speedily, disappear.*

Caitlin

It's like whoever's on weather today's got the dial turned
up to *Arctic*
It's too cold to be out
You go in.   Stage left.

She does an impressive mime, opening a door, doorknob. Going in . . .

We're doing *Marcel Marceau* this term . . .

Shutting it behind her . . .

I'm after an 'A'.
You're *In.*

Caitlin

You're *IN.*

Lights up! Reddish *homey* filter.
You watch *CSI – Miami*

You play Game Boy

You're on Facebook

You're on YouTube

You're on your mum's nerves

A knot of **Mums** *appear.*
And **Mums***' behaviour as . . .*

Mums

Haven't you got homework to do?
Do you have to be *there*?
You're driving me *up the wall*!

Cameron

You're on your dad's nerves

A fistful of **Dads** *appear.*
And **Dads***' behaviour as . . .*

Dads

Haven't you got coursework to catch up?
Who's finished *the beer*?
When I come home after a hard day's work all I want's .
   a *bit of peace*!

Caitlin

Your mum and dad row a lot.

Mums

Don't just put your cup down in that sink I've just this
   minute / cleaned all the work surfaces . . . cup! No!
   I mean it . . .

Dads

I'll do it in a minute can I have just one moment first with
a biscuit and my paper . . .? Moment! Biscuit! Paper!
I mean it . . .

Mums

Ken / Phil / Sanjay / Ronny / Desmond / Luv /
Mustapha /   Daddy!

Dads

Denise! / Audrey! / Amrit! / Jocelyn! / Houdna! /
Mummy!

Mums

You did you put it in my clean sink you did you did you.
did!

Dads

For a couple of minutes for a couple of minutes!

Caitlin

Lights dim.
Time for bed.

Cameron

Time for bed.

Dads/Mums

For pity's sake – *go to bed!!*

Dads

I'm off *out*!

Mums

GOOD!
I'm off to bed!

Mums and **Dads** *disappear magically in opposite directions . . .*

Caitlin

And you look out

Cameron
And you look out

Caitlin
It's got dark

Cameron
It's got dark
That weird girl's looking out of her window

The **Weird Girl** *looks out.*

Stay still

He photographs her.

Got it.

He turns back into his room so he doesn't see . . .

The **Weird Girl** *bringing up an old threadbare teddy bear to look through the window.*
She makes the teddy bear look left and right.
The teddy bear sees everything.
It looks up at her.
She looks at the bear.
They both look back out of the window.
Then she disappears it.
Then she disappears.

Caitlin
Then it's like whoever's on weather today's turned the
    dial off *Arctic*
Down to just *cold*
The sky looks heavy
A bit glittery.
You get under *two* duvets
You sleep.

Cameron
Air's full of frost.
You pile *all* your coats

And your bedside sheepskin rug
On top of your duvet
You sleep.

Caitlin

Lights down.
Single small spotlight on the juvenile leading lady.
   Rose pink.

You have these dreams.
About flying   and horses
You're on a horse riding away over   the dark green hills

Cameron

You have these dreams

You're fighting   with superhuman strength
   superhuman calm
With a superhuman ability to disable but not kill each
   of your dastardly enemies

Not kill   unless you *feel* like killing

Caitlin

Dream changes!

You're at a party on a big yacht and God you look fit
   you can see it in everybody's eyes . . .

Cameron

Dream changes!

You're at a party in *Hello!* in *GQ* in Heaven where even fit
   girls really fit girls treat you with *respect*   and   *longing*

Caitlin

You totally *love* dreaming

Cameron

You're *so* into dreaming!

They sleep.

The **Weird Girl** *appears at her window.*
She is screaming.
She beats the window with her fists.
None of us can hear her.
She disappears.

Cameron
You wake suddenly / in the middle of the night!

Caitlin
You wake suddenly in the middle of the night!

Cameron
What?

Caitlin
Yes . . .?

They both lie listening.

The **Weird Girl** *appears at her window with paper and marker.*
She writes a note.
Puts note up at the window.
The words are too small for us to read.
She takes down the note. Turns away.

Cameron
It's weirdly dark

Caitlin
It's weirdly dark   and   *warmer*
You chuck one of your duvets

Joy . . .

You remember it's posh Marlee Holmes-Spalding's party
tomorrow

Cameron
You've woken in a cold sweat
You chuck your sheepskin rug and five of your coats

Horror . . .

You remember
There's the incredible embarrassment factor of posh
    Marlee Holmes-Spalding's party tomorrow

Caitlin
And you're a *great* dancer

Cameron
And you're a *shit* dancer

Caitlin
Please   *Whoever*   Don't let anything happen to spoil it.

Cameron
Please   *Anyone* up there   Let something happen
    to spoil it.

The **Weird Girl** *appears with teddy bear and note.*
Fixes the note in among the teddy bear's stuffing via a split in its chest.
Safety-pins the split.
Tosses teddy bear out through window.
It falls through the air, turning over and over.
It lies on its back in the street below.

Caitlin
End of Scene One. Nightlight glow.
Black fading slowly to   dawn.

They sleep.

Scene Two
IT'S HAPPENING

Everybody
Morning
Morning
Morning

Caitlin *starts to wake as . . .*

Everybody
> You open your eyes
> You yawn

Everybody *yawns . . .*

> You look
> And you look out
> And you look out
> And you look out

Everybody, *plus* **Caitlin**, *looks out.*

Caitlin
> And the sky today somebody on *weather's*
> breaking off bits of white sky
> And the bits the *minute* bits of cloud are falling

Cameron *starts to wake up . . .*

Caitlin
> And
> It snows

Everybody
> It snows
> It snows

Cameron *blearily goes to window.*

Looks . . . goes from zero to wide-awake in a nano-second.

Cameron
> *IT'S SNOWING!*
> *IT'S SNOWING!*

Everybody's *watching!*

Cameron
> Even the girl in the window opposite is watching it snow . . .

> Stay still

He photographs her.

Got it.

As he looks away, she looks down, points frantically to her teddy bear on the ground below.

Everybody
   It snows

Eyes up!
Everybody *watches the snow fall. All the community.*
Everybody *catches snowflakes in their mouth.*

It's different

Things change

Things happen when
It snows

It's getting thicker!
It's settling!
It's going to be really really deep!

Brrrrrrrrrrr!

I NEED TO GET MY SNOW GEAR ON!

Everybody *starts to get dressed in various qualities of snow gear as:*

You can't wait to get outside

It's the clothes on the line frozen

It's the possibility of sledging!

SLEDDDDDDGGGINGGG!

It's the possibility of the pond freezing over therefore
   skaaaaaaaaaaaaaaaating!

It's the possibility of   loooooong   sliiiiiiides!

It's the white
It's the white

The white

The difference

The other

Brrrrrrrr!

Everybody *puts on mittens as . . .*

It's the clean surface the clean slate you get

It's the car driving through town with the foot of snow
on its roof

It's the hexagonal composition of snow

Hexagonal shape dance.

It's the steamed-up windows
It's how it covers everything up

Even the teddy bear that the weird girl in the window
threw down.

Everything

Gets covered.

And the teddy bear disappears as the **Weird Girl** *watches helpless.*

It snows

It's the joy of it
The joy of it
The joy of it.

And everybody is dressed and ready!

Scene Three
IT'S HERE!

Everybody ready for the snow . . . ?

Cameron
The world's new.

The space is clean and white.

Nobody was ever here before.

Caitlin
We go MAD!

Cameron
We go MADMADMADMADMADMADMADMAD!

Lads
We go maaaaaaaaaaaaaaaaaaaaaaaaad!

Girl Gang
Soooooooooooooo madmadmadmadmad!!!

Okay, this section is 'The Snow Piece'.
People make patterns in the snow.

Cameron
You start to see the patterns in life

People make snow angels.

Caitlin
Centre stage – *wings*!

People walk about with piles of snow on their heads!

Cameron
At the bus stop there's some penguins . . .

He photographs businessmen looking like penguins with Styrofoam-cup
beaks, etc. . . .

There's some blood in the snow.

He photographs it.

Snow in the tree

Photographs it.
Where the teddy bear is under the snow . . .

Small mysterious pile of snow

Photographs.

Weird girl's window. Empty. But with snow on it.

Photographs.

Caitlin
And still the snow's falling
Its getting deeper and deeper . . .

Horror . . .

I hope Marlee Holmes-Spalding's party's still on!

Cameron
This snow's gonna be too deep for people to find their
way around!

Joy . . .

Marlee Holmes-Spalding's party's looking problematical!

Everybody
Somebody discovers something . . .
This snow is the sort of snow that makes . . . .

One of the **Lads** *bends down.*
Discovers the snow is now the sort that makes snowballs!

Lad
Snowballs

Lads
SNOWBALLS!

Girls
Oh no, not SNOWBALLS!

People start to make snowballs as . . .

Everybody

Even THE DADS AND MUMS LIKE SNOW!

They *all* come out of the buildings . . . .

Mums *and* **Dads** *come out of the buildings.*

Mums
Snow! Everywhere!

Dads
Best clear some paths!

Caitlin
The *Dads* Make The Big Snowball!

Dads *make the 'big' snowball which carries all before it.*

Dads
Careful!
Careful . . .
CAREFUL!

Cameron
The Mums *watch* the Dads make THE BIG SNOWBALL.

Mums *watch and smoke. Proud.*

Mums
Careful Dad / Ken / Phil / Sanjay / Ronny / Luv /
   Derek / Mustapha . . .
Careful Careful . . .

And now . . .
The Big . . .
Snowball Fight!
Not gender versus gender . . . more . . .
Threatening characters versus wimps.
Dads' 'Big Snowball' threads through.

Dads
What d'you say to *that*, Denise / Amrit / Audrey /
   Mummy / Jocelyn . . . ?

Mums
OOOOOOOOOOOH!
You are *clever*, Dad / Ken / Phil / Sanjay / Desmond . . . !

Cameron (*with perfect snowball*)
You've never been great at sports

But
Just *once* in your loser life . . .
You have the perfect snowball in your hand
The right size
The optimum weight!

You *have* to throw it!

Caitlin
You're fit
You're bendy
You've dodged every snowball
Because   you're like that
Graceful
Swift . . .

As she says this, **Cameron**'s *snowball flies through the air. Hits her square in the mouth.*

Cameron
It's suddenly not such a good day.

Caitlin
You've suddenly a gobful of sn . . .
(*To* **Cameron**.) You *pillock*!
Then you see it's Cameron Huntley . . .

Cameron
You're suddenly a pillock . . .

(*To* **Caitlin**.) Sorry! Not meant for . . .

Suddenly feels dark

Like the world's ending . . .

Like a familiar pattern's emerging . . .

Mobiles start to go.
Everybody has to find their mobiles in the depth of their snow gear in their mittens.

Everybody
Yes?

Yo?
Oh?
So?
Say what?

Marlee Holmes-Spalding's ringing round saying 'My party's
still on!'

I got to get my Best Knock-'Em-Dead Gear On!

Everybody gets into knock-out gear ready for the party.

The **Weird Girl** *is at her window, looking out.*
She turns back into the room.
There is a boy sitting in a chair. Saying nothing.
She dresses him in warm, warm clothes. He says nothing.
She leads him to the window, shows him the snow.

Weird Girl
   It's snow
   Come on.

She leads him to a door.
But he won't go through it. He resists.
She leads him back to his chair.
Sits him down.
She goes back to the window and looks out.

Cameron
   You're inside.
   Snow's got very frosty.
   Its *got* to be too slippery for Marlee Holmes-Spalding's
      party

Caitlin *with her two friends* . . . **Delisha** *and* **Tamara** . . .

Caitlin
   Lights up.
   You're inside Delisha's building with Delisha and Tamara.
   You look fabulous, they look fabulous.
   You're waiting for your cab to take you to Marlee
      Holmes-Spalding's party.
   It's not coming.

The three make a picture of waiting for a cab.

You're waiting.

They wait.

Then . . .

Lights down.

Cameron
Sky with stars
Moon.

He photographs it.

Caitlin
Lights up.

Another configuration of three waiting for the cab. Desperate.

You're still waiting.

They wait.

Then

Lights down.

Cameron
Weird girl at window
Looking   down

Stay still

He photographs her.

Got it.

Caitlin
Lights up.

Another configuration of three waiting. One of them is on the phone, others listening. More desperate.

Still. Waiting.

They wait. Then . . .

Lights down.

Cameron
You could *not go*.

He considers this . . .

Caitlin
Lights up.

Another waiting configuration . . . very desperate.

Still waiting.

Wait desperately . . . then . . .

Delisha
We could 'not go'

Tamara
We could rethink the plan
We could go up to your bedroom, Delisha, invent a
    dance routine.

Cameron
You prayed for an excuse
You got one.
Snow. Deep snow. Freezing.
Slippery as f –

Delisha
Thinking outside the box, Tamara.
I like it.

Caitlin
But there'll be people at the party you might want to *see*

Cameron
But something might *happen*

You might cop off.

Caitlin

You might be like 'Hi, Cameron!
Dance?' 'Sure. Why not?'

Cameron

You might be like 'Oh. Caitlin. What say?
Admirin' my shapes? Join me?' 'Yo! Sure!'

Tamara

We can choose popular upbeat music!
Possibly like a medley   steady beat   go up-tempo
Segue into a like *manic* beat cool it into slo-romantic
    vibe . . .
Make it really complex!

Then audition for *Britain's Got Talent*!

Delisha

I'll go to the kitchen get some Tangos and Doritos and
    some of my mum's Pernod!

Tamara

I'll go clear your bedroom floor, Delisha . . .

Come on, Caitlin . . . Forward plannning! Fame! Fortune!

They exit . . . where 'fame' awaits them.

Caitlin

You shout up.

(*Really quietly.*) I might just go to the party . . .!

Okay

Just *DO IT*!

Even by *bus*!

Cameron

Just *be A MAN*!
Get a bus!

And they both leave their buildings.
Caitlin *with an impressive through-the-door mime as always . . . lots of bolts and locks and chains to undo this time . . .*

Everybody
> Meanwhile
> At Marlee Holmes-Spalding's party . . . .

Everybody else is, as if by magic, at the party, very squashed up, doing really really wonderful group dancing!

Among them, very squashed, our hostess **Marlee** *. . .*

Marlee
> So Many of You! Lovely! Come in!
> Coats There! Shoes Off!
> No, Seriously Shoes Off!
> Drinks in There!
> Dips Crisps Eats Stuff in There!
> No Going in the Dining Room.
> No Going in Dad's Drinks Cabinet!
> Come In! Lovely! Welcome!

As . . .
Caitlin *and* **Cameron**, *on the street, arrive at the same bus stop.*

Cameron
> Oh. No. Oh.

Caitlin
> Oh. God. Oh.

They queue.
They watch for the bus coming.

Meanwhile, the squashed party continues.
Marlee, *squashed within . . .*

Marlee
> Don't lean on the walls!
> They've just been redecorated!
> Who are *You*? Who are *YOU*?
> I don't know *ANYBODY* here!

Dad said *twenty* guests! Don't let anybody else in!
No Gatecrashers!
No More! No!

Back at the bus stop . . .
It's getting unbearable, and colder . . .
Cameron *points his camera at something very small.*

Cameron
Stay still

Got it.

Caitlin *practises mime-walking in a very strong wind.*

Caitlin
It's *mime*.

Cameron *tries to photograph his own face*

Cameron
Stay still

Got it.

Caitlin *practises being trapped in a mime glass box.*

Back at the even more squashed party . . .

Marlee (*even more squashed*)
Put that *Down!* That's my *dad's twenty-five-year-old malt!*
There's *a scratch* on my mum's *dining-table-for-twelve!*
Don't bring the dips out of the kitchen you'll get it all over
    the furniture, the paintwork. Oh look the carpet!
Why did I say I'd have a party?
I *hate* parties!
I Hate You!
I Hate You ALLLL!

Back at the bus stop, everybody is very very very cold . . .
After what feels to them both like for ever . . .

Cameron
Don't think it's coming.

Caitlin

No

Cameron

I'm freezing

Caitlin

Me too.

They sit. This is the journey of the shiver.
They shiver. Apart. In stereo.
Both their teeth chatter for a bit.
Then he, very tentatively, starts to warm her.
And then, they warm one another . . . little bits of each other's cold
extremities, going from freezing and shaking through everything . . .
blowing on one another . . .
To warmth.
To amazing closeness.

Caitlin

Thanks

Cameron

You're . . .

Caitlin

Welcome

Think I might give up on the party

Cameron

Me too.

Gutted to miss dancing, though.

Caitlin

Always.

She rummages through her snow gear for her mobile . . .
Finds a dance track on it.
They dance.
Miraculously, **Cameron** *can dance with* **Caitlin.**

Cameron
Er   so   well   um   walk you home?

Caitlin
No!

Caitlin
No. Of Course Not.

Caitlin
Don't walk me

Dance me home.

And they do.
Lights: many brilliant bright colours glitterball.
End of Scene Three.

Scene Four
IT'S GOING (SLUSH)

A 'slush damce' . . . as **Everybody** *discovers . . .*

Everybody
Snow
Is always followed
By slush

Morning
Morning
You come out

It's all slush!

Slush!

Slush!

The snow on roofs starts to slide and

Dush!

Trees hurl the snow off their branches

Dush!

The snowman falls over

Dush!

The snow creeps back from the buildings

Dush Dush Dush

White turns to
Soot grey
Dog-urine-yellow

That blood on the snow   it's gone

Real world starts to re-emerge

It's not pretty

Everything goes back to dull old ordinary old *normal* . . .
Here comes normal . . .

Lads *return to threaten.*

Lads
    Oi!
    Yo!
    No!

Girls *return to threaten.*

Girls
    Say What?
    Don't Think So!

Lads
    Yo . . . *Cuntley?*

    Yo . . . *Twatley?*

Girls
    Oh . . . *Cameron?*

    Hey . . . *Amoretti?*

But no Huntley or Amoretti.

Lads

Nobody to threaten!

Girls

Its sooooo *boring*!

Delisha *and* **Tamara** *appear.*

Lads

Oi!
Yo!

Girls

Say What?

Delisha / Tamara

Don't Think So !

Delisha

Watch this!
Then text *Britain's Got Talent.*

They dance ambitiously.
Lads, **Girls** *watch.*

Lads / Girls

Yo!

Impressed, they get out their mobiles.
Start to text . . . then . . .

Lads

ORRRRR . . .
Put you on YouTube, yo!

Girls

Build your reputation up *slowly* give you a cool indie feel . . .
Say what?

Tamara

Forward planning!
Fame!
Fortune!

Everybody films the top dance.
Marlee Holmes-Spalding *appears* . . .

Lads / Girls
Great party, Marlee!

Marlee
I know!
House? Trashed!
Mummy and Daddy? Ballistic!
Starting next Saturday, I'm grounded for *five years*!

And she joins the dance.

Everybody
Mums return to work.

Mums
See you tonight!

Everybody
Dads return to work.

Dads
See you tonight!

Darling!

Sweetheart!

Mums
You big soft thing!

Weird Girl *looks out of her window.*
Cameron *looks out of his.*
Caitlin *looks out of hers.*

Cameron
Not going out in *this*!

He watches the street . . .

Caitlin
I'm not going out in *this*!

She watches the street.
After a while, both turn from their windows to their mobiles.
Cameron *texts* **Caitlin**.

Cameron
　R U going out in this?

Caitlin *texts back.*

Caitlin
　R U?

Cameron
　No.

Caitlin
　Nor Me.

Ponders.
Texts.

　　X.

Cameron
　X.

Both behave as if they have received a Shakespearean sonnet.

Weird Girl
　Doesn't matter.
　It's all turning to slush anyway.
　Everything's melting.
　Doesn't matter.

Cameron
　Sleep
　I dream

Caitlin
　Night
　Sleep
　I dream

Cameron
Caitlin – Caitlin Amoretti

Caitlin
Cameron – Cameron Huntley

X

Cameron
X

Weird Girl
It's gone.

Caitlin
X   that's *a kiss* that is!

Caitlin
Lights down   goldish glow   fades slowly.

End of Scene Four.

Scene Five
IT'S GONE

Everybody
Snow's gone.
Buildings naked again.
Streets bare.

When the snow's gone
Nobody wants to go out.

Place is deserted.

Cameron (*with his camera*)
The day in's good
Because
You spend it fiddling about with your camera
And
You discover

Pillock!
It has a facility for making
Short films . . .

Caitlin

The day in's good
Because
You finally work out your three-minute mime routine . . .

She shows us.
It is quite complicated, busy with opening and closing doors, story and very impressive . . . a journey through quite severe weather conditions, etc. . . .

The **Weird Girl** *appears in her window, looking out.*
Then she turns back to the room.
Her **Brother** *sitting. Suitcase beside him.*
Two people come in, gently, professionally, take him out.

Person (*to* **Girl**)

Would you like to bring his stuff?

Cross-fade to . . .

Cameron

You have this idea
Make a short film
Outside
On the street
Say . . . near Caitlin Amoretti's building . . .

Caitlin

You're not *convinced* by what you're doing in your
    showing *cold* mime
You think why not go out *experience* cold
On the street
Say . . . near Cameron Huntley's building . . .

Then

Just opposite his building
You see on the pavement
This teddy bear.

Cameron (*as he does it*) . . .
    You're doing a tracking shot from the weird girl's window
    Through your building
    Out of your door . . .
    Across the street
    And   there's Caitlin Amoretti
    With

Caitlin
    Look

She picks it up.

    This was under the snow.

Cameron
    Keep going

He's filming . . .

Caitlin
    What?
    Improvise?

She does. She picks up the teddy bear tenderly . . .

    Poor Teddy   you're soaked through.

    Your little jacket   wet through.

    Safety pin through your heart.

    There's something sticking in your little chest . . .!

Caitlin
    Keep going . . .

Caitlin
    Piece of paper! Could be a *secret* message!

    You open it carefully it's really fragile . . .

She opens out the paper. Reads:

    'Help.'

They look at each other.
They look at where the teddy bear was.
They look up to the window.

Cameron
Knock on the door.

Caitlin *knocks on the* **Weird Girl**'s *door.*
Waits.

Cameron
If a weird girl answers, say, 'Are you okay?'

Caitlin
Okay.

She knocks on the door again.
Waits.

Hell . . . it's windy!

She does some mime-fighting against an invisible wind.

I'm after an A.

Knocks again.
Waits.

Nobody.

Cameron
Stop.

Battery's got really low. *Pillock.*

He takes out the batteries. Warms them. Rearranges them . . . as . . .

Caitlin *(mimes as . . .)*
No door can stop you
No locks no bolts
You're *in* . . .

She is, with a mimed but effective Uzi . . . she checks in many possible dangerous rooms . . .

Place is deserted
It's the start of a long, dark, complicated case for
DSI Caitlin Amoretti . . .

She props the teddy up somewhere.

Somebody might come back for it.

Cameron
Yes.

This will still do stills.

He photographs the teddy sitting there.

Caitlin
I might leave here.
Pursue Acting.

Cameron *(as he photographs the empty window)*
I might come with you.

Caitlin
Yes, you might.

Cameron
I might become a photographer.
World famous.

Caitlin
Yes, you might.
I might become a famous actress.

Cameron
Yes.
You might.

I take a still picture of . . .
This street
This building
My dad
My mum
Caitlin Amoretti
This bare tree against a sky

Caitlin

I *do* get an A for my mime project.

Caitlin

Obviously!

Caitlin

That's all.

They both look up and out at the sky.
The **Weird Girl** *appears in the empty window.*
She is dressed for leaving.
She blocks out each of the four window panes with her paintings of . . .
Opposite building in snow . . .
Woods bare . . .
Sun . . .
Field of flowers.

Caitlin

Lights fade slowly   to
Blackout.

And they do.

The End.

It Snows

BY BRYONY LAVERY
AND SCOTT GRAHAM & STEVEN HOGGETT
FOR FRANTIC ASSEMBLY

*Notes on rehearsal and staging drawn from a workshop
with the writer held at the National Theatre, October 2015*

*From workshops led by Vicki Manderson and Damian Cruden,
with notes by Emily Kempson and James Blakey*

How Bryony came to write the play

Bryony wanted to write a play that was 'a celebration',
although not one that was 'religious or about Christmas. I
wanted to write a love story. I want the audience to leave the
theatre having had a great time. I wrote it out of joy.' She
acknowledged that *It Snows* is different to a lot of her other
work in that 'most things work out, except for the story of
Weird Girl. You can't fix everything.'

Bryony said that the play 'shouldn't be heavy'.

When discussing the final image, she expressed a feeling that
the tone (whether hopeful or not) should be left up to
individual groups.

It was Scott Graham who first had the idea of writing about
snow. He realised that snow had a shape to it – it's not there,
it's coming, it's here, it's slush, it's gone.

The challenges of the play

The workshop participants discussed the challenges of the
play. These included both creative challenges, such as how to
deal with the swearing in the play, how to communicate the
sense of snow, the multi-location setting, and landing the play
in the appropriate era.

It is important to identify and confront the challenges of any
project in the early stages. These shouldn't be seen as
problems – get excited about the ways in which you can
tackle the challenges of both the play and the circumstances
in which you are working.

The groups generated some 'top tips' for each other in response to the challenges they identified:

1 Embrace the freedom of the language – try layering it in lots of different ways and applying lots of different contexts until you find what feels right for your vision of the play.

2 Empower your cast to make decisions, in order to give them some ownership over the creation of the piece.

3 Workshop your ideas for the production early, perhaps before introducing the text.

4 Celebrate the idea of ensemble early, perhaps before introducing the text.

5 Keep set and production elements simple so as to prioritise working with the cast.

6 Make a contract with the cast that allows them to work in as professional a way as possible.

7 Keep it playful.

8 Love the play.

9 As director you are in an editorial role. Often less is more.

10 Embrace the gender demographic that you are working with. The play leaves room for both gender-blind casting and changing the gender of certain characters as you see fit.

Approaching the play

Building an ensemble

The ensemble is at the heart of this play. Building an ensemble takes time and work and is based on giving everyone involved in the show a sense of ownership over its creation and performance. Allow each actor to create a character with a name and back-story so that you can have a proper dialogue about who they are and their attitude to the unfolding action of the story.

The play breaks down into groups of people, for example THE
LADS, THE GIRLS, MUMS, DADS, COMMUNITY MEMBERS. It may be
helpful to structure your process around these groupings. But
remember an ensemble is not an amorphous mass that all
respond in the same way. Rather, they are a group of
individuals, who all have their own thoughts and feelings in
response to stimulus. If all the members of the group have
their own point of view, the group will be more dynamic,
allowing for more interesting textures in the storytelling.

Once the ensemble understands that they do not just follow
the narrative but that they *are* the narrative and have choices
to make all the time, they will be with you all the way.

Deconstructing the play

Break the play down in a way that makes sense to you. What
are the signposts or gearshifts in the play that help you to tell
the story? The play is already chaptered according to the
characters' experience of the snow:

1   It's Not Happening
2   It's Happening
3   It's Here
4   It's Going
5   It's Gone

Try breaking it down further in terms of place and time to
identify the moments where the story changes.

Once you have identified these units of the play, you can
begin to ask questions of the nature of each unit. Look for the
anchors that deal in absolutes. For example, we know that a
scene of the play takes place at a bus stop. Use the evidence
of the play to imagine your version – what sort of a bus stop
is it? What are the buildings and streets like? Imagine the
setting you would choose and all of its details if you were
making a film version.

Now look for ways to abstract that 'real' bus stop so you can
make its theatrical version through design and/or with your

actors. When we make a piece of theatre, nothing is real –
everything is an abstraction of a real situation because a room
full of people are watching. As a way into this, Damian
recommended asking the following questions of each unit of
the play:

- If it were a colour, what colour would it be?
- If it were a shape, what shape would it be?
- If it were a time, what time would it be?
- If it were a weight, what weight would it be?
- If it were a space, what type of space would it be?
- If it were a flow, what type of flow would it be?

In this way you can develop a language for communicating
ideas to your actors that can be translated into action on
stage.

Exercises for use in rehearsals

It Snows leaves much space for layers of physical expression
and Vicki Manderson introduced several 'starting points' and
ideas for approaching movement with your company.

PREPARATION FOR WARM-UP

- Inhale.
  Lift shoulders to your ears, and release.
- Align the body in to a 'neutral' position:
  – feet hip-width apart;
  – hands by your side – imagine they are heavy and filled
  with blood;
  – chest wide and open;
  – shoulders back.
- Inhale – screw face up and make it as small as you
  possibly can.
- Exhale – release into a big open face, look around the
  room.

- Rub hands together to create warmth, then spread this warmth to the rest of the body by rubbing every part of it.
- Massage face, temples and jaw.

CIRCLE SWAP

This exercise helps to build a strong ensemble, and to develop energy and focus:

- Stand in a circle.
- One person starts the exercise (this could be the director/ teacher/group leader):
    - make eye contact with someone across the circle;
    - start walking towards your chosen person;
    - as you approach them, and it is clear that you are looking at each other, that person makes eye contact with someone across the circle, and you slot in to their place.
- This swapping of places continues.

If you have a larger group you may wish to initiate subsequent rounds of swapping by setting off yourself again.

To develop this exercise:

- Walk with purpose and energy.
- Progress from faster-paced walking to a jog and even into a run.

WALKING ROUND THE SPACE WITH COMMANDS

This exercise is a great way of beginning to build a community of people moving together:

- Walk into any gaps you see.
- Keep eyes up.
- Remain present in the room.
- Think about your focus being wide.
- Keep an awareness of where other people are in the room.
- You can have eye contact with your fellow cast members.

Add in a few commands:

– WALK

Imagine a hand on the middle of your back, pushing you forward in space.

– STOP

– CENTRE

Get into a clump in the centre of the room.

How condensed can you get? No gaps!

Once in position rest your right ear on someone's shoulders. (Get into position first before resting head to avoid collisions!)

Whatever the next command is, explode away from the centre with a burst of energy.

– CLEAR

Clear the space as swiftly as possible – move to the walls.

– SWAP

Move in to a place on the opposite side of the room.

Everyone must arrive at their new position at exactly the same time.

This may take a few tries – think about how you are going to achieve this.

Similar to 'Circle Swap' – you need to have a wide focus and be aware of everyone else in the space.

– FAVOURITE

Point to your favourite object or area in the room.

There should be a clear shift from a medium energy to something very sharp.

It should be dynamic.

– PERSON

Find a person close to you. Hug them. Squeeze their chest towards your chest. No gaps allowed!

Repeat this a few times. You can also allocate 'Person A' and 'Person B'– you must remember who your 'Person A' is – when this instruction is called you must find them and hug them.

GRID IMPROVISATION

This extended improvisation helps to build a strong ensemble and to develop a company's physical vocabulary.

- Walk around the space – but this time imagine you are on a grid. You can only move in straight lines and at right angles.

- You might experiment with being still.

- You might experiment with walking backwards.

- Is your grid the whole of the space, or just a small section of it? Experiment with changing the size of your grid.

- Keep carving through the space, looking for gaps.

- Now take the grid into your physicality. How can you make your body more grid-like?

- How do your arms swing?

- Where is your focus?

- Where does the head sit on the spine?

- How do your legs move?

- What does it do to your breath? Is your breathing easy or restricted? Does it sit in your belly or your chest?

- Experiment with your speed, playing with levels zero to ten (where zero is stillness and ten is a fast run). How fast can you shift between speeds? Try a sharp shift in speed that takes 1 to 2 seconds. Then explore a longer shift in speed, perhaps from 10 to 20 seconds.

- You can also try moving side to side. Keep experimenting with a 'grid-like' and angular way of moving.

- Now start playing with your spatial relationship to other people. You can decide to form a relationship with someone else in the room – perhaps following their path or mirroring their speed. They might not know you're doing it. This is just something for you to play with in your own head. You can become independent again at any time. Or find someone new to interact with.

- Try not to get stuck in a pattern. Notice where your comfort zone is; if it's always walking very slowly, then mix it up and try going really fast. Surprise yourself and surprise the group. If you are feeling uninspired, don't be afraid to be still and look around the space – wait for someone else's movement to inspire you.

- Now imagine that your grid has halved in size. As a group you must now continue the improvisation in one half of the room.

- There is now less space, more people around you – how does that feel?

- Now squeeze the grid even more. You can only move in a quarter of the space now.

- Keep forming relationships with people in this new, condensed space.

- You are now allowed to have physical contact with other people. You might touch backs, or place a hand on a shoulder.

- Now make that contact more human – maybe a smile, a handshake. You can speak. You can ask a question. Really talk. Don't just pretend to. Then move on to someone else.

- To finish the exercise – open the space back up. Now you are free to walk anywhere. Shake the 'grid' off.

LEVELS OF SPEED – MOVING TOGETHER

- Walk around the space at level 5.

- Keep your focus open.

- Be aware of everyone in the space.

- Walk in to any gaps, change direction.

- Now shift up to level 7, then 8, then 9, then 10.

Continue to call out different levels.

- Now, you have two minutes to move together as a group from level 7 down to level 0 (stillness). There will be no leader to guide you. Watch each other. Try not to lead. Keep 360-degree awareness.

- You should all take the last step at the exact same time.

- Don't be a soloist, be a team member.

Once the group has got to zero:

- You're not frozen. Not a statue. Be a human being. Just breathe.

- Again as a group, and with no direction, move from level zero back up to level 7.

- All the time keep aware of what level you think you're at. Think about what that level feels like in your body.

- Shout out what level you think you're at.

- Call out level seven when you think you're there.

CREATING CHARACTER GROUPS: STARTING POINTS

Vicki suggested that when doing initial work on character groups, gender shouldn't matter. Boys can help create the movement for the MUMS and girls can contribute finding the physicality for the DADS. This approach opens up and develops young people's physical vocabulary. It also makes for a richer creative process – what the girls come up with for the LADS might be much more interesting than what a boys-only group may have produced on their own.

Initial stage: responding physically to words

In this exercise the director asks the group to match their physicality to certain words that they call out:

- Walk around the space at level 5.

- Think about where your own physicality is at: Where is your focus? How are your arms moving? Where are your shoulders? How do your feet press into the floor?

Call out a series of words. In the workshop Vicki used these words as examples:

MENACING   AWARE   NOSY   OVERBEARING

- The first thing you do might not be the right thing. Feel free to play.

- Think about how to embody each word.

- What is it like when you're still? When you move at different levels of speed? How do you react to other people?

- Note how the word affects your face.

- Remember what each word feels like in your body. Feel where your shoulders are, where your breath is. Where is your focus? How is your head sitting on your spine?

- After experimenting fully with each word, shake it off then, walk around the space at level 5, before we move on to the next word.

CREATING CHARACTER GROUPS: SECOND STAGE

Vicki divided the participants into four groups – LADS, GIRLS, MUMS and DADS.

Each group was given a list of words that one might associate with that group of people. What these words are would be up to each individual director. Vicki used the following examples:

Words for the LADS

Grounded
Confident
Menacing
Swagger
Night time
Underground
Shifty

Words for the GIRLS

Pink
Showing off
Aware

Copy

Excited

Giggles

Friends

Bitchy/Catty

Words for the MUMS

Nosey

Prodding

Preoccupied

Busy

Knowing

Caring

Strong

Words for the DADS

Protective

Gruff

Overbearing

Lazy

Silent

Awkward/Embarrassing

Caring/Loving

INSTRUCTIONS TO EACH CHARACTER GROUP

- Find a way of entering the space and leaving the space.
- Find a way of travelling from point A (entering the space) to point B (leaving the space).
- You can move as a group or as individuals.
- The words are there to help you find the genre that the movement sits in.
- Think about changes of speed, levels and energy.

- You can use sound, or even perhaps a repeated line from the play.

- You have ten to fifteen minutes to complete this task.

Towards the end of the allotted time, Vicki gave each group an additional word and an idea for a physical shape. These were in contrast to the somewhat stereotypical list of words that the groups had been given initially. The groups were instructed to layer this new idea or 'flavour' on to what they had already created. These 'counterpoint' words were:

LADS   Grace/Huddle

GIRLS   Ugly/Prom

DADS   Femininity/First

MUMS   Unpredictable/Know

Vicki advised that when doing material-generating sessions like this, it is important to be able to edit. It is best to pick out a few standout ideas, or even just one, to develop. You will get rid of most of what you come up with. Don't feel you have to use everything that you generate in rehearsal. Be brave about what you discard.

The group discussed the idea that creating stereotypes might be a useful approach for *It Snows*. It would help the audience to recognise who a character or a group of characters was very quickly. Setting up stereotypes also allows you to undercut and subvert them. Adding an element of surprise, or a counterpoint, as shown in this exercise, can be powerful.

Hexagonal-shape dance

Many of the participants expressed that this was a moment in the script that they felt unsure about!

Instructions for a suggested starting point:

STAGE ONE

- Draw an imaginary hexagon on the floor. There are six points – also picture one in the centre of the shape.

- Create a journey where you start in the centre and travel to each of the six points. You can move from point to point or travel through the centre.

- Your hexagon can be any size – from large to small.

- At this stage keep the movement simple and just walk.

- Memorise your route and repeat it. Do it a few times so that you feel confident you can remember it.

STAGE TWO

- The hexagonal dance occurs at a point in the story when the snow has arrived but no one has experienced it yet.

- Imagine you are at this point in the story.

- Now make each part of your hexagon journey have a different intention.

- Perhaps you are moving to one point to put your mittens on, or to look out of the window. One journey could just be full of anticipation about the fun you're going to have. Or imagining what it will be like to step on the snow for the first time. Maybe you're nervous about going out into the snow. The whole sequence might be about not being able to find your hat. It's entirely up to you.

- Make sure all the journeys aren't the same in terms of energy. Explore a contrasting range of speeds.

These sequences were shared in groups of five or six. The groups noticed how there were happy accidents when these individual sequences were performed in this way. Vicki talked about how a great way of creating movement sequences, such as this, is to develop something separately, and then put them together to see how they work as a group.

This exercise was built up in layers; it started with a simple task (just a walking journey). Breaking tasks up into stages like this can be a manageable and effective way of approaching what might seem like complex moments of choreography.

Ideas that came out of hexagonal-dance exercise

Vicki discussed how effective it can be to have repeated sections of choreography in a performance. Audiences enjoy repeated moments – their eyes recognise them and that can be exciting. Perhaps individual performers could teach other members of the group the steps they created.

A soundscape could be effective for the sequence – moments when we heard gasps were powerful.

When working through the hexagonal-dance sequence, some participants mimed putting on a scarf, or doing up boots. This proved to be really useful as it led to considering 'how to not mime'. Caitlin is the only character in the story who mimes.

Vicki gave some examples of how mimes could be abstracted into something more interesting. Perhaps putting on a scarf could morph into an exaggerated roll of the head (look at how the head actually moves when putting on a scarf – extract and develop this movement).

The group also discussed the possibility of using real clothes for this sequence as another way of avoiding mime.

If no actual 'snow clothes' are used, Vicki suggested that it might be interesting to explore how we move differently when we are all bundled up in winter layers (moving like the Michelin man, feet heavier when in boots). This could be a way of telling that story physically, without costume or props.

SNOWBALL FIGHT

Stage One

Vicki divided the group into pairs, who then labelled themselves A or B.

- Person B finds five points on person A's body where they might be hit by a snowball.

- To mark the moment of impact for this exercise Person B might place a hand on the area (e.g. put a hand on the back of the neck).

Person A must come up with a physical reaction to being hit by the snowball in that specific place.

Each pair develops a five-point snowball fight sequence.

Stage Two

- The pairs separate in the space.

- Each pair must continue working on their five-point sequence, but Person A must now find alternative ways of 'throwing' the snowball at Person A, from across the room.

- No miming a throw allowed!

- Some ideas – a header, a blow of air from the mouth, a kick, a thrust of the left hip

- We must 'see' the snowball travel through the air. Achieve this with clear eye-focus – watch it travel.

Thoughts after watching snowball-fight sequences

A cartoonish whistling sound as a snowball approaches was effective – perhaps a soundscape would be worth exploring here.

Playing with proximity could be fun – sometimes a snowball could be 'thrown' close to a partner, sometimes from far across the space.

Varying the speed is something to consider – moments of slow motion, then sharp bursts of speed worked well.

BUS-STOP SHIVER DANCE

Divide the group into pairs.

Stage One

- Find a point on your partner's body that is shivering. You can stop the shivering by using any of the following five methods:
  - Blowing.
  - Wrapping.

- – Massaging.
- – Squeezing.
- – Caressing.

- Apply one of these methods until that part of the body has softened and stopped shivering (partner decides when the attempt has been successful).

- Repeat this – finding four parts of each person's body. Take it in turns to be the person shivering.

- This can be developed into a sequence, or eight separate moments.

Stage Two

- Begin to develop a physical sequence using your moments of shivering and warming.

- Now make your eyes tell a story.

- Create a journey with eye contact.

- Does one person never look at the other?

- Do you go from no eye contact to tentatively looking at each other?

- Think about what your eyes are doing at every moment.

Developing the house-party sequence: starting point

The group talked about what actually happened at house parties. Vicki discussed the idea of them being essentially a series of encounters.

You meet one person you're really keen to talk to, the next person you want to touch, then there's someone you haven't met before, and so on.

A sequence of encounters could be developed.

Perhaps in a tight, condensed space on the stage.

Perhaps in a condensed space that stretches in a line across the stage, resembling a corridor.

Bursts of dance could occur within this sequence.

Music

Using sound and music could help to enhance the musicality of the text. Try and find music that gives the actors space to move in the same way that the text does and that complements rather than smothers the text.

Vicki suggested the following artists:

Dustin O'Halloran

Kiasmos

A Winged Victory for the Sullen

Ólafur Arnalds

Hybrid

Nils Frahm

Max Ritcher

John Hopkins

Ekko

Floating Points

Deadmau5

Múm

Yann Tierson

Phil France

Use of explicit language in the play

As a group we discussed the potential difficulty in some communities of using the nicknames in the play ('Cuntley' and 'Twatley'). Bryony acknowledged that this often comes up but felt that, 'These are the right words. They are about bullying. The style of the play told me that it should be "Cuntley" and "Twatley", not anything else. My first position is, if you *can* do it, then do it. If you need to argue it, I will try and support you. I can say why those words are there. If you absolutely cannot use those words then I would ask you to be creative about censorship.' We discussed ideas at this point, such as a hooter, a buzzer or perhaps a sign which could be held up to the actor's mouth when they are about to swear.

Bryony did feel that the audience 'have to know what the word is' even if they don't hear it (through rhyme)' No alternative words are to be used.

Following stage directions

Bryony said that the stage direction 'No videos to be used' did not necessarily need to be adhered to. She made the general point that while no alterations to the text were to be made, the stage directions should be taken as suggestions only.

Setting

Bryony was asked whether she had a particular place in mind for where *It Snows* is set: 'Clearly, I come from a small town in Yorkshire. When I was there it was a mill town, it was very grey. But when the snow came it was utterly transformed. I have a sense that this play is set somewhere unbeautiful, which then becomes beautiful. The environment alters, there is a change. That is a gift when you are putting on a play.'

Mime

The play states that only Caitlin does mime. Vicki encouraged the participants to be 'bolder and braver than mime. Don't do something that your group has done before.'

Damian said, 'Caitlin has got to be different. Her movement is in a different language to everyone else's. It stands proud.' It is also useful to consider the following questions:

- Does Caitlin's use of mime evolve or develop throughout the play? She is changed by the end of the story – is that change reflected in her physicality?
- What does mime mean to Caitlin?

Set

Bryony said that she felt how the play is designed, and how much physical set there is, is very much up to each individual director. However, she said that one of her most important notes is to 'keep it moving'. It is important that a heavy or substantial set doesn't delay or slow down the action. The action needs to move quickly from one location to another.

Themes

Damian said that, as a director, he was drawn to the ideas of 'inside' and 'outside' in the play. There is lots to explore in terms of interior and exterior landscape. Windows, and looking out of windows, is a recurring image. Somehow there is a notion of the future in that. Ideas of inside/outside also play into an exploration of the difference between a person's external sense of self and their interior lives. The snow is a force that brings everyone out of themselves.

Rehearsals

There are logistical challenges such as limited rehearsal time, how to create the right atmosphere for rehearsal in a busy school environment, attendance and dropouts, convincing your young people of the value of ensemble work rather than a play with traditional protagonists. When planning your rehearsal schedule, work backwards from your production dates, not forward from your first rehearsal. If you plan backwards you give yourself a much better chance of not running out of time. Only schedule 80 per cent of your time. Leave yourself a 20 per cent contingency.

The Musicians
by Patrick Marber

The orchestra of Ridley Road, a state school, is to give a concert in Moscow at the European Festival of Youth, playing Tchaikovsky's Fourth Symphony before an audience of cultural bigwigs. But their instruments have been impounded by customs. Luckily, Alex, the Russian boy who cleans the hall, is a devout 'Pinball Wizard' fan who comes up with a plan that saves everyone.

Age suitability: any age

Cast size
many named characters, plus ensemble

Patrick Marber's plays for the National include *Dealer's Choice* (also Vaudeville and MTC in New York), *Closer* (also Lyric, London, and Music Box, New York), *Howard Katz* (also Roundabout, New York); and *The Musicians* for NT Connections. Other plays include *After Miss Julie* (also Roundabout, New York) and *Don Juan in Soho* at the Donmar Warehouse; and *Hoop Lane* for BBC Radio 3. TV includes co-writing *Knowing Me Knowing You with Alan Partridge*, *Paul & Pauline Calf Video Diaries* and *The Curator*. Film includes *Closer*, *Notes on a Scandal*, *Old Street* and *Love You More*. Radio includes co-writing *Knowing Me Knowing You with Alan Partridge* and *Bunk Bed* (with Peter Curran). *The Red Lion* and *Three Days in the Country* opened at the National in 2015.

Characters

Alex
Roland
Second Flute
Cello
Second Trumpet
First Violin
Viola
Double Bass
Second Horn
First Horn
Timpani
Oboe
Clarinet
First Trumpet
Bassoon
First Flute

Except where obvious the musicians can be male or female.

A larger company may perform the play with a greater number of speaking roles by, for example, judiciously allotting some of Violin's lines to a new character called 'Second Violin', etc.

Alternatively, the company could keep the roles as written and have a much larger orchestra some of whom don't have speaking parts. They will still have plenty to do.

Scene One

The stage of a concert hall somewhere in Moscow.

Chairs arranged for an orchestra to play.

A young man in overalls, **Alex**, *ambles on from the wings with a broom and dustpan. He idles to the centre of the stage and peers out at the auditorium.*

Suddenly, he raises his broom as if it's a guitar.

Alex (*in Russian*)   Good evening, Moscow!

He makes the sound of two thousand people applauding – they whoop and scream – he modestly acknowledges the applause.

(*In Russian.*) Thank you, thank you!

Fantasy over, he reaches into his pocket, turns on his Walkman and starts sweeping.

He sings to himself as he works. He is Russian, but sings in English – though with a Russian accent.

He is listening to 'Pinball Wizard' by The Who.

He knows the song well and starts humming the opening guitar riff and then goes into Pete Townshend-style gyrations when the big chords come in.

Once the vocals start, the broom becomes his microphone.

Alex (*singing*)
   Ever since I was a young boy,
   I played the silver ball,
   From Soho down to Brighton,
   I must have played 'em all,
   But I ain't seen nothin' like him
   In any amusement hall,
   That deaf, dumb and blind kid
   Sure plays a mean pinball!

Guitar break. He mimes with the broom. When the vocals return he becomes the pinball wizard on his machine.

Alex (*singing*)
    He stands like a statue,
    Becomes part of the machine,
    Feelin' all the bumpers,
    Always playin' clean.
    Plays by intuition,
    The digit counters fall.
    That deaf, dumb and blind kid
    Sure plays a mean pinball!

Roland (*seventeen*) *appears in the wings. He is intense, dedicated – but not without humour. He watches* **Alex**, *somewhat embarrassed to be witnessing this private display of insanity.*

Alex (*singing*)
    He's a pinball wizard, there has to be a twist,
    A pinball wizard's got such a supple wrist.
Very high voice.
    How do you think he does it?
Response.
    I don't know!
Further response.
    What makes him so good?

He is freaking out. A one-man concert with full imaginary lasers and dry ice. **Roland** *coughs but* **Alex** *can't hear.*

Alex (*singing*)
    Ain't got no distractions,
    Can't hear no buzzers and bells,
    Don't see no lights a-flashin',
    Plays by sense of smell –

Roland *strides on to the stage so* **Alex** *can see him.*

Alex   Hey! Sorry! Hello!

He turns off the Walkman. **Roland** *nods to him and carefully places his small, black leather case on a table.*

Alex   'Pinball Wizard', The Who!

Roland *gives him a 'thumbs-up' then surveys the stage and the auditorium.*

Alex   You like The Who?

Roland *considers what will best prevent further conversation.*

Roland   I have no opinion.

Alex   Okay, I get message, shut cake-hole.

He resumes his sweeping but watches **Roland** *with curiosity.*

Alex   Are you in group?

Roland *is lost in thought.*

Alex   Hey! Britishman, are you make music?

Roland   What?

Alex   Speak English?

Roland   Sometimes.

Alex   You play music, la la la.

Roland   Oh, yes.

Alex   I like music! Alex.

Roland   Roland.

They shake hands.

Alex   You orchestra, yes? From UK.

Roland   Correct.

Alex   How is Queen?

Roland   She was fine when I last spoke to her.

Alex   That is joke?

Roland *nods.*

Alex   British jokes, I know all about. Very ho ho ho.

He gestures to **Roland**'s *small leather case.*

Alex   What instrument you have in box? Don't tell me, I'm guessing . . .

He goes up to the case and inspects it.

You have double bass! (*Beat.*) That is Russian joke.

Roland   And most excellent it was.

Alex   *I* play guitar.

He briefly demonstrates using his broom.

(*Wistfully.*) I don't have guitar really but can pretend . . .

Roland *looks sympathetic.*

Alex   I like all English music: The Who best, then also Beatles, Stones, Pistols, Davie Bowie, The Smiths, Oasis, Coldplay, Radiohead –

Roland   Sorry to stop you but is this list much longer? You see, I've got all day, so why don't I pull up a chair and you sing me every single song you've ever heard?

Alex   You take piss?

Roland   Just a bit.

Alex   English humour: take piss, right?

Roland   It's our national sport. Sorry.

Alex *looks at the case again.*

Alex   So you play little erm . . .?

He mimes a flute.

Roland   Flute?

Alex *nods.*

Roland   No.

Alex   Play what you play?

Roland   I'm not playing anything today.

Alex   You singer? *I* sing.

Roland   No, I'm not a singer.

Alex   What are you do?

Roland *goes to the case, dramatically releases the catches and produces a conductor's baton.*

Alex   You wave stick?

Roland   I'm the *conductor*!

Alex   Duh, I *know*! Who you conduct, famous people?

Roland   The Ridley Road School Orchestra.

Alex *conceals his disappointment.*

Alex   You are boss man?

Roland   Well, kind of . . .

Alex   Kind of what?

Roland   Well, usually I play the cello, but I've been conducting a few rehearsals recently. That's what I've always wanted, to be a conductor. Our music teacher's given me this one-off opportunity. So, if it goes well, who knows . . .?

Alex   This big break for you?

Roland   Yeah.

Alex   Big scary break, wake in middle of night in sweat and screaming fear, yes?

Roland   You could say that.

Alex   Where from school?

Roland   Croydon (*or wherever the company performing the play are based*).

Alex   I have been in Wolverhampton. You know? I live Wolverhampton six week. On exchange. I stay with family Henderson.

Roland   Please don't ask me if I know them.

Alex   Do you know them?

Roland   No!

Alex   Ken and Valerie Henderson. They have daughter, Donna. She love Rio Ferdinand, football player. She say he have good body, tall and slim.

Roland   Have you finished your cleaning yet, your sweeping? I don't mean to be rude, it's just that I really need to prepare.

Alex   Okay, I get. I bugger off.

Roland   The stage looks perfect.

Alex   I been sweep all day for you.

Roland   Thank you.

Alex *starts to exit.*

Roland   By the way, where is everyone? The technicians, sound people, lights?

Alex   All take break.

Roland   What, tea break?

Alex   Vodka break, take longer.

Roland (*worried*)   They'll be back for the concert, tonight?

Beat.

Alex   *Concert?* I thought you just practise?

Roland *starts to panic.*

Roland   We're giving a concert *tonight*, right *here*!

Alex   *Here?* No one say nothing.

Roland   It's for an invited audience of dignitaries and cultural luminaries.

Alex   Huh?

Roland   'The European Festival of Youth' – there are posters all over town!

Alex   I not see poster.

Roland   We're representing our country, it's *incredibly* important!

Alex   No one say about concert, you make wrong mistake?

Roland *mops his brow, sweating with anxiety now.*

Roland   No! Look, here's the leaflet, it's *tonight*!

Alex (*reading*)   Oh my God, *tonight*?!

Roland   Yes, tonight!

Alex   But it's impossible tonight!

Roland   It's a catastrophe!

Alex *starts laughing.*

Alex   I piss take! I take piss! They come back in half hour!

Roland (*relieved but angry*)   Are you familiar with the word 'bastard'?

Alex   And you with word 'tight-ass'?

Roland   That's *two* words.

Alex   Yeah, but only *one* tight-ass.

Roland *shrugs, acknowledging the truth.*

Alex   So you practise music now?

Roland   Once the musicians arrive, we'll be *rehearsing*, yes.

Alex   I stay watch? Please?

Roland *looks wary.*

Alex   Please, I silent. I never see orchestra before.

Roland   Really?

Alex   Only TV, not living.

Roland (*correcting him*)   Live.

Alex   Living, live, same thing?

Roland   Not exactly. Now please, no more talking.

Alex   I can see orchestra?

Roland   If you *really* want to, yes – but you must be *quiet*, we desperately need this time to practise.

Alex (*confidentially*)   Orchestra shit, need practice?

Roland   *All* orchestras need practice – *rehearsal*. Now, *please*!

Alex   I zip. (*He mimes zipping his mouth shut.*) Also zip other place of talking.

He mimes zipping his arse shut. He takes a chair and goes and sits near the wings with his broom and dustpan.

Roland *takes up a position centre stage and practises with his baton. He silently goes through the opening section of the music.*

Alex *watches, fascinated, as* **Roland** *communes with the music. Eventually:*

Alex   What is meaning of 'Pinball Wizard'?

Roland   I don't know!

Alex   Is he wizard who like to play pinball? Or is he very good pinball player so people call him wizard?

Roland   The latter – the second one. Now, *please*.

He starts conducting again. As he's getting into it:

Alex   Where is Brighton?

Roland (*furious*)   On the south coast of England!

He starts conducting again but **Alex** *can't stop himself:*

Alex   Last question: what like please, Brighton?

Roland   It's got a beach! Sad, middle-aged businessmen with dandruff take their equally sad menopausal secretaries there for dirty weekends.

Alex   Huh?

Roland   They go there to have sex!

Alex   But not Pinball Wizard, he go there to play pinball only?

Roland   So it seems.

Alex   And there is amusement hall in Brighton, like in song?

Roland   I believe there are many amusement halls in Brighton.

Alex   I like go Brighton. Have sex, play pinball, meet wizard. Have sex with wizard, who knows!

Roland   May your wish come true! Now I really *must* get on!

Alex   But what is *meaning* of song?

Roland   I DON'T KNOW! It's just a bloody song! It doesn't MEAN ANYTHING! There is no Pinball Wizard, he doesn't exist, he's like the Tooth Fairy or Father Christmas!

Alex (*very serious*)   There *is* Pinball Wizard, he exist.

Roland   NO THERE ISN'T! HE DOESN'T!

Alex   YES HE DOES!

Roland   NO HE DOES NOT!

Alex   YES! TO *ME*, THERE IS PINBALL WIZARD!

Roland   HE DOESN'T EXIST!

Alex   I BELIEVE IN HIM!

Roland WELL, YIPPEE FOR YOU – YOU BLOODY
MUSCOVITE MORON!

Alex Okay, okay, no need get shitty shirty. Everyone in
world hate British people. Wonder why.

Roland *sighs, pinches his brow.*

Roland Oh, help me, Lord. I'm very sorry, er . . . Alex.
Forgive me? If you really want to know what the *meaning* of
Pinball Wizard is, in my opinion, it is this: the song is
metaphorical – symbolic, yes?

Alex *nods.*

Roland The Pinball Wizard is deaf, dumb and blind. He is
therefore wholly unsuitable for his chosen field of endeavour
– i.e. pinball. And yet, against seemingly insurmountable
odds, he succeeds to such an extent that he is anointed a
'Pinball Wizard'. The song is testament to that tedious but
seductive cliché, 'the triumph of the human spirit in
adversity'. Now will you please SHUT UP!

Alex *takes in the information, satisfied.*

Alex Thank you.

Roland *continues to go through the music as* **Alex** *vaguely sweeps in
the wings.*

*After a while thirty musicians (more is preferable, less is acceptable)
approach from offstage. A rumble of voices and noise from all sides.*

Roland *looks panic-stricken as the sound intensifies. He rushes for the
safety of his lectern.*

*The musicians enter, talking and shouting in high spirits. Some of them
acknowledge* **Roland** *but most of them are too preoccupied to notice
him.*

*They wear winter coats and stamp the snow from their shoes. It's
freezing outside.*

Entrance dialogue to be improvised. It lasts twenty seconds maximum.

Roland *shouts above the hubbub:*

Roland   Members of the orchestra, welcome! Welcome! Quickly, please! Please take your seats!

The musicians do so, knowing exactly where to sit.

During this **Second Flute** *– a very keen young girl – has staggered in with* **Roland***'s score – a big, heavy book. She positions it on the lectern in front of him.*

Then she hovers in readiness. By now, the orchestra are seated.

Second Flute   Anything else, maestro?

Roland *hands her his baton which she cleans with a special cloth.* **Cello** *observes her:*

Cello   What a creep!

Second Flute (*to* **Cello**)   What a loser!

She goes to sit with her fellow flautists.

The musicians are now all seated, facing **Roland**. *He taps his baton and after a while they pipe down.*

Roland   Is everyone alright?

General murmurs of assent until **Second Trumpet** *stands up.*

Second Trumpet   Yeah, we're all marvellous, 'cept for one tiny thing: where's our *instruments*?!

Roland   Ah, yes, apparently there was a bit of a mix-up at the airport. Mr Carmichael is in a van collecting the instruments as we speak.

First Violin   What mix-up?

Roland   Something to do with the hauliers, no need to panic

Cello   Who's panicking?

Roland   Sorry?

Cello   You said 'no need to panic', implying that we were panicking. Who's panicking? I don't see anyone panicking.

Roland   My apologies, I meant in a manner of speaking.

Viola (*to* **Cello**)   Stop having a go, arsehole.

Murmurs of agreement from fellow viola players.

All the way from Gatwick to Moscow, whinge, whinge, whinge.

Cello   I'm only making a point.

Viola   Your point is pointless.

Roland   Well, no harm done. Now, is everyone happy with their accommodation?

Double Bass   My shower doesn't work.

Second Horn   So what, he never had a wash in his life!

First Trumpet   Only soap he knows is *Emmerdale*!

Double Bass   Sod off!

First Horn   We're whiffing you from here!

Timpani   And here! It mings like a farm!

Roland   Members of the orchestra! Please let's behave like the ensemble we are! Now, while we're waiting I thought we could use this time to discuss Tchaikovsky's Fourth Symphony.

Murmurs of dissent and mock yawning from brass section.

Picture the scene: it's February 1878, the first performance of the Fourth Symphony right here in Moscow – not literally *here*, though it is in fact perfectly possible that Tchaikovsky may have once stood on this very stage. He might have actually stood where I'm standing now . . .

He can't speak, he stares at the floor, overcome by the enormity of the thought. After a pause conversation breaks out:

Oboe   My telly's bust.

Cello   There's nothing to watch anyway, it's all in bloody Russian.

Viola   See! Always moaning, always got the hump.

Clarinet   What I don't get is Chekhov. In *Three Sisters*, they're all going, 'Ooo, if only we could get to Moscow.' *Why?*

Murmurs of agreement.

First Trumpet   At breakfast, they gave me black bread. It wasn't burnt toast, it was black bread. What's that all about?

Vociferous agreement.

Oboe   You go outside, it's so cold your breath turns to snow. It like goes solid coming out your mouth.

Bassoon   Snow's not solid.

Oboe   What is it, then? It ain't liquid or gas, so it's gotta be solid. There aren't any other forms of matter – unless you've invented one, Einstein.

Bassoon   For your information, snow is a liquid.

Timpani   Only when you piss on it!

Roland   As I was saying, it's 1878, Tchaikovsky's in *despair*; his marriage is a disaster, he's attempted suicide and, guess what, he doesn't even attend his own premiere! He's written this magnificent masterpiece and he's too distraught to hear it . . .

Once more he can't continue, too moved to speak.

Second Horn   Anyone see those birds in the hotel lobby last night? I reckon they were prozzers.

Viola   Did they talk to *you?*

Second Horn (*proudly*)   Yeah!

Viola   They must've been!

Second Trumpet   Wonder how much they charge?

First Flute   For *you* – about a billion roubles.

Timpani   What's that then, ten p?

Roland   Members of the orchestra! I must insist –

First Flute   Anyone see those blokes with the big 'taches?

Viola   Yeah, and the leather car coats – bet they were Mafia!

First Flute   I wouldn't mind a bit of that!

Viola   Yeah, you could end up owning a football club!

First Flute   No, I'd make them buy me a castle like that Dr Zhivago.

Bassoon   You what? He lived in a shack in the middle of nowhere!

First Flute   Only at the end, not at the beginning *before* the Revolution.

Roland   Can we please –

First Trumpet   Anyone see that beggar?

First Horn   What, the one passed out on the pavement?

First Trumpet   D'you see all his snot and dribble had gone hard? If you gave him a little flick his whole head would shatter. It's sad really.

Second Trumpet   When are the bloody instruments coming?

Clarinet   Where's my clarinet?

First Violin   Where's my violin?

Cello   I want my cello!

Bassoon   Where's my bassoon?

Second Trumpet   Who's got my trumpet?

First Horn   I want my horn!

Suddenly the whole orchestra stand and demand their instruments, like a many-headed beast. Pandemonium.

Roland   SOON! SOON! SOON! The instruments will be here soon, *please* be patient! (*Beat.*) Now, please, let's discuss the music we're going to perform tonight.

First Violin   *Murder* more like.

Roland   I'm sorry?

First Violin   You heard.

Roland   Well, if we all adopt that kind of attitude we probably *will* murder it. So let's be positive.

First Violin   Positive?! We spend so much time quarrelling and bickering and, quite frankly, listening to complete and utter garbage from 'certain persons', that we never actually get any proper rehearsal time. We need to practise, practise, practise!

A few sarcastic 'oohs' from the 'certain persons'.

Roland   Actually, it's a fair point. Can I urge you all – just for today – to put aside your personal grievances and really commit yourselves to the music, just this once?

Clarinet   I mean, how on earth did we ever *get* this booking? We're an absolute shambles.

Oboe   It's obvious, there must've been a cancellation –

Second Horn   And Carmichael wangled us in!

First Trumpet   I bet he's taking a cut!

Second Trumpet   And he's nicked our instruments!

First Horn   He's pawning the lot in Vladivostock!

The brass section start singing, softly at first and then getting louder as others begin to join in:

Brass Section   We're shit and we know we are, we're shit and we know we are!

Woodwind   We're shit and we know we are!

Strings   We're shit and we know we are!

The entire orchestra are now at full volume, all pointing in unison at the beleaguered, cowering **Roland**.

All   WE'RE SHIT AND WE KNOW WE ARE! WE'RE SHIT AND WE KNOW WE ARE!

Second Flute *leaps up, screams with frustration:*

Second Flute   STOP IT! STOP IT! STOP IT!

The singing fades away. **Second Flute** *speaks with great passion:*

Second Flute   You're all horrible! Horrible, nasty, mean and unfair. *You* might be here for a jolly old piss-up at the British taxpayers' expense but *Roland*'s here because he *lives* for music! This is supposed to be the greatest night of his life! Why can't you give him a chance? Why can't you behave like human beings instead of – of spoilt animals! There are people in Russia who would kill for the privileges we have, they *dream* of playing in an orchestra with proper instruments. You don't deserve Roland, he's too good for the whole mouldy lot of you!

Deathly silence. **Second Flute** *sits down.* **Roland** *puts his head in his hands. He is, perhaps, the most embarrassed of them all.*

Roland (*softly, to* **Second Flute**)   Thank you.

She nods, unashamed.

Timpani (*murmurs*)   We're still shit.

Others hush him up. **Double Bass** *puts his hand up.*

Roland   Yes?

Double Bass   'Scuse me, but erm . . . (*Whispering.*) Who's *he*?

He points to **Alex**, *who has been quietly observing throughout. As one, in perfect unison, the orchestra turn to look at him.*

Roland   Oh, this is Alex.

Alex *waves, shyly, vaguely raises his broom.*

Roland   He was sweeping up when I arrived. He's never seen an orchestra before, he asked me if he could watch us rehearse. I hoped you wouldn't mind . . .

Silence. They are all ashamed of themselves.

Alex (*amiably*)   Hello, British orchestra!

Chastened murmurs of 'Hi', 'How ya doing', 'Hello', etc. **Clarinet** *stands up, mortified.*

Clarinet   May I officially apologise for our wholly unreasonable criticisms of your beautiful city.

Others murmur similar apologies. **Second Flute** *is triumphant.*

Second Flute   Well, it's a bit late now!

Oboe   Better late than never.

Second Flute   No, better to have never been so horribly rude!

Cello   Why don't you button it for once in your life!

Viola (to Cello)   Leave her alone, you big bully!

Second Flute (*to* **Viola**)   Thank you, but I'm perfectly capable of defending myself against the rabble!

A row breaks out between the woodwind and strings.

Roland's *mobile rings. He shushes them to receive the call.*

Roland (*in phone*)   Mr Carmichael!

He crouches at the front of the stage, finger in his ear. The orchestra strains to earwig the conversation.

Yes, yes, all fine. Just in the middle of a fascinating debate about . . . Excuse me . . . ? (*Listens.*) Right . . . When? (*Listens.*) I *see . . . Right . . .* Yes. I will.

He rings off. He is ashen. Everyone looks at him. Without warning he lets out a huge wail – a primal scream of incredible and surprising volume.

AAAAAAAAGGGGGGGHHHHHHH!

The entire orchestra shrink back as one – in fear and astonishment.

You bastards! You shitting bloody bastards! Russian customs have impounded all your instruments! You're giving the most important concert of your lives in two hours' time and you've got no instruments, you stupid, stupid bastards!

Consternation and panic break out in the orchestra.

Do you want to know *why*?

All   Yes!

Roland   Well *one* of you knows, don't you?

All   No?

The entire orchestra turn to him:

Roland   A Russian sniffer dog found a *spliff* hidden in one of the instruments!

Gasps and shock. Everyone looks at everyone accusingly, improvised protests of innocence and denial ring out.

Cello   Well, it wasn't me!

Viola   We *know* that! You wouldn't know what a joint looks like!

Cello   Oh, and I suppose you think it's cool to take drugs?

Viola   In moderation, yes.

Oboe   Who was it, Roland?

Second Trumpet   Yeah, I'll kill him!

Clarinet   It might be a *her*.

Clarinet *glares at* **Viola**.

Viola   Wasn't bloody *me*!

Double Bass   Yeah, she only does crack!

Second Flute *begins to emit a high-pitched wail. A strange, sad sonic scream through her nose. All eyes gradually turn to her . . .*

Second Horn   No!

Second Trumpet   No way!

Oboe   It's impossible!

Bassoon   Still waters run deep . . .

First Flute   Leave her alone, it wasn't her!

Second Flute   It was! It was! It was *me*! (*She rushes for the exit.*) I'm going to kill myself!

Various musicians prevent her leaving.

Roland   Why, *why*?

Second Flute   I did it for *you*. It was for *you*!

Roland   *Me*? I don't even smoke!

Second Flute   But you get so anxious before a concert, I've seen you pacing around backstage, wearing a sad little strip in the carpet. And that's when you're only going to *play*. Now you're *conducting* I was scared you'd die of nerves. I thought a few quick puffs might relax you. I stole it from my sister. (*Sobbing.*) I didn't think anyone would check a flute.

Roland *crumples into a chair, head in hands. Everyone else is in shock.*

Second Flute   Is Mr Carmichael going to expel me from the orchestra? He will, I know he will, my life is over!

Roland   You're one of the top two flautists in Croydon (*or wherever*). No one's kicking you out.

Double Bass   What are we going to do?

Everyone turns to **Roland** *hoping he's got the answer.*

Roland (*gutted*)   No other option. We'll have to cancel.

They are devastated.

First Violin   Can't we borrow some instruments, from another orchestra?

Bassoon   There aren't any others playing here tonight.

Oboe   And who'd risk lending us lot?

Second Flute   I'll never forgive myself!

First Violin   We could play tomorrow instead . . .

First Trumpet   We're flying home tomorrow, it's all booked.

Second Flute   Please, someone, kill me now!

String Section   We will if you don't shut up!!

Suddenly, **Alex** *raises his hand.*

Alex   Erm . . . hello? Can speak?

Roland *nods.*

Alex   My father works in airport.

The entire orchestra turn to him as one – full of hope. Freeze.

Maybe he can speak to . . . how say . . .?

Roland   Customs?

Alex   Yes.

Roland   What does he do, in the airport?

Alex *raises his broom.*

Alex   He's cleaner.

As one, the entire orchestra sighs, downcast.

He know lots people, maybe he explain . . . er . . . ?

Roland   The situation?

Alex   Yeah . . . who knows?

First Violin (*to* **Roland**)   It's worth a go, isn't it?

Roland *nods, hands his mobile to* **Alex**.

Roland   Thanks, mate.

Alex *dials, gets through and has a quick murmured conversation in Russian. The orchestra strain to hear.*

Alex   They find him.

He waits, listens and then speaks into the phone in Russian. A fairly brief but animated conversation with his father. Everyone watches him intently, trying to discern what's happening. Finally **Alex** *rings off and hands the phone to* **Roland**.

Alex   He say he scared make fuss, might lose job. Sorry.

Roland (*to* **Alex**)   Thanks for trying. (*To orchestra.*) I'd better wait here for Mr Carmichael. I think you should all go back to the hotel.

He nods to the flautists consoling **Second Flute**.

First Flute   Yeah, come on, we'll walk back with you.

They help her up.

Second Flute (*sniffling*)   So sorry, everyone.

They lead her out. The other musicians slowly troop out.

First Trumpet   Sorry, Roles.

Oboe   Bad luck, mate.

Viola   Maybe you'll get your chance another time.

Cello (*quietly sarcastic*)   Yeah, right.

First Violin   I didn't mean what I said. I mean, I did, but we do all appreciate you.

Double Bass (*to* **Alex**)   See you, mate.

Others shake **Roland***'s hand as they exit disconsolately.*

Eventually the stage is empty. **Alex** *begins to tidy up.*

Roland *picks up his baton and then places it back in its case.*

Alex   In situation like this, have to ask very important question: what would Pinball Wizard do?

Roland *manages a slight smile. He stares at his score for a few moments then closes it.*

Roland   I really wanted you to hear this.

Alex   Tchaikovsky?

Roland   Mmm. Shall I send you the CD?

Alex   Or maybe we meet in Brighton and you give to me?

Roland   It's a deal.

He paces and stands where Tchaikovsky might have stood.

He raises his face to the heavens.

Pyotr Il'yich . . . I only wanted to honour you. I'm sorry. (*To* **Alex**.) The irony is that old Tchaikovsky was condemned to death by his own schoolmates.

Alex   They kill him?

Roland   There was this sort of committee and they kind of forced him to kill himself.

Alex   Why?

Roland   Oh, he'd been having an affair with the son of some posh bloke.

Alex   Tchaikovsky is poof?

Roland   Er . . . yeah . . .

Alex   Hmm. My brother is poof.

Roland   Right . . .

Alex   Are *you* poof?

Roland (*embarrassed*)   Erm . . . I haven't decided yet. You?

Alex   I think maybe *everyone* is bit of poof.

Pause. **Roland** *sits in abject misery.*

Roland   You were right. I'm not a conductor. I never will be. I'm just a schoolboy waving a stick.

Pause.

Alex   What is word? *Describe* this music you were to play?

Roland   Oh, well, you're asking me to describe the indescribable.

Alex   Please, if can.

Roland *thinks for a while. He speaks softly, slowly formulating his thoughts.*

Roland   Well, it's beautiful. Really beautiful . . . (*Beat.*) It's joy. And passion. And hope and despair . . . it's *life*. It's like silk and velvet and slate and fire. (*Pause.*) When we play – and we're really pretty awful – but just occasionally, almost by accident, we hit it right and everyone plays *together*. Just for one bar. And it's incredible. Everyone knows they did something wonderful. It's our secret, for a moment. And then it's gone. (*Beat.*) It makes you forget who you are and it reminds you you're alive.

Silence. They listen.

Alex   I can hear . . .

Roland (*quietly*)   Me too . . .

They listen some more, both lost in thought.

Alex   And I think maybe I have idea . . .

Roland *turns to him, curious. They look at each other.*

Blackout.

Scene Two

That night. The concert.

Same configuration of seats. **Roland**'s *score on its lectern.*

The house lights are up, the stage lights dim, just picking out the empty chairs. Murmur and buzz of the waiting audience. The house lights go down and the stage lights come up to concert state.

Roland *walks on stage holding his baton. He is now wearing tails and a white bow tie.*

The audience applaud. **Roland** *bows nervously and gestures for silence.*

Roland *(in Russian)*   Good evening, ladies and gentlemen. *(In English.)* I'm afraid that's the full extent of my Russian. But a friend has very kindly offered to translate. *(Gestures to the wings.)* Alex!

Alex *strides on in a hastily improvised, ill-fitting dinner suit and bow tie.*

Alex *(in Russian)*   Good evening, Moscow!

He takes the applause, blinking in the bright lights, enjoying himself.

Roland *shoots him a look – enough!*

Roland   You might have heard a rumour . . .

Alex *translates into Russian.*

Roland   That tonight's concert was to be cancelled.

Alex *translates.*

Roland   This was due to the unfortunate loss of our instruments.

Alex *translates.*

But his speech is considerably longer than **Roland***'s.*

It becomes obvious that he's decided to tell the audience about the incident of the smuggled spliff.

Interspersed with his words, he mimes the custom dog sniffing the instruments, the joint in the **Second Flute***'s case and* **Roland** *taking the call from Mr Carmichael.*

Then he imitates **Second Flute** *screaming and weeping her confession, the orchestra's shock and their sad acceptance that all was lost.*

Roland *conceals his fury as best he can.*

Roland   *However*, due to a last-minute piece of inspiration . . .

Alex *translates but inserts a reference to the Pinball Wizard –* **Roland** *gives him a dirty look.*

Roland   *We are able –* I hope – to give you our 'version' of the Second Movement of Tchaikovsky's Symphony No. 4 in F Minor.

Alex *translates.*

Roland   May we humbly request your indulgence . . . and your imagination.

Alex *translates.*

Roland   The Ridley Road School Orchestra!

Applause. As the orchestra take the stage **Alex** *shakes* **Roland***'s hand, wishing him luck, and then exits.*

The musicians are now wearing the appropriate dress for an orchestra. Evening wear / black and white, budget permitting. They enter with surprising grace and ease and stand at their seats.

Second Flute *is the last to come on.*

Roland *hands her his baton, she gives it a good-luck wipe with her special cloth and then goes to her seat.*

The orchestra have no instruments. But they will act as if they do.

Roland *turns to them and with one neat movement directs them to sit. Which they do. In perfect unison.*

On **Roland***'s cue – after the third tap of his baton on the lectern – as one – they mime their instruments into life.*

Brass section have brass. Strings have bows. Timpani has sticks. Woodwind have instruments at their mouths, their fingers at the ready. They hold their positions, poised to commence playing, focused, concentrating – as one.

Audience – hush of expectation.

Roland *turns to the auditorium, holds up his baton and very seriously and symbolically places it in his inside pocket. He too will mime. He turns back to the orchestra, nods to* **First Violin***, who nods back. All is ready.*

And **Roland** *begins to conduct. The music begins with a slow oboe melody and plucked strings. The oboist plays, the strings pluck and* **Roland** *conducts.*

In complete silence.

But gradually, imperceptibly, the actual music begins to flood the auditorium – as if the audience are really hearing it.

By the time the strings bring in their melody (around forty seconds in) the sound level is approaching concert volume and fairly soon the orchestra are in full flight.

They mime as the music plays. And they must mime as if they know the music well.

The 'concert' miming need not be wholly naturalistic. The 'instruments' might be larger than life. The orchestra might even stand during the climactic sections. They might even dance. But whatever they do, they must do it as one.

After five minutes the movement reaches a climax and over the next twenty seconds the sound dips under and out as we start to hear the musicians' inner thoughts. It may seem like they're talking to each other but they're not. The 'tone' is not dialogue but rather, interior monologue.

During this they continue to 'play'.

Second Horn   Hey, it's sounding quite good!

Cello   Eh?! It's not *sounding* like anything!

Second Trumpet   All I can hear is my own breath.

First Horn   My fingers are sweating.

First Violin   Concentrate!

Bassoon   They're listening! The audience are listening!

Clarinet   They can *hear* it!

Double Bass   They're not walking out!

Cello   Only cos it's sub-zero out there!

First Flute   They can hear it!

Viola   It's a miracle!

Oboe   Shit! I made a mistake!

First Trumpet   Did Roland hear it?

Oboe   Oh God, he's scowling at me!

Bassoon   No, he's smiling, he's encouraging us!

Timpani   I've never seen him smile before, he looks insane!

Second Flute   He looks lovely, he's an angel!

Second Horn   I never thought this would work.

Timpani   That Alex bloke's a genius!

Second Trumpet   How can we thank him?

Double Bass   We did a collection, weren't you there?

First Trumpet   I think I was in the bogs, throwing up.

First Flute   Nerves?

First Trumpet   No, that black toast.

Second Horn   Roland's going to get him a present tomorrow.

First Violin   Concentrate everyone, it's nearly the end . . .

Viola   Gently – remember what Roland says . . .

Second Flute   Play each note as if it's your last . . .

And now we hear the last two minutes of the movement. **Roland** *brings the piece to its slow, beautiful conclusion.*

The audience applaud.

Roland *gestures the orchestra to stand. They rise as one and bow together.*

Alex *rushes on with a bouquet and presents it to* **Roland**.

Roland *plucks a single stem and motions* **Second Flute** *forward. He presents her with the flower and she immediately swoons with the emotion of it all.* **Alex** *catches her as she falls backwards into his arms, he slaps her back to consciousness.*

Alex, **Roland**, **Second Flute** *and the orchestra bow together one last time.*

Blackout.

Scene Three

The following morning.

Empty stage. Just the chairs.

Alex *wanders on in his cleaning overalls with his broom and dustpan. He comes to the centre of the stage and looks out at the auditorium. He half-raises his broom in a desultory fashion. He is in strangely low spirits.*

Alex (*in Russian*)   Good morning, Moscow.

He makes the vague sound of his own voice echoing in the empty auditorium:

Moscow – Moscow – Moscow . . .

He shrugs and starts to slowly sweep the stage, murmuring listlessly to himself:

> Ever since I was a young boy,
> I played the silver ball,
> From Soho down to Brighton,
> I must've played 'em all,
> But I ain't seen nothin' like him,
> In any amusement hall –

Roland (*singing loudly*)
> That deaf, dumb and blind kid
> Sure plays a mean pinball!

Roland *strides onstage, full of beans, a changed man. He leaps in the air and does a few Townshend-style rock gyrations as he grinds through the chords.*

(*Singing.*) Duh, duh, duh, duh, duh!

Alex *nods to him.*

Alex   Hello.

Roland   Hey! How are you?! Great party last night!

Alex   Excuse. Have to clean stage and stick chairs.

Roland   *Stack* chairs?

Alex   Stick, stack, who cares?

Roland   Alright, let me help you . . .?

Alex *shrugs,* **Roland** *starts to stack the chairs with him.*

Roland   God, I'm totally wrecked!

Alex *doesn't respond.*

Roland   Hey, what's up with you? It was a triumph!

Alex   For *you*, yes. I pleased for you. But I clean, sweep, slave. You come, you go, I stay. Never change.

Roland   Ah, the famous Russian temperament.

Alex   Huh?

Roland   It might change, what about your trip to Brighton?

Alex   No money. And can't leave, have family here. This home.

Roland   Okay, but what about your music?

Alex   Yeah, I write songs on broom. Stupid. All make-believe.

Roland   But you're the Pinball Wizard of Moscow!

Alex (*despairingly*)   No! I am *cleaner*! My father clean, my mother clean, I clean. My kids will clean!

Roland *glances offstage and nods. The orchestra come on quickly and stand together in a tight group.*

Second Flute *is carrying a black instrument case.*

The shape is unmistakable – a guitar case.

She gives it to **Roland** *who goes on one knee and presents it to* **Alex**.

Roland   Alex, in recognition of your contribution to our concert and for helping me to be less of a tight-ass and for helping us to be an orchestra and not just a bunch of bickering musicians –

Cello   It'll never happen again!

Viola   Shh!

Roland   We'd like you to have this. We wish you all the best with your music. And please don't forget to come and visit us when you're a huge rock star touring the world.

The orchestra applaud. **Alex** *is beside himself with joy and excitement.*

Alex   Thank you! Thank you! I love British people!

He snaps the catches open and excitedly lifts the lid of the case . . .

His joy turns to abject sorrow as he takes out . . . a broom.

The lads of the brass section all laugh. **Alex** *is devastated.*

Alex   British piss-take! Very shit funny. Bastards! British bastards!

Roland *looks very apologetic – and furious. He turns on the orchestra:*

Roland   How could you?!

A huge improvised row breaks out between the brass section and woodwind and strings – the new-found unity is rapidly disintegrating . . .

(Pleading.) Orchestra! Orchestra! *Please*!

The argument is reaching a climax when **Second Flute** *shrieks:*

Second Flute   QUIET, EVERYONE! LOOK!

She points to the wings, **Double Bass** *runs on with the real present: a brand new electric guitar.*

The orchestra applaud. **Alex** *is overcome. He holds the guitar aloft and then quickly straps it on in case he's dreaming.*

Roland *takes out his baton and with a grand gesture, like a wizard, he points to the heavens. Immediately, the lights snap to a single spot on* **Alex***.*

Roland *conducts, readying the orchestra. On his cue they start to hum the opening riff of The Who's 'Pinball Wizard' loud and clear – in perfect* a cappella *unison. Different sections of the orchestra make the sound of each instrument.*

And on the first big guitar chord **Alex** *thrashes along, the full Pete Townshend whirling motion.*

The stage lights start to come up so we can see the orchestra clearly again. And once more they're in unison. The vocal starts and their voices join in with **Alex***:*

Orchestra *(singing)*
    Ever since I was a young boy,

I played the silver ball,
From Soho down to Brighton,
I must have played 'em all,
But I ain't seen nothin' like him
In any amusement hall,
That deaf, dumb and blind kid
Sure plays a mean pinball!

Guitar break. **Alex** *does his stuff. When the vocals return he mimes the Pinball Wizard on his machine.*

Orchestra (*singing*)
He stands like a statue,
Becomes part of the machine,
Feelin' all the bumpers,
Always playin' clean,
Plays by intuition,
The digit counters fall,
That deaf, dumb and blind kid
Sure plays a mean pinball!

He's a pinball wizard,
There has to be a twist,
A pinball wizard's got such a supple wrist.

Half the Orchestra (*high voice*)
How do you think he does it?

Other Half (*response*)
I don't know!

Whole Orchestra
What makes him so good?

Alex *continues to freak out as* **Roland** *jubilantly conducts.*

A final round of vocals:

Whole Orchestra
Ain't got no distractions,
Can't hear no buzzers and bells,
Don't see no lights a-flashin',

Plays by sense of smell,
Always gets a replay,
Never seen him fall,
THAT DEAF, DUMB AND BLIND KID
SURE PLAYS A MEAN PINBALL!

Suddenly – the whole company freeze as one.

Tableau. Everyone. Still. Silent. Together.

Blackout.

The Musicians

*Notes on rehearsal and staging drawn from a workshop
with the writer held at the National Theatre, October 2015*

*From workshops led by Lisa Spirling and Philip Breen,
with notes by Rosemary McKenna and Edward Stambollouian*

How Patrick came to write the play

'I wanted to write something that celebrated what NT
Connections is all about. It seems to me that it's about releasing
the imagination of young actors and working collectively to
produce a little rough magic. I like the metaphor that you can
make music without having instruments just as you can make
theatre anywhere, with any group of people, trained or
untrained, in a theatre, in a garden, on a street, in a shed.
In a sense the device of the orchestra was retro-engineered as
a situation where I could have lots of kids of non-specific age,
race or gender, and which would be a good catalyst for a
dramatic situation.

'In 2003 my son Fred, to whom the show is dedicated, was
born. I was feeling happy about children. I'm generally quite
a bleak playwright, I tend to be drawn towards the darker
side of things, so I wanted to show my sunny side. When I
was at school I got such pleasure from being in plays. I had
great English and Drama teachers.

'When selecting a piece of music for the play I knew it had to
be Russian. I asked a viola player friend of mine what to pick
and he suggested Tchaikovsky's Fourth Symphony. It's very
Russian and it's also potentially playable by a youth orchestra,
even if they have to struggle through it. It's a beautiful piece
of music as well.

'In the end, the spirit is the most important thing. It is very
moving to see young people coming together to achieve
something great, with vigour and a smile on their faces. However
well drilled the actors are their spirit is what's most important.

'I'd like the adults in the audience to be left with a sweet nostalgia for youth, and the kids to think, "That looks like fun." Those kids are a bit like me, and they figured it out and learned how to get along. I'd like to be on that stage!'

Approaching the play

Below are a number of exercises that can be employed by the director and the actors early in the rehearsal process. These exercises are designed to help unearth the director's vision for the production, and to begin to explore the some of the key elements of the play.

CONTEXT TRIANGLE

Philip suggested that the directors look at three points of a context triangle:

1   What was going on at the time the play was written (2003/2004)? What was art like? What other plays were on? What was in the news?
2   What was going on in the writer's head at the time he wrote the play? Where was he in his career? What was he making? What was he doing?
3   What is going on in the world today? Try to root your understanding of the play in what it might mean now.

Context is everything. Philip talked about a Native American dream-catcher. It is an interesting object for about ten minutes, but it only really becomes interesting when you know what the Native Americans thought of sleep and dreams, where it was hung in relation to a bed, or teepee or totem. It is embedded in its culture.

As directors, it is useful to consider the period and context of the play. Is *The Musicians* a period piece? Patrick questioned whether setting it now would be consistent with what happens in the play. The development of mobiles and online technology is a big shift. Patrick thinks it needs to remain set in 2003, which is part of its charm now and is interesting for young people to consider what it was like twelve years ago. There was no social networking in 2003, no Snapchat, no Twitter . . . Young people might enjoy experiencing that other world and thinking about being on a school trip and not being able to communicate via technology.

SOME ANSWERS TO THE THREE QUESTIONS

1   WHEN THE PLAY WAS WRITTEN: 2003

- Russia came third in the Eurovision Song Contest.
- Theatre hostage crisis in 2002, with theatres being bombed.
- A bombing in Red Square, December 2003.
- Russia requested extradition of Boris Berezovsky. Britain refused.
- Roman Abramovich bought Chelsea.
- No Google maps, no technology, no Twitter, no Snapchat.
- Putin was three years into his presidency.
- The youth of Russia might have been more open to the West than they are now.

2   THE PLAYWRIGHT: PATRICK MARBER

- Patrick's interest in making work for young people: the world of the play and the play itself are in parallel with each other. The students in the story have to put a performance together without their instruments, as do the students in NT Connections putting on the play. Patrick is clearly interested in what that experience is like for the young people – the act of theatre and taking part having the power to transform people's lives.
- Patrick had recently become a parent. Children becoming adults. How your children are simultaneously part of you, but also nothing like you. Children growing up and doing their own thing, solving their own problems, doing it without a teacher.

Philip suggested the group start by reading the playwright's other plays and gave as examples *Don Juan in Soho*, *Closer*, *Dealer's Choice*, *Red Lion* and *Notes on a Scandal*.

3   WHAT IS HAPPENING NOW?

- Today, a British school going to Russia is a big deal.
- There are heightened political tensions between the UK and Russia.
- An increase in attacks on homosexuals and suspected homosexuals in Russia, and the introduction of Putin's LGBT Propaganda Law (banning teaching minors about non-traditional sexual relationships). This is interesting considering Tchaikovsky was one of Russia's most famous homosexuals.

Philip suggested that these questions could act as jumping-off points for deeper research and investigation. The more you go into it, the more you find the rich texture of the play. For example, Philip talked about the classical music in the piece. He suggested you might start by looking at Tchaikovsky. His mother died when he was fourteen and a lot of his work comes from his early experiences. Philip said it might be interesting to look at the similarities between Roland and Tchaikovsky.

It could be useful to consider how you will introduce the classical music to your young people and the challenges of demystifying it. One of the participants suggested that you must first take them into the world of the composer in an uncomplicated, accessible way, not making it too serious, but making it seem like it's nothing unusual. It is not unusual, it is just new. You don't need to be clever to understand it, Philip suggested, you just need a soul. Is it possible for the young people to go and see an orchestra or to take a trip to a concert hall?

Unearthing the vision

Lisa developed a list of seventeen questions that are designed as a starting point to enable directors to develop their individual approach to the text.

1 What part of this play do you personally connect to?

2 Why do you like this play?

3 What style is the play written in?

4 How long is the play?

5 What are the three most important things about this play?

6 What is the writer exploring with this play?

7 If you could stage this play anywhere, where would it be?

8 Think of three pictures related to the play. What are they?

9 What three colours come to mind when you think of the play? (Be specific: e.g. gun-metal grey, stage-curtain red).

10 Think of the most vivid image from the play. What is it?

11 Think of three sounds from the play. What are they?

12 Think of three pieces of music (not necessarily from the play) that connect you to the script. What are they?

13 Aside from 'Pinball Wizard', what would the theme song of this play be?

14 Which character do you most relate to?

15 Who are your references for the three main characters in the play? (These could be celebrities, fictional characters or people you know.)

16 If the play were a type of movement, what would it be? (Be specific: e.g. starlings in flight, sheep being herded.)

17 What feeling do you want to leave your audience with after they have seen the play?

It may also be useful to get the actors to complete this exercise. Their answers may provide a source of new ideas or perspectives that the director can utilise.

Questions

Philip suggested that directors spend some time asking questions about the play. They can be the most basic, simple questions possible, no matter how silly or straightforward.

What is he doing at that point? Why is he there? Etc. This is something you can do alone before rehearsals or with your cast as part of your rehearsal process.

EXAMPLES OF QUESTIONS

- What are they doing in Russia?
- Why do the children play instruments, how good are they?
- Why are they unsupervised in Russia?
- Why is Alex sweeping the stage?
- What kind of school is Ridley Road?
- Why didn't the students collect their instruments individually from the airport?
- Where are all the adults?
- What does the concert hall look like? (This is an important design point as well.)
- How many people are they expecting to attend?
- Who are the dignitaries?
- How old are the people in the orchestra?
- What is the festival?
- Why is Alex not with the rest of the staff? Why is he there?
- The kids know the Chekhov reference; why? (Patrick says they could be doing English A-level.)
- Is Alex any good at music; can he play guitar?
- What is Roland's sexuality?
- Why is Roland so passionate about the music?
- Why 'Pinball Wizard'? Why does Alex love that song?

Having compiled a list of questions, try and answer them using the text. Anything that you can't answer with the text becomes a decision that you make as a director. These questions give you a solid structure to work from. Like a detective, you work out the clues that the playwright has left for you, and use that information to open up the play with your own imagination. You can do this exercise as preparation before rehearsals, and/or you could do it with your company as part of the exercise below:

THE READ-THROUGH

Lisa suggested the following method for reading through the play that helps highlight the events, ideas and questions in the script. To do this, it is useful to arrange six desks in a large square with a space in the middle.

For each scene, the actors involved stand in the centre of the square. One of the group should be assigned to read the stage directions. The job of the remainder of the group is to slap the table with an open palm when something 'occurs' and to slam the table with a fist when a character expresses an opinion. The actors or spectators can also interrupt the scene at any time with a question. The questions that are asked will form the basis for the production. The choices you make in answering these questions will be the vision. It is important not to have too many assumptions about how things should 'obviously' be in the early stages. It is not necessary to answer the questions at this stage, but it important to take note of them, so that when it comes to rehearsing the scene, you have a list from which you can work.

Lisa worked through a section of the script with a participant to demonstrate this process. The following is a record of the facts, opinions and questions noted by the group on pages 552–3 of the script:

After a while thirty musicians (more is preferable, less is acceptable) approach from offstage. A rumble of voices and noise from all sides.

    Fact: Musicians approach from offstage.

    Question: What time of day is it?

    Fact: A rumble of voices from all sides

    Question: How big is the door?

Roland *looks panic-stricken as the sound intensifies. He rushes for the safety of his lectern.*

Fact: Roland rushes for the lectern.

Question: Does anyone notice his panic?

Question: Why is he panic-stricken?

The Musicians enter but are immediately silent for five seconds as they take in their new surroundings.

Fact: Musicians enter and are immediately silent for five seconds.

Question: Is this their first time on stage?

Question: What are they thinking/seeing?

The musicians enter talking and shouting, in high spirits. Some of them acknowledge **Roland** *but most of them are too preoccupied to notice him.*

Fact: They start talking and shouting.

Question: Why are they in high spirits?

They wear winter coats and stamp the snow from their shoes. It's freezing outside.

Entrance dialogue to be improvised. It lasts twenty seconds maximum.

Roland *shouts above the hubbub:*

Roland   Members of the orchestra, welcome! Welcome! Quickly, please! Please take your seats!

The musicians do so, knowing exactly where to sit.

During this **Second Flute** *– a very keen young girl – has staggered in with* **Roland***'s score – a big, heavy book. She positions it on the lectern in front of him.*

Then she hovers in readiness. By now, the orchestra are seated.

Second Flute   Anything else, maestro?

Roland *hands her his baton which she cleans with a special cloth.* **Cello** *observes her:*

Cello   What a creep!

Opinion: Cello thinks Second Flute is a creep.

Question: Why does Cello think/say this?

Passions

Divide the group into pairs. Each person has two minutes to explain their 'geeky passion' to their partner (e.g. West Ham United, maps, unusual coins . . .). Then each person introduces their partner to the group and describes their partner's passion. Not only is this a good way for groups to get to know each other, it is also a useful exercise in encouraging the actors to access the energy and vitality that goes along with being passionate about something. The actors can then channel the energy that they have for their own 'geeky passion' into their character's passion for music. This exercise can be repeated later in the process, but from the perspective of the character.

Wants

Lisa introduced an exercise for directors to explore what it is that drives and motivates individuals. The following questions could be answered first by the actors as themselves, and later in the process by the actor as their character. Individuals should only share whatever level of information they are comfortable with.

- What do you want by the end of the day?
- What do you want by the end of the month?
- What do you want in a year's time?
- What do you want in five years' time?
- What do you want in ten years' time?
- What do you want in twenty years' time?
- What do you want in forty years' time?
- What do you want by the end of your days?/What would you like your legacy to be?

School trip

Patrick suggested that it is worth spending time with the actors discussing and improvising around the idea of being on a school trip, and the implications of this. The orchestra are liberated by the strange and unforgettable experience of being away from home, and this is a crucial factor in persuading them to go to such extreme lengths. This is a once-in-a-lifetime opportunity and they will never see this audience again. The actors can share stories about their own experiences of being on a school trip (romances, dramatic events, unfamiliar surroundings) in order to build a picture in their minds of the world their characters inhabit. They should consider what it must be like for these students to be caught up in such unusual circumstances.

Themes

Patrick: 'All plays have a story, which is the action of the play, and an understory. The understory is what makes it shapely, and it is worth a mention because audiences perceive stories in an unconscious way, taking in very basic elements.

'At its simplest, it is a play about a Russian boy who loves British music, and a British boy who loves Russian music. It is an exchange of ideas and a crossing of hands between two cultures. Alex imagines his broom is a guitar. For him it is absolutely real. This is where they get the idea to mime the missing instruments.

'In the end, the kids do it for Roland. They know they're not extremely talented, but he believes in them. He's not a teacher – he's one of them. The orchestra recognise Roland's integrity and passion, and he takes them on a journey with him. It's about a bunch of kids doing it for him. The final section of the play, the British students presenting Alex with a real guitar, is a simple, hopeful and satisfying ending.'

It is useful to think about the song 'Pinball Wizard', and the meaning of this song as a central metaphor for the play. As Roland asserts, 'And yet, against seemingly insurmountable odds, he succeeds . . . ' This is exactly true of what the orchestra achieves, managing to make the audience suspend their disbelief through their sheer conviction in playing invisible instruments. The idea of working together to achieve greatness in the face of adversity is a central theme of the play.

Structure

Patrick warned directors against spending so much time on the section in which the orchestra mime playing their instruments that they forget to put sufficient work into the final scene in which the group perform 'Pinball Wizard'. This is where the two worlds of the play intersect; the British orchestra with a classical Russian repertoire, and Alex, the young Russian with a passion for British rock music. It should have the feeling of being a final, joyous, hopeful moment.

Patrick noted that the stated maximum length of the ad-libbing sections should be adhered to.

Lisa suggested breaking the script down into units: manageable sections which will help with structuring rehearsal. This 'sectioning' should be done with the cast, and it is a good idea to allow them to give memorable titles to these units, creating a common language and shorthand for the scenes.

Language and accents

Patrick does not give permission for any changes to the script (including the removal or softening of profanities) without prior written consent to be obtained via the National Theatre.

Patrick noted that it is essential for the actor playing Alex to play the character as Russian as opposed to any other nationality.

PRONUNCIATION

Russian is a phonetic language, you pronounce every letter and sound and there is no silence.

- There are twenty-nine sounds in the Russian language.
- All 'r's are rolled.
- They speak a little slower, landing more on each syllable.

- 'O' is pronounced as in 'oar'.
- 'Horror show' phonetically is the Russian word for 'good'.
- 'Drug' or 'droog' phonetically is Russian word for 'friend, mate'.
- Speaking it in the body can help find the accent.
- There are fewer unnecessary words, which means there is a directness.
- 'E' is always like in 'pet'.
- The 'ch' sound is like in 'loch'.
- 'Eh' is closer to 'yes'.

The films of Andrei Tarkovsky are useful references for the Russian accent. You could also listen to Russian footballers – for example, Andrey Arshavin or Roman Abramovich. Philip talked about the Russian sensibility. They cry. They laugh with their whole bodies, throw back their heads and laugh. Nobody in Russia smiles, it's a sign of madness if you smile. There are no Russian pleasantries.

Character and characterisation

Patrick described the many similarities between Alex and Roland. They share a mutual intensity and have a great passion for music. While their life experiences are radically different, they have a shared sensibility. It is their love of music (albeit very different genres of music) that binds them together.

The group discussed how to create a sense of character with the smaller ensemble parts. It may be useful for the actors to invent back-stories for their characters, so long as these support the narrative of the play. It is a valuable exercise for all the actors to consider their characters' place within the orchestra. Questions like 'Who am I friends with?', 'Who do I dislike?', 'What is my status within the group?' and 'What are the characteristics of my instrument section?' will all be beneficial in creating a vivid portrayal of a real orchestra and avoiding generalisation.

A number of directors expressed concern about making the smaller or non-speaking members of the company feel included and valued within the process. It was suggested that in the early stages of rehearsal, the company could learn things as a group; for example, everyone could practise doing Russian accents. It may also be a worthwhile exercise to get all the actors to write a monologue or diary entry about themselves. When working with a large cast, the trick may be to pull out little moments of non-verbal interaction between the characters.

Patrick described the choir as the 'nerdy kids', although noted that this is a relative label. In the grander hierarchy of a school, the orchestra members are at the lower end of the social spectrum. However, as a group they exist within their own relative ecosystem that has its own factions (some are cool, some are studious, some are quiet, etc.). Directors may want to think of particular instrument sections having their own traits and characteristics. It is important to note that these young people have not been forced to join the orchestra. While they may not be the world's greatest musicians, they all have a passion for their instrument and quite enjoy classical music.

They are all essentially good people. They feel deeply embarrassed and ashamed when they realise that they have been denigrating Russia in front of Alex, and despite playing a joke on him with the broom, they make it up to him with the gift of a guitar.

Casting

Patrick feels that it is important to retain the gender of the characters where gender is obvious from the script (e.g. Roland and Alex are male, Second Flute is female). Where the director is working with a single-sex group, it is preferable to have males play females or vice versa.

Patrick pointed out that there isn't a right or a wrong way to do *The Musicians* and that the script is very open. Directors need to find out how to make it work for their own groups and their own specific needs.

Before casting, it may be useful to discover if any of your group has an instrument that they think they know well. It is also possible to consider physical type and to try and match or contrast this with a specific instrument.

Production, staging, design

Patrick suggested the use of different levels on stage, to enable the audience to have a clear view of the different orchestra parts.

Setting the play is 2003 was determined as being important, because these are not children who are carrying iPhones or constantly documenting their experiences via social media. They are present and in the moment.

Lisa also encouraged 'pulling actors out' during rehearsals, so each actor has a chance to view the stage and the stage pictures from the perspective of the audience. This will help the actor to more fully understand their place within the living and fluid dynamic of the production. There is also the potential for the actors to have some personal props (bags, coffee cups, etc.), which can contribute to a more full and realistic image.

Style and technique

The group discussed the shift in style and tone during the section in which the actors narrate their internal feelings to the audience while miming Tchaikovsky's Fourth Symphony. This is a highly stylised moment and it is important for the actors to deliver their lines straight to the audience, seemingly unaware of one another. This section can prove technically difficult, but a good sound designer can help achieve the right sound balance.

It is important to teach the real audience and the imagined audience at the concert that the school orchestra are not pretending they have instruments, they are showing the audience what they would have done had they had instruments. Roland sets this up by saying 'tonight's concert was to be cancelled, this was due to the unfortunate loss of our instruments [. . .] May we humbly request your indulgence, and your imagination.' That is an important distinction to make. Moments of non-naturalism and stylised movement are useful to establish prior to the main event. The play operates in a slightly magical realm; it is almost a fairy tale.

Exercises for rehearsal

MOVING IN UNISON

On page 559, the stage direction states: 'As one, in perfect unison, the orchestra turn to look at him.'

Patrick described this as a non-naturalistic moment, which demonstrates that the orchestra has the capacity to behave as a single unit. This moment should be slightly stylised and is a pre-echo for the moment when the orchestra mime playing together in the third act. Lisa offered an exercise to help groups develop the technique of moving as one.

The actors should stand in a circle with their eyes closed and their fists held at chest height. When the director says 'Go' they must count to twenty inside their heads, slowly reaching their hands above their heads, so that there are fully outstretched with open palms on twenty seconds. Other actors or observers can then comment on how well the group managed to stay in sync. The group then repeat the exercise, but this time with eyes open. This exercise can be applied specifically to the scene, by instructing the actors to turn and look at Roland over a specific number of seconds.

INCENTIVISED MOVEMENT

Movement director Gary Sefton asked the group to play a game in which they walked around the room, trying to get one another 'out' by teaming up with another player and encircling a person between their arms with their hands clasped. If the player under attack does not duck in time, they are out. In order to avoid the game slowing down too much, Gary made the playing space smaller as the number of players in the game decreased. You could also give the rule that everyone must be moving all the time. You could also introduce fictional stakes (the winner gets £200,000 in cash). When only two players are left, the first person to touch the back of the other's knee is the winner.

The objective of the game is to win. After the exercise, ask the company whether they had been moving because they *could*, or because they *had to*. Encourage them to think about the difference between 'want' and 'need' in relation to the play. A need is immediate and is much stronger than a want. Why does the group not get back on the plane and go home the next day? Why does Roland need to do the gig? Why does he need to get the orchestra on side? Why do the orchestra need to go along with it?

Gary stated that when directing movement, the objective is to get actors to move because they need to, not because they can. Often, these kinds of games can unlock movement that is playful, inventive and explorative without any thought or discussion. Think about this game in relation to the orchestra playing. The orchestra *need* to play their instruments (even though they don't have any). Why? This can lead you on to looking at the stakes.

STAKES

Split the group into pairs and invent a scenario that has a clear objective, high stakes and a physical obstacle that the group have to overcome in order to achieve the objective. You could also introduce a condition – how are they feeling about the task?

For example: 'I must collect the bag from the other side of the room (*objective*), because it contains a heart which is needed for a transplant (*stakes*), but the ground is very fragile and will break if I apply too much pressure (*obstacle*). I am nervous (*condition*).'

To avoid the group getting cerebral about it, ask them to stay physical and don't spend too long talking about it. Ask that they try and achieve their task with the highest possible stakes and investigate the different ways they might be able to achieve their need. These are their tactics, or choices.

Having tried the task once, give the actor a new rule. For example, they can't use chairs. Each time a choice is made, create a new rule, which forces them to come up with another choice. This will encourage actors to make physical, playful choices. Gary suggested that the fifth or sixth choice is usually the most interesting. Once you stop using your brain and start using your body and instinct, wonderful things can happen!

Gary explained that directors shouldn't have to tell their actors how to move. Instead they should focus on making sure the stakes and obstacles are in place, which will enable the actors to find the movement for themselves. Movement on stage should always be connected and motivated.

Improvising outside the text

Gary suggested improvising a scene outside the play where Roland has to convince the orchestra to try Alex's imaginary instrument idea. In this scene, the need could be to perform the music well, to honour Tchaikovsky. The stakes could be that the orchestra wants to do it for Roland. The inner obstacle could be Roland's lack of self-confidence. The obstacle in the scene could be resistance from the group; some of them are nervous, worried about making a fool of themselves, fed up, wanting to go home. The condition could be varied: excited, nervous, frustrated, angry.

You could play the scene with one person as Roland and everyone else as the orchestra. Every time a tactic doesn't work, ask the actor playing Roland to change his approach, to try something different. Note that there is never a wrong solution, it is always either more or less interesting than the previous one. Eventually the tactic has to work; the other actors must let it work. To keep the momentum of the exercise, you could introduce a time pressure: for example, the curtain goes up in two minutes.

MIMING THE INSTRUMENT

Many of the participants expressed apprehension about the scene in which the actors mime playing their instruments. Gary suggested that it may be useful to for the actors to apply a practice similar to 'animal studies', which is often used as a part of actor training. Each actor must get to know their instrument inside out. Where possible, they should spend some time handling their instrument, paying close consideration to its weight, shape and size. They should also spend time watching videos with close attention to detail, observing the specifics and intricacies of the movement. It is very important to be specific and to avoid generalisation.

Gary then asked the directors to split into groups and assigned instruments to each. He then led a ten-step improvisation:

1 Players enter the space and sit down in their instrument sections. Be specific about how this happens. Where do you get your instrument from? Do you have a music stand? Be aware and attuned to the other players around you. Following the conductor's instruction, begin to play.

2 Become more specific with your playing. Think of your breath and of what is at stake.

3 Play with increased passion, fervour and specificity.

4 Up the stakes again. You are playing for your life.

5 The instrument and the player start to mould into one another.

6 The player becomes the instrument.

7 The instrument has completely taken over.

8 The instrument becomes monstrous.

9 The instrument starts to become the music.

10 The instrument has become the music.

This improvisation can then be played backwards, starting at ten, moving back down to one.

You could also get your imaginary orchestra to play a version of 'Pinball Wizard'. Do the scale of one to ten physically with the orchestra playing along to the track. The performance of 'Pinball Wizard' shouldn't just be a crazy free-for-all, but a fabulous, joyous expression.

Lisa suggested that it may be interesting to do an exercise like this very early on in the process to allow the actors to find the world of the play and to establish a sense of being part of an orchestra. Directors could also ask the company to bring in improvised instruments such as rubber bands between sticks, shakers or pots, and ask one member of the group to conduct a 'music circle'.

Another way to think about the different instruments in the orchestra and their characteristics could be to look at Gabrielle Roth's 'Five Rhythms'. This is another language with which you can find the specificity in the movement and can be helpful to use when describing the dynamic of a scene. For example, 'I think this scene might be lyrical, or it might be chaos', and so on.

GABRIELLE ROTH'S FIVE RHYTHMS

1   Slow – cello, floating movement, sustained and low.
2   Lyrical – higher in the heart, more classical, string instruments, fast and fluttery.
3   Staccato – sharp, spiky, angular, severe, brass instruments (samba music).
4   Chaos– no rules, urban, tribal, normally becomes quite aggressive (punk music).
5   Stillness – which is a movement itself, suspension.

PUSH/PULL

Lisa introduced the directors to an exercise to help free up their thinking regarding the delivery of the lines. This exercise is titled 'Push/pull' and is based on the idea that in life we are either pulling people closer to us, or pushing them away with the things we say.

Lisa asked the directors to get into pairs and to take turns pushing or pulling one and other to opposite sides of the room. She then asked them to add the line 'I hate you' when pushing and 'I love you' when pulling.

The next step is to introduce text from the play. The group used page 544 of the script, beginning with Alex's line 'Hey! Sorry! Hello!'

The person playing Alex decides to either 'push' or 'pull' the person playing Roland with this line. Roland responds instinctively whether to 'push' or 'pull' in return. The pair play this out over about ten lines of dialogue, pushing or pulling with each of their lines.

Lisa then asked the group to follow the opposite impulse. How is the delivery of the line affected if you push instead of pull? The actor's first choice is not always the most interesting, and it is important in the early stages of rehearsal to keep things fluid and not to settle into a way to saying a line too quickly.

Line feeding

This exercise is designed to help generate interesting and unusual staging ideas. Ask the actors to form groups of four. Two of the group hold scripts and are responsible for 'feeding lines', one at a time, for the other two members to perform. The performers must enact the lines physically with their scene partner, without concern for naturalism.

This exercise should be almost like an interpretive dance. The members of the group who are feeding the lines should also be looking out for any interesting pictures or moments that transpire in the physical enacting of the lines. These will often be much too heightened to use in the play, but they can be a useful way of unlocking feelings or impulses which can then be utilised in a more pared-down fashion.

Points of focus

Lisa noted that it is useful to introduce things you want your group to work on incrementally throughout the process, and having points of focus for the day or week is a good way to do this. For example, the point of focus over one week could be establishing relationships between the characters through eye contact. Once the actors have had sufficient time to concentrate on this, you can layer on another point of focus, building the scene in small, cumulative steps.

References

Guide to Russian accent:
prettyaccents.blogspot.co.uk/2011/05/russian-accent.html?m=1

Jeremy Seipmann, *The Instruments of the Orchestra.*

Whiplash (film, dir, Damien Chazelle, 2014).

Brassed Off (film, dir. Mark Herman, 1996).

School of Rock (film, dir.Richard Linklater, 2003).

Fantasia (film, Disney, 1940).

BBC Proms (radio, orchestral).

Victor Pelevin, *The Clay Machine Gun* (comic novel about a writer reinventing Western adverts for a Russian audience).

Benjamin Britten, *The Young Person's Guide to the Orchestra.* www.youtube.com/watch?v=Z0ltoiU8KEU

Tommy (album by The Who).

Useful illustration showing a traditional orchestra formation: www.thinglink.com/scene/636923039480545280

Citizenship
by Mark Ravenhill

Tom dreams of being kissed, but he's not sure whether by a man or by a woman, and he feels he should choose pretty quickly. His friends' homophobic teasing and interrogations about what he did with his friend Amy the other night leave Tom no space to make up his mind, and he's got no one to ask for advice, except maybe people on the internet.

Age suitability: 15+

Cast size
fourteen named characters:
eight girls, six boys

Mark Ravenhill's first full-length play, *Shopping and ********, opened at the Royal Court Theatre Upstairs in 1996. Other plays include *Mother Clap's Molly House* (National, 2001); *Product* (Traverse, Edinburgh, 2005); *The Cut* (Donmar Warehouse, 2006); *Citizenship* (National, 2006); *pool (no water)* (Lyric Hammersmith, 2006); *Shoot/Get Treasure/Repeat* (Edinburgh Festival, 2007); *Over There* (Royal Court/Schaubühne, Berlin, 2009); *A Life in Three Acts* co-written and performed with Bette Bourne (Traverse, Edinburgh 2009); *Nation* adapted from the Terry Pratchett novel (National, 2009); *Ghost Story* (Playhouse: Live, Sky Arts 2010); *Ten Plagues*, a song cycle with music by Conor Mitchell (Traverse, 2011); *The Coronation of Poppea*, a new English version (Opera UpClose, King's Head, 2011); and a new English version of *The Life of Galileo* (Royal Shakespeare Company, 2013). As Writer in Residence at the RSC, his play inspired by Voltaire's *Candide* played in the Swan (2013). He recently wrote a new play for the Lyric Hammersmith's Secret Theatre series and a new libretto for the Norwegian National Opera.

Characters
in order of speaking

Amy
Tom
Gary
Ray
Stephen
Kerry
Chantal
Alicia
De Clerk
Melissa
Tarot Reader
Tarot Reader's Daughter
Baby
Martin

One

Amy, **Tom**.

Amy   You got the Nurofen?

Tom   Yeah.

Amy   Take four.

Tom   It says two.

Amy   Yeah, but if you're gonna really numb yourself you gotta do four.

Tom   I dunno.

Amy   Do you want it to hurt?

Tom   No.

Amy   Then take four. Here.

She passes him vodka. He uses it to wash down four Nurofen.

Amy   Now put the ice cube on your ear.

Tom *does this.*

Amy   Now you gotta hold it there till you can't feel nothing.

Tom   Thanks for helping

Amy   It's gonna look good.

Tom   Yeah?

Amy   Yeah, really suit you.

Tom   Thass good.

Amy   You got a nice face.

Tom   I don't like my face.

Amy   I think it's nice.

Tom   Sometimes I look in the mirror and I wish I was dead.

Amy   I got rid of mirrors.

Tom   Yeah.

Amy   Mum read this feng shui thing and it said I wasn't supposed to have them. You numb now?

Tom   Almost. You got a nice face.

Amy   You don't have to lie.

Tom   I'm not. You're fit.

Amy   I know I'm plain. But that's okay. I talked to my therapist.

Tom   What did she say?

Amy   That I have to love myself in case nobody else does.

Tom   Your mum loves you.

Amy   I suppose. You ready now?

Tom   I reckon.

Amy *produces a needle.*

Tom   Is that clean?

Amy   I put it in Dettol.

Tom   Alright.

Amy   Let's start.

She starts to push the needle into **Tom***'s ear but he pulls away.*

Amy   I can't do it if you do that.

Tom   I know.

Amy   You gotta sit still.

Tom   Maybe we should leave it. Maybe not today.

Amy   I thought you wanted an earring.

Tom   I know.

Amy   Thass what you been saying for weeks: I wanna earring, I wanna earring.

Tom   I know, only –

Amy   I'll go careful. Come here. You're a baby.

Tom   No.

Amy   I'll treat you nice and soft. Like a baby.

Tom   Alright.

He comes back.

Amy   Bit more vodka.

Tom *drinks.*

Amy   Bit more.

Tom *drinks.*

Amy   Bit more.

Tom *drinks.* **Amy** *pushes the needle into his ear.*

Tom   Aaaggghhh.

Amy   Thass it.

Tom   It hurts.

Amy   Nearly there.

Tom   Do it quickly. Do it. Aaaggghhh.

Amy   Soon be finished.

Tom   Right. Right. Is there blood?

Amy   What?

Tom   Is there blood?

Amy   I dunno.

Tom   I can feel blood

Amy   Maybe a bit.

Tom   Shit. Shit. Shit.

Amy   It's not much. You're gonna be alright.

Tom   Yeah. Yeah. Yeah. Yeah. Yeah. Yeah. Yeah.

He faints.

Amy   Tom? Tom! Shit. Shit.

She drinks a lot of vodka.

Tom – please.

Her mobile rings.

(*On phone.*) Kez? No. I'm fucking – I'm having a panic attack. Like I used to, yeah. Tom's dead. He's died. Just now. Shit. I killed him. I've killed Tom. I wanna kill myself. Shit.

Tom *groans.*

Amy (*on phone*)   He made a noise. Yeah, well. He came back to life. I gotta go. Kez – I'm going now.

Tom   Whass going on?

Amy   You sort of went.

Tom   Who's on the phone?

Amy   Thass Kerry. She's getting stressed out cos she's gotta give the baby back tomorrow.

Tom   Baby?

Amy   Life Skills.

Tom   Oh yeah.

Amy   You remember Life Skills? Each of the girls has gotta take it in turns to look after this baby – plastic baby. It puts you off having a real one. You could have memory loss.

Tom   No.

Amy   Like Shareen after the overdose. Her mum and dad went to see her in the hospital and she didn't know who they were.

Tom   I haven't got memory loss.

Amy   Alright.

Tom   Fucking stupid idea letting you do that. I should have gone to a fucking professional. Fucking go to somebody who knows what they're fucking doing 'stead of letting you fucking fuck the whole thing up.

Amy   I was trying to help.

Tom   Yeah, well, you're no help – you're rubbish. You're total rubbish.

Amy   Don't give me negative messages.

Tom   Trying to kill me with your stupid needle.

Amy   I can't be around people who give me negative messages.

Tom   I fucking hate you.

Amy   No. I'm sorry. I'm sorry. I'm sorry.

She cries.

Tom   Come on. Don't. No. No.

Amy   I can't do anything right. I'm useless.

Tom   No.

Amy   I am. Thass why I cut myself. Cos I'm totally useless. Ughhh.

Tom   Hey hey hey.

He holds **Amy**.

Tom   Come on. Alright. Alright. Alright. You better?

Amy   I dunno.

Tom   You're alright. You're a good person. I like you.

Amy   Yeah?

Tom   I really like you.

Amy   Thass good.

Tom   You got a nice face.

Amy *kisses* **Tom**.

Tom   Oh.

Amy   Was that wrong?

Tom   I didn't mean you to do that.

Amy   Oh. Right. Right.

Tom   I didn't wanna kiss you. Only –

Amy   Yeah?

Tom   I'm not ready for . . .

Amy   You're fifteen.

Tom   I know.

Amy   You gotta have done . . .

Tom   No.

Amy   Why?

Tom   It doesn't matter.

Amy   Tell me.

Tom   I have this dream. And in this dream I'm kissing someone. Real kissing. Tongues and that. But I can't see who I'm kissing. I don't know if it's a woman. Or a man. I try to see the face. But I can't.

Amy   Are you gay?

Tom   I don't know.

Amy   There's bisexuals.

Tom   You won't tell anyone?

Amy   No. Are you going to decide?

Tom   What?

Amy   What you are?

Tom   I don't know.

Amy   Or find out?

Tom   I don't know.

Amy   Don't waste yourself, Tom. You've got a nice face.

Tom   Yeah.

Amy *gets a text message.*

Amy   It's Kerry. She says the baby's gone to sleep.

Tom   It's not real.

Amy   It is to her.

Tom   I'm gonna go.

Amy   Finish off the vodka.

Tom   No. Thanks. Forget what I told you.

Amy   You're still bleeding. There's still some –

Tom   I got coursework.

He exits. **Amy** *drinks.*

Two

Gary, **Tom**. *They are smoking a joint.*

Tom   Good draw.

Gary   Got it off my mum's boyfriend for my birthday. Ten big fat ones for my fifteenth.

Tom   Thass cool.

Gary   Thass the last. He had a fight with his dealer last night. Dealer come round the house and they had a big barney. An' me mum's ragga CDs got smashed in the ruck.

Tom   Shit.

Gary   Yeah. She is well gutted.

Enter **Ray** *and* **Stephen**.

Ray   Wass 'appening?

Gary   Chilling.

Ray   You shag Amy last night? We wanna know. You get jiggy?

Stephen   Jiggy-jiggy.

Ray   Is she your bitch? You ride her like your bitch?

Tom   Fuck's sake.

Gary   You got problems.

Ray   What?

Gary   I'm saying: you got problems.

Ray   What you saying? I got problems.

Gary   Yeah, you got problems. No respec'.

Ray   I respec'.

Gary   No respec' for woman.

Ray   I respec' woman.

Gary   Ride her like a bitch? Didn't he say?

Tom   Yeah.

Ray   That's what I said.

Stephen   He said it.

Ray   That's what I said. I ride her *and* respec' woman.

Stephen   Yeah. Ride and respec'.

Ray   You chat shit. What are you? What is he?

Stephen   He is gay.

Gary   All I'm saying –

Ray   So gay. You are so totally gay, Gary.

Gary Just sayin' –

Ray You are like the most totally gay person anyone knows.

Gary I'm not.

Ray Gay Gary. Thass what you are. Respec'? What are you chattin'? You're chattin' gay. You are fucking wrong, man. Wrong in your head. Wrong in your, your . . . hormones, man. Totally totally wrong.

Gary Thass not right.

Ray (*to* **Tom**) Come on, man. Say something. Tell him.

Tom I . . .

Ray You're always watching. You're never talking. Tell him.

Tom Listen, I wanna –

Ray You fucking tell him.

Stephen Tell the battyboy.

Ray You fucking tell him.

Tom . . . You're gay, Gary.

Gary Shit.

Tom Everyone says it. Everyone calls you it. Gay Gary.

Gary I know what they say.

Tom You shouldn't talk gay.

Stephen Thass right.

Tom Cos no one likes a person who talks gay.

Gary You chat shit, Tom.

Ray Listen, he's tellin' you –

Gary Same as them. All of you. Chattin' shit. All day long. Mouths moving but it's just: chat, chat, chat. Shit, shit, shit.

Tom   No, no.

Gary   Yeah, yeah.

Tom   No.

Gary   Yeah.

Ray   Fight fight fight.

Stephen   Fight fight fight.

Ray   Fight fight fight.

Stephen   Fight.

Tom *pushes* **Gary**.

Ray   Thass it.

Stephen   Do it back or you're gay.

Gary   Fuck's sake.

Gary *pushes* **Tom**.

Ray   Fucking insulted you, man. The gay boy insulted you.

Stephen   Batty hit yer.

Ray   Get him.

Tom   Listen –

Ray   Use your fist.

Stephen   Fist for the battyboy.

Gary   Go on.

Tom   Yeah?

Gary   Do what they tell you. Do what they want to.

Tom   Yeah?

Gary   Follow the leader.

Tom   Yeah.

Tom *punches* **Gary** *in the stomach.*

Ray   Respec', man.

Stephen   Total respec'.

Gary   Fuck you.

Gary *punches* **Tom** *in the stomach very hard.* **Tom** *falls over.*

Ray   Nasty.

Enter **Amy**, **Kerry**, **Alicia**, **Chantal**. **Chantal** *carries the baby.*

Kerry   You're not carrying her properly.

Chantal   Leave it, Kez.

Kerry   But you're not doing the head right.

Chantal   It's my baby, Kez.

Kerry   I know.

Chantal   Yesterday it was yours and now it's mine.

Kerry   I'm only telling you.

Chantal   An' I can do whatever I want with it.

Amy   She's got withdrawal symptoms.

Chantal   Over plastic?

Kerry   Don't say that. You're not fit.

Alicia   Iss the Blazin' Squad. You mellowin'?

Ray   Totally chilled, me darlin'.

Stephen   Totally.

Alicia   Sweet.

Ray   Hear Tom was round yours last night.

Amy   Thass right.

Ray   Gettin' jiggy.

Amy   Do what?

Ray   Jiggy-jiggy-jiggy.

Stephen   Jiggy-jiggy-jiggy.

Amy   You say that?

Tom   No.

Ray   What? You never?

Amy   Thass right.

Ray   What? He not fit enough for you?

Amy   Iss not that.

Ray   You frigid? She frigid, Tom?

Tom   No.

Ray   Wass wrong with 'em? Why ain't they gettin' jiggy?

Alicia   I dunno.

Ray   Thass gay.

Tom   What?

Ray   Youse two are so gay.

Tom/Amy   No.

Ray   Oooo – sore.

Amy   Your ear's started.

Tom   Yeah?

Amy   You started bleeding again.

Alicia   Shit. There's blood.

Kerry   I don't wanna look.

Amy   You wanna look after that. You got a hanky?

Tom   No.

Amy   Chantal?

Chantal   Here.

She tucks the baby under her arm to find a paper hanky.

Kerry   You can't do that.

Chantal   Juss for a moment.

Kerry   You got to hold it properly all day long.

Chantal   Juss while I'm lookin'.

Kerry   Give it me. Give it me.

She takes the baby from **Chantal***.* **Chantal** *finds the hanky, passes it to* **Amy***.* **Amy** *holds the hanky on* **Tom***'s ear.*

Kerry (*to baby*)   Alright. Alright.

Amy   You wanna hold that there?

Ray   She bite you?

Stephen   Yeah.

Ray   While you were doing it?

Tom   It'll be alright now.

Amy   You sure?

Tom   Yeah.

He continues to hold the handkerchief on his ear.

Chantal   Give me the baby, Kerry.

Kerry   Later.

Chantal   Now.

Kerry   Bit longer.

Chantal   I gotta have it for Life Skills.

Kerry   I know.

Chantal   So . . . ?

Alicia   Give it, Kez.

Kerry   Juss . . . do the head properly.

Chantal   Alright.

Kerry *hands* **Chantal** *the baby.*

Alicia   Thass it. Come on.

Exit **Alicia**, **Kerry**, **Chantal**.

Amy   Laters.

Exit **Amy**.

Ray   How do you do the ear? She do that ear? Was she like eatin' you?

Tom   Won't stop bleeding.

Ray   What do you do?

Tom   It was . . . we were doing an earring?

Ray   Earring? Earring? Earring? Shit man. In that ear? You was doing an earring in that ear? Shit, man. Thass the gay side. Shit. You was doing an earring in the gay side. Shit.

Stephen   Shit.

Tom   No. No. I'm jokin'. It was –

Ray   Yeah? Yeah?

Tom   It wasn't –

Ray   Yeah? Yeah?

Tom   It was bitin'.

Ray   Yeah?

Stephen   Yeah?

Tom   It was like love-biting.

Ray   I knew it.

Stephen   Thass right.

Tom   We were gettin' hot and biting and that and we –

Ray   Yeah?

Tom   And we got –

Stephen   Jiggy.

Tom   Yeah. Jiggy.

Ray   I knew it.

Tom   Yeah, totally jiggy. Like ridin' and ridin' and ridin'.

Ray   Oh yeah.

Tom   And she was wantin' it.

Stephen   Yeah.

Tom   And I was givin' like, like, like, like –

Ray   Yeah.

Tom   A big man.

Ray   Thass right. Big man.

Stephen   Big man.

Ray   Big man.

Stephen   Big man.

Ray   Big man.

Stephen   Big man.

Gary   Hey – that's sweet.

Ray   Shut it, gay boy.

Stephen   The big man is talkin', battyboy.

Ray   Out of ten?

Tom   She's a six.

Ray   So you see her again?

Tom   Maybe. I'm thinkin' about it.

Stephen   De Clerk.

Ray   Run.

Gary   Give us a hand.

Ray   On your own, man.

Ray *and* **Stephen** *exit rapidly.* **Tom** *goes to help* **Gary**. *Enter* **De Clerk**.

De Clerk   Tom.

Tom   Sir?

De Clerk   A word – now. Gary – move.

Gary   Sir.

De Clerk   You're a stoner, Gary.

Gary   The herb is the people's weed.

De Clerk   Piss off.

Exit **Gary**. **De Clerk** *pulls out a piece of coursework.*

De Clerk   What's this, Tom?

Tom   My Citizenship, sir.

De Clerk   Your Citizenship coursework. And what's this?

Tom   Blood, sir.

De Clerk   Blood on your Citizenship coursework. Blood on the work which tomorrow inspectors are going to want to see.

Tom   I know, sir.

De Clerk   And it's not going to be you that's going to be bollocked, is it? No. It's going to be me. Didn't I say, didn't I say many, many – oh so many – times that your coursework should be neat?

Tom   Yes, sir.

De Clerk   Because I don't need the hassle from the inspectors. Because I'm very stressed out. I'm not sleeping. I told you all that I wasn't sleeping. Some nights nothing. Some nights just a couple of hours.

Tom   I know, sir.

De Clerk   The Head gives me grief, kids give me grief. And now tomorrow the inspection team arrives and what do I find?

Tom   I'm sorry, sir.

De Clerk   I find that you have been bleeding all over 'What Does a Multicultural Society Mean to Me?'

Tom   I didn't mean to.

De Clerk   I'm not showing this to the inspectors. You can stay behind tonight and copy this out.

Tom   But sir –

De Clerk   You want me to copy it out? I've got lesson plans, marking. I'm going to be here till midnight. I'm not copying it out. You'll see me at the end of school and you'll copy this out.

Tom   Yes, sir.

De Clerk   Right then. See you tonight.

Exit **De Clerk**. **Tom** *mops his ear. The bleeding has stopped. Enter* **Amy**.

Amy   Why you tell 'em you slept with me?

Tom   I never.

Amy   Don't lie. You tole Ray and Steve. Now they tole everyone.

Tom   I'm sorry.

Amy   But it's not true.

Tom   I know.

Amy   So why you – ? You gotta sort out what you are, Tom. You straight? You gay?

Tom   Don't say it in school.

Amy   You bisexual? If you want you can see my therapist. My mum'll sort it out.

Tom   I don't need a therapist.

Amy   I know somewhere they do tarot. The card might tell you.

Tom   I don't believe in that.

Amy   What you gonna do, Tom? You gotta stop lying. You gotta decide what you are.

Tom   I know.

Three

Tom *and* **De Clerk**. **Tom** *holds a bloody handkerchief to his ear.*

Tom   I'm still bleeding, sir.

De Clerk   Just – copy it out.

Tom   I am. I'm just . . . worried.

De Clerk   Mmmmmm.

Tom   You know – worried that I might copy it but then I might drip blood on the, like, copy, you know.

De Clerk   Well, don't.

Tom   I'm trying, only –

De Clerk   Put the paper over there, lean your head over there.

Tom   Alright. (*Does this.*) It feels really weird, sir.

De Clerk   Shut up.

Tom   I'm not writing straight, sir.

De Clerk   Do the best you can.

Tom   I'm trying hard but it's not going straight, sir.

De Clerk   Fuck's sake, Tom.

Tom   Thought so. I just dripped. Blood on the folder.

De Clerk   Haven't you got a plaster?

Tom   I asked at the front office, but the rules say we have to provide our own.

De Clerk   Well, alright – just try not to drip any more.

Tom   Doing my best.

De Clerk's *mobile rings.*

Tom   You gonna get that, sir?

De Clerk   No.

Mobile stops.

Tom   Might have been important.

De Clerk   Nothing else matters. Nothing else matters but your coursework and the inspectors and that we don't become a failing school, okay? There is nothing else in the whole wide world that matters apart from that.

Mobile rings again.

Tom   They don't think so.

De Clerk   Well fuck 'em, fuck 'em, fuck 'em.

Tom   They really want to talk to you.

De Clerk   Uhhh.

He answers the mobile.

No. Still at – I told you. I told you. Because we've got the inspectors. No. No. Well, put it in the fridge and I'll . . . put it in the bin. I don't care. I don't care. I can't.

He ends the call.

Tom   Are you married, sir?

De Clerk   I'm not talking any more.

Tom   I was just wondering.

De Clerk   Well, don't.

Tom   Other teachers say: my wife this or my girlfriend that. But you never do.

De Clerk   Well, that's up to them.

Tom   It makes you wonder. We all wonder.

De Clerk   Listen, I'm here from eight in the morning until eight in the evening, midnight the last few weeks – maybe I don't have a personal life.

Tom   Yeah.

De Clerk   Maybe I'm not a person at all. Maybe I'm just lesson plans and marking.

Tom   Yeah. Maybe.

De Clerk   Oh. My head. Have you got a Nurofen?

Tom   Sorry, sir?

De Clerk   Have you got a Nurofen or something?

Tom   No, sir. I had some but I took them all.

De Clerk   Right.

Tom   If you want to go home – go home to your . . . partner.

De Clerk   I can't.

Tom   I can do a massage, sir. I know how to do a massage.

De Clerk   No.

Tom   It stops headaches. I done it loads of times.

De Clerk   Listen. Physical contact is –

Tom   Out of lessons now.

De Clerk   Difficult.

Tom   Shhhhhh. Our secret.

He moves over to **De Clerk** *and massages his shoulders and neck.*

Tom   You've got to breathe too. Remember to keep breathing.

De Clerk   Mmmmm.

Tom   There's a lot of stress about, isn't there?

De Clerk   It's all stress.

Tom   How old are you?

De Clerk   Twenty-two.

Tom   Lots of teachers burn out before they're twenty-five because of all the stress.

De Clerk   Mmmmm.

Tom   You're quite developed, sir. Do you go to the gym?

De Clerk   Sometimes.

Tom   With your . . . partner.

De Clerk   Back to your work now. That was wrong. Physical contact.

Tom   Sir – I'm really sorry, but I've –

He wipes **De Clerk**'s *shoulder.*

Tom   I've dripped on you, sir.

De Clerk   What?

Tom   You've got blood on your shirt.

De Clerk   Oh fuck.

Tom   I'm really sorry. It's a really nice shirt.

De Clerk   Shit. Shit. Shit.

He scrubs at his shoulder.

Tom   If you want me to get you another one, sir –

De Clerk   No no.

Tom   I get a discount. My brother manages Top Man.

De Clerk   Tom – get on with your work. You get on with your work and I'll get on with my work.

Tom   You've got good clothes, sir. For a teacher.

De Clerk   Tom.

Pause.

Tom   Sir . . . I keep on having this dream and in this dream I'm being kissed.

De Clerk   Don't.

Tom   Only I never know whether it's a man or woman who's doing the kissing.

De Clerk   This isn't Biology. I'm Citizenship.

Tom   I think I dream about being kissed by a man.

De Clerk   I don't want to know about that.

Tom   I really want to know: so I dream about a man kissing me?

De Clerk   Please. Don't do this. I'm tired. I'm exhausted. I've got the Head of Department chasing me. I've got the inspectors coming after me like wolves after blood. I've still got eight hours of paperwork. And I've done a full day's teaching. Please understand the pressure I'm under and just copy the work.

Tom   What do you do if you're gay, sir?

De Clerk   You talk to someone.

Tom   I'm trying to talk to you.

De Clerk   You don't talk to me. Talk to your form tutor.

Tom   He hates me.

De Clerk   I don't think so.

Tom   What do you do at the weekends, sir?

De Clerk   Alright. Go away. Go home.

Tom   What about the coursework?

De Clerk   I'll explain the blood to the inspectors.

Tom   Alright then.

He packs up his bag.

Bye then, sir.

De Clerk   Bye, Tom.

Tom   I want to talk to someone gay, sir. I don't know any.

De Clerk   Shut up, please shut up.

Tom   I really want to meet someone gay and ask them what it's like.

De Clerk   Well – it's fine. It's normal. It's just fine.

Tom   You reckon?

De Clerk   You know the school policy: we celebrate difference. You report bullies. Everything's okay. You're okay.

Tom   I don't feel okay.

De Clerk   Well – you should do.

Four

Gary, **Tom**. *Smoking a joint.*

Gary   Was it good?

Tom   What?

Gary   You know – when you done Amy?

Tom   Well . . .

Gary   Cos lovin'. There's so many types of lovin'.

Tom   Yeah?

Gary   Yeah. Between man and woman. There's so many types of lovin', in't there?

Tom   You reckon?

Gary   Oh yeah. There's sweet lovin' and there's animal lovin' and there's hard lovin' and there's dirty lovin'. There's millions of ways of lovin'. You follow?

Tom   I think so.

Gary   You lie.

Tom   No.

Gary   I'm chattin' shit, aren't I?

Tom   No.

Gary   Yeah, I'm chattin' shit. Thass the herb. I always chat shit when I'm blazin'. But thass the way I like it. I like to chat shit.

Tom   I like the way you talk.

Gary   Yeah?

Tom   You talk good. You're better than the knobheads. Ray, Steve – they're knobheads.

Gary   Then how come you –

Tom   Yeah yeah.

Gary   – hit me when they tell you?

Tom   I'm sorry.

Gary   No worries. Love and understanding. Peace to you, brother.

Tom   Yeah, peace.

Gary   To mellow, man. Love you, brother.

Tom   Yeah. Brother love.

Gary *puts his arm round* **Tom**.

Gary   You like the brother love?

Tom   Yeah, it's good.

Gary   Peace on the planet. No war. Herb bring harmony. Blaze some more?

Tom   Yeah.

Gary *produces another rolled joint from a tin.*

Gary   So tell me 'bout your lovin'?

Tom   Well –

Gary   Is she your woman now?

Tom   Well –

Gary   Or was it like a one-night lovin' ting?

Tom   Well –

Gary   Don't be shy. Take a big draw and tell.

He hands **Tom** *the joint.* **Tom** *draws.*

Gary   Harder, man. Draw as deep as you can.

Tom *draws as hard as he can.*

Tom   I need some water.

Gary   No. Not till you tell. Tell me what it was like. Come on, man.

Tom   I feel ill.

Gary   I gotta know. I gotta know about the ride.

Gary *pins* **Tom** *to the floor, knees over his arms, sitting on his chest.*

Gary   What was it like when you rode the woman?

Tom   Get off me – off me.

Gary   Jiggy-jiggy with the honey. Ya!

Tom   Off.

He pushes **Gary** *off.*

Tom   I never, alright? I never –

Gary   What?

Tom   I never done her. We never done anything.

Gary   What? Nothing? Oral? Finger?

Tom   Nothing, okay. We never done it.

Gary   Shit. You lied.

Tom   Yeah.

Gary   That's sad, man.

Tom   Yeah, it's really sad.

Gary   So – you not gonna tell me 'bout no lovin'?

Tom   No.

Gary   Shit, broth'. That was gonna be my wank tonight.

Tom   Yeah?

Gary   Yeah – your booty grindin' her. That was gonna –

Tom   Well, there's nothing.

Gary   You wanna pretend for me? Like make it up. So – you never done it. But you can make up like a story, like a dirty story so I got summat in my head.

Tom   I'm not good at stories.

Gary   Just make it dirty so I got something for tonight.

Tom   I'm still supposed to copy out my Citizenship for De Clerk.

Gary   Okay – tell me about your dreams. You gotta have dirty dreams.

Tom   Course.

Gary   Then tell me –

Tom   I don't know.

Gary   Come, brother love. (*Sits* **Tom** *down, puts his arms around him.*) Tell your brother.

Tom   . . . I have this dream. And in this dream I'm lying in bed. Not in my room. Not like my room at home. Like a strange room.

Gary   Like a dungeon?

Tom   No, maybe like a Travel Lodge or something, I don't know.

Gary   Right.

Tom   And I'm almost asleep but then the door opens and this stranger comes into the room.

Gary   Like a thief?

Tom   Maybe but this . . . person, they come over to the bed and they kiss me.

Gary   Right. And – ?

Tom   It's a person but I don't know, I don't know –

Gary   Yeah.

Tom   See, this person, are they a woman or are they . . . ?

Gary   Yeah?

Tom *leans over and kisses* **Gary** *on the lips.*

Gary   You're battyman?

Tom   I don't know.

Gary   Shit, blud, you're battyman. The battyman kissed me. Shit.

He moves away and takes several draws.

Tom   I don't know. Don't know. Just wanted to see, you know – just wanted to see what it felt like if I –

Gary   And did you like it?

Tom   I don't know.

Gary   Was my lips sweet?

Tom   I don't know.

Gary   No, blud, thass cool, thass cool, I can handle that. Peace to all. Everybody's different. I can go with that.

Tom   I'm sorry.

Gary   Hey – love you still, bro'.

He hugs **Tom**.

Tom   I just thought – you're Gay Gary.

Gary   Thass just a name. You touch my arse I kill you, see?

Tom   Okay.

Gary   No, see, I like the honeys. You should see my Myspace. Thass where I live out what's in my head, see?

He gets out his laptop, opens his website.

See, these are my fantasies. And I share him with the world on my message board. I got graphics, see?

Tom   Is that you?

Gary   Yeah.

Tom   You got muscles.

Gary   Yeah, well – thass me older, see. And thass my dick.

Tom (*laughs*)   I thought it was a weapon.

Gary (*laughs*)   Yeah. My dick's a lethal weapon. And I fight my way through the desert, see, through all the terrorists and that, see? Nuke nuke nuke. And then when I get to the city – there's all the honeys, see? And I ride 'em, see. And then I kill 'em.

Tom   That's sick, man. I thought you was all love and understanding.

Gary   Can't help what's in my head. Gotta let it out.

Tom   All that – it's . . . wrong.

Gary   Stuff that's in my head. I don't fight it. I let it out. Thass your problem. What's in your head, Tom? Who do you want? The honey or the homo?

Tom   I dunno yet. I want to find out. I gotta try different stuff.

Gary   You wanna get online.

Tom   You reckon?

Gary   Yeah. You start searchin', chatting, message boards, stuff. You can try everything.

Tom   Yeah?

Gary   You wanna do a search now? 'Gay sex'? 'Battyman'?

Tom   No.

Gary   What you want?

Tom   I don't know. Maybe I'll do Amy.

Gary   You reckon?

Tom   I could do if I wanted to, yeah.

Five

Tom *and* **Amy**. **Tom** *carries hair dye.* **Amy** *has a bandage round her wrist.*

Tom   See? It's baby blond.

Amy   Right.

Tom   I wanna go baby blond.

Amy   Right.

Tom   And I want you to do it to me.

Amy   I'm supposed to be doing my affirmations.

Tom   What's that?

Amy   I'm supposed to write out a hundred times 'I'm surrounded by love'.

Tom   Why?

Amy   Cos I cut myself again last night.

Tom   Why?

Amy   I dunno. I was bored. Or something. Or stress. I dunno.

Tom   You gotta know.

Amy   I don't. Mum took me down the healer and she told me I had to do the affirmations.

Tom   You can do them later. Do my hair.

Amy   They don't work anyway.

Tom   No?

Amy   I did them before and they never worked.

Tom   What works?

Amy   I dunno. Melissa says I need a shag.

Tom   Maybe you do.

Amy   You reckon?

Tom   Yeah. I reckon.

Amy   There's no one fancies me.

Tom   That's not true.

Amy   Says who?

Tom   Says me.

Amy   Yeah?

Tom   You gonna do my hair?

Amy   If you want.

Tom   We need a bowl of water.

Amy   Alright.

Tom   And a towel.

Amy   Yeah yeah.

Tom   Thanks.

Amy *exits.* **Tom** *removes his shirt. Folds it up. Arranges himself on the floor. Pause. Enter* **Melissa***.*

Melissa   Alright?

Tom   Alright.

Melissa   You seen my iPod?

Tom   No.

Melissa   She takes my iPod. Drives me mental. We're always having words. There'll be a ruck soon.

Tom   Right.

Melissa   You shagging?

Tom   Not yet.

Melissa   Do us all a favour and give her one, will you?

Tom   Do my best.

Melissa   Where the fuck's it gone?

She exits. **Tom** *arranges himself again on the floor to look as alluring and yet as natural as possible for* **Amy***. Enter* **Amy** *with bowl of water and towel.*

Amy   I got it.

Tom   I took my top off.

Amy   Right.

Tom   Cos I don't want to get bleach on it.

Amy   Right.

Tom   That alright? Me getting naked?

Amy   Whatever. You got the instructions?

Tom   Yeah.

He gives **Amy** *the instructions.*

Tom   I've been thinking about what you said.

Amy (*reading instructions*)   Yeah?

Tom   About sorting myself out and that. In my head. You know – about whether I wanted . . . you.

Amy   You seen a therapist?

Tom   No. I just been thinking.

Amy   Right.

Tom   About who I wanna kiss and that.

Amy   Right. You got any allergies?

Tom   Why?

Amy   Cos it says here – (*the instructions*) You got any allergies?

Tom   Dust and peanuts.

Amy   Dust and peanuts should be alright. You wanna get started?

Tom   If you like. What if you got bleach on your top?

Amy   It's a crap top.

Tom   Yeah, but you'd ruin it. Bleach down the front.

Amy   Mum'll recycle it.

Tom   Maybe you better take your top off too.

Amy   I don't think so.

Tom   Go on. I took my top off. Time you took your top off too.

Amy   No.

Tom   Come on. Take it off. Take it off.

He reaches out to **Amy** *– she pushes him away.*

Amy   I'm not taking my top off, alright?

Tom   Alright. Do you reckon I should go down the gym?

Amy   I don't know.

Tom   Maybe I should go down the gym. My body's stupid.

Amy   No.

Tom   I've got a stupid body.

Amy   No. You've got a fit body. I like your body.

Tom   Yeah?

Amy   It's a nice body.

Tom   Do you wanna touch it?

Amy   I dunno.

Tom   Come on. Touch it if you like.

Amy   Alright.

She reaches out to touch **Tom**. *Enter* **Melissa** *followed by* **Chantal**, **Kerry** *and* **Alicia**. **Alicia** *carries the baby.*

Melissa   Your mates are here. They're shagging.

She exits.

Chantal/Kerry/Alicia   Alright?

Tom   Alright.

Amy   We're not – we weren't gonna –

Chantal   Thass a buff bod.

Tom   Yeah?

Chantal   For a kid, you're fit. He's fit, isn't he?

Kerry   He's alright. I mean I wouldn't –

Amy   We weren't gonna –

Kerry   But yeah, he's alright.

Amy   I was gonna dye his hair.

Chantal   Go on then.

Tom   Forget it.

Chantal   No. Go on.

Tom   Another time. I don't want people watching.

Chantal   It's safe. Go on. We heard you cut yourself again. You alright?

Amy   Oh yeah. I'm fine. Come on – let's wash your hair.

*She pours water over **Tom**'s head.*

Tom   Owww! Hurts! Awwww! Burning, aagh!

Amy   Shit.

Tom   What you – ? You put cold in that? You never put any cold in that.

Amy   I forgot.

Tom   You forgot. Shit. I'm gonna be scarred. Ugh.

Amy   I'll get cold.

She runs out with the jug. **Tom** *paces around scratching at his scalp, groaning.* **Alicia** *gets out cigarettes.*

Kerry   Lish – don't.

Alicia   What?

Kerry   Not around the kid.

Alicia   Don't be stupid.

Kerry   It stunts 'em.

Alicia   Thass when you're pregnant.

Kerry   Not when you're mother.

She takes the packet of cigarettes from **Alicia**.

Alicia   Fuck's sake. I get stressed out without 'em.

Kerry   Yeah – well.

Alicia   See that, Spazz? Took my fags.

Kerry   Don't call it that.

Alicia   Whatever.

Enter **Amy** *with jug of cold water.*

Amy   Here.

Tom *kneels in front of bowl.* **Amy** *pours cold water over his head.*

Tom   Aaaggghhh.

He lies back.

Amy   You better now.

Tom   Is there red? Like burns?

Amy   A bit.

Tom   Thought so.

Chantal   Are you gonna shag? Cos we can leave if you're gonna shag.

Tom   No. We're not gonna shag.

Chantal   You sure?

Tom   Yeah. I'm sure. We're not gonna shag. We're never gonna . . . no.

Six

Tom, Tarot Reader. *Nine cards spread out in a fan – three lines of three.*

Tom   And that one. What's that one?

Tarot Reader   There's the tower.

Tom   What does that mean?

Tarot Reader   The tower means… This is a time in your life when . . . The foundation on which – you see here these are your emotions – the foundations on which your emotions are based is unstable. It may collapse at any time.

Tom   Yes. That's how I feel. Nothing feels . . . fixed. I don't know who I am. I want to know. What does the tower mean?

Tarot Reader   The tower means change. You are facing a moment of great change. A moment of great decision. Yes?

Tom   Yes.

Tarot Reader   All the time, we've got choices.

Tom   But how do we chose? They tell you choose – but how do you choose?

Tarot Reader   The cards. That's the way. My life. I was confused. I was lost. I got as low as anyone can go. The future was nothing but darkness and fear. But then – a gift. A stranger taught me how to read these signs and now I turn to the cards. Do you see?

Tom   I think so. Can we look at my future?

Tarot Reader   Of course.

Tom   Then let's do it.

Tarot Reader   Now this is – the cards are very strong here. The future is so –

Tom   Am I going to kill myself?

Tarot Reader   I don't see that. No.

Tom   Sometimes I wonder . . . pills and that, y'know. Maybe that's my future. When the pain gets really bad I . . .

Tarot Reader   No, no. You're a beautiful boy, you . . .

Tom   I mean don't think I could, I'm too scared, but if that's my future . . .

Tarot Reader   No. You will live a long life.

Tom   Right.

Tarot Reader   Are you pleased about that?

Tom   Yeah. Course. S'pose.

Tarot Reader   A great long happy life.

Tom   How? How? You say that to everybody –

Tarot Reader   I only tell the truth. If you can't believe me.

Tom   I just can't.

Tarot Reader   The cards will tell us. They've always helped me. Here. Two of the major . . . We call these the major arcane, you see? Here – the pictures. The High Priestess – here. Drawing back the veil. Drawing back the veil to let you into her world.

Tom   It's a woman?

Tarot Reader   She's a feminine energy.

Tom   It's a woman letting me into her – I've got to know – that's a woman –

Tarot Reader   It's more complicated than that. We prefer the masculine and feminine energies.

Tom   But is she a woman?

Tarot Reader   Or a man with a feminine energy.

Tom   Oh.

Tarot Reader   Men can have feminine energy. You could have feminine energy –

Tom   No

Tarot Reader   But your energy could –

Tom   What you calling me? Are you calling me a girl? I'm not a girl.

Tarot Reader   What are you doing?

Tom   I'm going if you call me a girl.

Tarot Reader   Alright. Go. If you have to – go

Tom   I will.

Tarot Reader   Give me your money and go – but you'll never know – Here . . . the lovers. The cards are so strong for the lovers.

Tom   The lovers?

Tarot Reader   Yes. You are about to enter the gate, pass through the threshold and embrace the lovers. A lover for you. Yes? You've got a question?

Tom   I've really got to know. Is it? Is it a . . . a man or a woman?

Tarot Reader   Ah. I see. I can't tell you that.

Tom   You have to tell me that. Tell me. Otherwise what's the – Please – please –

Tarot Reader   I can't tell you that. But if you look at the cards. Look at the cards. Really listen to the cards. You are about to pass through the gateway and meet your lover. Man or woman? What do the cards say? Look at them. Listen.

Tom   I can't . . . Nothing.

Tarot Reader   Make yourself comfortable. Be patient. Listen.

Tom   No. I really can't . . .

Tarot Reader   We have time. You will choose a course of action. With the cards you will choose a course of action. Just watch and wait and listen.

Tom   Nothing. Nothing. No future. Nothing.

Tarot Reader   Shhhh. Listen. Listen. Listen to the cards.

Tom *looks at the cards. Long pause.*

Tarot Reader   Yes?

Tom   Yes.

Tarot Reader   You know what to do?

Tom   I know what to do.

Seven

Tom, Amy. Amy *carries the baby.*

Tom   You got the baby.

Amy   She made me. Said I'd have detention for a week.

Tom   That's harsh.

Amy   Totally harsh. I told her – I'm not fit to be a mother, look at my arms. You can't be a mother when you've got cuts all over your arms.

Tom   And what did she say?

Amy   Said it would take me out of myself – think about another life.

Tom   Bit of plastic.

Amy   And now I have to write down all my thoughts and feelings in my baby diary.

Tom   What you written?

Amy   Nothing. Don't feel anything. It doesn't do anything. Just sits there. It's heavy.

Tom   Let me feel.

Amy   Go on then.

She gives **Tom** *the baby.*

Tom   Yeah. Really heavy.

He drops the baby.

Whoops.

Amy   You did that on purpose.

Tom   Maybe.

Amy   You're trouble.

Tom   That's right. Do you reckon it's damaged?

Amy   Shut up.

Tom *picks up the baby.*

Tom   No – it's fine.

Amy   Don't tell Kerry – she'll go mental.

Tom (*to baby*)   You're alright, aren't you? Aren't you? Yes.

He throws the baby up in the air – lets it fall on the floor.

Amy   You're mad.

Tom   I'm rubbish at catching. Catch it!

He throws the baby to **Amy**. *She catches it.*

Amy   I'll be bollocked if it's damaged.

Tom   Throw it to me. Come on.

Amy *throws the baby. He lets it fall to the floor again.*

Tom   Why can't I catch it?

Amy   You're not trying. Give it here.

She goes to pick up the baby. **Tom** *stops her.*

Tom   No – leave it.

Amy   Why?

Tom   Cos I'm here. You can hold the baby later.

Amy   What am I gonna write in my baby diary?

Tom   Make it up.

He takes his shirt off.

Amy   What are you doing?

Tom   I went down the gym. See?

Amy   How many times you been?

Tom   Three.

Amy   I don't think three's gonna make a difference.

Tom   Course it is. Have a feel.

Amy   Yeah?

Tom *flexes a bicep.*

Tom   Feel that.

Amy   Alright.

She feels his bicep.

Tom   See?

Amy   What?

Tom   It's stronger. Harder.

Amy   You reckon?

Tom   Oh yeah – that's much harder.

Amy   I dunno.

She picks up the baby.

Tom   Do you wanna have sex?

Amy   Maybe.

Tom   I think maybe we should have sex.

Amy   I've never had sex before.

Tom   Neither have I. I've seen it online.

Amy   Yeah?

Tom   Round Gary's.

Amy   Gay Gary's?

Tom   He's not gay.

Amy   Right. Are you gay?

Tom   Come here.

Amy *goes to* **Tom**. *He takes the baby out of her arms and lays it on the floor. They kiss.*

Tom   Did you like that?

Amy   Yeah. Is it me?

Tom   What?

Amy   In your dreams? Is it me you're kissing in your dream?

Tom   No.

Amy   Are you sure? If you can't see the face . . . ?

Tom   Yeah, well. But I can feel it.

Amy   And it's not me?

Tom   It's not you. Does that bother you?

Amy   No.

Tom   Good.

They kiss again.

Melissa (*off*)   Amy.

Amy   What?

Melissa (*off*)   You got my camcorder?

Amy   No.

Melissa (*off*)   You sure? I can't find it anywhere.

Amy   I'm sure.

Melissa (*off*)   If you've taken it again . . .

Amy   I haven't taken it again.

Melissa (*off*)   I'm coming to look.

Amy   No.

She exits. **Tom** *waits. Enter* **De Clerk**.

Tom   How did you get in here, sir?

De Clerk   Through the floor.

Tom   What? You just . . . ?

De Clerk   Come through the floor.

Tom   Shit.

De Clerk   Just something I can do. Don't tell the Head. We're not supposed to have special powers.

Tom   Alright. Are you here cos I'm still a bit gay – is that it?

De Clerk   Let's not talk about that.

Tom   I sort of decided I wasn't gonna be gay any more – now you sort of – well, it's a bit gay, isn't it, coming through the floor like that?

De Clerk   Are you going to have sex with her?

Tom   Yeah, I reckon. What – don't you think I should?

De Clerk   We can't tell you yes or no. That's not what we do.

Tom   Why not?

De Clerk   Because you have to make your own choices.

Tom   But why? Everything's so confusing. There's so many choices. I don't feel like a person. I just feel like all these bits floating around. And none of them match up. Like a jigsaw that's never going to be finished. It's doing my head in.

De Clerk   And what would you prefer?

Tom   Someone to tell me what to be.

De Clerk   No one's going to do that.

Tom   I wish they would.

De Clerk   When I was growing up: everyone told you who to be. They told you what to do. What was right and what was wrong. What your future would be.

Tom   I'd like that.

De Clerk   No. It made me very unhappy.

Tom   I'm unhappy – too many choices. You were unhappy – no choices. Everyone's unhappy. Life's shit, isn't it, sir?

De Clerk   That is I would say a distinct possibility.

Tom   Are you still unhappy, sir?

De Clerk   If I stop. If I stop working and rushing – the inspection, the continual assessment – trying to pay the mortgage every month, trying to please the Head, trying to get home before nine every night – then, yes, I'm unhappy. But only when I stop.

Tom   You've got a boyfriend?

De Clerk   I can't talk about that.

Tom   You're gay, sir. I don't mean that in a bad way. I just mean – like you know who you are. And you're gay. I'm going to have sex with her.

De Clerk   If that's what you want.

Tom   So you better get back through the floor. I'm not having you watching us.

De Clerk   I don't want to watch. Use protection.

Tom   I know.

De Clerk   If you're having sex, use protection.

Tom   That's telling me what to do.

De Clerk   It's advice.

Tom   It's telling me what to do. You should tell me more of that.

De Clerk   I can't. Promise me you'll use protection.

Tom   I might do.

De Clerk   Promise.

Tom   Do all gay people come through floors?

De Clerk   Now you're being silly.

Enter **Amy**.

Amy   She's gone now.

Tom   Good. (*To* **De Clerk**.) You going?

De Clerk   Take care.

He exits.

Tom   Is everyone out?

Amy   Yeah. They're all out. Got the place to ourselves.

Tom   That's good.

Amy   Are you scared?

Tom   A bit. Are you?

Amy   Scared and excited.

Tom   We'll take it slow.

Amy   Yeah. Let's take it really slow. You got anything?

Tom   Like what?

Amy   Like condoms and that?

Tom   No.

Amy   Oh.

Tom   Does that bother you?

Amy   No. Does that bother you?

Tom   No.

Amy   Do you love me?

Tom   I don't know. Maybe later. Is that alright?

Amy   Yeah. That's alright.

Tom   After – we can do my hair. I still want blond hair.

Amy   Alright.

Tom   Turn the light out.

Amy   I want to see you.

Tom   No.

He turns the light off. The **Baby** *comes forward and speaks to the audience.*

Baby   And so it happened. My mummy and my daddy made me that night. Neither of them enjoyed it very much. But they did it. And that's what they wanted. And that night I started to grow in my mummy's tummy. And by the time she did her GCSEs I was almost ready to come out of her tummy.

I think that night as they lay together in the dark she thought they might spend all their time together from that day on. But that didn't happen. In fact, once that night was over, they were sort of shy and embarrassed whenever they saw each other until – by the time I was born – they weren't speaking to each other at all. And Mummy says for a few moments – she's sure there were a few moments that night when he did really, really love her. And I believe her.

They did talk to each other once more after they left school –
but there's one more bit of the story to show you before we
get to that.

Eight

Tom *and* **Martin**. **Tom** *has a hat pulled down, completely covering
his hair.*

Tom   You've got a nice place.

Martin (*off*)   Thank you.

Tom   Yeah, really nice. Trendy.

Martin (*off*)   Thank you.

Tom   What do you do?

Martin (*off*)   My job?

Tom   Yeah. Your job.

Martin (*off*)   I'm a systems analyst.

Tom   Right. Right. Is that alright?

Martin (*off*)   I enjoy it.

Tom   And the pay's good?

Martin (*off*)   The pay is ridiculously good.

Tom   Well – that's good.

Martin (*off*)   And you?

Tom   What?

Martin (*off*)   Do you have a job?

Tom   Yes.

Martin (*off*)   What do you do?

Tom   Well, actually, I'm looking.

Martin (*off*)   I see.

Enter **Martin**, *with two bottles of beer. He gives one of the bottles of beer to* **Tom**.

Martin   Cheers.

Tom   Right. Cheers.

Martin   If you want to take off –

Tom   I'm alright.

Martin   Maybe – your hat . . . ?

Tom   No.

Martin   Alright.

Tom   It's just I had a disaster.

Martin   Yes?

Tom   With my hair.

Martin   I see.

Tom   Yeah, this mate tried to dye my hair but it went wrong.

Martin   Right.

Tom   Yeah, tried to dye my hair, but I had a bit of a reaction and it's gone really weird, like ginger bits and green bits and that. Last month. I'm waiting for it to grow out. I look weird so that's why I'm wearing –

Martin   It suits you.

Tom   Yeah?

Martin   The hat. It's a good look.

Tom   Thank you.

Martin   You're a good-looking guy.

Tom   Right.

Martin   Was it your boyfriend?

Tom   What?

Martin   With the hair dye?

Tom   No.

Martin   Have you got a boyfriend?

Tom   No. Have you?

Martin   Yes. Is that alright?

Tom   I suppose. How old are you?

Martin   Twenty-two.

Tom   Right.

Martin   How old are you?

Tom   Eighteen.

Martin   You said nineteen in the chatroom.

Tom   Did I?

Martin   Yes.

Tom   Well, I'm eighteen.

Martin   But actually you look younger.

Tom   Really?

Martin   You actually look about sixteen.

Tom   Everyone says I look younger. That's what they said when I was at school.

Martin   Right. Do you want to come through to the bedroom?

Tom   In a minute. Are you happy?

Martin   What?

Tom   You know, in your life and that? Does it make you happy?

Martin   I suppose so.

Tom   With your boyfriend and your job and that?

Martin   I never really think about it.

Tom   You seem happy.

Martin   Then I suppose I am.

Tom   That's good.

Martin   And you?

Tom   What?

Martin   Are you happy?

Tom   I reckon. Yes, I am.

Martin   Well, that's good. Look, we really should get into the bedroom –

Tom   Right.

Martin   My boyfriend's coming back at five and I don't want to –

Tom   Right.

Martin   Sorry to hurry you, but –

Tom   That's alright.

Martin   You can keep your hat on.

Tom   Thanks.

Martin   You're cute.

Tom   Thanks. I've never done this before.

Martin   Chatrooms?

Tom   This. All of it.

Martin   Sex?

Tom   No. I've done sex. Only . . .

Martin   Not with someone so old?

Tom   Not with . . .

Martin   Twenty-two too old for you?

Tom   No. Not with . . . a bloke. I mean, I did it with girls, a girl, but . . .

Martin   Did you like it?

Tom   It was alright.

Martin   If you like that kind of thing.

Tom   Yeah. I'm shaking. Sorry. I feel nervous. Is it gonna hurt?

Martin   Not if we do it right.

Tom   How will we know?

Martin   I don't know. You just have to . . . er . . . suck it and see.

Tom (*laughs*)   You dirty bastard.

Martin   Yeah.

Tom   I shouldn't have come.

Martin   Alright then – another time. How are you getting back?

Tom   No, no.

He kisses **Martin**.

Martin   Mixed messages.

Tom   You're right. I'm sixteen.

Martin   I know.

Tom   I'm legal.

Martin   What do you want?

Tom   This.

He kisses **Martin**.

Tom   Come on then. Where's the bedroom? Or do you want your boyfriend to find out?

Martin   The bedroom's through there.

Tom   Your boyfriend, he's not . . . ?

Martin   Yes?

Tom   He's not . . . is your boyfriend a teacher?

Martin (*laughs*)   God, no. He's a mortgage broker. Why?

Tom   Nothing.

Martin   Ready?

Tom   Ready. Just – don't touch my hat, alright?

Martin   Alright.

Nine

Amy, **Tom**.

Amy   Your hair's alright.

Tom   Yeah. Took a few months. But in the end it went back to normal.

Amy   You should still do an earring.

Tom   You reckon?

Amy   Yeah. I always reckoned an earring would really suit you.

Tom   Maybe one day.

Amy   Yeah. One day. What you up to?

Tom   Not much. I'm going to college next year.

Amy   That's good.

Tom   Fashion.

Amy   Nice.

Tom   And I'm doing coat-check.

Amy   In a club?

Tom   Sort of pub-club.

Amy   Gay club?

Tom   Just Fridays and Saturdays. You should come along.
It's a laugh.

Amy   You got a boyfriend?

Tom   I dunno.

Amy   You got to know.

Tom   There's a bloke . . . We . . . meet up. A couple of
times a week. But he's living with someone.

Amy   His boyfriend.

Tom   Yeah. He's got a boyfriend. He keeps on saying
they're gonna split but they haven't. Still – we have a laugh.
He's got money.

Amy   Right.

Tom   You seeing anyone?

Amy   Yeah.

Tom   Who?

Amy   Nosy. I mean, I can't go out much but, you know, if
I get a babysitter –

Tom   Right.

Amy   I'm gonna do college in a couple of years.

Tom   That's good.

Amy   Just gotta wait till she's a bit older.

Tom   Of course. If you need me to babysit –

Amy   No.

Tom   I don't mind.

Amy   I've got mates do that for me. Kerry loves it.

Tom   Yeah, but if you ever need me to –

Amy   I don't need you to.

Tom   I want to.

Amy   I don't want you to, alright?

Tom   Alright. I still . . . think about you.

Amy   Right.

Tom   Like . . . fancy you and that.

Amy   You told your boyfriend?

Tom   Sometimes, when he kisses me, I think about you. He kisses me but I close my eyes and it's your face I see.

Amy   You can't have it both ways.

Tom   That's what I want.

Amy   Well – you can't have it.

Enter **Gary**, *pushing a pram.*

Gary   Alright, babe?

Amy   Yeah. Alright.

Gary *kisses* **Amy**.

Amy   She been alright?

Gary   Yeah. Fast asleep the whole time.

Amy   She'll be awake all night now.

Gary   You want me to wake her?

Amy   No. Leave her alone.

Gary   Alright, Tom?

Tom   She told me she was going out with someone.

Gary   You guess who?

Tom   No. You gonna bring the kid up to be a stoner too?

Gary   No. I give up the weed, didn't I? Can't be blazing around the kid, can I? Once you got a kid to look after – that's the time to grow up, I reckon.

Tom   Yeah – suppose that's right.

Amy   Tom's gone gay now.

Gary   Thass cool.

Tom   Can I have a look at her?

Amy   We gotta go in a minute. Mum's booked us up the naturopath.

Tom   I just want to have a quick look.

Amy   Go on then.

Tom   She's beautiful.

Amy   Yeah. She's alright.

Tom   Can I pick her up?

Amy   No.

Tom   I'll be careful.

Amy   I don't want you to.

Tom   Alright.

Amy   Not now she's settled.

Tom   Alright.

Amy   Best to leave her alone.

Tom   Alright.

Amy   I want to keep her out of the sun.

Tom   Of course.

Gary   We've got to get the bus.

Amy   Yeah.

Tom   Will I see you again?

Amy   Maybe.

Tom   I wanna see you again. I'm the dad.

Amy   Gary looks after her – don't you?

Gary   Yeah.

Tom   Yeah – but still.

Enter **Martin**.

Martin   Sorry, I tried to get away only –

He goes to kiss **Tom**. *He steps away.*

Tom   Don't.

Amy   You his boyfriend?

Martin   I wouldn't . . . sort of . . .

Tom   Yeah. Only sort of.

Amy   Better than nothing though, isn't it?

Martin   That's right.

Amy   See ya.

Exit **Amy** *and* **Gary** *with pram.*

Tom   Did you tell him?

Martin   What?

Tom   You know. About me. You were supposed to tell him about me.

Martin   He's away this weekend. What do you want to do?

Tom   Do you love me?

Martin   You know I don't like to use that word.

Tom   Because?

Martin   Because.

Tom   Tell me.

Martin   What does it mean? It doesn't mean anything.
'Love'? It doesn't mean . . .

Tom   You've got to say it.

Martin   No.

Tom   There's no point to this. There's no point to
anything. What's the point?

Martin   Money. Sex. Fun. That's the point.

Tom   No. I want –

Martin   What?

Tom   Say you love me.

Martin   No.

Tom   Say you love me.

Martin   No.

Tom   Say you love me. Please. Please. Please – say you love
me.

Martin   Okay. I love you – okay?

Beat.

Tom   . . . No.

Martin   Fuck's sake. Why can't you . . . moneysexfun?

Tom   Because I want more. I want everything. I want . . .

Martin   Yes?

Tom   I want everything and I want . . . I want . . . I want to
find out everything.

Martin (*laughs*)   You're a baby. Treat you like a baby.

Tom   No. Not any more. No.

Citizenship

BY MARK RAVENHILL

*Notes on rehearsal and staging drawn from a workshop
held at the National Theatre, October 2015*

*From a workshop led by Nadia Fall,
with notes by Richard Weinman*

How Mark came to write the play

'I think, from the age of six or seven, I wanted to be an actor.
So any youth theatre I could join, amateur theatre groups
and so on. And I would write plays for myself to perform. *The
Life of Louis Braille* was one . . . But even before that, before I
even knew what plays were, as an extension of playing games
and dressing up, I'd make up plays. I forced my brother to be
in plays with me that I'd make up and get people to watch.

'I think I was very keen to write a Connections play because
I remember how exciting it was to get a play to be in when
you're a teenager, just how important a play is. It may be the
first play you come in contact with, so that play really matters
to you. Whereas for an audience member or an actor later on,
when it's their three-hundredth play, they can be a bit jaded.

'The first time I wrote one, I did want to know what the
elements were of a popular Connections play: large cast,
good parts for girls, comedy . . . and I wrote *Totally Over You.*
which was very popular. But, having done that . . . I wrote
Citizenship because I fancied writing something quite
challenging, that some schools may turn down. I'd seen a
TV documentary about teenage sex and it had this boy-girl
couple at the centre of it and he was gay and she was saying,
'Yeah he doesn't really fancy me and we do have sex but I
know it won't last long cos he's gay.' And they were so funny
and painful that when it came to this play – and I knew I
wanted to write about teenage sexuality – I used them as a
springboard for the central characters. Even so I think
seventeen groups did it.

'Often you walk into a school hall to see your play and you can feel the level of commitment of everybody in the room, audience included. I saw such a range of productions. I had one production pulled at the last minute. The teacher had gone ahead and chosen *Citizenship* and rehearsed it and the Head found out about the content of the play only a week or so before the performance, and it was cancelled. Poor group – they'd done weeks and weeks of rehearsals and it got pulled. But it was the only one.

'I think the appeal of theatre is in its simplicity. With a film, with all its layers of money-making and bureaucracy and technology, you're quite far from that fundamental act of 'playing'. I was once in a massive rehearsal room at the National Theatre and looking around thinking, this is just some people, a few props, messing around; it's not even one remove, it's half a remove, from me and my brother in my bedroom, making up plays. The theatre, at whatever level, is always so close to that basic level of 'let's pretend.'

Approaching the play

The workshop focused on offering exercises that raised questions about the play and that might be useful as part of a rehearsal process. All the exercises aim to allow a process that can be shaped to reflect each group and are based on creating a safe space within which young actors can then be challenged.

Themes

By way of approaching the play Nadia encouraged a read-through of the script in order to extract its themes. She encouraged the group to share the obvious themes that immediately stood out but also to challenge what is underneath and at the core of the play – the deeper and more subtle ideas which underline the events and characters. The group offered the following themes:

- love
- sex and sexuality
- citizenship
- fantasy vs. reality
- drugs and alcohol
- no choice vs. too much choice
- responsibility
- life choices
- therapy
- coming of age
- expectations
- conflict
- social pressure
- rebellion
- consequences
- privacy
- role of education/teachers
- body image
- technology and porn
- time pressure
- expectations
- therapy
- gender stereotypes – innate vs. learnt
- parents, and the lack of

The participants were asked to challenge and unpick these words and to be specific about how they are represented in the world of the play and the current social context of the young actors. This highlighted some of the following points and questions:

- All the characters have their own or similar struggles, whether they are a teacher or a young person. There aren't really any 'bad people' in the play yet they all have flaws. Tom's questions to De Clerk raise interesting ideas about education – De Clerk as a teacher is seemingly unable to answer these even though we sense that he wants to. Many of the characters have a desperate need for answers or clarification, even De Clerk.

- This conflict of what each character wants, versus the social pressure of what they should want and what they are able to do, seems relevant to all the characters. It raises the question: who are the protagonists in the play putting pressure on the other characters? And what are the expectations that the characters put on themselves?

- In the play there seems to be a constant time pressure to do things or to get answers to things, as if success is measured by how old you are when you do things. How can this pressure manifest itself in your production – physically, through transitions, the presence of other characters onstage?

- The conflict of choice again feels relevant to nearly all the characters. No choice or too much choice, the consequences vary but the stakes to make the right choice seem really high.

- The idea of privacy feels even more relevant now in the age of social media, but in the play what or who are the forces that want to know everything?

- How do you update the play? It is not easy to just interchange Myspace for Facebook, etc. as the play is set just as the internet and communicating via it are starting to surface, whereas now the landscape of how young people communicate has completely changed.

- How do you extract the comedy in the play while still honouring the dilemmas and struggles of the characters? It can be easy to explain some of the struggles as simply coming of age – questioning your sexuality, impressing friends, having sex for the first time; there is comedy in everything and it is important that this is found in order for us to care about the characters. However, it is important to remember that the stakes are always high for a fifteen-year-old. The Tarot Reader is an example of how you need to explore this balance – if you play her

completely straight you can lose some of the comic
potential, but a lot of what she says makes sense and it is
important that this character does not become generalised
or a stereotype.

The play represents how life is made out of a series of choices,
mistakes and rebellions. Each character is struggling with these.

It is useful to reflect on the various themes and questions
raised by the play and to consider which themes/questions
you have an affinity with. It might also be useful to recognise
other themes which you might not be drawn to but are
important to the story. As a way of developing this and
demonstrating how a simple theme might be useful when
making work, Nadia set the group a physical exercise,
outlined below:

EXERCISE – PHYSICALLY INTERPRETING THE THEMES

In small groups, discuss which themes you think are important
or that you are drawn to. Pick one theme and create an
image – animated rather than frozen or a tableau – that
represents or is inspired by that theme. If you want to include
text, try to use words taken directly from the script. Think
about where you would put this image in the story? When
sharing these images with the rest of the group, think about
your reaction to each one and what each might symbolise –
what are you trying to distil? Think about where you might
put this in terms of your production – could it work as a
transitional moment, an opening image or something that
features in the background of scenes, or could it weave its way
through the play?

The aim of this exercise was to allow the themes to become
physical starting points – to encourage participants to think
about what themes were important to them, to talk and
challenge these ideas and to start thinking about how they
might tackle the play aesthetically, sparking instant physical
ideas which they could maybe incorporate or play with.

The discussion around the images created and the reaction of the audience raised the following points:

- Who is massaging who? The group explored the idea of different characters massaging each other and experimenting with the way in which this could be done. It could be interesting to observe whether who is involved makes it sweet or lewd? This raises the idea of perception and how it can be played with.

- There was a recurrent theme of 'asking' for answers, help or clarification and the representation of being met by a 'shut door'. The physical repetition of asking and being shut down was an interesting physical motif that could be useful to explore.

- The adults in the play are not resolved – they are still different and flawed in much the same way as the young people in the play. It is important to expose these flaws and not to play characters as too 'nice'. If we see the flaws and regret, it exposes the characters' natural vulnerability and allows the audience to empathise rather than pity.

- It can be really powerful to unpick the subtext and allow this to come through. This doesn't have to always be obvious, but again what is underneath adds a truthful vulnerability to the characters. Nadia talked about how this can often be done using music, highlighting how a character is feeling through a particular song. This allows moments where you can show 'the mask off' and might be something you can build into transitions or stylised moments – what is this person like when they are on their own?

- It is important to find ways to show how high the stakes are for the characters, but this doesn't necessarily mean you need to play the scenes 'big'. Think about how repetition can be used to build pressure. Can the transitions be used to build pressure before a scene starts so that the actors can play against the subtext? Think of the arcs in the play and how the pressure can build to a crescendo.

OPINION THERMOMETER

Nadia divided the room into three areas – 'agree', 'undecided' and 'disagree'. She then asked the participants a series of questions based on the themes and events in the play and asked them to stand in the area of the room which represented their thinking. The first example she gave was 'You're born gay'. With each question, she asked people to explain and justify their decision and facilitated the debate that these discussions provoked.

The following is a list of provocations that might be useful to think about, although there are many others that might be interesting to look at or be specifically tailored to your group:

Young people shouldn't watch porn.

Only girls should look after a plastic baby.

Tom is deliberately seducing De Clerk.

It is a school's responsibility to educate pupils about sex.

Weed isn't harmful.

De Clerk is inappropriate.

Sexuality is fluid.

Self-harm is attention seeking.

Therapy is essential for young people.

Amy and Tom are too young to be parents.

We should discuss our fantasies – no matter what the content.

Teachers and students should discuss their personal lives.

Nadia highlighted that there is a big responsibility in doing this play with young people; the struggles within the play are very real. There is something interesting in allowing these struggles to be present rather than feeling you have to make conclusive decisions around every issue.

Exercises for intimacy

Nadia talked about the general rules for creating a safe space within which to work with young people before you can even begin to look at the physical intimacy of characters. This involves understanding your group so that you are clear where you put boundaries and how far you can push individuals within them.

The following are exercises designed to encourage a group to develop physical intimacy.

EXERCISE ONE – CONNECTIONS IN SPACE

Instruct the group to walk around the space, filling any gaps so that they balance the space. Encourage them to become aware of the group and to really see each other as they move around. Develop this so that they actually meet each other and naturally say hello. Once this genuine atmosphere has been established, give the instruction that each time they meet someone they should stop opposite each other and find a moment to jump together without verbally communicating. Once the group has established this, develop it by encouraging them to find and play with the negotiation of when to jump.

The next stage of this exercise is to find a pair and for both people to close their eyes. The pair must try to identify each other's little fingers and link them. Once this has been achieved they should put their hands down by their sides and repeat, but this time interlinking two fingers. This is repeated with three fingers, four, and so on, until you have both hands connected. Once the pairs are palm-to-palm they can open their eyes.

Within the pairs assign an A and B. Still palm-to-palm, ask A to close their eyes and B to lead A around the space. On the instruction of the facilitator, encourage A and B to instantly swap who has their eyes open/closed and who is leading. Build the frequency of the swap and encourage the pairs to push how instantly and smoothly they can make this transition.

Building on this intuitive and trusting energy that you have begun to establish, ask the group to walk around the space, keeping an awareness of the group as a whole. The group must keep open to the idea that at some point, uninstructed to do so, they will pick a moment to gather around the door and stop there all at the same time. It is important that individuals do not try to lead this moment but that the group strives to find a connected moment where this decision is taken. Now encourage the group to move around the space together and to repeat the exercise, but stopping somewhere in the space – finding a moment where they will all come to a standstill together.

These exercises are designed to build up trust within the group and to encourage them to work in a way that doesn't require too much thought. This requires a vulnerability, which helps to develop a safe space and creates a genuine intimacy within the group and its members. It is important to remember that it is not necessarily the exercise but how it is played that can lead to intimacy. These exercises are really important to generate an ensemble feeling in a cast, encouraging intimacy within the whole group rather than simply the actors who have an intimate moment in the play. Encourage the cast to understand that they are all responsible for the storytelling no matter how big their part may be; in this way it is important that every character has a name even if it is not in the script. Remember to give feedback to these actors no matter how small their role.

EXERCISE TWO – TEXT FRAMES

Split the group into two, either side of the space. Set a framework so that each side represents a character and that they have a relationship in the play. Encourage two people to come up and pick a folded piece of paper with differing text frames, for instance 'I like it when' and 'I'll never forget when'. Each person must finish the text frame using the learnt or imagined knowledge of the character and must try to do this instantly. This might be something factual that we know happens within the story, for example, 'I'll never forget when you told me you were pregnant', or it might be something more imagined outside the story or a general feeling, for example, 'I like it when you listen to me'. Encourage both parties to really listen to the other and react as the character's imagined history might dictate.

This is a really nice exercise to build characters and test the imagined corners of their psyches. It creates a fairly safe structure from which to begin exploring the potential of improvising and focuses the thoughts of the performer on what their character might be feeling and their relationships with others. Other examples of text frames are:

I like it when you . . .

You were ridiculous when . . .

You scare me when . . .

You make me laugh when . . .

You confuse me when . . .

I hate it when you . . .

I'll never forget when . . .

I was proud of you when . . .

You let me down when . . .

I don't understand why you . . .

Having watched these back, the group commented on the power of simplicity – that many of these moments, where just two lines were spoken, held a real power and truth allowing the interaction to be believable.

Staging and solving the magic realism

How could you address the moments of magic realism – for example, where De Clerk comes through the floor or when the baby talks to the audience? Participants were split into small groups and asked to stage one of these sections using the text and looking specifically at potential solutions to the moments of magic realism/surrealism. Below is what the different groups came up with:

REPRESENTING SEX AND PREGNANCY

The groups explored how these moments could be stylistically represented. One offer was to have Tom and Amy use the hand exercise that has been demonstrated earlier, where they slowly interlinked their fingers with their eyes closed – this has a vulnerable clumsiness paired with the delicate intimacy of touch, which seemed to represent well the act of conception. Intimacy in these moments was often found through the suspension of the pace, where the naturalistic rhythms were broken or held to heighten the moment. This can be effective if it contrasts the more natural rhythms in other scenes, allowing the moment to stand out rather than playing the whole play at this pace. Similarly the use of unbroken eye contact between Tom and Amy seemed to hold a far greater intimacy when representing the sexual act than something more explicit.

THE BABY

Nadia gave the groups weighted dolls to use as required in the scene. Two were lifelike and one was a more symbolic weighted rag-doll/blanket. One of the solutions explored by the groups was to puppeteer the baby – with either Tom and Amy or separate puppeteers – allowing it to stand independently when addressing the audience. Groups explored the possibilities of the puppeteers voicing the baby or a different actor placed next to/elsewhere on the stage. This is a difficult moment as it can almost become comical and the group talked about fighting against the need to dramatise this moment and to play the voice of the baby as simply and restrained as possible to counter this. Another alternative was the use of an ensemble who passed the baby between them and subsequently became the collective voice of the child.

DE CLERK ENTERING THROUGH THE FLOOR

The appearance of De Clerk in this moment can have many different interpretations and symbolic connotations for the story. Is it Tom's psyche or De Clerk's or both? Is it Tom's fear or confusion about having sex with Amy or is it that he wants to be stopped from having to go through with it? Is it a longing to be helped or De Clerk's desire to be able to help? Is it a fantasy about De Clerk?

There are also decisions to play with about *how* the actor playing De Clerk enters the space 'through the floor'. Do you play it with an element of disguise or surprise so that it is as if he just appears? Or do you play against this and simply allow him to walk into the space and note the fact that something about this doesn't sit in the naturalistic world of Amy's bedroom – for instance if he blatantly enters in Amy's view but she shows no signs of seeing him.

One group played with the notion of De Clerk having the ability to freeze Amy before she exits the room in order to very clearly suspend the naturalism and visually highlight Tom's turmoil and dilemma. Another group played with the notion that De Clerk enters earlier in the scene unnoticed by Amy but seen by Tom. This created an interesting tension whereby Tom wasn't sure if Amy was aware of De Clerk, which led to Tom being pulled between the two worlds. In this example De Clerk simply entered the space and sat at Amy's desk and started marking homework. This again created an interesting dynamic for the audience because it could have been that he was simply existing in a separate world and it made us question whether he was really there.

Improvisation

Improvisation could be a very valuable rehearsal tool. Nadia outlined some of the techniques, frameworks and parameters that can help to make it useful. She suggested that improvisation needs clear boundaries to be safe and putting constraints on an improvisation often allows more focused and interesting outcomes. Examples of this might be to set a length of time – for instance, 'This improvisation will last exactly one minute.' It might be that as a director you offer a word or a line or the last sentence of the improvisation. It can also be really helpful to give the actors clear intentions to play – for exanple, you are trying to belittle the other person or you want to amuse them.

Think about the context for improvisations – a good starting point might be to take the facts that you already know and improvise around these. For example, we know that Amy sees a therapist, so this might be a scene that you could choose to play out. Other possible moments might be:

De Clerk and his partner at home.

Amy, her mum and sister at home.

Amy telling Tom she is pregnant.

The phone call between Martin and Tom arranging to meet.

De Clerk talking honestly to Tom about his personal life.

Another approach might be to start with tableaux, asking the actors to create a still image based on the situation that you give them. This must be done quickly and without comment and then using this image as a starting point the actors can bring it to life. Again it is important to keep the young people held in these situations so you might give them the starting line, a thought, an emotion or an intention.

It might be helpful to the actors to do some preparation work around their characters beforehand. This might include writing down all the facts about their character that are revealed in the script, every stage direction which directly applies to them, anything that anyone else says about their character or anything they say about another character. This might also prompt a list of questions that the actor has about the character that aren't given in the script. This might be done individually or as a group but it offers a good grounding from which to build improvisation and allows them to discover some of the unanswered questions in an active, instinctive way.

Using the example of Amy meeting her counsellor, Nadia offered another technique, which was to provide the counsellor with a series of pre-written questions. These acted as a guide to help structure the improvisation, but actors did not have to stick rigidly to them and were encouraged to keep reacting to what the other actor offered. The questions were as follows:

What brings you here?

Have you ever seen a therapist before?

What is the problem from your viewpoint?

How does this problem typically make you feel?

What makes the problem better?

If you had a magic wand, what positive changes would you make in your life?

Overall, how would you describe your mood?

What do you expect from the counselling process?

What would it take to make you feel more confident, happier and more satisfied?

Do you consider yourself to have a low, average or high interpersonal IQ?

Once this scene had been established, Nadia asked them to try it again six months later with the detail that Amy was now comfortable in these surroundings and liked her counsellor. She then got them to do it again with the context that Amy wanted to tell her therapist that she was pregnant. This way of developing improvisation can be really helpful to creating rounded characters and allowing improvisations to have a learnt context. The ability for the director to control the scene by freezing it keeps the actors safe and allows them to encourage certain directions that they might want to explore.

Additional questions and offers.

Is De Clerk gay? The script doesn't explicitly say that De Clerk is gay but it is inferred by the young people. Nadia felt that even though it is not said, the instincts of the young people in the play, who seemingly just know that he is, is telling and that it can be assumed that he is gay.

Explore what 'citizenship' is and what it actually means. What was a Greek 'citizen'?

While it is important to allow the young actors a voice in the space, sometimes it can be helpful to distance them from their personal feelings when looking at themes and ideas. One offer is to create a framework for debate where you give them a statement to agree or disagree with and encourage them to argue the point even if they don't believe it; this removes it slightly from personal opinion while still pushing the extremities of the subject. Similarly a good way to challenge stereotypes is to use strong images as starting points for discussion.

Explore the physicality of how someone walks into the space or leaves it – this physical storytelling is an extremely powerful tool outside the text. When looking at the text you might want to encourage the actors to improvise moments, putting them into their own language. This can be useful for them to relate to it and find their own instincts and rhythms. Encourage them to go back to the original script and see how their discoveries might translate.

Put props and objects into the rehearsal space early so that they can be played with as part of improvisations and rehearsals. These can be interesting stimuli in their own right but often will also affect the action and may end up being useful differently from how you intended, or become a motif within the storytelling.

You might want to produce a timeline for the play so that as a company you are clear over what period the story takes place. It is useful to be really specific as this offers tangible anchors for the imaginations of the actors.

Encourage the 'many-headed director' where you take suggestions from the rest of the cast when looking at an improvisation or moment in the play. This can really help to promote a feeling of ownership over the work and encourages a sense of playfulness whereby the cast knows that they can try something that may or may not work.

Bedbug

by Snoo Wilson,
Gary Kemp
& Guy Pratt

A musical based on Vladimir Mayakovsky's 1929 satire on the distrust of authority and the threat of the independent voice to the socialist system during a time of growing disillusion with the Soviet Union. Ivan Varlet is making a class change. As he prepares to marry his bourgeois bride, the former mechanic casts off his socialist acquaintances and re-invents himself as 'Ivor Violet'. Before he can embark on his new life, however, a fire at the wedding kills all the guests, and sees Ivan trapped in the ice cellar, frozen into a state of cryogenesis. Fifty years later, after the creation of a global socialist state following a world war, Ivan is unfrozen into an unrecognisable Russia.

Age suitability: any age

Cast size:
many named characters,
plus chorus, plus songs

Book adapted by Snoo Wilson
from the play *The Bedbug*
by Vladimir Mayakovsky

Music by Gary Kemp and Guy Pratt

Lyrics by Snoo Wilson
with additional lyrics
by Gary Kemp and Guy Pratt

Snoo Wilson (1948–2013) was a founding director of the Portable Theatre, Brighton and London. During his career, he was script editor for the *Play for Today* series (BBC TV), dramaturg for the RSC, director of the Scarab Theatre and also taught film scriptwriting at the National Film School. In 1980 he was awarded a US/UK Bicentennial Fellowship and worked at Santa Cruz University and with the New York Theatre Studio in New York. In 1989 he was Associate Professor, lecturing in playwriting, at University College San Diego. With a writing career from the 1960s, his place as an important and distinguished playwright was confirmed in his many award-winning plays both in Britain and across America. He received the John Whiting Award in 1978 for *The Glad Hand*, the San Diego Theater Circle award in 1988 for *80 Days* and the Eileen Anderson/Central Broadcasting Premiere Award for *Best Night Out* for HRH. He wrote films, libretti, radio plays and two novels. His libretti include an acclaimed adaptation of Offenbach's *Orpheus in the Underworld* for the English National Opera and the book for *80 Days* at the La Jolla Playhouse in California.

Gary Kemp is one of the UK's most successful songwriters of the past thirty-five years. He is the guitarist and was a founder member of eighties band Spandau Ballet. He was responsible for writing the words and music of all of Spandau Ballet's twenty-three hit singles and albums, including modern-day standards like 'Gold' and 'True' as well as classics like 'Through the Barricade', 'Only When You Leave', 'To Cut a Long Story Short' and 'Chant No. 1'. After Spandau Ballet split up in 1990 he decided to return to acting, starring in numerous films including the British crime thriller *The Krays* and the Hollywood blockbuster *The Bodyguard*. He recorded an acclaimed solo album called *Little Bruises* and has written two musicals with Guy Pratt. In 2009 Spandau Ballet re-formed to successfully tour the world for the first time in nineteen years. In the same year Fourth Estate published his memoir, *I Know This Much*. In 2012 he was awarded the prestigious Outstanding Song Collection Award at the Ivor Novello Awards.

Guy Pratt was born in London in 1962, the son of songwriter/actor Mike Pratt. Internationally renowned as a bassist, Guy has performed and recorded with artists including Pink Floyd, Madonna, Michael Jackson, Tom Jones, Sophie Ellis Bextor, Roxy Music, Bryan Ferry, Robert Palmer, David Gilmour, Jimmy Page, Iggy Pop, The Pretenders, Echo and the Bunnymen, Lemon Jelly, Nathalie Imbruglia, All Saints, Bond, Elton John and McFly. He has co-written and produced songs for artists including; Pink Floyd, Robert Palmer, The Orb, Fat Les, Jimmy Nail, Marianne Faithful, Debbie Harry and Chris Difford, along the way picking up two Ivor Novello nominations and a Grammy. For TV he wrote scores for *Spaced*, *The Young Person's Guide to Becoming a Rock Star*, *Randall & Hopkirk (Deceased)*, *Linda Gree*, Dawn French's *Wild West* and Jimmy Nail's *Crocodile Shoes 2*. Documentaries include *Riddle of the Skies*, *The Roswell Incident*, *Terror in Texas*, *Gloria's Toxic Death* and *The Underboss*. For theatre he scored *The Remarkable Piety of the Infamous* (Baron's Court) and *Lena* by Carla Lane (Valley Theatre, Liverpool, and the Pleasance, Edinburgh). He was also Musical Director of *I Just Stopped by to See the Man* by Steohen Jeffreys (Royal Court).

Characters

Ivan Varlet, *also known as Ivor Violet, Party member,*
    former worker, now the fiancé of
Elzevir Bornagin, *manicurist and cashier of a beauty parlour*
Rosalie Bornagin, *her mother*
David Bornagin, *her father*
Zoya Byrioshka, *a working girl*
Oleg Bard, *an eccentric female life-stylist*
Vladimir Mayakovsky, *poet and narrator*

Market Vendors
Button Seller (m), **Doll Seller** (m), **Fruit Seller** (f),
Herring Seller (m), **Lampshade Seller** (f), **Bra Seller** (f)

Balloon Seller	**Hairdressers**
Bookseller	**Mechanics**
Barefoot Youth	**Reporters**
Second Youth	**Paperboys**
Inventor	**Girls**
Cleaner	**Zoo Director**
Intellectual Girl	**Workers**
Mechanic	**Chairman**
Best Man	**Orator**
Chief of Police	**High School Students**
Policemen	**Master of Ceremonies**
Professor	**Members of Presidium**
Zoo Director	*of City Soviet*
Fire Chief	**Children**
Revolutionary Firemen	**(Future) Man and Woman**
Future Firemen	**Vets**
Usher	**Historian**
Choreographed	**Zoo Keepers**
Stenographers	**Old People**
Doctors	**Animals**
Matron of Honour,	**Animated Voting Machine**

Prologue and Scene One

Screen, then exterior of Russian department store and market.

Enter the author, Mayakovsky, in an explosive fashion. Everything that Mayakovsky does is performed outsize. The wild-eyed, cloth-capped poet harangues the audience confidently, revolver in hand. He is wielding a pair of pistols, bursts through a screen which is showing a collage of Russian images from the twentieth century: everything from the storming of the Winter Palace to babushkas selling wooden Gorbachev dolls in Red Square and queues outside the Moscow McDonald's.

Mayakovsky
    'In my end is my beginning.' Who am I? A poet. Right.
    My first poem was 'Mayakovsky, a Tragedy',
    I am Vladimir Mayakovsky, come from the dead.
    Like other visitors from the nether world, my time here
        is brief.
    Relax, I explain everything. The only brains blown out
        tonight will be mine.
    For those who have not read their programmes yet
    This prologue is pronounced by the shade
    Of the former author – who long ago shot himself.
    Some say I, Mayakovsky, knew
    My time was up: Stalin was always behind a bad review.
    My advice to you is, enjoy tonight! It could be your last,
    Any artistic shock could be a trembling prelude to delight.

    The Bedbug, work of genius, begins in a street market after
        that false dawn of the assassination of the Tsar, the
        Russian Revolution ushering in
    A brief and comically deluded season of hope.
    Audience! Do your best. If not moved, pretend. To be alive
    Is not always to be sincere; unless you are a genius.
    You might say I foresaw
    The revolution would turn to ashes, and burnt straw.
    I left a note, to be found beside my brains. 'The love boat
        has crashed.'
    Hell's devils tell me it loses everything, in translation.

But they would, wouldn't they?
The poetic heart is subject to perturbation.
My love life was not in tip-top condition, plus
I was subject to arrest by Comrade Stalin
And the condemned man calls in vain for pen and paper.
I had a flair for gesture that enabled me to pinch out
My own deathless flame – and what can I tell you?
Darkness! No more taper.

Cue Prologue and 'The Sellers' Song'.

My pen, you will observe, skewers many hearts;
I wield it like a stake, to drive through the hypocritical left
    ventricle of all later Stalinist, Socialist-Realist, fear-
    beshitted so-called 'art'!
A glowing Futurist electron storm returns
To illuminate the tundra of the Russian soul!
I hereby conjure up before your eyes
A Russian state department store
In front of it here, a People's Market.
Begin my play, and
Unfold here, its lethal prophecy.

He fires pistols, and exits through broken screen. Scene begins. The cries of the street vendors all overlap in a scene-setting panorama. The sellers begin a market number, each pitching their wares, building the song to a choral crescendo.

THE SELLERS' SONG

Button Seller
    Dutch press studs,
    Dutch press studs,
    Better than buttons are Dutch press studs.
    Dutch press studs, Dutch press studs,
    Twenty-four-hour control. (*Repeats.*)

Doll Seller
    Dancing dolls, dancing dolls,
    Light as a feather are dancing dolls,

Dancing dolls, dancing dolls,
Ready and willing are dancing dolls. (*Repeats.*)

Fruit Seller
No kiwis, no melons,
We got socialist bananas,
Not twenty, not eighteen,
Fifteen's all I'm asking.
Bargain bananas
Are yours for the gobbling –
Put the best Russian manhood to shame! (*Repeats.*)

Herring Seller
Herrings! Non-Tsarist herrings!
And herrings! Republican herrings! (*Repeats.*)

Lampshade Seller
Lamspshades, lampshades! (*Repeats.*)

Bra Seller
Lovely brassieres trimmed with mink,
Ladies, you never seen anything like it.
Not just thermal, decorative too.
Be surprised what your husband'll do. (*Repeats.*)

Singing continues under dialogue. **Balloon Seller** *is making up animals with long thin balloons.*

Balloon Seller   What am I doing? I'll tell you. With these all-socialist balloons at five kopecks, you can make animals – see – like a sweet little post-monarchist sausage dog – you try.

He gives an untied balloon to a small boy. **Boy** *lets go and balloon deflates.*

Balloon Seller   You got to hold on tight to its arse. Have another try now. Thing is, even with with socialist balloons, it all whooshes out. That's right – whoops –

Balloon flies out of **Boy***'s hand again.*

Bookseller   Books, books. 'How to' books on all subjects. This one – special offer – *How to Commit Adultery*, a spicy rib-tickler by ex-Count Leo Tolstoy.

All

> A modern souk, a new bazaar,
> Though not the first, the best by far.
> You'll be surprised, you'll be amazed,
> Amazement is our stock in trade.
>
> You might presume the state provides,
> But you don't need to shop inside.
> Unless you take that foolish step,
> The choice is yours, selection wide.
>
> It's every Russian's right to choose
> State or private enterprise.
> We can obtain in any size
> If you supply a crate of booze.
>
> You want some cheese, you want a hat,
> A bit of this, a bit of that.
> A dream come true, we promise you –
> The marketplace is where it's at.
>
> Marxists all, in Marx we trust,
> He will prevail when we are dust.
> But even Lenin will admit,
> It's only fair to earn a crust.

Music fades under dialogue.

Enter **Varlet**, *his mother-in-law*, **Rosalie Pavlovna**, *and* **Oleg**.

Varlet   I say, look at these aristocratic nightcaps! Is it real fur?

Varlet *puts a bra from a stall on his head.*

Bra Seller   Real? Is this lovely fur real? Was Cleopatra a snake fancier? Feel that silkiness. It's from the inside legs of the animals. But there wasn't no suffering involved. These little minks were sleeping on silk, crammed with cream, before they finally sacrificed themselves for the Soviet people's comfort.

Rosalie   Comrade Violet, I wouldn't advise trying to put your head in one of those. There are two, see?

Varlet   Away with you, foolish creature. I always have two of everything that catches my fancy.

Rosalie   But they're not for your sort. They're for supporting parts of outstanding female Party members.

Varlet   What nonsense. After I marry your daughter Elzevir, these trinkets will dress what comes to pass.

Rosalie   Get away! You're not one of them cross-dressers, are you? And I thought he was an honest prole, not a decadent capitalist!

Varlet   I'm talking about what comes to pass exactly nine months after. I know they will make superior hats for your future grandchildren. They can put them on when they go out together in the park.

Rosalie   They'll have to be twins if they're going to put their two heads into one brassiere!

Varlet   Of course we'll have twins – because I am going to have two of everything I want in the future. It is written! You just have to read Comrade Marx.

Oleg   I think what the former Ivan Varlet, now known as Ivor Violet here, is doing is bringing an innocent proletarian eye to bear on everyday creations, and transforming their use-value with his incisive intelligence, don't you?

Rosalie   I didn't realise that union with the proletariat meant that my grandchildren will have to go round for ever with their heads crammed into one fur-trimmed brassiere as if they were Siamese twins.

Oleg   Rosalie, don't provoke His Working Classness – don't forget, with your kind of background, you need to get that HWC union card in your front room.

Doll Seller (*background*)   Dancing dolls, dancing dolls, light as a feather, ready and willing in all kinds of weather.

Oleg   If he wants two of everything, it's his by right! We've had the revolution, the proletariat are the men of the hour!

Varlet (*to* **Doll Seller**)   Hither, fellow. (*Examines dolls.*) 'The fruit of the proletarian loom must be able to step out of its cradling, into culture and elegance.'

Rosalie   You'd better have two of them, too, then.

Varlet   No. I don't just want two, I want a whole regiment of those.

Rosalie   But Comrade Violet!

Varlet   Don't comrade me in public till after the marriage. For now, you are still unredeemed bourgeoise, so watch what you say.

Oleg   How about Future Comrade as a correct form of address and you can call her future mother-in-law?

Rosalie   I take your point, Future Comrade Violet, but for the money we're spending, we could smarten up any number of your compatriots – shave and shampoo a dozen of the grottiest proles. If the wedding's going to go off with a bang, we're going to need to budget for some booze.

Varlet   Do you imagine I would forget to order drink? Of course not.

Oleg   That is so true! The trouser pockets of Future Comrade Violet, however repellent, contain within them the socialist horn-of-plenty! As the wedding is the promised union of the working and bourgeois classes, the Future Comrade has committed to several bottles of vodka already for the occasion.

Herring Man   Finest post-Tsarist herrings! Essential accompaniment to all kinds of vodka!

Rosalie (*brightening*)   You hear that? Salted herrings are the very thing for a wedding! Out of my way, young prole-gentleman. (*Looking.*) Oh dear, how disappointing.

Oleg   Let me carry them – I won't charge a penny –

Rosalie   How much do you want to get rid of these horrid little stunted sardines?

Herring Man   I can't let these salmon go at under two roubles sixty. They weigh a full kilo each.

Rosalie   Two-sixty for a piddling minnow like that?

Herring Man   That's no minnow, that's an apprentice sturgeon! Look at the fat on those gills!

Rosalie   Sturgeon? More like a twiglet fish.

Music stops.

Well, I'm not standing here arguing, we've had a revolution in case you haven't heard. I'm going to get some decent fish from the Soviet State Co-op!

Herring Man   Pull the other one!

Rosalie   Don't you try to stop me bypassing the private sector!

Exit **Rosalie**.

Herring Man   Go ahead, go on, see what they've got in there. It's rubbish. You'd be lucky to find a fish head that hasn't gone off.

Oleg   Oh, this is all so upsetting and unnecessary. Future Comrade Violet, why let your dear future mother-in-law get involved in tasteless street polemics when, if you refer to me, I can personally guarantee the most luxurious and stylish wedding that you'll ever have in your life! (*To* **Varlet.**) Fifteen roubles and a bottle of vodka, how about it?

Varlet   Others are going to be handling the petty-bourgeois details. I don't care to be involved.

Oleg   Alright, then have you thought of having your nuptials conducted along the lines of the ancient Rites of Eleusis? Eleusis of the ancient world, the fountain of our culture, where sacred drama and religion both drank from the same stream? We can reconstruct the rites for your ceremony. When the wedding procession advances, holding sheaves of corn in front of the bride, I will sing in praise of Hymen.

Varlet   Hymen? Hymen who?

Oleg   Hymen's the ancient goddess of marriage and fertility.

Varlet   No no. I want an honest to goodness modern Red wedding, with no decadent foreign trimmings.

Oleg   Then the wedding will obey our socialist dramatic unities – I refer to the coming unities, of class . . . let's see . . . a Red . . .

Romantic music begins.

We envision the red-dressed Red wife-to-be stepping out of her carriage as she arrives on the arm of the Red accountant, the universal proxy father-in-law, representing the state. She's looking pretty steamed up, but he's ooh, red as a beetroot. And then the Red red groom is ushered in by the Red ushers, and the red tablecloth is covered with bowls of steaming borscht and juicy red hams.

Music stops.

How does that envision for a start?

Varlet   I like it. How does it go on?

Enter **Zoya**, *circles them suspiciously.*

Oleg   Very well.

Music begins again.

The blushing guests tear the red red tops off the vodka bottles with sweaty fingers and pour the proper vodka down their red throats, and when they look down at you again to draw breath, they shout, 'Kiss, kiss!' and your brand new encarminated red-hot spouse with her tongue weaving like a red cobra inside her mouth comes towards you closer and closer till her panting embouchure closes succulently on your own rosy face sphincter, sploosh! – recipe for mutual rapture. All taking place exactly as modernity stipulates, in a divinely atheistic ambience, you note.

Zoya Just a minute. Ivan!

Music stops abruptly.

What's this old cow going on about? What wedding? Who's getting married?

Varlet Nothing's happened yet, Zoya. But as clear as the recent triumph of the working class, we cannot continue our romantic acquaintance.

Zoya Why not? What are you two talking about?

Varlet Nothing that concerns the objects of my previous affections.

Oleg We are discussing the impending rubicund nuptials between Elzevir Davidovna Bornagin, and this eminently titled prole-gentleman here, His Working Classness Ivor Violet.

Zoya His name is plain Ivan Varlet, and he is engaged to me! Or was. What's going on? What about me, Ivan?

Varlet Ivan? Who he? Ivan exists only in memory. Enter Ivor, the new man!

VARLET'S SONG

So sorry, Zoya,
If I destroy ya

Hopes for the future, but you're an annoyance.
Class credentials take a battering,
Pinstriped pants prove more flattering.

All (*except* **Zoya**)
The bourgeoisie's the new norm,
This is how proles should reform.

Varlet
Ivan is dreaming his dream of advancement,
Turning his previous fiancée down flat.
Changing his name, his cap for a top hat,
Drink up to that, brothers, drink up to that.

All (*except* **Zoya**)
Destiny beckons and Ivan's arising,
He's got the bridegroom's right answer down pat –
I do, I do, and the bride says, I do too,
Drink up to that, brothers, drink up to that.

The bourgeoisie's the new norm,
This is how proles should reform.

Varlet
Call me a fool, say that I will fall hard
But the ace in this game is my red Party card.

Zoya
Dumped at the altar – world-shattering,
No thought for me, not a smattering.
Carry on joking and chattering,
This poor heart's taking a battering.

All (*except* **Zoya**)
The bourgeoisie's the new norm,
This is how proles should reform.

Ivan is dreaming his dream of advancement,
Turning his previous fiancée down flat.
Changing his name, his cap for a top hat,
Drink up to that, brothers, drink up to that.

Destiny bekons and Ivan's arising,
He's got the bridegroom's right answer down pat –
I do, I do, and the bride says, I do too,
Drink up to that, brothers, drink up to that.

Varlet
I do, I do, and the bride says, I do too,
Drink up to that, brothers, drink up to that.

Zoya   You're not that different!

Varlet   I am too! Ivan drank like a fish, as if his life depended on it, and his wretched guitar was the extent of his cultural horizons. He's gone, I have disinvented him.

Music stops.

Zoya   Ivan! You once said Ivan and Zoya belonged together for ever, like pork and beans!

Varlet   That wretch Ivan would say anything to have his way with a girl.

Zoya   Ivan – you once said our hearts beat as one. And that we would work for the good of our class together for ever . . . Don't tell me it's over, Ivan.

Varlet   Our former love which you wish me to recall has been liquidated, citizen. I shall summon the people's trusty law enforcers if you try to obstruct my heart's new direction with your plebeian fisticuffs. All that is behind me.

Re-enter **Rosalie**.

Rosalie   The bleeding fishmonger was right, the fish I saw in there are even smaller . . . (*Sees* **Zoya**.) Just a minute, what's going on? Who's this little slut?

Rosalie *starts to pull* **Zoya**, *who is holding on to* **Varlet**. *A crowd gathers, cheering.*

Zoya   Piss off! Who are you?

Rosalie   Has she got her hooks into you, Future Comrade Ivor? Piss off yerself, you little tart, he's going to be my son-in-law!

Zoya   His fate is tied to mine. Irreversibly.

Rosalie   Aha! You mean you're pregnant and you want money. Alright, fair's fair, I'll pay you off here and now.

Zoya   You lot can only think of money!

Rosalie   Not true! When I've paid you off I'm going to split your nostril in the bargain, you little slut. Come here!

Cue:

THE POLICEMAN'S SONG

Police
   Citizens! Please stop this ugly scene!
   Admit the law must throw itself between.
   We arrest every action underhand
   And if you're drunk we'll put you in the can.
   Citizens! Please stop this ugly scene.

Girls
   Now we know there is no God
   Post-revolutionary mode.

Boys
   We seek the higher things in life,
   Come with us up the red red road . . .

Transformation to:

Scene Two

Grubby dormitory of unhygenic hostel for young inner-city workers.

Barefoot Youth *screams and runs around.*

Barefoot Youth   Oi! Me grass shoots!

Intellectual Girl Yer wot?

Barefoot Youth Some capitalist swine's nicked me daisy roots again! The last time, I tried to leave 'em in hand luggage at the railway station, last thing, but they say they won't take anything that ripe. What am I supposed to do, sleep with the effing cheesers on?

Cleaner I meant to tell you. Ivan Varlet's borrowed them to see that bourgeois cow he's going to get hitched with. He was effing and blinding trying to get them on.

Barefoot Youth I'll effing blind him if he ruins 'em, the poxy class traitor! What does he think he's doing in my shoes?

Cleaner Moving up the social ladder!

Barefoot Youth Can you see it working out? I know he's trying to improve, you just have to look at all the crap he leaves around – before it was old sardine tins and empty beer bottles and dog-ends, now it's bottles of aftershave in amazingly poncy wrapping paper. Effing ponce.

Cleaner Now now, stop that or the warden'll –

Barefoot Youth Ponce, ponce, that's what all class traitors are.

Intellectual Girl Class traitor, arse traitor. Just because he's got a flash new tie an' gear you're going on like he was a poncing enemy of the people.

Barefoot Youth He is a poncy bloody enemy of the people. I'm the people, aren't I? I told him not to take my boots and look what he done. But you know, he's not going to fool anyone into thinking he's not still a prole. He's so thick, when he tightens his tie, it stops any blood getting to his brain at all.

Inventor He seems to have reinvented himself. Seen this box of calling cards? (*Shows them round.*)

All (*mocking*) Ivor Violet! Wooooo!

Displays of extravagant and contemptuous mirth. **Inventor** *takes bottle of aftershave.*

Barefoot Youth   'Ere, are you nicking that?

Inventor   'Ivor Violet' won't need aftershave. He sounds like he smells good enough already! I'm sure I could use it in one of my inventions.

Barefoot Youth   Leave it, mate, it's got class contamination written all over it! Go on, pour it away!

Intellectual Girl   You can mock, but he's started a one-man cultural revolution in the domestic sphere, from right here in the hostel! He's made an effort to change himself.

Barefoot Youth   I agree he's recently been smarming this horrible-smelling stuff all over his sideboards. They hang off the side of his face like something nasty off a dog's behind. No wonder they call 'em buggers' grips.

Inventor (*surprised*)   Oh, is that why sideboards was invented? There's a reason for everything in this world.

Intellectual Girl   Lotsa movie stars have sideburns now.

Barefoot Youth   But Ivan's not a movie star. He makes steering wheels. He's a factory mechanic, third-class!

Enter greasy **Mechanic.**

Mechanic   Not any more. That's all in the past. Comrade Ivan Varlet came in and chucked his job in today. I saw him as he was leaving the gates. Said factory work was incompatible with his new life and new wife.

Intellectual Girl   Who is this lucky girl, then?

Barefoot Youth   Not you, obviously.

Intellectual Girl   Piss off! Just cos I'm not against him for trying to better himself! I'm curious, that's all!

Mechanic   A posh hairdresser's daughter is what he's landed. Yep. The poodle-fancying class, hearing a genuine card-carrying member of the proletariat was available, threw out a lure, and the lucky girl is reeling her prize in now. She'll sort his new side-whiskers out for free in the salon by day, and then, come the night, his proletarian short an' curlies will get a seeing-to. From any angle, Ivan will be unrecognisable.

Intellectual Girl   Lucky for him.

Mechanic   Yeah, but it doesn't alter the fact that marriage across class lines is deeply decadent. Take me for instance. I'm a socialist. To build a new state, with occupations and living space for everyone, I know you gotta stick to your guns.

Barefoot Youth   The war's over. It stopped being 1917 a while back. The revolution's finished, dad! Anyone who can afford it can get as many new pairs of shiny shoes as they like!

Enter **Oleg** *and* **Ivan**, *who is wearing new shoes and clothes.* **Ivan** *throws the boots to* **Barefoot Youth**.

Barefoot Youth   Thanks for nuffin'!

Oleg   The new couture is the middle, not the end of the transformation. We need a dancing lesson to accompany your striking new outfit. Meinheer Ivor will complete the schooling for admission to your new class. We'll do it right here in the hostel. Music, ho!

Dance music.

When you leave this squalid boarding house for your red wedding, you will truly have been transformed into a new graceful creature. Head up now. Now, follow my instructions. At the nuptial climax of your modern wedding, the seductive rhythm of the foxtrot will insinuate itself into the guests' consciousness. And we will all . . . step out onto the dance floor!

Varlet   These new shoes are playing Old Harry with my corns. Can't I take them off?

Oleg   Certainly not! This rehearsal should be in full dress. Step up, sir, imagine your bride-to-be standing here and one, two, three and off!

Varlet *dances.*

Barefoot Youth   Class traitor!

Oleg   Very nicely, sir! Now, Monsignor Violet, the moon is riding high, filling your soul with longing and passion – the night-scented stock fills the air with heavy perfume, and what are you doing? Imagine you are weaving dreamily back from a well-stocked taverna. The Rites of Eleusis were always concluded with a dance. Don't wiggle your rear end, you're supposed to be leading your lovely partner, not carrying a sack of spuds. Too high! Watch that hand!

Varlet   It won't stay up!

Oleg   Alright, well, just locate the lovely lady's brassiere, and hook your thumb in it; easy for you, and it's very pleasant for the lady too. Now you can experiment with the other arm. What on earth are you doing with your shoulders?

Ivan*'s dance gets wilder and wilder.*

Oleg   That's not a foxtrot. It's something greater! You have a talent and no mistake. You're too big for this country! You should break into Europe and astonish them all! Beyond socialism! The song of the body beautiful! More, more! Encore! Bravo! Magnificent!

Varlet *falls over. Music stops.*

Oleg   The Moulin Rouge will never be the same when you've conquered Paris! But I must go and finish the preparations – if I don't keep the ushers off the booze we'll never get there. Tuck your shirt inside your trousers but not inside the underpants. (*Makes to leave, turns.*) That is, if you have underpants . . .

She leaves.

Barefoot Youth   Oy, dog's dinner! What's going on then?

Varlet   Etiquette would say, none of your business, respected Comrade. But I will tell you. I have fought for the good life, and I have won. Furthermore, I'm doing my class, the proletariat, a favour by raising the average standard of living. What do you say to that?

Gunshot, offstage followed by a commotion. They all look off. Enter **Second Youth**.

Second Youth   'Ere! You know Zoya, Ivan Varlet's rejected fiancée? Well, she gone all demented with romantic woe and shot herself! I don't know how she's going to explain herself at the next Party meeting!

Voices   Help! First aid! Help! First Aid!

Zoya *is carried in by an excited crowd.*

Man   Someone phone for an ambulance!

Mechanic   There's no phone here!

Crowd (*enthusiastic*)   Find a phone! Emergency! Find a phone! Emergency! Find a phone! Emergency! Emergency!

Crowd exits, leaving **Zoya** *on the floor. Music stops.*

Man   Missed the heart, thank God – only shot herself through the tits! Did they say you knew her?

Varlet   I knew her once, but my past is behind me.

He steps over **Zoya** *and comes downstage to hail cab.*

Varlet   Cabbie! Seventeen Lunacharsky Street, otherwise known as Hairdresser Hall. Don't forget my baggage! Farewell to poverty, lice and cheap propaganda – (*As he exits.*) Hello to relaxed summer evenings with trivial chatter upon the veranda.

Exits, leaving **Mechanic** *alone with body of* **Zoya**. **Mechanic** *kneels, weeping, to hold her hand. The crowd comes back and surrounds them.*

Mechanic   Don't die, my love!

Zoya (*faintly*)   To think I tried to kill myself over a greasy worthless jerk like Ivan. There's nothing stupider than misplaced love.

Mechanic   I know what you mean. (*Cloth cap off, hand on heart, he sings.*)

THE MECHANIC'S SONG

The road towards Utopia
Is paved with blood and stone.
There's many with me, comrades,
I know I'm not alone.
The godless Party promises
A heaven for our eyes,
But who will pay for this?
We're paying with our lives.

We've been building a road to a better world
For nigh on seven years,
But now the mists have moved away
To show the path we steer –
The road to Utopia leads straight to a wall,
And our work was in vain,
'Cos the wall don't want us,
The wall don't us,
The wall don't want us at all.

See how sleek our masters get
While we sit in our dirt and sweat.
Still it isn't finished yet,
Our Utopia.
Our Utopia.

Hark to what our masters said,
'Swing your hammer, swing with dread.
Hit that rivet on the head.'
But the dream will fall,
But the dream will fall.

And the wall don't want us,
The wall don't want us,
The wall don't want us at all.

Scene Three

A beauty parlour for a Red wedding.

Onstage: **Varlet, Oleg** (*Mistress of Ceremonies*), **Elzevir** *and* **Rosalie Bornagin**, **Best Man** (*accountant*), **Matron of Honour** (*accountant's wife*), **Hairdressers** *and* **Mechanics**.

Elzevir   I think we could start, Ivor darling, don't you?

Varlet   Not so fast!

Elzevir   What's the matter? Don't you want to get married after all?

Varlet   You bourgies have a thing or two to learn about protocol in this new world! On these important occasions of inter-class mingling, protocol has to be strictly observed. In addition to the Best Man, the accountant, and Matron of Honour, his regularly fulfilled wife, the Secretary of the Committee of our glorious steering-wheel factory has graciously accepted our invitation. And look, here he comes!

A guest runs in holding a memo.

Elzevir   Oh, is Mr Steering-Wheel the guest of honour? Some sort of super-prole? I see. Alright, I'm sure that will be convenient.

Varlet   Deigning graciously to illuminate our nuptials with his working-class brilliance and repartee – the highest representative of socialised motor vehicle assembly, Comrade Lassalchenko! (*Pause.*) But you're not Comrade Lassalchenko, are you?

Guest   Party greetings and apologies for absence from Comrade Lassalchenko's message reads – (*Reads.*) 'Tomorrow I can go anywhere – even into a church. Today, however is a

Party day, and like it or lump it, I have to report to my Party committee in full.' Message ends. (*Exits.*)

Varlet   So that's that. Apologies having been tendered, we should move on to the next item on the agenda.

Opens champagne bottle and sprays it over **Elzevir***.*

Elzevir   Just a minute – what sort of celebration is this? You're ruining my dress!

Varlet   I hereby declare this wedding – open!

Cheers and the guests rush for the food.

Rosalie   Comrades, proles, nuptial sponsors of the hour from all sexes – please help yourselves from the generous buffet. I've been saving the ham for a rainy day ever since the end of the war. It's impossible to find porkers tasting like they do nowadays. They just don't feed piggies the right food.

A musical interlude, during which everyone eats furiously.

Best Man   Next item – drink!

All stop eating, rush to drinks, take and raise bottles. Music stops.

Best Man   And now, the smooch that proclaims the twin fleshes one inseparable for ever more till divorce do 'em part!

All   Kiss! Kiss!

Elzevir *and* **Varlet** *kiss.*

All   Kiss! Kiss!

Elzevir *kisses* **Varlet** *with passion. He returns kisses stolidly.*

Best Man   We witness here the historic embrace of the broad masses, by the bourgeois! C'mon let's hot it up! We Russians know how to celebrate –

Oleg   Now about this union we are celebrating. I predict it will be a reconciliation of the two classes and all their inherent contradictions, for ever and a day.

Applause.

All   Kiss – kiss!

Oleg   And there's something about this union that we should not forget when we see a twinkle in both the bride and groom's eye. I predict we will soon hear the patter of tiny feet around the beauty salon! Tiny socialist hands raised to be manicured! What is happening here is the rebirth of family life which over the years has been so damaged by the economic savagery of the marketplace.

Guest   Shut up, you old windbag. Get them to kiss!

All   Kiss! Kiss!

Oleg   Not Marx, not Engels, could have dreamed in a thousand years that what we are witnessing could ever take place – Labour and Capital together. What a winning combination! Neither lived to see the heroic class, then obscure, if promising, rise up and seize the reins of history. They never dreamt that in a dramatic development, the conquering hero, Labour would take such a shine to Capital – now dethroned but clearly, enduringly alluring.

Usher   Who's that trying to make off with a case of vodka over there! Come back!

Guest   I was just putting it somewhere safe, honest.

Oleg   Well spotted, comrade usher. But no need to bust a blood vessel, just get everyone to relax – (*Calls out.*) Attention please, everyone!

Guests finally fall silent as **Usher** *holds the vodka-thief* (**Best Man**) *by the lapels.*

Usher   You're one of those bleeding bourgies, aren't you?

The two sides – **Hairdresser***s and* **Mechanics** *– divide and square up for a fight.*

Oleg   People, listen to me! We shouldn't be getting snooty about occupations! 'She's a hairdresser and he's a mechanic, so they can't get on!' One look at the bride and groom would dispel that nonsense. (*To bride and groom.*) I think that if the hairdressers could all find a mechanic to demonstrate their art on, then both classes will discover exactly why the bride and groom are going to live happily ever after.

A pairing off of hairdressers and mechanics, mutually suspicious. Tension. The hairdressers begin to do the mechanics' hair, against their wishes.

THE HAIRDRESSERS' SONG

Oleg

There's a class of persons present, maligned, misunderstood,
Who in this dawning new age can still do simple good.
I sing in praise of hairdressers all around the world –
It's an international movement –
Let's hear it for them, girls!

Hairdressers

We like to chat a little bit, it helps us pass the hours,
You won't believe the stories that we hear under the dryers.
Oh, don't you think we raise the tone
And we deserve a union of our own.
Don't you think we raise the tone
And we deserve a union of . . .

Oleg

Hairdressers can change a woman's thoughts about herself,
Her hair done right, she'll never stay fore'er upon the shelf.
Why should Mother Nature rule and make us all unchanged?
Now the revolution's come, dear,
Men! don't be ashamed.

Hairdressers

Admittedly beside the gossip other passion pales.
We follow fashion fearlessly
And do each other's nails.
Attending weddings is our bliss,
We'll give the bride a loving kiss.
Oh, don't you think we raise the tone
And we deserve a union of our own?
Don't you think we raise the tone
And we deserve a union of our own?

Don't you think we raise the tone
And we deserve a union of our own?

The **Mechanics** *fight off the* **Hairdressers**. *Brawls break out.
A stove is knocked over and smoke starts to fill the stage. Smoke increases.
The* **Hairdressers** *are winning, pinning* **Mechanics** *down in the
mêlée to perm their hair with monstrous combs and spraycans of lacquer,
as the stage darkens and pandemonium breaks out.*

All (*variously*)   Kiss! Kiss! / Where's the bride and groom – /
Can't see them – / We're on fire! / Who said fire? / Fire
brigade! – It's out of control! / Heeelp!

Conflagration. The fire roars. Blackout.

Scene Four

Outside the burnt-out beauty parlour.

Firemen *inspect rows of charred corpses. Enter* **Fire Chief**, *with
further group of* **Firemen**, *officials.*

Fire Chief   Alright, what's going on? Twelve hours I hear
it took you to come to a blazing hairdresser's salon. Twelve
hours, from ten streets away. You lot should have rescued at
least some of these hapless folk, innocently celebrating what
was to have been the happiest day in the life of the bridegroom.

Fireman 1   There was nothing we could do, Chief. Like,
when we arrived, the whole bleeding place was like an oil
refinery. Vodka musta been feeding the flames.

Fireman 2   What a bloody barbecue, eh?

Fire Chief   But a hundred per cent casualties! It's not
going to look good in the records. Dear oh dear. We better do
an inventory. What have we got here, anyway?

*They review the corpses, pulling back the shrouds and dropping them in
place again.*

Fireman 1   One bod, bonce all spoiled, probably falling
beam . . .

Fireman 3   One charred bod, sex NK, hairdressing tongs in hand . . .

Fireman 4   One female bod, with wire thingummyjig fried tight on her upper bonce.

Fire Chief   Spare us the details, sonny. I've just had me tea.

Fireman 2 *gives charred notes to* **Fire Chief.**

Fireman 2   One, back of the site, criminal and pre-revolutionary build, was found with a cash register in his hands.

Fire Chief *(pockets notes)*   Something for the firemen's ball at last. Check the cellar too.

Fireman 2   Can't get down there. It filled up with our water straight off, and froze solid. We did manage to rescue this.

Fire Chief *examines a blackened box, then opens it. It is a case of vodka. Bottles of vodka from the case are handed out to* **Firemen***, and they line up for their drinking song.*

Fire Chief   What you see when you clear up afterwards is enough to drive anyone to drink. But I'm amazed you lot can even take any more. You were all pissed out of your heads when you left the fire station and drove off the wrong way!

THE FIREMEN'S SONG

Fire Chief
  Traditional! The marriage feast
  Which ends in Armageddon,
  It's quite surprising anyone survives
  A Russian weddin'.
  And you firemen are so legless
  That you cannot point a hose.
  Proof alcohol's a killer, avoid the dreaded dose!

Hear my dreadful warning, people,
Hear it loud and clear –
With each and every cork that pops
Rehearse it in your ear.
If you like a drink you well may think
That it won't end in tears,
But you're risking full combustion
When your liver changes gear.

Firemen

Oy! Oy! The red-nosed fireman strives in vain
To douse the flames
(We cannot get the ladder up,
We call each other names.)
Oy! Oy! It's never too late to celebrate!
As the flames go higher, the flames go higher,
What was once a bride and groom
Becomes a funeral pyre.

Ding dong, the bells all clang, emergency,
We're coming soon
(But if at first we don't arrive
You still can hear our tune.)
Ding dong, it's best to drown your sorrows first.
As the flames go higher, the flames go higher.
What was once a bride and groom
Becomes a funeral pyre!
Om tiddly om tiddly om, oy! oy! (*Repeats.*)

They exit. Enter **Mayakovsky**, *with pistol.*

Mayakovsky   It is I, Mayakovsky. With a wedding that
leaves Ivan in a state of cryogenic suspension, he is forgotten
for half a century as socialism re-engineers men's souls and
the promised Utopian world paradise is forged.

Shoots pistol. Music stops.

On, to 1975!

Scene Five

Futuristic conference hall with crazy Futurist electronic voting system.

Old worker and his apprentice are polishing bits of machinery feebly.

Old Man   It's a vital vote, this one today, young shaver. Oil the Agricultural Zone's voting apparatus. We don't want no little mistakes again.

Youth   Yeah the Central Zones were a bit off as well, and the Smolensk apparatus was coughing a bit.

Old Man   Are we forgetting, sonny, that all this grew from a socialist blueprint? Everything works, more or less. Just needs a drop of oil. Urals factories are go, Kursk metalworks sections is spanking new with sealed bearings. Runs with 'all the smoothness of a military operation'.

Youth   I thought you must remember military operations, Vlad, 'cos you're so bloody Jurassic and wrinkly.

Old Man   Nah. I was a baby when they had the revolution. I'm not that old. I do remember in the old days, just after the revolution, people voting by hand. My mother had to hold me in her arms. And the whole hall was filled with a thousand and one people, and there was all this argy-bargy, and they was split down the middle, exactly on the vote. My mother couldn't vote, of course, she was carrying me in her arms and this stopped her.

Youth   That could never happen now with this modern voting equipment.

Old Man   Exactly. In the old days, some people stood at the back and waved a cut-out and pretended they had twelve hands; that can't happen nowadays.

Enter **Orator**.

Old Man   Here comes the President of the Institute for Resurrection. I say!

Youth   What's he doing here?

Old Man   I'd guess there must be something of great national importance to be made public in the resurrection department! What can it be?

Orator   Citizen functionary mechanic and apprentice – plug in the interactive response registers for all the federation zones! We have an urgent consensus to hold.

Old Man *and* **Youth** *hurry to their places.*

Old Man   Yes suh! Green Register go!

Young Man   Green Register on!

Old Man   Red Register on!

Young Man   Red Register go. All systems go!

Orator   Testing testing. One, one, one.

Old Man   Test transmission verified, President, transmission commencing forthwith!

Orator (*coughs, announces*)   Now hear this! At the corner of 62nd Street and 17th Prospect in the town of Tambov, a building brigade working at a depth of seven metres has unearthed an ice-filled cellar of a previous building. Visible in the midst of the ice is a free-floating, frozen human figure. In the opinion of the Institute for Human Resurrection, this individual, who froze to death very rapidly in the immediate post-revolutionary era, could be reactivated. This motion has been circulated by telegram and discussed and we will now proceed to register the different opinions on this proposal. Remember, the Institute for Resurrection reminds you that the life of every worker must be used until the last possible instant. What we have found is definitely a worker – the hands are callused, and this is the distinguishing mark of workers around the decade of his entombment. I would also remind you that after the wars that swept over the world, and led to the creation of our World Federation, human life was declared inviolable by decree. But we should note the objections to resuscitation, from members of the Institute of

Prevention of Disease, who fear a renaissance of many of the bacilli and bacteria known once to have infested the inhabitants of what was formerly Russia. But remember, comrades, I cannot emphasise this too strongly, we are voting for a human life here!

Lights, bells, buzzers.

In order to further anthropo-cum-archaeological comparative studies into the age in question, the Resurrection Institute itself votes for resurrection! (*He reads message.*) 'A warning from the sanitary inspection stations in the Don Basin. The hazard to humankind of reviving these archaic bacteria is great, so the sample must remain in a deep frozen state for ever!'

Hubbub.

The Siberian Agricultural Zones request that the defrosting indeed take place, but only after harvest in the autumn so that the Tractorate, who have naturally all heard of the monster on their cab radios while harvesting, can be witnesses to this prodigious event. I can take no more amendments, before voting. All in favour of immediate action, raise hands!

A forest of steel hands goes up.

Voting on the Siberian amendment?

Two hands only.

The Assembly of the Federation hereby accepts the motion for full and immediate resuscitation.

All   Resurrection! Resurrection! Resurrection NOW!

Stage floods with **Reporters**. *They speak, overlapping, in great haste and urgency.*

Reporter   Eskimo *Isvestia*? Clear the front page. It's resurrection!

Second Reporter   Vladivostok *Pravda* – news desk. Conference has voted for resuscitation – pictures by wire to follow –

Third Reporter   Berlin and Warsaw *Komsol Pravda* – Resurrection confirmed as predicted –

Fourth Reporter   Chicago Soviet *Isvestia* – it's go for resurrection –

Fifth Reporter   *Red Gazette* of Rome – resurrection gets green light –

Sixth Reporter   Shanghai *Weekly Pigeon-Fancier* – it's go for resurrection –

Seventh Reporter   Los Angeles *Weekly Embalmer* – shock horror decision on near-corpse. Ex-guitarist to swear and smoke again.

THE REPORTERS' SONG

First Reporter
Despite the risks, it's been decreed,
Early man is to be freed.
Will he be vermin free?
Tune in tomorrow to know. (*Repeats.*)

Second Reporter
This just in! This just in!
We're witness to history! This just in! (*Repeats.*)

Third Reporter
The state has decided,
Although he's retarded,
Homo vulgaris, with archaic virus,
Suspended in block-ice,
This Cro-Magnon man
May put our best Russian bridegrooms to shame. (*Repeats.*)

Fourth Reporter
Danger, ignoring the danger.
Danger, from yesterday's stranger. (*Repeats.*)

Fifth Reporter
Bedbug bovver-boys, booze and vice!
We'll be bringing you an exclusive.

Read it first in *Izvest-ia* . . .
He may just be your caviar! (*Repeats.*)

Newsboys *come on with papers.*

Newsboys   Resurrection!
                              Resurrection!
                                          Resurrection!
                                                      Resurrection!

All

Our brave new world will set him free,
The white heat of technology.
When he awakes this will all seem
The perfect futuristic dream.

Science shows us how to feel,
How to vote and how to heal.
Science plays the starring role –
Reanimates the humble prole.

As they sing, **Zoya**, *much older, comes on and buys a paper, reads the news.*

Zoya   Oh no! They can't be! They're bringing him back to life! No! No!

Screams.

Scene Six

The defrosting chamber at the Institute for Resurrection.

Zoya *is waving her newspaper at the* **Professor**, *who is working in the central cryogenic unit with a huge frozen ice-block which can be seen to contain* **Varlet**.

Zoya (*panting*)   Comrade! Comrade Professor! Don't go through this! Don't pull the lever or the bleeding shenanigans will start all over again.

Professor   Shenanigans . . .? Comrade Zoya, in your excitement you appear to have slipped back into a language unknown to today's scientists. Excuse me. (*Takes up dictionary.*)

Zoya   Oh, you know what I mean!

Professor   I'm afraid to say I don't. Modern life has a very different language, and we have no use for these old words. Slobberchops . . . Shibboleth . . . Here we are. Shenanigans. 'Useless occupation or activity that prevents anything being done.'

Zoya   Exactly! Fifty years ago, this 'shenanigans' which you are about to unfreeze caused me to attempt suicide!

She mimes shooting herself, graphically.

Professor   Suicide? What's that? You've got me guessing again, comrade. (*Dictionary.*) Suppositious . . . Swabber   . . . Suppository . . . Suspender . . . (*Pause.*) Suicide. (*Reads.*) Oh dear. I suppose they were turbulent times in those days, and we understand there were injustices. Did you try to shoot yourself after receiving a court order from a misguided tribunal, perhaps?

Zoya   No. I acted entirely alone.

Professor   Then it must have been an accident. It is irrational to end life before it stops being of use to the Party.

Zoya   I acted out of disappointed love, comrade.

Professor   Oh, that is impossible. It is well known that love for the Party means we have children and railway bridges and tractors, and so forth.

Zoya   I can't stay if you continue with the reverse cryogenic programme.

Professor   But I can't let you go, if you know it! There is specialised information which we in the Party may need from you to ensure his survival. To survive the trauma of awakening after all these years.

Zoya   I think I am going to try and kill myself again.

Professor   I beg you to submerge your personal feelings for the good of the Party.

Zoya   He's going to be extremely dangerous to bring back. All the vodka inside him could ignite when you run the defrosting current through him.

Professor *goes to phone.*

Professor   Good point. People's Fire Brigade? Prepare to saturate Resuscitation Room 451 area with carbon dioxide.

Zoya   What's so wonderful that's he's got that needs to be brought back?

The **Firemen***, completely modernised with extinguishers, all arrive at the back, at the double, very brisk and efficient. They each squirt the room with a quick test-blast of carbon dioxide from their extinguishers.*

Professor   The past, comrade, is a puzzle that modern socialism seeks to explore, for the further enlightenment of mankind.

Switch on the current when I say.

Doctor   Alternating current standing by.

Professor   Now!

Bring up the temperature to 98.6 Fahrenheit with fifteen-second bursts.

Doctor   Fifteen seconds and counting!

Professor   Have the oxygen ready.

Doctor   Surgical oxygen cylinder and mask ready to go!

Professor   Replace the ice with air pressure as you draw off the melt-water, and I want a full description for the Institute of every physical change he goes through –

Choreographed Stenographers*, taking down the narrative.*

Sixth Doctor   Natural colour returning . . . Subject
appears almost ice-free . . . Chest movement now perceptible!
But some very unusual manual spasms now apparent!

Professor   That's a trapped sensory-reflex from the time
he was frozen. Musical, probably: unimportant. They had
things which they used to strum with one hand like that,
didn't they?

Zoya   Oh no, he's coming back with his bloody guitar as
well!

First Doctor   Temperature 98.6.

Second Doctor   Pulse is 68 per minute.

Sixth Doctor   Breathing regular.

Professor   Stand back, gentlemen! Observe the triumph of
science!

Varlet *comes to life, dishevelled. He rises up, clutching his guitar,
bending over it, retuning it, croaking along in a broken, cracked voice.*

Varlet
   The party went over the top,
   Then someone musta shouted stop . . . (*Twang.*)

I think we're in a police station, me old guitar! I musta have
slept it off. I'm starting to feel rough.

   I'd prefer by far to be in a bar. (*Twang.*)

The **Firemen** *surround him and put an end to the song with a burst of
dry ice. Music stops.*

Professor   Comrade Neanderthal, this is not a police
station.

Varlet *faces* **Professor**.

Varlet   What?

Professor   Drunk tanks are no longer necessary. This is
Reverse Cryogenic Room 451 in the Institute for

Resurrection where specimens can be thawed out under scientific conditions.

Varlet   Specimens? I'm a person – I've got documents to prove it! Come off it! You're pissed! You're all pissed! I know doctors – they're never far from the surgical spirit, and – it's glug, glug, glug all the time with them . . . what's the date?

Professor   The tenth day of the revolutionary month Blossomy.

Varlet   Not Blossomy, already? I musta been asleep for . . . What year is it then?

Professor   Revolutionary year fifty-nine!

Varlet   You're kidding. Don't tell me it's fifty-nine years . . .

Professor   That's exactly what we are telling you.

Varlet   Oh no! I'd better get the wife a bunch of flowers. She's going to be really pissed off.

Professor   You do not have a wife, specimen.

Varlet   I don't have a wife?! Look, here's my marriage certificate. (*Searches.*) Oh no! Where the bloody hell is it? I can't find it –

Doctor   What's it doing now?

Varlet*'s hands go in and out of pockets faster and faster, trying to find the documents. Two* **Doctors** *move forward with a straitjacket and try to put it on* **Varlet**.

Varlet   Oy! Lemme alone, you wankers!

Professor   Dictionary again, please!

Varlet *frees himself from the jacket and throws it down.*

Varlet   There's a woman out there, waiting for me – She's been waiting there for fifty years!

Professor   The creature acts as if still trapped in fantasy. Comrade Zoya, see if you can obtain the animal's trust, alone.

Zoya *steps forward to be recognised by* **Varlet**. *He stares at her. The rest of the* **Doctors** *and the* **Professor** *step back.*

Varlet   Who's this? Just a minute, don't I know you?

Lighting change: 'The Loveboat Theme'

Zoya *and* **Varlet** *approach each other.*

Varlet   Blow me down, it's got to be the ex-girlfriend's mother. If not you're the spitting image –

Zoya   Fifty years have passed, comrade.

Varlet   You're not Zoya, are you?

Zoya   Yes, I am Zoya. I was Zoya. What a fool Zoya was to care about you.

Varlet   Tell me it's not fifty years on.

Zoya   Find out for yourself.

Music stops. **Zoya** *throws open a huge door, and traffic noise and fumes pour in and fill the stage.* **Varlet**, *dazzled by the light, peers out into the new world.*

Varlet   There's not a horse in sight. Cars, cars, cars! It's inhuman! Where am I? What's going on? Is this Moscow, Paris or New York?

The door closes, and the noise and fumes die away abruptly.

Zoya   You'll never survive in the modern world. They should never have unfrozen you.

Varlet   That's a cruel thing to say, Zoya. But then you always had a cruel, sarcastic side to you.

Zoya   Cruel? I was the one who was given the push by you! (*Exits.*)

Varlet   I don't know what I remember any more. This is all so confusing. I don't like this modern world. It's all machines. And the people have turned into machines too. Just a moment, here's a little animal friend I recognise! A bedbug! Perhaps you can you take me to 17 Lunacharsky Street, little bedbug? Take me back in time again, to where there is singing and dancing, and people there, admittedly drunk, stupid, laughing – but alive.

THE KLOP SONG

Varlet (*sings to bedbug, with guitar*)
Little bed, little bug,
Where you go, my heart goes with you.
Little bed, little bug,
So familiar to me.

The cast come on to take up the refrain en masse as the scene changes.

Cast
Little bed, little bug,
Where you go, my heart goes with you.
Little bed, little bug,
So familiar to me.

Varlet
You don't complain, you make your home
Where'er your little legs may roam.
Hot or cold, you'll survive,
You remind me I'm alive.
I once had dozens, now there's one,
Will you be my only one?
Little Klop, in the seams
Of my trousers and my dreams.

Cast
Little bed, little bug,
Where you go, my heart goes with you.
Little bed, little bug,
So familiar to me.

Scene Seven

A Futuristic city street.

*Futuristic city noises. A **Man** and a **Woman** move around, as if on conveyer belts, holding newspapers. They reach up and eat fruit which is hanging on trees overhead.*

Woman   What's going on with these diseases spreading everywhere?

Man   I dunno. Nothing in the world newspapers!

Woman   It's scary! Who can you trust?

*A **Reporter** eating a slice of melon glides on.*

Reporter   Pssst! If you step off your pedestrian travellators, comrades, and come under the shade of our civic omni-arborials, I can tell you more, in confidence, of the worrying situation that has followed on the vote to thaw out the sub-human.

He points to men hurrying across stage, each with a black bag with a dog's head wearing a stethoscope sticking out of the bag.

We have three epidemics now raging in the town.

Cue music: 'Epidemic Dances'.

See that? Those men are vets. This particular epidemic started when the resurrected early mammal made contact with some of our advanced domestic animals – and now the dogs don't bark any more, they don't play, they only go around on their hind legs, smirking, winking and generally ingratiating themselves with diners in restaurants, and then – they bite.

All   Disgusting! Outrageous!

Reporter   Now look at this! Disease number two!

*Several **Firemen** roll by, drunk.*

Fireman 1

> Walk backwards with me to the good old days,
> You could get legless in so many ways.

Firemen 1 *and* **2**

> With a chum on each arm, and a bottle in hand . . .

Fire Chief

> Boys, keep down the noise, you know it's bin banned.

All Firemen

> No reading or writing, just fighting, fart-lighting.
> Liver on fire, heart's desire.
> Cast not the first stone, we're merry,
> And the effects are revolutionary.
> I'm tiddly, I'm . . . oh, oh.
> I'm tiddly, I'm . . . oh, oh. (*Repeat.*)

Reporter   See that? He's done for as well! There are already one hundred and seventy-five workers infected just like him.

Several **Firemen** *take up the tune and hum softly as they weave backwards and forwards, all over the stage.*

Reporter   They say this one may be even more contagious.

Historian   This is dreadful! How on earth did it start?

Reporter   To revive the unfrozen early mammal, a fermented mixture you may have heard of was used, called 'beer'. During the preparation great care was taken, but some has escaped and been accidentally ingested. Five hundred and twenty workers have been hospitalised and the numbers are growing every day!

Historian   As a historian, I know about this 'beer'.
I predict the mysterious illness can only be conquered if enough volunteers come forward – and for the good of the people, I will put myself forward immediately as a test case to be inoculated!

Applause from the crowd. **Firemen** *stop singing.* **Man** *bows and exits. Enter* **Girl**, *dancing by herself.*

Reporter   This is the third variety of plague the subhuman has brought. Any women who live within earshot of the crazed infected mammal hear him at night, when the town is silent, hear the plunk of his horny plectrum on his depraved instrument through the thin walls – finally this noise becomes too much for our girls – they go out of their minds –

Man   This I do not believe! How can this be? Does this illness yet have a name?

Reporter   Infection rates of 'Lurve', as it is known, are running at over seventy-five per cent of all within earshot!

All   'Lurve' microbes are poisoning every cubic centimetre of our air!

The single **Girl** *is joined by several others, inhaling imaginary roses and swooning about the stage. They swoop around, to music, humming in a trance.*

Reporter   At a certain stage, 'Lurve' victims respond to a further set of stimuli. They come together on a hidden signal, and somehow the parasitic infection synchronises all infected legs, in a low parody of decadent bourgeois art!

The **Girls** *come together to do high kicks, in an intense, professional-looking, insect-like conga.*

Man (*amazed*)   How on earth is that done??

Reporter   The epidemic is reaching crisis proportions! It's as if some sort of depraved primitive consciousness is taking over the world!

Enter **Zoo Director**, *with a magnifying glass. The* **Girls** *keep dancing in conga round him.*

Zoo Director   Attention please!

Music stops. **Girls** *keep dancing.*

I am your Zoo Director. A search party has reported that the precious sole living example of the unique bloodsucking creature, the Klop, or bedbug, has been sighted here a quarter of an hour ago, heading for the fourth floor, with a top speed of one and a half versts per year it won't be far away – comrades, search the premises immediately!

Everyone searches while the **Girls** *dance through them.*

Reporter   The only way to capture a bedbug is to lay out some bait –

Voice   Put a naked man on a mattress in every window!

Voices   Don't shout, you'll frighten it away!

Zoo Director   Anyone who finds it is warned not to try to secrete it about their person. This bedbug is state property and a severe fine will be levied if it is found on any person!

Voice   Here it is! Here it is!

Spotlight on one spot on stage. The **Girls** *stop dancing.*

Zoo Director   Yes, that's it.

Music stops.

Firemen, over here!

Charade with drunken **Firemen**, *trying to trap it in helmet, and ladders. Each time they go to get it, it escapes and they chase the follow-spot around the stage, perhaps even into the audience.*

Zoo Director (*variously as they chase*)   It's over here now! Bastard got away! Never fear, quick – Don't let it fall – it'll kill itself! Do not crush the insect's legs! Careful!

Fireman (*eventually, after many efforts*)   Got it!

Voices   Got it, hurrah!

Zoo Director   Quiet, folks, please. It has crossed its legs and wishes to rest! This is an unique specimen of Bugus Normalis, extremely popular at the beginning of the revolutionary era and believed extinct subsequently. Now our zoological gardens will be the first to exhibit it and, if we're not on the tourist map after this, I'll eat my tricycle.

Cue 'The Klop Song Reprise'.

I invite all present, including gentlemen of the press, to a formal inauguration of Bugus Normalis' new life in captivity.

THE KLOP SONG REPRISE

Chorus
Little bed, little bug,
Where you go my heart goes with you.
Little bed, little bug,
So familiar to me.

Exit all, to music, as bedbug is taken off ceremonially, on a velvet cushion.

Music ends.

Scene Eight

The cryogenic ward. **Varlet** *strums 'The Klop Song' on his guitar.*

Varlet   Can we liven up this cryogenic ward please? Professor, c'mere – gimme some more hair of the dog, will you? The drink you gave me just now doesn't have a chance in hell of curing a hangover. What about a litre of vodka?

Professor   I could not be responsible for giving you a lethal dose.

Varlet   If a litre was lethal I'd have been dead years ago. Did I ask to be sober when I was resurrected? No! If you can't get me what I want, freeze me back! (*Slurred.*) What 'smatter? Scared?

Professor   The state acknowledges that the life of each worker is sacred.

Varlet   But your charter doesn't have to include me. I'm not working here, am I? I'm just waiting by a hatch for my rations like an animal. So what is sacred about a research animal? Gimme a proper drink, or put me out of my misery.

Enter **Zoya** *with books.*

Professor   Comrade Zoya, please explain to the animal we are not empowered to act against the collective vote.

Varlet   A collective vote which took none of my feelings into account!

Professor *exits.* **Varlet** *turns to* **Zoya**.

Varlet   Get me a drink!

Zoya   They won't allow it here at the Institute. But I've got some books for you. I don't know whether they are what you want, the ones we talked about. Nowhere carries books about 'Lurve' nowadays, for us it's a new, frightening disease. I couldn't find anything on daydreams, and the closest I could get to roses was a textbook on horticulture.

Varlet   Am I alone in finding this glorious future unacceptably sanitised?

Cue: 'The Loveboat Has Crashed'.

Do you remember what it was like, Zoya?

Zoya   I remember. But, in the collective, regret has no part to play.

THE LOVEBOAT HAS CRASHED

Varlet
This is why I would rather die –
What did we fight for in the old days?
Memory's in short supply,
Censored, sanitised.
All the chips were stacked on red,
We took our chances with the gun,

We danced and sang, we thought we'd won.
What happened?

Why did you let it go,
Sweet proletariat?
A beautiful plan, the perfection of man –
I would have died for that.

Zoya

How can you blame me now?
You never worked for this.
Didn't you feel that our noble ideal
Was more than hypothesis?

Varlet *and* **Zoya**

I would have died for that,
Now we're all out of time.

Varlet

We were afloat on dreams,

Varlet *and* **Zoya**

But the loveboat has crashed.

Zoya

We're out of step with love,
Time hasn't been our friend.

Varlet

The world's lost its passion
Now feelings are rationed,

Varlet *and* **Zoya**

But we can't start again.

Why did we let it go,
Sweet proletariat?
A beautiful plan, the perfection of man –
I would have died for that.

I would have died for that,
Now we're all out of time.

Varlet

We were afloat on dreams,

Varlet *and* **Zoya**

But the loveboat has crashed.

The past is ashes now,
We are both out of time.
Feelings are rationed here
Now the loveboat has crashed.
The loveboat has crashed.
The loveboat has crashed.

Enter **Doctor** *and* **Professor** *of the Cryogenic Institute.*

Doctor   The Professor of this Cryogenic Resuscitation Unit tells me you are not satisfied with your existence in our modern state, but here's an old tradition you'll like we have kept alive. Dancing! Tomorrow, you can watch twenty thousand male and female workers celebrating the collective harvest with a dance around a thousand-tractor rally in the people's arena.

Varlet *(contemptuous)*   Aw, I can't wait. It's pretty obvious that you haven't the faintest idea what to do with me here. I'm redundant. *(Pause.)*

Professor *(to* **Zoya***)*   There is a sort of sub-human logic to what he is saying. We just don't have the resources to provide the beast's natural environment.

Varlet *starts throwing books.*

Varlet   Crap, crap, and more crap! These are some of the most boring bloody books I've ever had the misfortune to open. What's this leaflet advertising?

He has found a flyer in one of the books.

Zoya   I'd freeze him again without a second's regret, if it was up to me.

.

Varlet (*pointing at the leaflet*)   Zoya – explain – please. What's this about?

Zoya (*reads*)   'Situations vacant.' It's a jobsheet. They give them out on the streets. The city is committed to full employment. I must have picked one up . . .

Varlet   But have you read it, you dumb woman? It's the way out. It says, look, 'Human being wanted.' Human being! That's me. None of the rest of you are qualified any more, are you?

Zoya (*reads*)   Job at . . . Civic Zoo?

Varlet   'Ordinary human being wanted!' See – someone wants me! Get on the blower now and call this number, you brain-dead oaf!

Professor   If you are sure this is suitable for you –

He goes to phone and dials.

Varlet   I could do this! I could do this job!

Professor (*on phone*)   Zoo Director? This is the Institute for Resurrection. We think we may have a candidate who would fit your advertisement. (*Pause.*) Right away. (*Pause.*) No, he won't need to be tranquillised for conveyance to you – he *wants* to come.

Scene Nine

*The city zoo. As music plays, the stage fills with zoo animals, elephants, giraffes, etc. Upstage centre is a curtained cage, which contains **Varlet** and the bedbug. They're followed by many city **Workers**, who have come to attend a special event in the zoo.*

Music stops.

*Enter **Chairman** and **Committee**.*

Committee
> We send fraternal greetings to the workers of the zoo.
> We Soviet city workers all applaud what you do.
> Heroes of labour, with rhinos for neighbours!
> We send fraternal greetings to the workers of the zoo.
> Oy!

Applause. **Zoo Director** *enters and walks up onto the podium next to* **Varlet***'s cage.*

Zoo Director   If it had not been for the kind offer of my colleague, the Professor at the Institute of Resurrection, these – two – specimens of a bygone era, present here, would not be available for our edification tonight. Initially, we were only aware of one. We first caught Bedbugus Normalis, it was on its own, but we knew we would need a Homo Sapiens feedsource to keep the specimen alive. But how? We have evolved far beyond them. I put out an advertisement, and to my utter astonishment a mammalian specimen was made available. When the specimen arrived at the zoo, we discovered that it was Bourgeoisius Vulgaris, not noble Homo Sapiens. However, Bedbugus Normalis is not too choosy, thankfully, and both have settled into their little routine quite happily. Bourgeoisius Vulgaris, in the era this specimen is from, affected horrid passions for what was called 'culture'. It was not possible to avoid Bourgeoisius's cultural droppings filling the insteps of your shoes, wherever you stepped.

Zoo Keepers *wearing masks carefully sweep around* **Varlet***'s curtain-draped cage.*

Zoo Director   In the past, it was disgusting and contagious but today we have a system which continuously removes any culture that the animal deposits so you are all quite safe.

Zoo Keepers *shovel 'culture' from underneath the cage into buckets labelled 'Culture' and take off.*

Zoo Director   Comrades and comradesses, Bedbugus Vulgaris and Bourgeoisius Normalis in an exact replica of their natural habitat. Behold!

He pulls a cord. Curtains fall away to show **Varlet** *on a bed with a bottle and guitar. Crowds carefully approach.* **Varlet** *plucks guitar listlessly.* **Zoo Director** *steps into the cage, puts on rubber gloves, draws a gun, and turns a listless* **Varlet** *round for the zoo visitors.*

Zoo Director   Come closer, comrades, don't be frightened. It's quite tame. Look, this is something you won't have seen before. It's going to have a 'smoke'.

Voice   Disgusting! The children shouldn't be allowed to contribute to the fire risk!

Zoo Director   And then – this part is for strong stomachs only – it's going to have some 'booze'.

Voice   This is cruel – watching animals take poison! We shouldn't be tormenting it!

Zoo Director   Would you like to come for a little walkies, Bourgeiosius? Come on! See, it knows its name. Come on, leave your little chum under the bed and come for walkies. Bourgeoisius dropped a whole lot of culture after his breakfast before you arrived – he generally only does that once a day. So you have nothing to fear in the way of impromptu missiles from that quarter.

Zoo Director *opens the cage door and retreats. Slowly* **Varlet** *comes out and peers around.*

Zoo Director   Say hello to the nice people!

He slowly backs away from **Varlet***, who looks at the crowd, disinterested, then turns back to the theatre audience, and starts to peer at them, excited for the first time. Recognition.*

Varlet   Hey – just a minute – citizens! Hundreds of them. Brothers! My own, my very own people! People like me! How did you get in here? So many of you? When were you all unfrozen? Oh, this is marvellous – but why am I kept all alone in the cage when there are so many of you? We could have a party. Come and join me please, immediately! All of you! (*Yells.*) I'm so lonely – it hurts to be alone. So alone! Do you know what it's like to be alone?

He sinks to his knees.

Cue: 'Behold The Noble Prole'.

I'm sad, so sad, sad, sad. Life has cheated me . . . Join me . . . Why am I suffering like this?

Children scream again.

Varlet   Touch me. Come closer! (*Sobs.*)

Zoo Director   Comrades, you are witnessing an anomaly. The bright lights must have caused it to hallucinate. How unfortunate and pathetic. Please remain calm and wait for it to return to its cage. Remain still, children, and none of you will be in danger; it will not attack unless provoked.

BEHOLD THE NOBLE PROLE

Varlet
> The road towards Utopia
> Was paved with blood and stone –
> We were so great in number
> How could we have known?
>
> I am the myth incarnate,
> Your liver and your soul;
> And I've come back to haunt you –
> Behold the noble prole.
>
> We were building a road to a better world,
> Free of want and fear,
> But now the mists have moved away
> To show the path we steered –
> The road to Utopia leads straight to a wall,
> And our work was in vain,
> 'Cos the wall don't want us,
> The wall don't us,
> The wall don't want us at all.
>
> See how sleek our masters get
> While we sit in our dirt and sweat.
> Still it isn't finished yet,

Our Utopia.
Our Utopia.

Hark to what our masters said,
'Swing your hammer, swing with dread.
Hit that rivet on the head.'
But the dream will fall,
But the dream will fall.

And the wall don't want us,
The wall don't want us,
The wall don't want us at all.

All

Marxists all, in Marx we trust,
He will prevail when we are dust.
A dream come true, we promise you . . .

As the song ends, it's as if **Varlet** *can't see the audience any more. He retreats into his cage, watched by all.*

End.

Bedbug

BOOK ADAPTED BY SNOO WILSON FROM
THE PLAY 'THE BEDBUG' BY VLADIMIR MAYAKOVSKY
WITH MUSIC BY GARY KEMP AND GUY PRATT

*Lyrics by Snoo Wilson
woth additional lyrics by Gary Kemp and Guy Pratt*

*Notes on rehearsal and staging drawn from a workshop
held at the National Theatre, October 2015*

*From a workshop led by Anthony Banks and Tom Brady,
with notes by Alice Hamilton*

How Snoo came to write the play

In 1995, Snoo was commissioned by the National Theatre
to contribute to the newly established NT Connections
programme. Snoo had been interested in Mayakovsky's 1929
satire, *The Bedbug*, but had been unsure what to do with it. In
1994, he wrote a play version, before being introduced to the
composers Gary Kemp and Guy Pratt and collaborating with
them to create a musical version of the story.

In creating the music for the play, Gary and Guy were keen
not to be unduly influenced by the Shostakovich compositions
that accompanied Mayakovsky's original work; they therefore
avoided listening to the original score until they had produced
something of their own. Guy describes the musical approach
they decided to take as 'very vaudeville', and they later found
it to be inadvertently in sympathy with Shostakovich's
original 'circus influences'.

Themes and approaches to the play

The play is a satiric study of the class system, disillusionment
and a distrust of authority during the Soviet Union.

Snoo was not interested in naturalism or dramatic social
realism, and he avoided sentimentality at all times. He was
drawn to the European epic style of theatre, and his work
took the form of a surreal, subversive and darkly humorous
social critique. Snoo was interested in channelling other time

zones – as with *Brave New World* and *1984*, he created a dystopian futuristic world. He was also very interested in suicide and particularly in the suicide of the artist – there is a suicide in many of his plays.

A key theme of this play is the battle of social class. This can be a challenging subject to address with younger groups, and may perhaps be approached through status exercises. It could also be helpful to go through the text picking out 'examples of snobbishness'.

When approaching this play for performance, it might be useful to ask who is going to watch this and what will illuminate their souls. The play is strongly rooted in a specific socio-historical context, but there is room to hit contemporary resonances within that.

Approaching the music of the play

If you don't have a musician who could play through the music on piano or guitar, a good starting place might be to listen to recordings of the songs to familiarise performers with the music.

Performers should not worry about sounding 'pretty' but should rather focus on bringing out the characters and sense of the lines through the singing. It might be helpful – particularly for younger groups – to begin with one of the 'fun' songs such as the Sellers' or Hairdressers' songs, to build confidence and spark enthusiasm.

The workshop participants looked in detail at the *Sellers Song*. This is orchestrated for six voices, but groups can expand to accommodate the number of singers available. Anthony talked about layering the acting onto the singing. He advised identifying and hitting the adjectives within the line for sense and colour: '*Dutch* press studs', '*Dancing* dolls', '*Socialist* bananas', '*Non-Tsarist* herrings', '*Lovely* brassieres'.

Participants then focused on the Hairdressers' and Firemen's songs. They were asked to perform them once 'neutrally' and once 'in character'. This exercise shows how important character and attitude are to bringing these songs to life, and can be very helpful when working with less experienced singers. It is also helpful to ask the actors to choose the most important words in the song to land, to ensure the sense of the words is conveyed.

Tom led an exercise using Varlet's first song, which begins with the 'speak singing' – 'So sorry Zoya, if I destroy ya . . . ' The performer was encouraged to try this section in various different musical styles – opera, indie pop, and finally in plain naturalistic speech. Exploring the extremities of vocal styles can expose different possibilities for performance and also help to unlock meaning.

Language, style and technique

The style and density of the text would defy an entirely naturalistic representation of the play. Companies will need to find a way to embrace and manage the distinctive 'sculpted' language. It was acknowledged that this language can be challenging for untrained actors, and it is important to get to the end of the line hitting significant syllables. It was suggested that the 'target practice' exercise should be employed, in which the five most important words in a line are identified and hit. The group were also encouraged to look after internal rhymes, and be sure to take care of important information such as the differentiation between 'Ivan' and 'Ivor'.

Through various exercises the participants were encouraged to try out different ways of approaching the language. Two people were asked to enact the exchange between Varlet and Oleg on page 686, in which Oleg advises Varlet on the best way to conduct his wedding. Attention was drawn to certain unusual phrases such as 'petty-bourgeois details', and Anthony suggested putting energy behind the consonants to make them stand out. The scene was then re-enacted in various different styles – once like 'Wagnerian cardboard cut-outs' performing on the Palladium stage. In this version, every word is opened out thereby exposing things that may have gone unnoticed. It was then tried again as an intimate encounter for television. These different readings prove the elasticity of the text and offer a number of different options for performance from which it is possible to mix and match. It is worth taking time to perform a 'forensic investigation' on the text.

Characters and characterisation

It is important to begin by asking who these characters are – age/status/weight and so on. Anthony suggested trying to come up with modern parallels for the characters in the play to provide enlivening points of reference, and to help illuminate their specific roles within the play. It was suggested, for example, that a modern equivalent for Oleg might be Gok Wan, Gillian Keith or Trinny and Susannah. These references should help casts to access their characters.

A similar exercise might be conducted when looking at the status/class issues within the play. Modern parallels for the Russian 'bourgeoisie' could be the Kardashians or the 'Made in Chelsea' set. It is also interesting to reference our concept of the 'hipster' – that is, someone who is rather well-off but who deliberately and consciously dresses against this.

In creating characterisations, it will also be necessary to think about questions of age – how to transform a teenager into a middle-aged Russian aristocrat. The ages are not given in the text, so there is some room for flexibility, but in most cases there will be some degree of 'ageing up'. This might be done purely through the actors' physicalisation, or you may wish to look at using masks, beards or other distinctive means to convey this.

In addition to the named principals, there is also the question of how to approach the CHORUS. It is important to decide to what extent they should appear as a unified group or as a collection of individuals. It would be possible to play up to the uniformity and make them look and behave in a similar way, which could contribute to an uneasy and sinister atmosphere of the dystopian future. Alternatively, you may wish to spend time differentiating these characters and giving each performer something distinctive to play. It can be galvanising – particularly for younger performers – to feel that they are developing their own characters, and they may enjoy building up their own personal backgrounds and characteristics which can emerge through the ensemble scenes. In such a scenario, it might be interesting to give each performer a list of questions to answer about their character – best friend, biggest fear, favourite food and so on – which will enable them to invest in their role and bring their performance to life. Another approach would be to give them each a single defining characteristic, gesture or prop; this could allow for a nod towards individuality within a cohesive whole.

Casting

The casting for this play can be quite complex, and it is likely that it will involve a certain amount of doubling.

The play is about class divisions, not gender divisions, and for this reason it might be best to mix up the casting of the hairdressers and the firemen – it would be possible for example to have male hairdressers and females who like to hold a hose!

Some of the roles with solo numbers – Varlet, Zoya, Oleg, Chief Fireman – are more challenging vocally, so it would be wise to bear this in mind when casting.

Think about the smaller roles – it is important to have someone with a strong presence and great energy to play the Professor for example. Similarly, the part of Mr Steering Wheel is a great comic cameo role for somebody.

Production, staging and design

The participants discussed the various options, challenges and potential pitfalls to look out for in staging this show:

While the socio-political landscape of the play is overt and firmly rooted, individual companies must decide upon the extent to which this will be carried into the design of the show.

It has been acknowledged that there are strong Brechtian influences running through the piece, and it may be that this is something to embrace in the design and staging. Snoo has titled each of the scenes, and companies may choose to display these captions on banners or placards, in the style of Epic Theatre. It was observed that the play's nine scenes are akin to a series of Hogarth paintings, and the captions could perhaps be projected on to screens.

The opening was felt to be crucial for establishing the magical tone and mood. Anthony advised the directors to create something that would give the audience a sense of what they are to expect from the performance. In the stage directions, Mayakovsky 'bursts through a screen which is showing a collage of Russian images from the twentieth century: everything from the storming of the Winter Palace to babushkas selling wooden Gorbachev dolls in Red Square and queues outside the Moscow McDonald's'. This immediately establishes a vivid theatricality as well as giving a clear introduction to the historical political context of the piece. Directors should think about all the possible ways of setting this scene in a way that will hook the audience without being alienating or distracting.

Other staging challenges include the presence of the Chorus – how much of an onstage presence should they be and how to differentiate between their multiple roles? This will be dependent, in part, on the size of the company. On page 690, for example, the company must decide who the police are and how they appear. It may be that this closing song is delivered by the whole company, dropping out of their previous characters for this moment. The song could also usefully be used to transition the scene from the market into the hostel, thereby functioning as a sort of front cloth for the transition.

Another staging challenge identified was the section involving the dance on page 694. It was observed that companies would have to come up with something that was funny. What kind of dance is it? Is Varlet a good dancer? And is this choreography repeated when Varlet dances again at the end of the play? It might be useful to improvise something in this section using the rest of the company. Other onstage characters at this moment include the 'intellectual girl' and the 'barefoot boy'. Try asking them to begin an improvisation starting from these basic characteristics and explore how the scene might develop and escalate. The cast could perhaps get involved by playing onstage instruments or joining in with the dancing.

Within these scenes, the response of the ensemble will be really important. It might be helpful to rehearse the songs as text in the first instance to allow the company to respond to the ideas before layering in the music. Similarly, you may want to run the scene allowing everyone to speak the thoughts of their character aloud so that the memory of this exercise may be carried into their performances later.

Another important consideration is the differentiation between the world of the 'present' and the world of the 'future'. Anthony suggests that designers might like to think about colour: he sees the two parts dividing into 'hot red' and 'cold blue'. It might be interesting to draw up two lists citing the polarities across the two halves – for example, Part One might be seen as 'curved lines' and Part Two as 'straight lines'. In the first half, characters are differentiated by characteristics such as 'intellectual girl', in the second part by occupation – 'reporter'. It is worth considering the different sound quality – perhaps Part One is warm hubbub, while Part Two is beeping machines. Do people look different in the futuristic world? It seems a good idea to make strong visual statements.

It was suggested that the 'bits of machinery' in Scene Five might be created from the ensemble. The company could experiment in rehearsals with different ways of using their bodies to create machines. The Orator in this scene might be a recorded voice or projected image rather than a physical presence.

Perhaps the most significant staging challenge is the 'unfreezing' of Varlet. In discussions, the National Theatre 2011 production of *Frankenstein* was cited as a point of reference where the creature emerges from a piece of material within a vertical frame; movement work could be done on this transformation for maximum dramatic interest. The effect could also be created using a clearly defined and coloured block of lighting, spray on snow/icicles, or even, again, using human bodies.

At the end of the play the fourth wall must be broken as Varlet 'turns back to the theatre audience, and starts to peer at them excited for the first time. Recognition.' Companies must decide how to achieve this effectively; it could be by bringing up the house lights, for example.

In staging this piece, companies are encouraged to bring some of their own world to bear on the one presented here. Though obviously set in Russia, there is a London vernacular with Cockney rhyming slang – 'me grass shoots!' Guy Pratt attributes this dialect to the writers' own particular backgrounds, but says there is no reason why these communities could not be shifted to wherever the play is being performed, with the accents changing accordingly. He suggests that the peasants could happily be scouse rather than cockney, for example.

Groups should feel free to explore any number of different ways of approaching this play. In a general response to various questions about staging ideas and possibilities, the directors in the workshop were told 'the answer is yes'.

Participating Companies

#HFC Youth Theatre
1812 Youth Theatre
20Twenty Academy
360 youth theatre
5 Dollar Shake Productions
Aberconwy
Acorn Young People's Theatre
ACT 2 Drama School
Act Now Kids
Act Up
ACTAcademy UK
Active8 Theatre
ACTS
Ark Globe Academy
ARK Helenswood Academy
Artemis Studios in partnership
    with Reading Studios
Arts1 School of Performance
artsdepot Youth Theatre
ArtsSpark Youth Theatre
Ascendance Theatre Arts
Astor Youth Theatre
Atlantic Coast Theatre
Australian Theatre for Young People
Aylward Academy
Bablake Theatre
Barbara Priestman Academy
Bare Bones Drama
Bath Area Play Project
BDC Company
BEA Theatre Company
Belgrade Theatre Community and
    Education Company
Berzerk Productions
Bethany School
BH23
Bideford Kingsley Community
    Theatre Company
Birmingham Repertory Theatre
Bishop Gore School Performing
    Arts Company

Bishop Ramsey School
Bishops High School
Blackheath Youth Theatre
Blatchington Mill School
Bloxham School
Blue Bee Productions
BOA Acting
Bolton Sixth Form College
Borders Youth Theatre
Brewery Youth Theatre
Bridgend College
Bridport Arts Centre
Bristol Grammar School
Bromsgrove School
Brooklands College
Brylights
BTEC Extended Diploma
    Performing Arts (Acting)
Burnage Academy for Boys
Buxton Opera House Young
    Company
Caerleon Comprehensive School
Caerphilly Youth Theatre
Calderdale Theatre School
Camberley Youth Theatre
Canley Theatre Group
CAPA College
Cardinal Pole School
Carney Academy
Cavendish School
Cedars Theatre Company
Central Youth Theatre
Centre Stage Youth Theatre
Centrestage
Chadsworth Stage School
Chadwick School
Chagford Youth Theatre
Chapter 4 (Mansfield Palace Youth
    Theatre)
Characters Stage Company
Cheltenham Youth Theatre

Chesil Youth Theatre
Chew Valley School
Chichester Festival Youth Theatre
Chickenshed Kensington &
    Chelsea
Chiswick School
Church Stretton School
Churchill Academy and Sixth Form
Churchill Theatre Connections
    Company
Cirencester School of Acting
City Academy Bristol
City of Westminster College
Class Act Drama Academy
Cockburn School
Colchester Institute
Core Actors
Crescent Arts Youth Theatre
    (CAYT)
Dalbeattie High School Drama
    Club
Darwen Youth Theatre
David Game Drama Society
Daydreamer
De Aston Drama
De Warenne Academy
Deafinitely Theatre
Debden Park High School
Debut Theatre Company
Delante Detras
Denton Community College
Dorchester Youth Theatre
Dorothy Stringer school
Drama at Crest
Drama Lab Jersey
Dudley College Performing Arts
Dukies Drama Society
Dumfries Youth Theatre
Dundee Rep Youth Theatre
Easy Street Theatre Company
Eden Court Young Company
Edgbaston High School Youth
    Theatre
Everyman Youth Theatre

Exposure Theatre
Felixstowe Academy
Felsted Theatre Company
First Act Theatre
First Floor
Fisher Youth Theatre Group
Flame Theatre Company
Flipside Theatre Co
Fluid Motion Theatre Company
Flying High Theatre Company
Forge Theatre
Found in the Forest Youth
    Theatre
Foundations Youth Theatre
Fowey River Academy
Frederick Bremer School
Freemen's Theatre Company
Further Stages Theatre Company
    Wimbledon
FYA Youth Theatre
Gaelic Youth Theatre Inbhir Nis
Garrick Youth Theatre
George Dixon Academy
George Green's
George Salter Academy
Get Stuck In
Gildredge House
Gloucestershire College
Grand Theatre Blackpool
Greasepaint Youth Theatre
    Company
Greenfields School Theatre
    Company
Group 64 Theatre for Young
    People
Grove Academy Youth Theatre
Gulbenkian
GYP
HA Sparks
Hackney New School
Halesowen College
Harris C. of E. Academy
Haste Makes Waste
HDHS Drama Company

Hemsworth Arts and Community
 Academy
Henry Beaufort School
High Tunstall College of Science
Hinchingbrooke School
HMTP
Holland Park School
Holyhead School
Homespun Youth Drama School
Hove Park School
HSFC Drama
Huntingdon Youth Theatre
Ian Ramsey Church of England
 Academy
Ignite Youth Theatre
Ilex Theatre
In Yer Face Productions
Indelible Arts Youth Theatre
Inspire!
Intangible Inc
InterACT Youth Theatre
Invergordon Youth Theatre
Invicta Grammar School
IV3YT
Jackass Youth Theatre
Jeugdtheaterhuis Zuid Holland
JKL Youth Theatre
John Cabot Academy
John Willmott School
Junction Young Company
Junk Shop Theatre Company
Kesteven and Grantham Girls
 School
Kidz R Us
Kildare Youth Theatre
King Edward's School, Bath
Kingsford Community School
KYT Leading Lights
Lady Manners School
Lady Manners School –
 Application 2
Lakeside Youth Theatre
Lammas School and Sixth Form
Langley Theatre Workshop

Leeds City College
Leighton Buzzard Children's
 Theatre Youth section
Lets Act
Lincoln Young Company
Lipson Cooperative Academy
Lister Company of Actors
Little Red Theatre
Lochaber Youth Theatre
Looking Glass Stage School
Loreto High School
LOST Youth Theatre Company
Lostleters
LS17
LSC Expressive Arts
Lutterworth College
Lyme Youth Theatre
Lymm High School
Macrobert Young Company
Mark Jermin Stage School
Marlborough Connections
Marple Drama
Marshalls Park School
Mate Productions
Mercury Young Company
Meridian School
Mess Up The Mess Theatre
 Company
Mezzamorphoses
MidKent Players
Midsummer's Theatre Company
Milfield School
Mishmak Youth Theatre
Montage Theatre Arts
Mulberry School for Girls
Narberth Youth Theatre
NCN Actors
Neale-Wade Acts
New College, Swindon
New Vic Youth Theatre
Newent Community School
North Durham Academy
North Kesteven School
Northampton College

Northampton High School
Northamptonshire County Youth
    Theatre
Northbrook College
Northern Lights Theatre Company
Northern Stage Young Company
Norwich School
Ockbrook School
Octagon Youth Theatre
Old Buckenham High School
Oldham Theatre Workshop
OP and MCS Company
Orange Tree Theatre Connections
    Company
Orchard Youth Theatre
Ormiston Rivers Academy
Oslo International School
Page2Stage Performing Arts
Panache Theatre
Patch
Patrician Youth Centre
Pensby High School
Peploe-Williams Academy
Perfect Circle Youth Theatre
Perpich Center for Arts
    Education
Perth Academy
Perth High School
Phoenix High School
Pike & Musket
Platform
Pump House CYT
Queen Ethelburga's Collegiate
    Foundation
Queen Mary's Grammar School
Queen's Park High School
Queen's Theatre Cut2
Queensbridge School
RAPA (Ravens Wood Academy of
    Performing Arts)
Ratzcool
Raw Academy
RCS Young Theatre Company
Redbridge Youth Theatre

Ricards Lodge High School and
    RR6
Riddlesdown Collegiate
Rising Stars Youth Theatre
Riverfront Youth Theatre
Rotherham College of Arts and
    Technology
Roundwood Park
Royal & Derngate Young
    Company
Royalty Theatre Youth Academy
Rye Studio
Sacred Heart High School
Sandwell Youth Theatre
SAVVY Theatre Company
Scrambled Eggs
Scrum Down Theatre Company
Seaford Musical Theatre Juniors
See and Eye Theatre
Senior Drama Company
Shazam Theatre company scio
Sheffield People's Theatre
Shenfield High School
Shenley Academy
Sherborne Girls School
Sherman Cymru Youth Theatre
Shetland Youth Theatre
Shooters Hill Post 16 Campus
Shotton Theatre School
SHS Theatre Company
Sinden Youth Theatre Company
Sion-Manning RC Girls School
Sir John Cass Redcoat School
Sirius Academy
Slow Theatre Company
Something out of Nothing Theatre
    Company
Something wicked this way comes
South Hunsley School
South West College
Sprungsters
SSYT Stamford Senior Youth
    Theatre
St Edmund's College

St Edward's School
St Francis College
St Gregory's School Bath
St Ives Youth Theatre
St Mark's Church of England
  Academy
St Mary's Catholic College
St Mary's Drama Club
St Monica's Theatre Company
St Saviour's and St Olave's School
St Swithun's School
St Teresa's School
St Thomas More Catholic School
St Wilfrids
Stafford Gatehouse Youth Theatre
Stagecoach Ashby & Burton
Stagecoach High Wycombe
Stagecoach Isleworth Further
  Stages Company
Stagecoach Theatre Arts
  Edinburgh
Stagecoach Theatre Arts Reading
  East & Wokingham
Stagecoach York
Stage-Fright Youth Theatre
Stephen Joseph Youth Theatre
Stockton Riverside College
Story Makers
Stratford-upon-Avon College
Strode's College Performing Arts
  Department
Suffolk New College Performing
  Arts
Sunderland Empire, Creative
  Learning
Sundial Theatre Company
Sutton High Drama
Swanwick Hall School
Take Part
Talisman Youth Theatre
TBAP (Tri-Borough Alternative
  Provision)
Temper Theatre Company
Thame Youth Theatre

The Actors Centre Theatre
  Company
The Barn Youth Theatre
The Blue Coat School
The Blue Room Theatre Company
The Bourne Academy
The Box School of Performance
  and Communication
The BRIT School – Theatre
  Department
The Captivate and Connect
  Theatre Company
The Customs House Youth
  Theatre
The Drama Studio
The Fallibroome Academy
The Garage Youth Theatre
  Compnay
The Glasgow Acting Academy
The Hastings Academy
The Ipswich School
The John Lyon School
The King's School Theatre
  Company
The Lewisham Southwark
  Collaborative
The Lowry Young Actors
  Company (LYAC)
The Marlowe Youth Theatre
The Minster School
The Norwood School
The Oast Youth Theatre
The Pauline Quirke Academy of
  Performing Arts Enfield
The Performance Factory
The Petchey Players
The Petersfield School
The Plough Arts Centre
The Priory City of Lincoln
  Academy
The Rochester Math School
  Players
The Roses Theatre Young
  Company

The St Leonards Academy
The William Allitt School
The Winston Churchill School
The Young Company
The Young Dramatic Arts Theatre Company
The Young Pretenders
The Young Theatre
Theatre Alba
Theatre Arts Starlight Youth Theatre
Theatre Royal Bath Theatre School
Theatre Royal Stratford East
Theatre Studio
Theatretrain Ashford & Maidstone
Theatretrain Reading
Thomas Clarkson Academy
Thurso High School Drama Club
Tomorrow's Talent
Tower Bay Youth Theatre
Trapdoor Theatre
Tricycle Young Company
Tyne Valley Youth Theatre
Ulidian Youth Drama Group
Unhinged Theatre Company
Unity Arts
Unity Youth Theatre
UROCK Youth Company
Uxbridge College
VENUE 2 VENUE
Vivid Theatre Company
Wallington County Grammar School
Walthamstow School for Girls
Walworth Academy

Warrington Collegiate Players
Warwick Arts Centre Connections Company
Watermans
WCTT Young Actors Company
Wellington School
Wellsway School
West Acre Young People's Theatre
West Park School
West Yorkshire Drama Academy
West Yorkshire Playhouse Youth Theatre
Weymouth Drama Club Curtain Raisers
wgytc
Whalley Range 11–18 High School
White City Youth Theatre
Whitefield Academy Trust
Whitley Academy
Winstanley College
Woodhey
Woolwich Polytechnic School
Worthing College
Yew Tree Youth Theatre
Young and Unique @ Callington Community College
Young Company – Theatre Royal Plymouth
Young People's Theatre
Youth Arts Centre
YT43
Yvonne Arnaud Youth Theatre

Partner Theatres

Aberystwyth Arts Centre
artsdepot, London
Belgrade Theatre, Coventry
Birmingham Repertory Theatre
Brewery Arts Centre, Kendal
Brighton Dome
Bristol Old Vic
Cambridge Junction
Cast, Doncaster
Chichester Festival Theatre/The Capitol, Horsham
Curve, Leicester
Derby Theatre
Dundee Rep
Eden Court, Inverness
Greenwich Theatre, London
Hall for Cornwall
HOME, Manchester
Lighthouse, Poole
Lyric Hammersmith, London
Lyric Theatre, Belfast
Marlowe Theatre, Canterbury
Mercury Theatre, Colchester
Northern Stage, Newcastle
Norwich Playhouse
Octagon Theatre, Bolton
Orange Tree Theatre, London
Queen's Theatre, Hornchurch
Royal & Derngate, Northampton
Sheffield Theatres
Sherman Cymru, Cardiff
Soho Theatre, London
Stephen Joseph Theatre, Scarborough
The Albany, London
The Garage, Norwich
The Lowry, Salford
The Lyceum, Edinburgh
The North Wall Arts Centre, Oxford
Theatre Royal, Bath
Theatre Royal, Plymouth
Theatre Royal Stratford East, London
Tricycle Theatre, London
Warwick Arts Centre
Waterside Theatre, Derry/Londonderry
Watermans, London
West Yorkshire Playhouse, Leeds

Performing Rights

*Applications for permission to perform, etc. should be made,
before rehearsals begin, to the following representatives:*

For *Bassett*
Curtis Brown Group
Haymarket House, 28–29 Haymarket, London SW1 4SP

For *Bedbug*
Micheline Steinberg Associates
Suite 315, ScreenWorks, 22 Highbury Grove, London N5 2ER
info@steinplays.com

For *Blackout* and *Citizenship*
Casarotto Ramsay & Associates Ltd
Waverley House, 7–12 Noel Street, London W1F 8GQ
rights@casarotto.co.uk

For *Children of Killers*
Creative Artists Agency
405 Lexington Avenue. 19th Floor, New York. NY 10174, USA

For *Eclipse*
David Godwin Associates
55 Monmouth Street, London WC2H 9DG

For *Gargantua* and *What Are They Like?*
The Agency (London) Ltd
24 Pottery Lane, London W11 4LZ

For *I'm Spilling My Heart Out Here* and *It Snows*
United Agents
12–26 Lexington Street, London W1F 0LE

For *Take Away*
Wylie Agency
17 Bedford Square, London WC1B 3JA

For *The Musicians*
Judy Daish Associates Limited
2 St Charles Place, London W10 6EG

Copyrights

Bassett © James Graham 2011, 2016
First published by Methuen Drama
in National Theatre Connections 2011
Published by Bloomsbury Methuen Drama
in National Theatre Connections 2016

Bedbug © Snoo Wilson, Gary Kemp and Guy Pratt
1995, 2004, 2016
First published by Methuen Drama
in *Making Scenes 2: Short Plays for Young Actors*
Published in Shell Connections 2004 by Faber and Faber
Published by Bloomsbury Methuen Drama
in National Theatre Connections 2016

Blackout © Davey Anderson 2009, 2012, 2016
First published in New Connections 2009 by Faber and Faber
First published by Methuen Drama with *The Static* in 2012
Published by Bloomsbury Methuen Drama
in National Theatre Connections 2016

Children of Killers © Katori Hall 2011, 2016
First published by Methuen Drama
in National Theatre Connections 2011
Published by Bloomsbury Methuen Drama
in National Theatre Connections 2016

Citizenship © Mark Ravenhill 2005, 2006, 2015, 2016
First published in Shell Connections 2005 by Faber and Faber
First published by Methuen Drama in 2006
in the Modern Plays series and in the Modern Classics series 2015

Eclipse © Simon Armitage 1997, 2000, 2016
first published by Faber and Faber with *Friendly Fire* in 2000
and in Shell Connections 1997
Published by Bloomsbury Methuen Drama
in National Theatre Connections 2016
with the permission of Faber and Faber

Gargantua © Carl Grose 2011, 2016
First published by Methuen Drama
in National Theatre Connections 2011
Published by Bloomsbury Methuen Drama
in National Theatre Connections 2016

National Theatre Connections Team 2016

Alice King-Farlow	*Director of Learning*
Ros Terry	*Connections Producer*
Thomas Freeth	*Connections Assistant Producer*
Adele Geddes	*Connections Assistant Producer*
Anthony Banks	*Connections Script Associate*
Paula Hamilton	*Head of Programmes, NT Learning*
Katie Town	*General Manager, NT Learning (to November 2015)*
Virginia Leaver	*General Manager, NT Learning (from January 2016)*

Play workshop production notes edited by Kate Budgen

The National Theatre

National Theatre
Upper Ground
London SE1 9PX

Registered charity no: 224223